SAVING CHRISTIANITY

*WHY MILLIONS OF CHRISTIANS ARE DROPPING OUT
OF CONGREGATIONS – AND HOW A RETURN
TO EARLY CHRISTIAN BASICS CAN GIVE
CHRISTIANS A NEW SPIRITUAL LIFE*

OWEN ALLEN

**Seymour Press
Capitol Heights, Maryland**

Saving Christianity
© 2020 Owen Allen

All rights reserved. No portion of this book may be reproduced, stored in a retrieval system, or transmitted in any form, or by any electronic, mechanical, photocopy, recording, scanning, or other means – except for brief quotations in critical reviews or articles – without prior written permission.

Published by Seymour Press, PO Box 5544, Capitol Heights, Maryland, 20791, in association with The Christian Family Online in America, Inc., PO Box 19125, Greensboro, North Carolina 27419.

All Scripture quotations are the author's personal adaptations of the original Hebrew and Greek.

ISBN: 978-1-938-37336-7
LCCN: 2020931562

Printed in the United States of America

3 4 5 6 7 8 9 10

Second Edition

Saving Christianity is available in bulk gifts for congregations, Sunday school classes, retreats, small groups, conventions, conferences, and other such uses through tax-deductible donations to The Christian Family Online in America, Inc. To request such bulk gifts, contact:

books@ChristianFamilyOnline.com

Or

Bulk Books Request
Christian Family Online
PO Box 19125
Greensboro, NC 27419-9125
www.ChristianFamilyOnline.com

Also by Owen Allen

Weatherization Production Control

Personal Profile Labs

Management Power the Specific Action Way

Personality Power the Specific Action Way

Master of Personal Excellence Program

The Specific Action Management System

The Specific Action Personality System

Spiritual Excellence

Preactive Leadership

Dedication

To my ol' pal, Joanna. God was our Matchmaker. He changed my life when He dug around in His toy box and put the two of us together. I'll always be grateful for my greatest blessing – you.

And to John and Kit Shields. My loving brother and sister in Christ who urged me to publish this book.

Contents

Author's Preface xi

Introduction xiv

Part I – The Source of the Trouble

Chapter 1
The Followers – *The Mysterious Phone Call* 1

Chapter 2
The Dropouts – *Bulldozing Christian Buildings* 11

Chapter 3
The Warlord – *The Murderer Who Became Emperor* 25

Chapter 4
The Contamination – *Courthouses, Sun Gods, and Crosses* 37

Chapter 5
The Current Crisis – *Program Christians and Ancestors* 55

Part II – The Early Christian Basics

Chapter 6
The Natural Person – *The First Spiritual Level* 67

Chapter 7
The Motivational Diagrams – *Flesh, Mind, and Spirit* 83

Chapter 8
The Infant Christian – *The Second Spiritual Level* 95

Chapter 9
The Growing Christian – *The Third Spiritual Level* 113

Chapter 10
The Mature Christian – *The Fourth Spiritual Level* 137

Part III – The Early Christian Lifestyle

Chapter 11
The Spiritual Behavior – *The "Fruit" of the Spirit* 163

Chapter 12
The Spiritual Gifts – *The Hospital Room* 173

Chapter 13
The Spiritual Experiences – *The Young Man at Breakfast* 201

Chapter 14
The Small Groups – *Holograms, Hosts, and Outlaws* 213

Chapter 15
The Spiritual Worship – *Mistakes, Choices, and Puppies* 239

Chapter 16
The Christian Life Today – *Habits, Styles, and Saints* 263

Appendix

Glossary 305

Early Christian Letters 329

Notes 335

Bibliography 367

Index 375

Acknowledgments 387

About the Author 389

Illustrations

Figure 1: Constantine's "Salutary Sign" 31

Diagram 1: The Basic Model of Motivation 88

Diagram 2: The Natural Person 89

Diagram 3: The Infant Christian 107

Diagram 4: The Growing Christian 127

Diagram 5: The Mature Christian 141

Table 1: The Spiritual Behaviors 167

Table 2: The Spiritual Gifts 185

Author's Preface

This book is about saving Christianity. It shows why millions of Christians are giving up and dropping out of their congregations; why thousands of Christian buildings are being abandoned; and why thousands of pastors, priests, and other Christian workers are resigning their posts to take up secular careers. This book also shows why returning to Early Christian basics can give any Christian a new Spiritual life – whether he or she is attending a Christian congregation, or has dropped out of one, or has never attended one.

This book gives the details. It shows the peace, healing, and hope that Early Christian basics can give Christians if they do what the original Christians did. It shows how we Christians can have the same love and miracles today that the original Christians had then – if we do some of the things that they did. I call that living the *Early Christian Lifestyle*. I often say, "If we *do* what they did, we'll *have* what they had." To give you a glimpse of what all this means, let me tell one true story that shows what Christianity can be like if we live it the way the Early Christians lived it.

The Children Who Wanted a Dog

When my children were school age, they came to me one day and asked if they could have a new pet dog. We'd previously had problems with pet dogs, so I said "No." They begged, but I cited all the reasons why we didn't need a new dog, and reminded them of our previous problems. They walked away disappointed, and I considered the matter closed.

A few days later, I was riding my lawnmower in the backyard on a quiet, clear day, when suddenly I saw the face of a beautiful dog floating in the air before me. He was staring at me intently. He was black and brown with handsome features, and he had a thick mane around his neck that gave him the appearance of a lion. I only saw him for a few seconds and then he was gone. I was late with my chores that day, so I continued mowing, only half-conscious of what I'd seen. And since the image had no meaning to me, it soon faded from my busy mind.

The following Lord's Day ("Sunday"), my children came to me again. This time they were waving the newspaper and pointing excitedly to a classified ad that said, "Wanted, Christian home for Collie-Shepherd dog." The children asked what harm it'd do to just *look* at the dog in the ad. I reluctantly agreed, and after worship and lunch that day, we drove out in the countryside to find the address printed in the paper.

Eventually, we pulled up a long driveway to a rural home, and stopped in front of a double-car garage with its door raised. No one was in sight and, as I sat with the engine idling deciding what to do next, a young dog stepped out of the garage and stood staring at me intently. He was black, brown, and handsome, and he had a mane that made him look like a lion. He was the dog whose face I had seen floating before me earlier in the week while I was riding my lawnmower.

I recognized him instantly, and I knew at once that God was telling me this dog was to be our new family pet. I got out of the car, rang the doorbell, and asked the owner if I could adopt the dog in the garage "that looks like a lion." The owner agreed, and we put the dog in the car and took him home. I was never sorry. He never caused me a moment's trouble and, throughout his life, he was a blessing from God that gave my children and me great comfort and joy. I loved him very much. He's gone now, but I miss him to this day.

Now – the point of this story (and of the other true stories I'm going to tell) is to show you this book's theme: That living the *Early Christian Lifestyle* in today's world is a life filled with miracles large and small. God has a solution for every need in our lives, no matter how huge or how tiny. The first Christians taught that God knows the number of hairs on our heads and knows every sparrow that falls in the forest. So the theme of this book is that Christians today can live the same kind of Spiritual life that the Early Christians lived in the early centuries of Christian history – if someone will tell them how.

But that's the problem. No one is telling them how. That's why today's Christians are giving up by the millions and walking away. That's why Christian buildings across the country are being bulldozed. And that's why Christianity's influence in America is drying up. So let's turn to the Introduction and start at the beginning. Let's talk about the kinds of experiences we Christians can have today if we live like the Early Christians lived, and let's start seeing more details of how and why those things can happen.

Owen Allen
Palm Beach, Florida
Jude 24-25

Introduction

I never realized how much I didn't know about Christianity until a time when I cleared my calendar of everything but sleeping and eating, and studied Early Christian history for three straight years. I read over 300 books on how the Early Christians thought and lived, many of the books rare and out of print. I also made research trips to study the Early Christian ruins in Italy, Greece, Israel, and Turkey.

I saw the ancient symbols of the "fish," the "shepherd," the "anchor," and the "ship" for the first time; and I saw Christian ruins and artifacts that showed how the first Christians thought, wrote, and acted. In Rome, I studied ancient Christian tombstones, dusty catacomb paintings, and faded etchings on pieces of broken pottery. On the island of Patmos, I prayed in the cave where the apostle John wrote the book of Revelation. In Jerusalem, I climbed the stairs that Jesus was dragged up by the mob the night He was arrested. In Athens, I stood in the place on Mars Hill where the apostle Paul gave his "Unknown God" teaching.

And I had dozens of other life-changing encounters with the sights, sounds, and smells of Early Christian history. I did those things because I wanted to understand Early Christian *behavior*. I wanted to know *why* the Early Christians had the marvelous Spiritual behavior, gifts, and miracles that they had. And during my research, it finally dawned on me that I had grown up without knowing anything about how the original Christians lived and behaved.

For example, I didn't know that they weren't originally called "Christians." I didn't know that they didn't have buildings called "churches." I didn't know that they didn't have preachers, pulpits, or pews. Or that they didn't have choirs, candles, or crosses. Or that they didn't have bulletins, Bibles, or bazaars. Or that they didn't have organs, offering plates, or orchestras. In fact, I didn't realize that they didn't have much of anything that we call "Christianity" today.

Then what *did* they have? They had incredible *Spirituality*. They were so incredibly Spiritual that they turned the whole world upside down Spiritually in only 70 years. Their lives were filled with healings, peace, love, and courage. Their behavior was so different from other people that the non-Christians of the day thought Christians were a *new kind of humans* that had somehow appeared on earth. As one example, a non-Christian in Second Century Rome was watching a group of Christians in the streets in amazement, and he turned to his friends and said:

> "Look at them! They love one another almost before they know one another!"[1]

But I never heard that story while growing up. I've been a Christian since childhood, but I'd never heard any of the things we just discussed. I didn't know Christianity was a special kind of *Spiritual behavior*. Actually, I didn't know that there *was* something called Spiritual behavior. So one of the biggest questions in this book is this: Why *wasn't* I told how the original Christians lived? After all, my parents were active in a Christian congregation. Our family attended every service and event. My parents sang in the choir and served on several committees. My brother and I attended services from the cradle roll on. We went to Christian camp in the summer, attended weekly youth meetings during the school year, sang in the youth choir, and did all the things that Christian children are expected to do.

In Sunday school, I learned about Noah's Ark; Daniel in the lion's den, and Joseph's coat of many colors. In morning worship services, I learned about Jesus healing lepers, calming storms on Lake Galilee, and feeding a crowd with only five loaves of bread and two little fish. Yet I never heard anything about the vibrant Spiritual *behavior* of average, everyday Christians in the early centuries. Why didn't someone tell me about Early Christian behavior?

Maybe there's a clue in something that happened to me once when I was about twelve years of age. Here's that story.

The Pastor Who Didn't Know the Answer

One morning after the worship service ended, I was walking through the lobby of our building with my Bible in my hand. I was puzzling over a verse I'd read. I don't remember the verse now. But I remember the pastor standing in the lobby shaking hands with members. He was an elderly man who wore a long white robe. I stopped nearby and waited until he turned to look at me.

When we made eye contact, I pointed to the verse in my Bible and said, "Excuse me, pastor, but what does this verse mean?"

He glanced at me, and glanced at the verse. Then he smiled a sad little smile and said, "Son, there are just some things we're not *meant* to know." And he turned his back and started shaking hands again.

I remember standing there feeling angry and frustrated. I remember thinking, *What do you mean we're not meant to know? Why would God put a verse in the Bible that we're not meant to know?*

I never got an answer to that question. In fact, I never got an answer to any of my youthful questions about why worship services sometimes seem boring and irrelevant, and why Christians sometimes seem hypocritical. Looking back on it all now, I see that nobody in my life – not pastors, parents, or friends – *knew* anything about Early Christian behavior. So like my parents and grandparents before me, I grew up without knowing anything about it either.

The years passed. I served in the military, went to college, got a job, got married, had children and, like many other people, I cooled off on Christianity. That coolness lasted until my own encounter with the Holy Spirit in a New York City hotel room many years later. More on that true story later. But right now, it's important to realize that *all* of us need to know how the Early Christians thought, lived, and acted. *All* of us need to know how and why they had such a Spiritual lifestyle. So here's the thing to remember from this Introduction: The services, rituals, and programs of today's Christian congregations – when compared to the lifestyle of the Early Christians – *are two very different things.*

Many people think that the services, rituals, and programs of today's Christian congregations *are* "Christianity." But they're not. That's one of the biggest lessons I learned in my three years of research. That's also one of the biggest lessons in this book. In coming pages, we're going to talk about how and why today's services, rituals, and programs are *different* from the vibrant behavior of the Early Christians. We're going to talk about how and why today's congregations don't teach Spiritual behavior. And we're going to use a series of simple diagrams to show how you and I can live the *Early Christian Lifestyle* in today's world.

So we have a lot to talk about. Just remember that our purpose is to experience the same peace, patience, and kindness that the original Christians experienced. Our purpose is to live with the same Spiritual power and miracles that they enjoyed. So let's turn to Chapter 1, and find out more about the Spiritual miracles that people like you and me can experience in our daily lives and – just as importantly – why many Christians today *aren't* enjoying those Spiritual miracles.

PART I

The Source of the Trouble

Chapter 1

THE FOLLOWERS

The Mysterious Phone Call

Once during my business career, when the economy was in one of its periodic recessions, my finances were at a low point. I was a private management consultant in those days, and my clients were loyal to me. However, all of them had been forced to delete consulting fees from their budgets until the recession was over. So I had unpaid bills on my desk and no income.

One morning, I sat at my desk reviewing my client list and praying until noon. Then I stepped out for lunch. I had just returned when my phone rang. I answered it, and a voice said, "Is this Owen Allen at phone number so and so?"

"Yes it is," I replied. "May I help you?"

The voice responded, "Yes, my name is John Jones (not his real name). I'm with so-and-so company (he named a *Fortune 500* company), and I'm returning your call."

"Pardon me," I answered, "who did you say you were?"

He repeated his words and said again, "I'm returning your call. What can I do for you?"

I sat at my desk puzzled. "Mr. Jones," I replied, "there's been some mistake. I don't know anybody in your company and I didn't call you."

He replied, "No, there's been no mistake. I came back from lunch and found a note on my desk saying, 'call Owen Allen at this number.' So I'm calling. What do you want?"

"Mr. Jones," I said, "I'm confused. Do you know who put the note on your desk?"

"No," he answered. "That's the odd part. I asked my secretary, but she didn't put it there, and we don't recognize the handwriting. So we don't know who put it there."

"Well," I said, "I'm sorry for the confusion, Mr. Jones. But you must have a wrong number. I hope you find out who caused the mistake, and I'm sorry for your wasted time."

"Well, wait a minute," he said. "As long as we're on the phone, what kind of business are you in?"

I described my consulting practice in a few words. He was silent for a moment. Then he said, "You know, this really *is* odd. My company is looking for a consultant in your field right now, and I'm the vice president in charge of finding the right person. Tell me more about what you do."

I told him about my private consulting, and our conversation resulted in a contract that carried my company through the recession. It also resulted in this vice president becoming a good friend who gave me contracts for the next 25 years. However, he never found out who put the mysterious note on his desk. But I think I know who put it there. I think an angel put it there.

A World Upside Down

Now – how does this miracle story apply to the theme of this chapter? It applies this way: Two thousand years ago, a unique group of people unlike any others who ever lived suddenly appeared in the city of Jerusalem in Israel. They identified themselves with a simple "fish" symbol,[1] and they were so Spiritual that the things they did seem impossible today.

However, the things they did *weren't* impossible. They *really* happened and, best of all, things like them still happen today. The lives of those unique people were as real as yours and mine are right now – except that they were so Spiritual that outsiders thought *a new kind of humans* had appeared on the scene.[2]

Most humans live with daily stress, anger, greed, and lust. But the members of this new group lived with peace, happiness, contentment, and purity. They spent their days teaching one another how to live their unique lifestyle, and in socializing, eating meals together, and gathering in small groups in one another's homes. They praised God continuously, and healings, wonders, and miracles happened among them daily. Visions, prophecies, and angels guided their comings and goings, and their Spiritual lives were so influential that millions of outsiders joined them – with the result that within 70 years their group spread worldwide and turned the nations of the world upside down Spiritually.

As we might expect, their moral behavior, individualism, and independence from the world's system angered the religious elites of their day. The religious elites were outraged because the members of this new group stopped attending their temples, stopped buying idols in their religious shops, and stopped tithing to their temples and shrines. These things infuriated the elites. But that didn't bother the new group. They *knew* they didn't fit what they called "natural" society, and they didn't *want* to fit it. They called themselves *foreigners* and *strangers* in the "natural" world, and a *priesthood* among "natural" people.[3] The truth is, they *were* a new kind of people. Nobody like them had ever lived before, and emperors, governors, generals, soldiers, priests, shop owners, and the people in the streets saw it and believed it.

Now – let's stop a moment to catch our breath. *Who* were these amazing people? *Where* did they get their unique Spiritual lives? *Why* did angels guide them? *Why* did miracles happen to them?

We're going to answer all these questions in this book. But to lay a firm foundation for the answers, let's talk about the *name* that this new group had. Then let's talk about their unique *lifestyle*. Then let's talk about how the citizens of a certain city *changed* the group's name.

The Trial of the Apostle Paul

Once, a courageous member of this new Spiritual group was arrested on false charges by the religious elites of his city. The elites claimed he was a troublemaker who had started riots and had violated the sacredness of their temple. Of course, he'd done none of these things. But those were the charges. That courageous man's name was Paul, and he served in the new Spiritual movement we're talking about as a teacher, a prophet, and an apostle.

After weeks of argument and false witnesses, during which the elites dragged him from city to city and from jail to jail, Paul finally found himself standing trial before the Roman governor of Israel in the palace at the capital city of Caesarea. The governor's name was *Marcus Antonius Felix*. After listening to the charges, Governor Felix turned to Paul and asked him what he had to say for himself. Standing alone in the governor's throne room, Paul looked calmly at Felix and said, "The only thing I admit is that I worship the God of our fathers as a *Follower of The Way*."

Now, the thing that makes Paul's strange reply even more interesting is that the record of his trial says that both Governor Felix and his wife, Drusilla, knew about *The Way,* although they weren't members of it. Felix and Drusilla had already heard about the new people who were spreading across the land calling themselves *Followers of The Way*.[4]

However, after a long trial, Governor Felix got cold feet – perhaps because he feared the religious elites – and he put Paul back in a cell without ruling on the charges against Paul. The details of what happened next are a story for another day. But briefly, angels guided Paul on a long journey that finally ended in Rome where he pleaded his case before the Roman emperor Nero, and where Nero found him innocent and released him. But then some months later, Nero arrested Paul again and had him beheaded.

But let's not tell Paul's full story here. Instead, let's find out what Paul meant when he told Governor Felix that he was a *Follower of The Way*. To understand Paul's meaning, we need to know the language in which the record of Paul's trial was written. His trial took place in First Century Israel, and many people in those days couldn't read or write. However, most of them spoke several languages "by ear" because they'd heard those languages since they were children. Thus, most Israelites spoke enough Latin, Greek, and Aramaic to transact business and participate in social events. Of those three languages, *Greek* was the official language of business and legal affairs – and that's the language in which the record of Paul's trial was written.

That helps us understand what Paul meant when he said he was a *Follower of The Way*. In First Century Greek, the words "the way" literally meant a road – but figuratively, they meant a special *lifestyle*; a special *course of conduct,* or a special kind of *behavior*. They referred to a special way of *thinking and acting.* So, when Paul told Governor Felix that he was a Follower of The Way, he was saying that he was a person who lived a special lifestyle, that he had a unique way of behaving that other people didn't have.[5] But what *was* Paul's unique behavior? Next, we need to understand the lifestyle that Paul and the rest of the Followers of The Way lived in the First Century. But to do that, we need to understand Christian *motivation*.

The Motivation of Christians

To begin, Followers of The Way *looked* like everyone else and had the same daily *routines* as everyone else. They dressed, ate, drank, and worked the same way other people did. They couldn't be picked out of a crowd by their clothing, appearance, or occupation. The reason for that is simple. The Followers of The Way were only different from other people in their *internal motivation*. They weren't different in their *external appearance*. We know that's true from the letters they left behind. Here are two quick examples of what the Followers of The Way wrote about their lifestyle:

> "We eat the same food, wear the same clothes, and have the same way of life as you. We live in the same world you do. We go to your forum, your market, your baths, your shops, your workshops, your inns, your fairs, and your other places of trade. We sail with you, farm with you, and engage in trade with you."[6]

> "(Followers of The Way as a group) are not distinguished from the rest of mankind by either country, speech, or customs. They use no peculiar language. They cultivate no eccentric mode of life. They conform to the customs of the people in dress, food, and mode of life in general. They marry like all others and beget children like all others. Their food they spread before all visitors. They may spend their days on earth, but they hold their citizenship in heaven."[7]

Now, the Followers of The Way who wrote these letters were saying that their group lived exactly like everyone else in *external* routines, schedules, and occupations. This meant that they bought and sold products, put money in banks, signed legal papers, paid taxes, and used the same names, pots, pans, clothes, homes, tools, and tombs as everyone else. They did everything that all other people did – except for one thing. They had a different *inner motivation* than everyone else. They were different from other people because they had *Spiritual behavior* – and other people didn't have that.

The Followers of The Way also had a Spiritual thought process that other people didn't have. When they wrote about their Spirituality, they used several different terms for it. In their letters, they called themselves: "saints," "chosen people," "a holy nation," and "people belonging to God."[8] They even described the term *The Way* with several different terms. They also called it: The Way of Peace; The Way of Righteousness; The Way of Truth; The Way of Life; The Way of the Lord, and The Way of God.[9]

These phrases meant that this group's outer behavior was motivated by an inner motivation unlike that of any other group. That unique and exclusive motivation gave the Followers of The Way supernatural healings, protection, encouragement, and guidance. But it's also what caused their *name* to be changed. Soon they were no longer called Followers of The Way, and that term was soon lost in the mists of time. Here's how that happened.

The Followers Lose Their Name

Later in the First Century, 31 years after the founding of the Spiritual movement known as the Followers of The Way, some of the Followers lived in the city of Antioch in Turkey. As was their habit, they spent their spare time socializing in the streets, standing around in happy, informal groups talking about "*Christus*." This was the Latin word for "Christ," the title given to Jesus, the founder of their movement. But, the citizens of Antioch, who weren't Followers of The Way, were irritated by hearing the Followers constantly talking about "Christ" in the streets and shops.

And in those days, the citizens of Antioch were known for the odd habit of giving everyone a nickname. So they did it again. They began to taunt the Followers in the streets, calling out at them scornfully, *Christiani*! *Christiani*! In Latin, that meant, "Little Christ! Little Christ!"[10]

Strangely, this new nickname – which the citizens of Antioch meant as an insult – stuck to the Followers and, as time passed, the camel caravans passing through the city picked it up and spread it worldwide. So within a few years, the Followers of The Way became known the world over as "Christians." Thus in this book, in addition to referring to this group as "Followers of The Way," we'll also refer to them as: the "Early Christians," the "first Christians," and the "original Christians." They were charter members of the new Spiritual movement that Christ Jesus founded in Jerusalem in the First Century. Their appearance changed world history and changed the world's relationship with God. But now, before we move on to Chapter 2 to find out what happened to these amazing new "Christians," let's pause to summarize Chapter 1.

Summary of Chapter 1

1. Jesus founded the Spiritual experience that we call "Christianity" 2,000 years ago in the city of Jerusalem in Israel.

2. Early Christianity was a special form of *Spiritual behavior*. Its members were the most Spiritual people who had ever lived on earth up to that time.

3. The members of the new movement were so Spiritual that other people thought "a new kind of humans" had appeared on earth – and that Spirituality turned the world upside down Spiritually in only 70 years.

4. Members of the new movement called themselves "*Followers of The Way*." In the Greek language of the day, that meant they

lived a unique and exclusive *Spiritual lifestyle*, a unique and exclusive *Spiritual behavior*, that other people couldn't live, and didn't live.

5. The Spiritual lifestyle that the Followers of The Way had was an informal, caring, supporting, lifestyle in which they spent their free time socializing and worshiping in small groups in private homes. They ate together, talked about "Christ" constantly, and gathered in relaxed groups to spontaneously sing, pray, and enjoy healings, answers to prayer, and other miracles.

6. The Followers of The Way looked and worked like everyone else. They were only different from others in one way: They had an *inner motivation* that other people didn't have. They kept the same routines, schedules, and jobs as everyone else. But they lived *Spiritually* in a manner that no one else had ever lived, or could ever live.

7. About 31 years after the movement was founded, the citizens of Antioch in Turkey began taunting the Followers by calling at them, "*Christiani! Christiani!*" That nickname stuck, and Followers of The Way eventually became known as "Christians." That's still their nickname today.

Now, as we close Chapter 1, several important questions remain to be answered: What *happened* to the Followers of The Way? Did they *continue* their wonderful Spiritual lifestyle? And *when* did Christian denominations as we know them today appear in history? How did those denominations *affect* the Followers of The Way? Finally, *how* are the Followers of The Way faring in America today? The answers to all these questions lie just ahead. Let's continue our discussion in Chapter 2, and let's start answering these questions.

Chapter 2

THE DROPOUTS

Bulldozing Christian Buildings

We've been talking about the first Christians who appeared on the world scene in the First Century, and about how they were charter members of the original Christian experience. We've been talking about how they were called "Followers of The Way" at first, and in the Introduction we even said they used a simple "fish" symbol to identify themselves. We said they lived a unique and exclusive Spiritual lifestyle of wisdom, joy, love, healings, and miracles that nobody else had ever lived before, and that nobody else *could* ever live unless they became a Follower too.

We said the unique and exclusive *Spiritual behavior* of the Early Christians was informal and supporting, and that they spent their free time socializing in shops, bazaars, streets, and private homes. They ate together, shared group activities, and broke into spontaneous singing and praying whenever the Holy Spirit prompted them to do so. They called themselves "strangers" in the "natural" world, and a "royal priesthood" among "natural" people.

History shows that as the years passed, emperors, governors, soldiers, priests, shopkeepers, and private citizens all witnessed the amazing Spirituality of the original Christians – and they were so impressed that they wanted that Spirituality for *themselves*. So millions of them in every city and nation of the world joined the movement and the planet was turned upside down Spiritually in 70 years.

In summary: The story of the original Christians is a *love* story unlike any other. They were a people united in peace, goodness, courage, and guidance. They loved one another regardless of the circumstances, and stood together regardless of the test, trial, or trouble. Their bond was so strong that they even stood with one another in torture and violent death. But that was then. This is now. Today we live in the Twenty-First Century. Almost 2,000 years have passed since the Followers of The Way lived their unique and exclusive Spiritual lifestyle in the ancient world. So now the question we need to ask ourselves is this: *How* are the Followers of The Way getting along today? For example, how are the people of the "fish" faring in America, the land of the "eagle"?

To answer that question, the first thing we need to know is that the people who were once known as Followers of The Way evolved over the centuries to become today's *denominational* Christians. The people who were once Followers of The Way are today's members of the *traditional congregations* that dot every town and city. So when we ask how the Followers of The Way are faring in America today, we're really asking how the members of today's traditional congregations are faring in American today. So let's answer that question.

The Shrinkage of Christianity

According to national polls and surveys, several decades ago *91 percent* of the American public said they were Christians. Today, those polls show that only *71 percent* of the American public says they're Christians – and that percentage is slowly declining each year.[1] The truth is, Christianity is slowly *shrinking* in America. It's slowly drying up. Instead of growing in numbers and social influence, it's declining in numbers and social influence. The people of the "fish" are slowly fading away in the land of the "eagle."

This shrinking of Christianity is happening in two ways. First, *fewer* new members are joining the traditional Christian congregations. Second, *existing* members of the traditional Christian congregations are giving up and dropping out. Researchers estimate that as many as *two million* members a year are dropping out of the traditional Christian congregations.² Read that last sentence again and think about what it means for a moment.

Because of this tidal wave of dropouts, an estimated 4,000 Christian buildings are closing their doors each year from a lack of attendance. Most of them will never reopen. Some are being bulldozed. Some are being turned into bars. And unless something changes, by the year 2050, an estimated 100,000 Christian buildings may stand empty and shuttered across our land. This trend means that an estimated 18,000 Christian workers – including pastors, priests, associate pastors, chaplains, choir leaders, youth leaders, and so forth – are dropping out of the Christian work force every year and taking non-Christian jobs.³

These statistics show that the American culture is slowly drifting *away* from its historical Christian culture, and is drifting *toward* a new non-Christian culture. Worst of all, research shows that while some of these millions of Christian dropouts join the New Age Movement or other religions – most of them *give up* on religion entirely and start living non-religious lives. But the big question about this trend is: *Why?* Why are so many Christians dropping out of a Spiritual experience that's so rewarding (or *should* be so rewarding)? Why are so many Christians dropping out of a Spiritual experience that's so helpful to society (or *should* be so helpful to society)?

The answer is simple, yet deeply disturbing. Christians are dropping out of the traditional congregations because attending those congregations isn't *rewarding*. Attending those congregations isn't *changing* people's lives for the better. Said another way, attending today's traditional congregations *isn't* the experience of love, joy, healings, visions, and miracles that it *was* for the Followers of The Way. For many Christians today, the services, rituals, and programs of the traditional congregations are the *opposite* of the wonderful experience that the original Christians enjoyed in the early years of the movement.

National polls show that many Christians today feel that the services, rituals, and programs of today's congregations are irrelevant, boring, and hypocritical. But – how can that *be*? Before we answer that important question, let's look at the practical result of today's congregational services, rituals, and programs. That practical result is this. Today's traditional congregational services, rituals, and programs create *unspiritual* Christians.

Today's Unspiritual Christians

Let's start with a question. If the majority of America's citizens are *Christians* (and polls say that 71 percent of them are), how do we explain all the *trouble* we have in our land? How do we explain the fact that we have so much crime, divorce, drug usage, adultery, suicide, profanity, and pornography in a nation that's *71 percent Christian*? After all, it wouldn't be fair to say that the *other 29 percent* of the population (the non-Christians) are causing all the nation's trouble, would it?

Let's look at that question a different way. If about seven out of every ten people we pass on the streets, in malls, in shops, in schools, and that we hear about on the radio or see on TV, are *Christians* – then why does our society have so much unrest, violence, stress, and unhappiness? How is it possible to have a divorce rate of 48 percent?[4] How is it possible for 41 percent of our children to be born out of wedlock?[5] How is it possible for us to have the worst child abuse record of any industrialized nation (with a child being abused every ten seconds and five children a day dying from abuse)?[6] How is it possible to have 10.3 million crimes per year, with 28,000 being committed every day – including murders, muggings, and mayhem on Christmas Day, Easter Morning, and every other day on the calendar?[7] How's all that possible in a country that has a population that's *71 percent Christian*?

We've already agreed that we can't blame the other *29 percent* of the population who're non-Christians for all of it. So let's just admit the fact that *Christians* play a big role in these gloomy statistics. Let's admit the fact that today's Followers of The Way are causing part of America's problems. To put it bluntly, a lot of Christians aren't very *Spiritual* these days. Some *are*. But many *aren't*. To see that even more clearly, let's take a closer look at the Spiritual condition of some of today's Christians.

The SuperChristian

Would it surprise you to know that the average Christian today is *no more Spiritual* than a non-Christian? (In other words, the average Christian today is no more *moral or ethical* than a non-Christian.) That's what the polls show.[8] Would it surprise you to know that many gangsters, prostitutes, drug dealers, child molesters, pornographers, and alcoholics tell the pollsters that they're Christians? They do.[9] But before we talk about more national polls and surveys, let's step back a moment to see a broader snapshot of Christian Spirituality. To do that, let's use a principle of arithmetic that pollsters use.

Pollsters know that any statistic that's true of a *large* group of people or things will also be true of the *small* groups of people or things within that large group. For example, if 10 percent of the new cars built in Detroit have defects in them, then we can expect 10 percent of the new cars in local town and city dealerships to have defects too. Or, if 10 percent of the people in Arizona eat broccoli, then we can expect 10 percent of the people in the city of Phoenix to eat broccoli too. See how the principle works?

Now let's apply this same arithmetic to Christianity. If *71 percent* of Americans are Christians nationally, then we can expect a high percentage of Christians to be the *causes* of many of our local town and city *problems*. And that's exactly what the research reveals.

For example, one survey of drug dealers revealed that 40 percent of them said they were Christians and were active in a Christian congregation. Surveys of divorcees reveal that the divorce rate for Christians is the same as the divorce rate for non-Christians, standing at 48 percent nationally. Other polls show that 91 percent of all Americans frequently lie; that 41 percent of them have used cocaine and marijuana; and that 61 percent of all children have premarital sex before the age of sixteen (many before the age of twelve).[10] Again, we know from our pollster's arithmetic principle that a high percentage of all this crime, pain, trouble, and disaster in American is being committed by *Christians*.

Now – let's stop here to regroup. We could cite more polls and surveys. But they'd only show the same thing. So here's our takeaway. It seems obvious that many Christians today *aren't* living the unique and powerful Spiritual lives that the original Christians lived. And we don't even need polls and surveys to tell us that. We already *know* that from personal experience. As you read these lines, isn't it true that you can think of friends, relatives, coworkers, and acquaintances who say they're Christians, but who behave like the people in these polls?

However, just to be sure we have a clear picture of the *unspirituality* of many American Christians, let's round out our research. Let's look at some newspaper and magazine stories that show it too. The following stories are true. They came from newspaper and magazine clippings I collected over the years while studying Christianity. Here are a few of those stories:

1. A certain national newspaper ran an article entitled "Church Shooting." The article reported that at a deacon's meeting in a Christian congregation, the fall program was being discussed. One of the deacons didn't like the plan, so he pulled a pistol, killed two members of the deacon board and wounded a third. Then he holstered

his pistol, walked calmly to his car, and drove home for dinner. The police later arrested him at his dinner table.[11]

2. A certain local newspaper printed an article entitled "We Did This Out of Love." The article reported that the elders of a Christian congregation decided that one of their members was insane. So they built a cage in the basement of the building and put the member in it. Someone tipped off the police, who raided the building and rescued the member. When questioned about their motives, the elders said they caged the member because they loved him.[12]

3. Another issue of that same newspaper ran an article entitled "Painted 'Beast' Gets a Fine." The article said that a Midwest courtroom convicted a man for driving around the city with a nude woman painted on his car. When asked by the judge why he did this, the man explained that he was a Christian, and that the nude woman represented his favorite Bible verse.[13]

4. In another issue of the paper, an article was entitled "Pastor Says He Robbed to Buy Sex." The article reported that in a Northern city, a man pleaded guilty to robbing fourteen local banks of a total of $50,000.00. Standing before the judge in court, he testified that he couldn't return any of the money because he had spent it all on prostitutes. He was the pastor of a local Christian congregation. The members of his congregation rejected the pastor's confession as unbelievable. They said the confession couldn't be true because the pastor was such a wonderful person.[14]

5. In yet another issue of the paper, an article was entitled "Man Plans 28th Marriage." The article told the story

of a man in California who had divorced his 27th wife (who was 19 years of age) to marry his 28th wife – who was his former wife's younger sister, and who was 15 years of age. When asked about this odd behavior, the man explained that he liked younger women. He was 81 years of age, and was the pastor of a local Christian congregation.[15]

6. Finally, we come to "SuperChristian." In another issue of this newspaper, an article was entitled "Breach of Faith." The article told the story of a Christian evangelist named "SuperChristian." He was famous for preaching sermons that lasted for hours, and was in the *Guinness Book of World Records* for preaching the world's longest sermon (72 hours). The man had the name "SuperChristian" because he often wore a Superman costume in the pulpit. He was building a school to teach his techniques to worldwide students when the FBI swooped in and arrested him. It turned out that "SuperChristian" had molested over 300 young boys over a period of 22 years during his evangelistic travels.[16]

Okay, I admit it. These are some of my most shocking and unbelievable news clippings. But I used them on purpose. I wanted you to see that, if we add these disturbing news stories to the list of national polls and surveys we've been discussing, there's crystal clear evidence that many Christians today (not all, but many) aren't living very *Spiritual* lives. And let's be totally honest. These polls, surveys, and news stories aren't just isolated events in the isolated lives of isolated Christians. These polls, surveys, and stories are the leading edge of a glacier of Christian horror stories that grinds its way across America every day. These polls, surveys, and news stories are just the ones that made the headlines. Thousands of similar stories don't make the headlines each day. So now we need to ask two vitally important questions:

1. Why *aren't* Christians living more Spiritual lives today?

2. Is it even *possible* for Christians to live more Spiritual lives today?

Now, we're only going to answer *question number one* in this chapter. Because you already know the answer to question number two. The stories we told in the Preface and Introduction of this book have already shown that the answer to question number two is, "Yes." It *is* possible for Christians to live more Spiritual lives today. So with that settled, let's talk about *why* Christians *aren't* living more Spiritual lives today.

The Problem of Unspirituality

In management classes, I used to teach the importance of identifying the *cause* of a problem before trying to *solve* that problem. If people ignore the cause of a problem, and instead fight the *problem* itself (trying to repair it or control it), they're wasting their time and money. Because the cause of the problem will continue to *create* the problem over and over in an endless cycle, and the people will have to fight the damage over and over in an endless cycle.

For example, if *defective* products are coming down a factory's assembly line, it doesn't matter how hard the operators work to *repair* those defective products – because defective products will continue coming down the line until the operators remove the *cause* of the defects. Doesn't that make sense? Fighting a problem without knowing its *cause* is illogical, hopeless, and demoralizing.[17]

Applying that principle of management to the problem of Christian *unspirituality*, we can't be Spiritual until we know why we're *not* spiritual. We need to know the *cause* of unspirituality before we can start thinking about how to be Spiritual. Also, as is normally the case in factories, we're actually dealing with a *chain* of linked causes, not just one cause.

There are actually *three* linked causes that are creating the unspirituality of today's Christians.[18] So let's start a "problem-solving case." Let's solve the problem of Christian *unspirituality*. Let's identify the linkage of three causes that's causing Christians to be unspiritual.

Why Christians Are Unspiritual

The problem we're solving is the documented fact that many Christians are *unspiritual* today. So, our first problem-solving question is this –

1. Why are many Christians unspiritual today?

The answer to this first question is *Cause #1* (or Link 1) in our problem-solving case. Here's the answer: Many Christians are unspiritual today because they attend (or used to attend) Christian congregations that don't teach the *Early Christian Lifestyle* of Spiritual living. So, that means that our second problem-solving question has to be –

2. Why don't many traditional congregations teach the Early Christian Lifestyle of Spiritual living?

The answer to this second question is *Cause #2* (or Link 2) in our problem-solving case. Here's the answer: Many Christian congregations don't teach the *Early Christian Lifestyle* of Spiritual living because it stopped being taught in Christianity many years ago in the Fourth Century. So, that means our third problem-solving question must be –

3. Why did Christianity stop teaching the Early Christian Lifestyle of Spiritual living in the Fourth Century?

Now – let's stop a minute. Let's press the pause button. In the next chapter we're going to answer this third problem-solving question. That third answer will be *Cause #3* (or Link 3) in our problem-solving case. That answer will be the *Root Cause* of Christian unspirituality.

But it's going to take another chapter to explain this Root Cause because it's been buried under a thick layer of institutional sediment of secrecy and mystery for over 1,700 years. Thus, before we turn to the next chapter, let's remember an important principle that we've already mentioned several times. It's this: Millions of Christians have dropped out of traditional congregations because they thought those congregations *were* "Christianity." The services, rituals, and programs that they saw in those congregations were the *only* "Christianity" they ever saw – and since that "Christianity" didn't meet their needs, they gave up and dropped out of what they thought was "Christianity" and started living non-religious lives.

However – as we've said – if we compare today's traditional congregational services, rituals, and programs to the *Early Christian Lifestyle* of Spiritual living, the two are entirely *different*. The two exist independently of one another. That means Christians don't need to give up the *Early Christian Lifestyle* just because they're dissatisfied with the services, rituals, and programs of some of today's Christian congregations.

The good news is that the two styles of Christian living aren't mutually exclusive. They can co-exist. They can operate at the same time. We'll see that in coming pages. So today's Christians can live the *Early Christian Lifestyle*, whether or not they attend a traditional congregation. That's why this book was written. It was written to show you the *difference* between today's traditional congregations, and the Spiritual lifestyle of the Early Christians – and to show you that you can have more peace, hope, and miracles in your life regardless of whether you're active in a traditional congregation. Now, before we go deeper into this surprising subject in the next chapter, let's pause to summarize what we've said here in Chapter 2.

Summary of Chapter 2

1. The original *Followers of The Way* in the First Century evolved over the centuries into today's traditional congregational Christians.

2. The American population was once 91 percent Christian. Today, it's only 71 percent Christian, and that percentage is dropping annually.

3. An estimated two million Christians drop out of traditional Christian congregations annually. Because of that, an estimated 4,000 Christian buildings close their doors each year, and an estimated 18,000 Christian pastors, chaplains, priests, and other institutional workers leave Christian work for secular jobs each year.

4. The average Christian today is no more *Spiritual* than a non-Christian.

5. We can't be more Spiritual until we identify and remove the *cause* of why we're *not* more Spiritual.

6. Today's average traditional Christian congregation doesn't teach the *Early Christian Lifestyle* of Spiritual living that the original Christians lived in the early centuries.

7. Christians make a mistake when they drop out of *Christianity* because the services, rituals, and programs of today's traditional congregations don't meet their needs. The *Early Christian Lifestyle* and today's congregational programs are two *different* things. They exist independently of one another, but they can co-exist. That means Christians can live with the same peace, hope, and miracles that the Early Christians enjoyed, regardless of whether they're active in a traditional congregation or not.

Now, in the next chapter, we're going to return to our discussion of *Cause #3* (Link 3) in our problem-solving case. We're going to talk about *when, where,* and *why* Christians in history stopped teaching the *Early Christian Lifestyle* of power and miracles. Let's turn to that next chapter now and find out what happened.

Chapter 3

THE WARLORD

The Murderer Who Became Emperor

We found in the previous chapter that today's Christian congregations are struggling. We found that millions of members are dropping out, thousands of buildings are being closed, and thousands of pastors, priests, chaplains, and other Christian workers are leaving Christian work for secular jobs. But now let's look at the same problem from a different viewpoint.

Several decades ago, *half* of all Americans (50 percent) were in a Christian worship service every week. Today, only 16.5 percent are. Worse, that percentage is expected to decline to 9.7 percent by the year 2050.[1] The sad truth is that traditional congregations are on the endangered species list. They're tired dinosaurs who're unable to cope with their changing environment and who're gasping for air. But *why* is that happening? We answered part of the riddle in the previous chapter. That's where we started our problem-solving case, and found that the traditional congregations are declining because they don't teach the *Early Christian Lifestyle* of Spiritual living. Said another way, they aren't meeting their member's Spiritual needs. They aren't teaching their members how to live with the same healings, peace, hope, and miracles that the Early Christians enjoyed. Because after all, if the traditional congregations *were* teaching those things, people would be *joining* their congregations – not dropping out.

So, the purpose of this chapter is to identify *Cause #3* (Link 3) in our problem-solving case. Because *Cause #3* is the *Root Cause* of America's shrinking Christianity. We want to answer the question of *why* today's congregations *don't* teach the original Christian lifestyle. Looked at from a different viewpoint, we want to know *who* designed the services, rituals, and programs that the traditional congregations use today. More, we want to know *why* those services, rituals, and programs were designed in the ineffective and inefficient way they're designed. So now let's start answering these vitally important questions.

The Greatest Whitewash

If you're like most people, you probably don't remember from high school or college classes a Roman army general named *Flavius Valerius Constantinus*. But it's important to remember him because *he's* the person who founded the Christian denominations that we have today. In simple English, his name was Constantine, and he was a cruel and vicious battlefield commander in the Fourth Century. (Notice carefully that Constantine lived three centuries *after* Jesus founded original Christianity in Jerusalem in the First Century.)

It's important to understand Constantine because he's probably the most *influential* person in Early Christian history after Jesus and the original twelve disciples. Think about that a moment. That statement is true because Constantine single-handedly founded what today we know as *institutional Christianity*. And he founded it in Rome, 300 years *after* Jesus founded the original Spiritual movement in Jerusalem.

However, before we start our discussion of Constantine, there are two facts we need to know on the front end. First, Constantine was *not* a Christian. Second, the institution he founded was *not* founded to teach the *Early Christian Lifestyle*. It was founded to suppress it. Constantine founded institutional Christianity to promote his own political and military career, and so he had to suppress the Spirituality of Fourth Century Christians to do that. And his plan worked. He *did* become one of the most famous emperors in history; and his plan *did* suppress Christian Spirituality. In fact, it has suppressed it now for over 1,700 years.

School books say that Constantine was the 57th emperor of the Roman Empire, and they call him such names as "Constantine the Great," "Constantine the First," and "Saint Constantine." But there was much more to Constantine's life than these glowing names reveal. The biggest problem with his story is that it was written by historians who were *sympathetic* to him, and thus he has been heavily *whitewashed*. Most history books describe him as a great, wise, and noble leader. Many call him the first "Christian" emperor of the Roman Empire, and claim that he was the emperor who "saved" Christianity from persecution.[2]

However, he *wasn't* any of these things, and he didn't *do* any of these things. The school books that sing his praises fail to mention that Constantine was a priest in the sun god religion, that he kept mistresses, that he murdered his wife and son, and that he routinely executed political and military opponents. The truth is, Constantine was a very different person from what the school books say about him. So let's tell his true story.

The Orphan from Serbia

To begin, Constantine was an illegitimate child. He was born out of wedlock in the late Third Century in what is now the city of Nis in the Republic of Serbia. (The Nis airport bears his name today.) Constantine's biological father was a Roman army officer named *Constantius Chlorus* – and his mother was one of Chlorus's many mistresses. Her name was Helena, and she owned a tavern in Nis where Roman officers often caroused, including Constantine's father.[3]

After Constantine was born, his father was away at war most of the time, so young Constantine grew up without a father's guidance. Instead, he was cared for as an orphan in the homes of various army officers who were his father's friends. Thus, in addition to being born out of wedlock and being raised as an orphan, Constantine also learned the cruelty and low morals of the military officers of his day. He began training on weapons and military tactics in childhood, and he learned by an early age how to be fearless and indifferent to pain.

Finally, when Constantine reached young adulthood in the Fourth Century, his guardians sent him off to the city of Nicomedia in Turkey for advanced military training in the palace of the Emperor *Valerius Diocletian* (pronounced "die-oh-<u>cleh</u>'-shun"). The result of this was that by the time Constantine reached his twenties, he was a hardened fighter from continuous training and coaching by visiting army officers and by the staff in Diocletian's palace.

Of course, like most Roman soldiers, Constantine was *not* a Christian, and he never became one. Instead, he worshiped *Sol Invictus* ("Ever-Victorious Sun"), the official god of the Roman Empire – and eventually he became the high priest of that religion, a position he held for the rest of his life. However, Constantine *did* encounter Christians while growing up, and it's important to understand the circumstances under which he encountered them.

Emperor Diocletian, in whose palace Constantine was training, was one of several Roman emperors who briefly but savagely persecuted Christians. And during the time Constantine was living in the palace, Diocletian imprisoned, tortured, and executed a number of Christians in his dungeons. And *that's* where Constantine encountered his first Christians. He encountered them as prisoners being tried, tortured, and executed in the dungeons of the emperor's palace. More importantly, Constantine attended some of these Christian trials and heard the evidence against the victims. And it was during these trials that he first heard the word "*Christus*." (This is the Latin word for "Christ," pronounced "<u>kree</u>'-stus.")

It was from these tormented victims that Constantine first heard that people can worship "Christ" (*Christus*) as God. The trouble with these youthful encounters with Christians in these dungeons was that Constantine held life and death authority over the victims, and probably helped torture and execute some of them. So from the very beginning, Constantine's attitude toward Christians was that they were criminals and beneath contempt. He held that attitude the rest of his life – which probably explains his later actions against Christianity. But now let's continue with the rest of his story.

The First Bloody Battles

Eventually, Constantine was old enough for combat, and Diocletian's staff sent him off to France to join his father, Chlorus, on the battlefield. Arriving in France, Constantine immediately proved his viciousness in battle and earned the respect and admiration of Chlorus's battle-hardened veterans. Then, just a few months into the campaign, Constantine's father suddenly fell gravely ill. Lying in his tent, Chlorus called his son to his bedside and begged him to take command of the army in case he should die. Chlorus's staff approved the idea, so Constantine agreed to accept the role in case the worst happened.

And the worst *did* happen. His father died in his tent, and at the tender age of 26, Constantine, a troubled and emotionally scarred young man, born out of wedlock and raised as an orphan, became the commander of a Roman field army. He was now the ultimate warlord and, for the next several years, he led his army from victory to victory in some of the bitterest fighting in world history. Then a strange event occurred that was to make Constantine the emperor of Rome, and that was to change the history of Christianity forever.

The "Dream" at Milvian Bridge

Constantine was now 32 years of age and a very tough character. He'd been engaged in hand-to-hand combat with swords and spears for seven long, bloody years. It's hard to imagine what a callous person he had become. Then he suddenly revealed his toughness in a surprising new way. He decided it was now time for his army to conquer the entire Western Roman Empire. So against the advice of his officers (his army was outnumbered and was low on supplies), Constantine launched a surprise attack against Rome. He unexpectedly marched his army out of France, into Italy and toward Rome, catching his enemies off guard. His plan was to confront the current emperor of Rome, *Marcus Aurelius Valerius Maxentius* (Maxentius for short), in a final desperate showdown on the outskirts of the city.

Constantine's army soon arrived on the banks of the Tiber River, just north of Rome, near a bridge called the Milvian Bridge. (The Milvian Bridge is still there today.) The army stopped near this bridge and pitched camp. Constantine knew that his enemy, Maxentius, would eventually be forced to come out of the city and accept his challenge of a fight to the end. But before that happened, it was there in Constantine's tent at the Milvian Bridge that the most controversial and debated event in his life is said to have occurred.

Constantine is supposed to have had a mysterious *dream* one night in his tent. Some researchers say the dream never happened. Some say it happened – but in a different way. Others say it wasn't a dream at all, but instead was a vision in the noonday sun. We'll never know the truth. However, if we accept the "dream" version of the legend, Constantine is supposed to have been asleep one night when he had an amazing dream.

In this strange dream, a man whom Constantine thought was "the god *Christus*" is supposed to have appeared to him. (Remember that years earlier in Diocletian's dungeons, Constantine had heard about "the god *Christus*" from tortured Christians.) In this dream, "the god *Christus*" is supposed to have showed Constantine an odd symbol.[4] The symbol was in the shape of a plus sign with a loop at the top, like this:

"The god *Christus*" then supposedly spoke to Constantine in Latin, and said, "*In hoc signo, vinces.*" (Translated, this means, "In this sign, you will conquer.") The legend continues that Constantine awoke from this incredible dream, rushed out of his tent in excitement, and told his officers about "*Christus*" and the odd symbol. Constantine then issued orders requiring his troops to paint the odd symbol – which he was now calling his "Salutary Sign" – on their helmets and shields with bright red paint. (A "salutary sign" is a sign of good luck or good health. People have used the *plus sign* as a symbol of good luck and good health throughout history.) Constantine told his troops that they'd be protected from wounds as long as they wore the Salutary Sign on their helmets and shields; and he told them to also create a large banner of the sign to carry before them into battle.

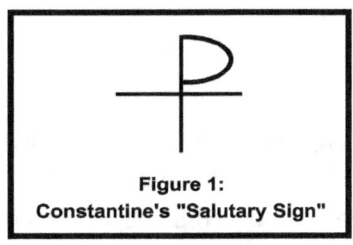

Figure 1: Constantine's "Salutary Sign"

Then, just as Constantine's men completed these preparations, Maxentius's army came marching out of the city to accept Constantine's challenge. The two armies soon clashed in violent combat on the banks of the Tiber – and Constantine's troops were so filled with zeal by the dream and the Salutary Sign on their equipment that they soundly defeated Maxentius's army. Constantine captured Maxentius, killed him, decapitated him, and threw his body in the Tiber River. Then Constantine marched triumphantly into the city of Rome with the severed head of Maxentius hanging from his saddle. Arriving in the city, he proclaimed himself the new emperor of the Western Empire, and the cheering citizens accepted him.

The Statue in Rome

As soon as Constantine got settled in Rome, he constructed a giant *statue* of himself and mounted it on the city square. The statue had one upraised arm in which it held a replica of the symbol of good luck that Constantine had supposedly seen in his dream (the plus sign with the loop at the top). At the base of the statue, Constantine engraved a message to the citizens of Rome. The message told them that he had saved the city and its citizens by means of his Salutary Sign, and that this proved that he and his sign were inspired and unstoppable. (Notice that Constantine was superstitious about the sign and believed it had magical powers. He also taught the people of Rome to think of the sign in the same terms. This becomes significant in later pages, when we talk about where the Christian symbol of the *cross* came from.)

Finally, to celebrate his victory at the Milvian Bridge, Constantine constructed a massive and beautiful triumphal *arch* over the city's main street. He did that to remind the citizens of his greatness as they walked beneath the arch each day. (This arch, and pieces of Constantine's giant statue, still stand in Rome today.) However, Constantine's plans didn't end with a statue and an arch. These were the least of his plans. He had a broader strategy in mind. He wanted to capture the Eastern Roman Empire too, and make himself grand emperor of a unified Roman Empire. He knew from his experience in the army, and from his training in Diocletian's palace, that the quickest way to gain control over people is to pass new laws to regulate them. So his next tactic was to start passing dozens of new laws that would eventually change the world.

The Great Law Giver

Constantine immediately began issuing a flood of new laws. Indeed, he became one of the most prolific lawgivers of all the Roman emperors, issuing over 300 new laws during his 25 year reign. The purpose of this torrent of laws was to tighten his control over the Roman people and strengthen his political and military mastery of the empire. But the most important thing about Constantine's tidal wave of new laws was that they suppressed the vibrant *Early Christian*

Lifestyle of the Fourth Century Christians. When Constantine came to power, Christians were still living the same way the *Followers of The Way* had lived in the First Century – except that the Followers were now called *Christians*. In other words, Christians were still living the same free, informal, loving way that they had lived since Jesus founded the movement in Jerusalem 300 years earlier. But Constantine's laws quickly changed all that.

Constantine's first law is called *The Edict of Milan*. An edict is a law, and so *The Edict of Milan* was a new law that Constantine passed in the city of Milan, Italy. What's interesting is that Constantine's first law didn't deal with taxes, or armies, or public safety. It dealt with *religion*. Its purpose was to increase Constantine's control over the *religions* of the empire (including Christianity). The new law decreed that, effective immediately, all of the religions in the Western Empire were to be considered *equal* under Roman law, and that persecution of all religions was to cease. This included the religion of the sun god (of which Constantine was a member), and all the other religions. So this new "equality" and "protection" of religions also applied to *Christianity*. Unlike what many school books say, Constantine did *not* outlaw the non-Christian religions, and he did *not* make Christianity the official religion of the empire. He also did *not* end Christian persecution. All he did was decree that all the religions in the empire were to be treated as social and financial equals, and that none of them was to be "unjustly" persecuted.

Now – at first glance, all this sounds "good" for the Christians of that day. It sounds like these things would "help" them. And that's exactly what most school books say. But Constantine's first law *wasn't* a good thing for Christians, and it *didn't* help them. Because for the first three centuries of its history, Christianity had never been recognized anywhere in the world as a *legal* religion. And now, with the stroke of a pen, Constantine had made Christianity a legal religion in the Roman Empire – and that was a watershed moment in Christian history. Because for the first time Christians could be identified, counted, categorized, and cataloged by government bureaucrats. For the first time, Christians were subject to government census-taking, taxation, regulation, conscription, and red tape. Constantine's first law was actually the first "brick" in the new "building" that would soon become *institutional Christianity*.

As for the Christians themselves, they suddenly realized that, whether they liked it or not, they now had the same legal rights, financial benefits, and social status that the members of all the other religions had. For example, they now had the same rights, benefits, and status as the members of the sun god religion – and those were among the most influential people in the empire. So Christians now faced social, political, and financial temptations and pressures that they had never faced before and, since many of them were illiterate and poverty-stricken, these temptations and pressures were overwhelming. Christianity had always been composed largely of socially powerless slaves, women, children, and the elderly. So the shock of suddenly having these exciting new legal, social, and financial rights disoriented and confused them.

Then something even worse happened. Constantine's first law triggered a lot of discussion and debate in the empire, so he began issuing follow up laws trying to clarify the new rights that Christians had been granted in the first law. But each follow up law only made Christians more visible, organized, taxed, regulated, and subject to public discussion than they had been before. And with each passing day, the informal, free, and loving lifestyle of the people who had once been Followers of The Way – and who had once been identified by a simple "fish" symbol – became more regulated and controlled. Yet the worst was still to come. Constantine's next series of dramatic actions completely perverted the original *Early Christian Lifestyle*. We're going to discuss that series of actions in the next chapter. But first let's summarize what we've said in this chapter.

Summary of Chapter 3

1. At one time, half (50 percent) of the American population attended Christian worship services each week. Today, only 16.5 percent do, and that percentage is expected to decline to 9.7 percent by the year 2050.

2. The most accurate way to measure the *Spirituality* of the services, rituals, and programs of today's traditional congregations is to compare them to the *Early Christian Lifestyle* that was lived by the original Christians in the first three centuries of Christian history.

3. In the Fourth Century, a cruel military general in the Roman army named Constantine laid the first "bricks" in the "building" that was to become *institutional Christianity*. He laid those bricks by passing a flood of new laws that regulated, monitored, and controlled Fourth Century Christians. The effect of that flood of new laws was to *suppress* Christian Spirituality.

4. Constantine lived three centuries (300 years, or about eight generations) *after* Jesus founded the original Spiritual movement known as Followers of The Way. This means that Constantine's institutional Christianity had *no* connection with the original *Early Christian Lifestyle*. The two were different organizational structures in history and weren't connected in any way.

5. Many history books say Constantine was a "Christian." But that's whitewash because Constantine was a priest in the sun god religion. Such books say Constantine was a "Christian" because of the legend that "the god *Christus*" supposedly appeared to him in a dream. However, many researchers dispute that legend. They say that if Constantine really had a dream, it was probably the result of unconscious memories of his experiences with tortured Christians in the dungeons of Diocletian's palace – not a real appearance by Jesus Christ.

6. Constantine's first law, *The Edict of Milan*, made Christianity a *legal* religion of the empire equal to all the other religions of the empire. But that made Christians visible, organized, taxed, counted, and regulated by the government for the first time in history.

In the next chapter, we're going to finish our analysis of *Cause #3* (Link 3) in our problem-solving case. We've going to continue analyzing the *Root Cause* of today's shrinking Christianity. We've seen why the services, rituals, and programs of today's traditional congregations are different from the free, easy, and loving original Christian lifestyle. They're different because Constantine laid their foundation in the Fourth Century, and he *wasn't* a Christian. But Constantine's damage isn't over. Next, we're going to talk about his most harmful series of actions against Christians – a series that injured and weakened Christianity forever.

Chapter 4

THE CONTAMINATION

Courthouses, Sun Gods, and Crosses

In the previous chapter, we talked about *Cause #3* (Link 3) in our problem-solving case, the *Root Cause* of America's shrinking Christianity. We found that *Cause #3* is the historical fact that Constantine appeared on the world stage in the Fourth Century and issued a flood of new laws in the Roman Empire that regulated, controlled, and subjugated the Christians of that day.

Of course, we'll never fully understand Constantine's motives. We know he had a low opinion of Christians because he had helped torture and execute them in the dungeons of Diocletian's palace. We also know that he was building a political and military foundation for conquering the eastern part of the Roman empire. But whatever motives were driving him, the moment he came to power, he began to aggressively mold Christianity into a legally regulated religion like the other legally regulated religions of the empire.

In this chapter, we're going to finish our understanding of *Cause #3* (Link 3) in our case. We're going to talk about *five* of Constantine's most ruinous actions against Fourth Century Christians. These five actions laid the final foundation for what would become institutional Christianity; and they suppressed Christian Spirituality so completely that it's virtually extinct today. Let's start with the most heinous of Constantine's actions: His decision to build *courthouses* for Christians.

The Courthouses

Let's start with an experiment. Let's ask you to remember the last Christian "church" building that you were in. Visualize how it was designed. The building was probably rectangular shaped, like a shoe box. You probably walked up several broad front steps from the street or lawn and entered a set of tall doors. That probably brought you into a reception lobby, where there may have been some literature racks, and perhaps a few potted plants, coat racks, umbrella stands, and so on.

Next, you probably opened another set of tall doors and entered a long, rectangular room. This rectangular room probably had a center aisle, with two side aisles running along the walls. Or if the building was large, the room may have had two middle aisles with rows of columns supporting a high ceiling. Depending on which Christian denomination built the building, and depending on the country in which it was located, the room probably had a stone or tile floor if it was old (as in Europe). Or it was probably carpeted if it was newer (as in America). If the building was ancient, the room probably only had a large open space for a crowd of people to stand. If the building was more modern, the room probably had pews or chairs. At the front of this rectangular room, with various screens, railings, and ornaments, there was probably a platform holding a table, a few chairs, a lectern, perhaps a pulpit and, in many cases, an ornate altar. The room probably had high ceilings, stone or plaster walls and, if the building was ancient (as in Europe), it may have been dimly lighted with banks of candles.

Now – we could continue discussing these details. But let's stop. Here's your first exam question: Allowing for different architects, ages, and denominations, weren't the details that you just read a fairly *accurate* description of a typical Christian "church" building? If so, here's your second exam question: *Why* are most Christian buildings designed that way?

The answer is simple. Most Christian buildings are designed that way because that's the design of a Fourth Century Roman *courthouse*. The Roman emperor Constantine built the first Christian "church" buildings ever built in history, and he chose the Roman *courthouse* design for them.[1] And now, although over 1,700 years have passed, today's Christian congregations still use that design.

Constantine's strategy was that if the non-Christian religions had temples and shrines, then *Christians* should have buildings, too. And he began construction of the very *first* Christian buildings ever built – and then passed laws mandating that Christians must attend them. It's important to remember that before Constantine, Christians *didn't* have buildings. Before Constantine, Christians met freely and informally in small groups in private homes, and that was one of the keys to their amazing *Spirituality*, as we'll see in coming pages.[2]

Now, the truth is that the very *first* Christian "church" building ever built still stands in Rome today, and it's still being used for Christian services, rituals, and programs. Its name is the "Basilica of St. John Lateran." It's in the *courthouse* design, and it's located on the Via Vittorio Emanuele Filiberto, in Rome. Of course, over the centuries it has been greatly restored, rebuilt, and remodeled, and today it's full of statues and art objects that weren't in the original building. But it's still there, standing on the foundations that Constantine laid in the Fourth Century.

The *second* Christian building ever built is also still standing. It's also in the *courthouse* design, and it's also in Rome, standing on the foundations that Constantine laid in the Fourth Century. Like the first building, it's also still being used for Christian services, rituals, and programs. Its name is the "Basilica of St. Peter," and it's located on the Viale Giulio Cesare, adjoining St. Peter's Square, in Vatican City. This second building is the international headquarters of the Roman Catholic denomination today and, like the first building, it has also been greatly restored, rebuilt, and remodeled over the centuries, and is full of statues and art objects that weren't in the original building.[3]

Now – before continuing, let's pause to understand the strange word "basilica" that Constantine used to name his Christian buildings. The word *basilica* is the Latin word for a *courthouse*. (It's pronounced "buh-<u>sill</u>'-uh-cuh.") In Latin, the word literally means "royal court." Basilicas were judicial buildings in ancient Rome. They were used for royal events, military and government events, as places to announce important news or laws, and as places to hold trials, executions, and funerals.[4] But these facts raise an interesting question. *Why* did Constantine choose the *courthouse* design for his Christian buildings? After all, he had unlimited time, money, labor, and building materials. He could have used any design he wanted. For example, he could have used the *round* or *square* designs of the non-Christian temples and shrines. But he didn't. He used the rectangular courthouse design. *Why* did he do that?

Let's think for a moment. In ancient Rome, basilicas were associated in the minds of the people with law enforcement, politics, and military events. To the people on the streets (especially slaves, women, children, elderly, poor, and the other socially powerless people), a *basilica* was a place where you were tried, sentenced, and executed. So average people dreaded basilicas and avoided them. That being true, *why* did Constantine choose such an intimidating design for his new Christian buildings? The answer is simple. As a cruel combat general and shrewd political dictator, Constantine wanted to suppress Christian *Spirituality*. He wanted to neutralize the free, easy, informal, and loving lifestyle of the Early Christians. So he built scary looking *courthouses* as their legally mandated meeting places.

And Constantine's scheme worked to perfection. As soon as Christians began gathering in Constantine's new basilicas, they became subdued, passive, and obedient – and that subdued attitude persists in Christian buildings to this day. I can remember my parents telling me to be quiet and reverent in Christian buildings. I also have another childhood memory of an aunt scolding me for laughing in a Christian building. So people's subdued attitude in Christian buildings is part of Constantine's legacy. But, we inherited much worse things from his basilicas, as we'll see in coming pages. However, before we get to those facts, let's ask another interesting question about Christian buildings. Where did the word *church* come from?

The Non-Christian Word "Church"

The full story of Constantine's rise to power is too long for this chapter. So let's summarize it by saying that Constantine eventually *did* conquer the eastern empire; and he eventually *did* achieve his dream of being grand emperor of a unified Roman empire. Then as part of his plan for his unified empire, he began to remodel a city in the east that he named "New Rome." That new city was intended to be the capital of the Eastern Empire. But as time passed and the situation changed, New Rome was eventually named after Constantine himself – and so the city was known as *Constantinople* for centuries. Today, "New Rome" is the modern city of Istanbul in Turkey. The point is that knowing about the city of New Rome is necessary because *it* is the place where the word "church" was invented. Here's how that happened.

While Constantine was remodeling New Rome, he built several Christian basilicas there, together with several non-Christian temples and shrines, often placing them side by side on same streets. And it was during that period of the Fourth Century – near the end of Constantine's reign – that he invented a new religious word in the city of New Rome. That new word started out as the Greek phrase *kuriakon doma*, meaning "the Lord's building," or "the Lord's hall." (The people of the city spoke Greek at that time.) Thus, the phrase *kuriakon doma* referred to the *physical structure* of religious buildings – both Christian and non-Christian buildings. In other words, Constantine's phrase *wasn't* a Christian phrase. It referred to *any* building used by *any* religion for *any* religious purpose to honor *any*

Lord. That included the temples of the sun god, and all the other non-Christian temples and shrines in New Rome.[5]

Then over the centuries, Constantine's phrase, *kuriakon doma*, was gradually shortened by people to *kuriakon*; and it slowly migrated to Europe, where it drifted across several different European countries and through several European languages (being modified each time), until finally it landed in England as the Old English word, *chirche*. In England it finally developed into today's modern word "church" – still referring to *any* religious building used by *any* religion for *any* religious purpose, to honor *any* Lord.

Then, in the merry old England of the Middle Ages, another unfortunate event occurred. English translators improperly used the Constantinian word *church* to translate the *New Testament* from Greek to English when the first English Bibles were published in the 1500s. And in 1611, with the publishing of the popular *King James Version* of the Bible, the use of the Constantinian word *church* spread worldwide and became the household word it is today. However, this improper use of the non-Christian word *church* has caused unbelievable grief in Christianity – because it keeps Christianity's attention focused on the care and maintenance of *buildings*, instead of on Spiritual behavior (exactly as Constantine intended back in the Fourth Century).

We'll return to our discussion of the non-Christian word *church* in later pages and draw more lessons from it. But for now, let's just remember that Constantine invented the word *church* in New Rome the Fourth Century, and that it *isn't* an original Christian word. Jesus and His disciples didn't know it, never heard it, and didn't use it. Neither did the Followers of The Way in Early Christian history. Next, as long as we're discussing non-Christian words that were invented by Constantine and not by the Early Christians, let's talk about another word he invented: the word *Sunday*.

The Non-Christian Word "Sunday"

In the First Century, the Early Christians put special emphasis on worshiping on the first day of the week. They called the first day of the week *The Lord's Day* because that's the day Jesus rose from the dead; and that's the day the Holy Spirit came to earth to give birth to Christianity. In those days, the first day of the week was a normal work day, so Christians met in their homes either before work, after work, or both, to share meals, pray, and worship.

But then Constantine changed "The Lord's Day" for Christians with one of his new laws. In the First Century, the days of the week were named in Latin after the sun, the moon, and the planets. For example, the first day of the week was *dies solis*, or "sun day." The second day was *dies lunar*, or "moon day." The third day was *dies martis*, or "mars day," and so on.

Constantine was the high priest of the sun god religion as well as emperor of Rome. So as part of his strategy to suppress Christians, it was easy for him to disrupt how they worshiped on the first day of the week. He simply passed a law *renaming* the first day of the week, and legally *mandating* what people could do on that day. His law said that everyone (including Christians) must now call the first day of the week *The Venerable Day of the Sun* (this means, "The Reverent Day of the Sun").

The new law also said that the first day of the week was now a legal *holiday* in the Roman Empire. All shops were to be closed and all work was to cease. Everyone was required by law to attend the approved basilicas, temples, and shrines – after which everyone was to take the rest of the day off for pleasure, chores, and recreation. (Later, this legal control over Christian worship on the first day of the week was tightened even more when *small groups* were outlawed, as we'll see in coming pages.)

Constantine's new law controlling worship on the first day of the week was implemented, and soon it upended the way Christians had been behaving on the first day of the week for 300 years. Christians began attending the basilicas more loyally – and more Christians stopped calling the first day of the week *The Lord's Day*. Then as the years passed, people began to shorten the lengthy phrase, "The Venerable Day of the Sun." First, they shortened it to "Day of the Sun." Then to "Sun Day." Then to "Sun-Day." And finally to *Sunday*, as we call it now.[6]

Today, Christians still call the first day of the week "Sunday," and they still treat it as a holiday. For many Christians, the first day of the week is simply a day for sports, picnics, hobbies, and family chores. Few Christians today call the first day of the week *The Lord's Day* – and even fewer meet in homes on the first day of the week for small group meals, prayer, and worship.

Now – let's pause to summarize what we know about Constantine thus far. We know that he made Christianity a legal religion. We know that he built the first Christian buildings; that he used the courthouse design for them, and that he named them "churches." We know that he named the first day of the week "Sunday," and made it a legal holiday. And we know that he passed many other new laws to regulate, control, and subjugate Christians. So, in the briefest of terms, we know that it was Constantine who laid the foundations of the *institutional Christianity* that we have today. But we're not finished yet. Next, we need to talk about the non-Christian word *clergy*.

The Non-Christian Word "Clergy"

We need some background before we can understand Constantine's next series of laws. It's important to remember that during the first three centuries of Christian history (about the first eight generations of Christians), Christians didn't have *bosses* in their small groups. That is, they didn't have a structure of human control – a pecking order, a hierarchy of authority. Instead, their groups were formed around two or three families who treated one another as equals. They treated one another as relatives and called one another "brother," "sister," "mother," and "daughter," even though they weren't blood kin. They loved one another irrespective of status, age, gender, nationality, and ethnic background, and they emphasized like-mindedness in all matters.

However, it's important to realize that the Early Christians *did* have special full-time "servants" moving freely among their small groups to help them grow Spiritually. Some of the Early Christians had "calls" from the Holy Spirit to serve the small groups in specific *Spiritual* ways. There were six of these Spiritual calls. A Christian could be called by the Holy Spirit to be an apostle, a deacon, an elder, an evangelist, a prophet, or a teacher. Some Early Christians even had multiple calls to servantship. The apostle Paul is an example. He had *triple* calls to serve small groups as a teacher, prophet, and apostle.

But here's the principle to remember. Paul served Christian small groups worldwide with giftedness, courage, discipline, and revelation. But he never had command-and-control *authority* over them. He never had a "job title" in the upper reaches of a lofty "organizational chart." The opposite was true. Paul was the social equal of the Christians in the small groups. The only thing different about him was that he had a call from the Holy Spirit to serve those groups.

Returning to our theme, these Spiritual calls to full-time Christian service were a *threat* to Constantine's plan to suppress Christianity. The free, easy, and informal way that these Spiritual servants moved among the small groups was a danger to Constantine's plan to subjugate Christianity. So next he passed a series of new laws that *legalized* these full-time servants and gave them the same legal and social rights as the priests in the other religions. He also *renamed* the full-time Christian servants. He named them *clerici* – the Latin word for "clerks," in the sense of government employees keeping records in an office. (By the way, that term reveals Constantine's true attitude toward the Christian servants.) Constantine's new Latin name, *clerici*, eventually stuck, and it's the source of today's denominational term, *clergy*.

Then Constantine passed more new laws to continue institutionalizing the Christian servants. He gave them immunity from debts, taxes, and lawsuits. Then he gave them the right to receive inheritances and government grants. Then he gave them the right to accept gifts of cash, land, and crops from the government. All these new "laws" were actually *bribes* designed to buy the loyalty of the Christian servants in the same way that he had purchased the loyalty of the other priests in the other religions of the empire.

And as the years passed, Constantine's financial and social pressures began to wear down the servant Christians. Many of them were everyday people whose *inner* Spiritual call wasn't visible externally. Externally, they were simply common people from the docks, farms, shops, trades, and camel caravans. Many were poor, illiterate, and powerless in the eyes of society. But Constantine continued to bribe them with new gifts, new rights, and new benefits they never thought they'd see in their lifetimes. And gradually Constantine's plan worked. Gradually, the Christian servants became more and more loyal and submissive to Constantine and his new institutional system.

And then Constantine drove in the final nail of his plan to subjugate Christianity. He created a *hierarchy* (a level of authority) among the full-time Christian servants. He created job titles that separated them from one other and from their groups. He decreed that some of the servants were now to be known as "deacons" in his new clergy. Others were to be known as "priests." Others were to be known as "bishops." And he made these appointments in *person*, so none of the servants could refuse their new titles. (Later, Constantine added "archbishops," "cardinals," and other job titles to his new clergy – until his structure finally evolved into the hierarchy of what became the Roman Catholic denomination.)

As Constantine continued passing new laws and adding new structure to his institutional "clergy," two things happened. First, a "caste" system developed between the clergy and everyday Christians. The servant Christians, now conscripted into the clergy, began to distance themselves from normal Christians, whom Constantine now called the *laity*. (The word *laity* is from the Latin root *laici*, and refers to people who are non-professional, non-consecrated, and non-priestly.) Now any Christian who wasn't a member of the *clergy* was a member of the *laity*, and was considered inferior in status and ability. This social chasm between the *clergy* and the *laity* persists to this day and is another part of Constantine's legacy.

Finally, something even more devastating happened. It suddenly dawned on the upper classes of Roman society – the royals and aristocrats – that they could *also* avoid debts, taxes, and lawsuits, and could *also* receive gifts of cash, land, and crops, if they joined Constantine's new clergy. So they did. Thousands of royals and aristocrats flocked to Constantine's clergy, and a new kind of *royal clergy* appeared. Most tragic of all, these royals and aristocrats were *not* Christians. So Constantine's new clergy soon consisted largely of non-Christians.

Then Constantine added a final intoxicating drug to his evil brew. He gave his new royal clerics the legal authority of *Roman judges*. His clergy now had the legal right to hold court in their basilicas and punish members who were disobedient. This finally separated the *clergy* from the *laity* in a profound and permanent way. Normal Christians (the "laity") now began to fear the clergy, and to be more loyal and submissive than ever.

This loyalty and submissiveness of the laity to the clergy is still evident in Christianity today, and is yet another piece of Constantine's legacy. And now, we're ready to talk about the last piece of Constantine's legacy. Let's talk about where today's Christian symbol of the *cross* came from.

The Symbol of the Cross

Although some Christians don't realize it, the "cross" was *not* an original Christian symbol. The Early Christians in the first three centuries of Christian history didn't use it.[7] In fact, since the *cross* is a symbol of an execution device (one of the most horrible execution devices in history), it wouldn't have made any sense for the Early Christians to use it as a symbol of the most loving and joyful Spiritual experience on earth. That'd be like using an *electric chair* today as a symbol of a loving, joyful Spiritual experience. It'd be illogical and confusing.

All of Early Christianity's original symbols have been discovered and studied in the *catacombs* around Rome. The catacombs are a series of underground cemetery tunnels dug by the Early Christians starting in the late First Century and ending in the early Seventh Century. When the Early Christians buried loved ones in these tunnels, they left artifacts, messages, symbols, poems, and inscriptions on the tombs; and that's how we know what the *original* Christian symbols were before the Fourth Century. The authentic Early Christian symbols include a fish, an anchor, a shepherd, a lamb, a sparrow, a dove, a peacock, a boat, and certain letters of the Greek alphabet used as abbreviations of Christian ideas.

But no *crosses* have been found in the catacombs before the *Fourth Century*. Said another way, no archaeological evidence for the cross as a Christian symbol exists before the Fourth Century. For example, "crucifixes," as we know them today, didn't appear until the Fifth Century, and they weren't officially accepted by institutional Christianity until the Eighth Century.

The truth is that the verses in today's Bibles where the word "cross" appears are actually weak translations of the original Greek, just as we saw with the word "church." The Greek word translated in today's Bibles as "cross" could be more correctly translated *pole* or a *stake* – and some First Century crucifixions actually did take place on poles and stakes.[8] But even if we translate the Greek word as "cross," that still doesn't make crosses an original Christian symbol.

So how did the "cross" originate as a Christian symbol? You'll recall from earlier pages that after his triumphal parade into Rome with his enemy's head on his saddle, Constantine built a huge *statue* of himself in the city. You'll recall that this statue had one upraised arm holding a replica of Constantine's *Salutary Sign* of good luck (the plus sign with the loop at the top). This was the symbol that Constantine supposedly saw in his dream in his tent at the Milvian Bridge. And finally, you'll recall that Constantine told the citizens of Rome that the sign was magical, and that it gave him unstoppable power to conquer the empire.

That's where researchers think the "cross" came from as a Christian symbol. They think it evolved from Constantine's *Salutary Sign* on his giant statue in the city of Rome in the Fourth Century. That explains why the earliest archaeological examples of Christian crosses ever found have only been found in *Rome*; and have only been dated from the middle of the *Fourth Century*.

Okay – everything we've discussed so far about Constantine now leads us to our final question about him. It's an obvious question. And it has an obvious answer. But history books sympathetic to institutional Christianity have made the answer fuzzy, confusing, and controversial. Here's our final question: *Was Constantine a Christian?*

The Non-Christian Emperor

As we've said, Constantine, the cruel combat general and emperor, was *not* a Christian and never *became* one. Like most Romans, he was a sun worshiper all his life. Indeed, he was a priest in the sun god religion, and later held the title *Pontifex Maximus* (greatest priest) in the sun god religion. Constantine never said – verbally or in writing – that he was a Christian. And he never joined the institutional Christianity that he personally created. Instead, all of his laws and actions point to the simple fact that he was a *non-Christian.*

For example, he never outlawed non-Christian religions in the empire. He never interfered with the non-Christian temples and shrines, and he never interfered with the often obscene and vulgar rituals in the non-Christian temples and shrines. More, he minted coins bearing the images of non-Christian gods, and he personally sacrificed to non-Christian gods until the day he died.

But worst of all, Constantine was cruel, vicious, and immoral. He was unfaithful to his wife, Fausta. He kept mistresses, and two of his sons were illegitimate. Later, he murdered his wife, Fausta, by drowning her in her own bathtub. He also murdered Crispus, one of his sons. He also murdered Sopater, his best friend. He also murdered Licinius, his father-in-law. And he routinely murdered any relative, military, or political rival who got in his way.

Here's the point. The big mistake that historians make when they say Constantine was a "Christian" is that they base that fuzzy claim on the legend that Constantine *dreamed* about Jesus in his tent at the Milvian Bridge. But even if that legend was true, people don't become Christians by *dreaming* about it. People become Christians by making a conscious *decision* to become one. And Constantine never made that conscious decision. Instead, he was a non-Christian priest, murderer, and dictator who for 25 years worked tirelessly to subvert and pervert Early Christianity. *That's* not Christian behavior.

But perhaps the final proof that Constantine wasn't a Christian is his legacy. After he died, the institutional Christianity that he founded grew into the Medieval Christianity of the Dark Ages, with its torture chambers, immorality, and levels of corruption that blacken the pages of history. And over the centuries, Constantine's institutional Christianity became the weak and shrinking Christian congregations that we have today. *That's* Constantine's legacy, and it's difficult to say with a straight face that it's a Christian one.

So, at last we've finished our problem-solving case. At last we understand *Cause #3* (Link 3) in the cause-and-effect linkage we started analyzing back in chapter 2. Now we know why today's Christian denominations don't teach the *Early Christian Lifestyle*. They don't teach it because they're descended from Constantine's institutional Christianity, and *he* didn't teach it. He suppressed it. And the tragedy is that his scheme worked in the Fourth Century and is still working today. So that leads us to the closing question of this chapter: *What can we do about it*? Assuming that we want a Spiritual lifestyle like the one the original Christians had in the First Century: *How can we get it*?

We're going to start answering that pivotal question in the next chapter. We're going to start discussing the simple and obvious solution to Christianity's present day weakness. We're going to start discussing how to live the *Early Christian Lifestyle* in today's world. But first, let's summarize all that we've said in this chapter.

Summary of Chapter 4

1. Most Christian "church" buildings today are in the rectangular shape of Roman *courthouses* because Constantine designed and built the first Christian buildings, and he built them in the shape of Fourth Century Roman courthouses.

2. Constantine invented the non-Christian word "church" as a name for his new religious buildings, including both Christian basilicas and non-Christian temples and shrines. The word "church" was unknown to Jesus and Christians before the Fourth Century, since they worshiped in small groups in homes and called themselves "groups." Then in the Middle Ages, translators inappropriately used the word "church" to translate the first English Bibles from Greek, and that made the word "church" acceptable worldwide. However, using the word "church" keeps Christianity focused on the care and maintenance of *buildings*, instead of on Spiritual growth.

3. Constantine renamed the first day of the week "The Venerable Day of the Sun." Over the years, people shortened this to *Sunday*, and we still call it that today. Constantine legally required people to attend basilicas and temples on the first day of the week and to the rest of the day as a holiday. These changes upended the way Christians had worshiped for 300 years, and helped dismantle their Spiritual lifestyle.

4. Constantine created the *clergy* by conscripting the full-time Christian servants into his new *clerici*. He corrupted them with bribes and gifts, and Roman elites rushed to join the clergy too, so that a *royal clergy* was born that still exists today.

5. Constantine drove a wedge in Fourth Century Christianity by dividing Christians into a *clergy* and a *laity*. Then he subdivided the clergy into *deacons, priests, and bishops*, and widened the gap by giving the clergy the power of judges. This created a subdued respect for the clergy that's still evident today.

6. The *cross* is a symbol of an ancient execution device, and was not an original Christian symbol. It evolved in Fourth Century Rome from the *Salutary Sign* Constantine had on his huge statue there. The original Christian symbols were the fish, anchor,

shepherd, sparrow, dove, peacock, lamb, boat, and certain letters of the Greek alphabet.

7. Constantine was not a Christian. He was high priest of the sun god religion, and held that title until his death. He minted non-Christian coins and sacrificed to non-Christian gods his entire life, and he was cruel, immoral, and a murderer. However, over the centuries, historians sympathetic to institutional Christianity have *whitewashed* him, so that few people today know who he was or what he really did.

After Constantine's death in the late Fourth Century, the emperors who followed him developed choirs and chants; incense and candles; "mass" ceremonies (called the "eucharist" or "communion" by some denominations); the use of sermons given by professional speakers; the habit of letting the clergy make all congregational decisions behind closed doors, and – most importantly – they outlawed small group worship in private homes, as we'll see later.

In closing, a wise philosopher once said that *institutions* are "The lengthened shadow of one man."[9] And so they are. Today's institutional Christian denominations are the lengthened shadow of one man in history. They're the lengthened shadow of Emperor Constantine in Fourth Century Rome.

Next, we're going to tie together everything we've said thus far, and we're going to talk about five important principles of Spiritual growth. So let's move to Chapter 5 and see those five principles.

Chapter 5

THE CURRENT CRISIS

Buildings, Programs, and Ancestors

This is a bridge chapter. It's going to connect everything we've said thus far to everything we're going to say in coming pages. We covered a lot of information in the past four chapters – all of it important for living the *Early Christian Lifestyle* of peace, hope, and miracles in today's world. But before we jump to the specifics of how to live that special lifestyle, let's keep our theme clearly in mind. Our theme is this: American Christianity is rapidly *shrinking* in both congregational *attendance* and in Spiritual *impact* on our nation.

We said that's happening because today's traditional congregations *aren't* teaching the Early Christian habit of living a Spiritual lifestyle. And that's happening because today's congregations are descended from the institution Constantine founded in Fourth Century Rome. That means we need to understand the cause-and-effect linkage between Constantine and today's Christianity even more clearly.

To understand that connection more precisely, let's compare the *Spirituality* of two different groups of Christians at two different points in history – and then draw a conclusion from the comparison. Here's our comparison:

1. As a *standard* for Christian Spirituality, let's use the behavior of the First Century Christians. Let's let the *Early Christian Lifestyle* be our test for Christian Spirituality in every century.

2. Next, let's compare Fourth Century Christians to that standard and see how well they matched (or didn't match) it.

3. Finally, let's compare Twenty-First Century Christians to that standard and see how well they match (or don't match) it.

But before we start, let's be clear about our *standard*. Let's remember that the Early Christians lived a lifestyle that was free, informal, and loving. They emphasized personal growth, freedom of expression, freedom of movement, and freedom to enjoy Spiritual experiences. They called themselves "Followers of The Way," and they lived with healings, peace, patience, courage, miracles, and angelic guidance. They worshiped in small groups in private homes without a hierarchy of humans to micromanage them. They were so Spiritual that even when they were persecuted, they walked to the lion pits holding hands and singing. That should be the standard for Christian Spirituality in every century, and it should be the acid test for all things Christian. So now let's see how well *Fourth Century Christians* met our standard.

The Basilica Christians

The Roman emperor, Constantine, built the first Christian buildings and built them in the Fourth Century *basilica* (courthouse) design. He invented the word *church* as a name for them, and passed a law requiring all Christians to attend them. He divided Christianity into a *clergy* and a *laity*, renamed the first day of the week *Sunday*, and passed 300 laws that ended the Spiritual lifestyle that Christians had been living since the First Century. Thus, because of Constantine, Fourth Century Christians weren't united, weren't like-minded, and didn't live with healings, peace, hope, and miracles.

So if we compare Fourth Century Christians to our *standard* of First Century Christian Spirituality, we have to conclude that, through no fault of their own, the Basilica Christians of the Fourth Century were *not* a good match to our standard. Their story is actually a story of abuse, tragedy, and failure. Next, let's see how well *Twenty-First Century Christians* meet our standard.

The Program Christians

Like Fourth Century Christians, today's Christians worship in buildings designed like *basilicas* and call them *churches*. Today's Christians are divided into a *clergy* and a *laity*, and they call the first day of the week *Sunday*. Their clergy is divided into a hierarchy (senior pastors, associate pastors, youth pastors, priests, bishops, archbishops, and dozens of other job titles). They worship with rigid *agendas* and are micromanaged by their clergy. They are *program-oriented*, and have covered dish meals, bingo games, bazaars, bus trips, sports teams, scout troops, preschools, musical concerts, choir rehearsals, dramatic presentations, fall pumpkin sales, nativity scenes, Bible studies, prayer meetings, and sunrise services – to name just a few of their many programs.

So if we compare Twenty-First Century Christians to our *standard* of First Century Christian Spirituality, we have to conclude that, through no fault of their own, the Program Christians of the Twenty-First Century are *not* a good match to our standard. Their story is a story of abuse, tragedy, and failure too.

Now – what did this comparison of these two groups of Christians tell us? It told us that today's Christians have the wrong "*ancestors.*"

The Wrong "Ancestors"

DNA tests are all the rage today. Everyone wants to send in a sample of their DNA and discover who their *ancestors* were. So let's ask a DNA question. *Who are the "ancestors" of today's Christians?* Are today's Christians descended from First Century Christians? Or are they descended from Fourth Century Christians?

The answer is easy, isn't it? Can't we agree that today's Christians act more like Fourth Century Basilica Christians than they do First Century Small Group Christians? If so, our next important question is: *What can today's Christians do to start being more Spiritual?*

The first thing today's Christians can do is "change ancestors." They can disown their Fourth Century ancestors and embrace their First Century ancestors. They can return to the basics of Early Christianity. And *that's* the solution we propose in this book. But before we discuss that solution in detail, let's slow down to deal with another huge issue. Today's library shelves sag under the weight of books teaching that the only thing Christians need to do to be more Spiritual is to renew, revive, and improve their spectator-type traditional "churches." They need to tweak the programs of today's "churches," and then work *harder* in those tweaked programs. But is that true? Is that a valid solution? Let's talk about tweaking today's traditional "churches."

The "Churches" That Never Existed

First of all, there were no such things as "churches" (or the word "church") in Christian history before the Fourth Century. That means writers, preachers, historians, and theologians make a mistake today when they use the non-existent word "church" to describe Christians as people, or Christian meetings. Of course, they've done that since the Fourth Century, so we can't really blame them.[1]

But when writers and speakers use the word "church," they're using a word that didn't exist in the First, Second, or Third Centuries. Jesus, Peter, and Paul never *saw* a "church," never *heard* the word "church," never *referred* to Christians as the "church," and never *referred* to Christian meetings as "church." Thus, when writers and speakers talk about renewing, reviving, and improving "churches," they're talking about renewing, reviving, and improving something that didn't exist when Jesus, Peter, and Paul walked the earth. This means that such renewal plans are false, futile, and frustrating. Not only that, but people have *tried* for hundreds of years to renew the institutional "church," and let's not forget what happened to them.

The Tweakers That Failed

Tweaking the spectator-type structures and programs of the institutional "church" has been tried before. Many times. The biggest attempts were made during the Middle Ages. That's when some of the institution's own *priests* realized that their institution was suppressing Spirituality – and they rebelled. History books call them "The Reformers." They lived in Europe from the late 1300s to the early 1600s. The peak of their efforts came in the 1500s, when The Reformers started what the history books call the "Protestant Reformation."

The Reformers wanted institutional Christianity to be more like First Century Christianity. But they failed. And after they failed, they resigned from the institution and tried to create new Christian movements that would be more like the Followers of The Way in the First Century. They wanted to return to the *standard* of First Century Spirituality – exactly as we discussed earlier. But that dream failed too.

The Reformers included such people as John Wycliffe, Jan Hus, Martin Luther, John Calvin, William Tyndale, John Knox, Jacobus Arminius, and many others. But the institution didn't appreciate their efforts. It didn't *want* to be renewed. So it imprisoned some of them. It exiled some of them. It tortured some of them. It beheaded some of them. And it burned some of them at the stake. And in the end, the sacrifices of The Reformers were all in vain. They failed, and the Protestant Reformation failed. It failed because the institution didn't *want* to be renewed.

Of course, The Reformers *were* able to change a few fringe habits around the edges of the institution. But since all of them were ex-priests themselves, and since all their followers were ex-members of the institution too, the movements The Reformers created were never able to shake off their institutional chains. The doctrines, rituals, habits, and hierarchies of the institution were too deeply embedded in their minds.

Thus today, institutional Christianity operates largely as it did in the Fourth Century – except that now it's divided into two large pieces: the Roman Catholic piece and the Protestant piece. Other than that, the institution is essentially the same one that Constantine founded over 1,700 years ago. That means Christians who want to grow Spiritually are going to have to do it *outside* the walls of the institution. They're going to have to do it using what we call para-groups. Let's get an early peek at *para-groups*, and then we'll discuss them in-depth in coming pages.

The Para-Groups

Since the spectator-type structure of institutional Christianity is cast in concrete and can't be changed, the only way for members (and non-members) to grow *Spiritually* is to do it the old-fashioned way – to do it like the original Christians did it. After all, the Followers of The Way in the First Century didn't have an institutional structure and *they* were Spiritual. That proves institutional structures aren't required for Spiritual growth.

Thus, one way for Christians to grow Spiritually today is to do what the original Christians did: meet in small groups in private homes. We're going to call that the "para-groups solution." In English, the prefix "para-" comes from the Greek preposition, *para*, meaning "by the side of, or parallel to."[2] So when we talk about para-groups, we're talking about a solution that works *by the side of*, or *parallel to*, traditional congregations.

This means that para-groups don't interfere with a traditional congregation's membership or programs. Christians can participate in para-groups whether or not they're active in a traditional congregation. The two systems can co-exist, and para-groups can actually increase the *attendance* and *Spirituality* of a traditional congregation. In the next chapter, we're going to start laying the foundation for para-groups. We're going to use diagrams and examples to show how Christians can worship in para-groups, and how they can experience miracles while doing it. But before we get to those details, let's slow down and look at *five* principles of Spirituality that we've developed. Then let's summarize and close the chapter.

The Five Principles of Spirituality

1. Institutional Christianity in the Fourth Century – and Christian Spirituality in the First Century – are *two different things* and should always be studied and discussed separately.

2. There was no "early church." Institutional Christianity was founded, and the word "church" was invented, 300 years *after* Spiritual Christianity was given birth by Jesus in Jerusalem. So if the word "church" is used at all, it should only refer to a *building* being used for religious purposes. The word "church" should never refer to Christians as people ("Good morning, *church*!"). Or to Christian meetings ("We're really having *church* tonight, aren't we!")

3. The institutional structure of today's Christian denominations *can't* be renewed, revived, or improved, and the institution will resist anyone who tries to do so.

4. Institutional Christianity was founded to *suppress* Spirituality – not to promote it – and through the centuries it has been very effective.

5. The *standard* for Christian Spirituality for every Christian, and every Christian activity, in every century, is how closely that person or activity matches the *Spiritual behavior* of the original Followers of The Way.

Summary of Chapter 5

1. The *Early Christian Lifestyle* must be our standard of Spirituality today. That lifestyle is free, informal, loving, and emphasizes supernatural experiences. The Early Christians worshiped in small groups in private homes with no religious hierarchy or rigid programs to distract them from Spiritual growth.

2. The Roman emperor Constantine came to power in the Fourth Century and began to dismantle the *Early Christian Lifestyle* with vigor. He built the first Christian buildings, invented the word "church," passed laws forcing Christians to attend the buildings, divided Christianity into a "clergy" and a "laity," named the first day of the week "Sunday, " and in general started the demise of original Christianity.

3. Today's Program Christians are direct descendants of Constantine's Basilica Christians. Like Constantine's Christians, they worship in buildings called "churches," they're divided into a "clergy" and a "laity," they call the first day of the week "Sunday," and they have an institutional "hierarchy" to micromanage them.

4. Today's Christians need to "change ancestors." They need to disown their Fourth Century ancestors, embrace their First

Century ancestors, and return to the basics of Early Christian Spirituality.

5. Since there were no "church" buildings and no word "church" until the Fourth Century, it's improper for writers, preachers, historians, and theologians to use the word "church" to describe today's Christians or today's Christian meetings.

6. The biggest attempt to tweak institutional Christianity happened in the Middle Ages. That's when some institutional priests realized that their institution was suppressing Spirituality and tried to stop it. They were called "The Reformers," and their movement was called "The Protestant Reformation." But they failed, and many of them were tortured and executed.

7. The way for Christians to be more Spiritual today is to do what the original Christians did – worship in small groups in private homes and emphasize Spiritual growth.

8. The para-groups solution is a return to the basics of Early Christianity without interfering with a traditional congregation's membership or programs. Para-groups work *by the side of* traditional congregations and strengthen their membership and Spirituality.

And now we're ready to talk about how to implement para-groups. We're going to do that with diagrams, examples, and true stories. But as always, we need to begin at the beginning. First, we need to understand *Spirituality*. Only then will we be equipped to talk about small group worship. And if we're going to understand Spirituality, we need to understand the people that the Early Christians called "natural" people. Let's turn to Chapter 6 and find out who "natural" people are.

PART II

The Early Christian Basics

Chapter 6

THE NATURAL PERSON

The First Spiritual Level

During the first three centuries of Christian history, the Early Christians taught *four* different levels of Spirituality. They didn't use the word "levels," but if we study their teachings, that's what they were saying. They said that all people are living on one of the following four Spiritual levels:

1. They're *natural* people,

   or

2. They're *infant* Christians,

   or

3. They're *growing* Christians,

   or

4. They're *mature* Christians.

As you can guess, Paul, Peter, John, and the other First Century teachers wanted all people to be *mature* Christians, since that's where the most peace, healings, and miracles occur. Now, so you can see the principles involved, we're going to start here in Chapter 6 with the "natural" level of Spirituality (the non-Spiritual level), and in following chapters, we're going to work our way up to the *mature* level.

However, before we start with "natural" people, let's agree on *three ground rules* that we're obeying in this book. These rules are important because they help us grow faster Spiritually. Here's the first of the three ground rules.

Ground Rule #1

Define Fuzzy Words

In management classes, I taught a technique called "defining fuzzy words." A "fuzzy" word is a word that has two or more common meanings, or that can imply two or more different actions. The trouble with fuzzy words is that when people hear them, they don't know specifically what *action* to take. They don't know exactly what *behavior* is being expected of them.

As a silly example, let's imagine that I hand you a toolbox and ask you to "fix" my car.

You'd have a vague feeling that I was asking you to do something to my car, but you couldn't actually start work because I used a fuzzy word on you. The word "fix" was fuzzy. It wasn't clear enough for you to know exactly what action to take. That means you'd have to ask me one or more defining questions. You'd ask something like, "Okay, I'll be glad to 'fix' your car. But what do you *mean* by 'fix'?"

That's how we handle fuzzy words. We ask defining questions. If we want people to *do* things (such as be Spiritual), we can't use fuzzy words while discussing it with them. So in this book, we're going to define all of the Christian fuzzy words we use. And we're going to do it clearly enough for you to know exactly what *behavior* the words imply.[1] Of course, you've already guessed where this is heading. Many of the words used by today's traditional congregations are *fuzzy*. The members of those congregations have a vague feeling what the words mean – but few of them know what specific *behaviors* the words imply.

For example, we've been using two popular Christian fuzzy words for many pages now, and the denominations use them too. The two words are: "Christian" and "Spiritual." Most Christians have a vague feeling what these two words mean but – if pinned down – few could clearly explain what *behaviors* the words indicate. So one purpose of this book is to *define* the fuzzy words "Christian" and "Spiritual," and to specify what *behaviors* they imply. We've been chipping away at that for several chapters, but by the end of this book you'll know exactly what the words mean and exactly what behaviors they indicate. However, if we're going to define Christian fuzzy words clearly, we need a "dictionary" to use. So here's the *second* of our three ground rules.

Ground Rule #2

Use Early Christian Definitions

The best dictionary for Christian word meanings is obvious once you think about it. The best source for clear *definitions* of Christian words is Early Christian writing *before* the reign of Constantine. That principle is more important than it seems at first glance – because many Christians today take their definitions from the writings of contemporary Christians. (The pastors of large congregations; the founders of large ministries; the authors of popular devotionals, or the hosts of popular radio or TV programs).

Some Christians today even take their definitions from writings of "The Reformers" of the Middle Ages. (John Calvin; Martin Luther; William Tyndale, and others). Still other Christians take their definitions from the writings of the famous evangelists of the "Great Awakenings" of the 1700s and 1800s. (Jonathan Edwards; Dwight L. Moody; Charles Spurgeon; John Wesley; George Whitefield, and others).

And to be perfectly honest, these writings can be helpful and insightful if kept in context. There's nothing wrong with them. Except for one thing. All of these writers lived (or are living) *after* the Fourth Century. That means they grew up in a Christianity that's descended from Constantine's institution. In fact, most of these writers are (or were) priests, pastors, monks, preachers, professors, theologians, evangelists, or missionaries in traditional denominations, and who make (or made) their livings from those denominations.

Thus, no matter how well intended the authors might be, writings produced *after* Constantine bear the imprint of his structure, rituals, habits, and ceremonies. Said a different way, Christian books, radio, and TV programs produced *after* Constantine always focus (at least partly) on the idea that what Christians need to do is renew, revive, and improve their traditional congregation – and then they need to work harder in that congregation. It's rare for writings produced *after* Constantine to focus on the principle that what Christians need to do is *act more like the Early Christians.*

The simple truth is this. The best place to find clear definitions for Christian fuzzy words is to jump all the way back in history to the Early Christian writings of the first 150 years of Christianity. These ancient writings are the only source of pure and original definitions for Christian words. But if we're going to use Early Christian writing to define today's Christian fuzzy words, we also need to do something *practical and useful* with the definitions. So here's the *third* of our three ground rules.

Ground Rule #3

Use Early Christianity as a Model

As we know, Christianity is a special kind of behavior. It's a unique lifestyle that only Christians can live. And that unique lifestyle is embedded in Early Christian writing *before* Constantine. This means that if we use those Early Christian writings as a *model* for our daily behavior, we're adopting the *Early Christian Lifestyle* in today's world.

None of us wants to return to the primitive physical conditions of the Early Christians. None of us wants to return to the ancient food, medicine, and sanitation of the First Century. None of us wants to give up our smart phones, smart TVs, and smart cars. But without giving up any modern conveniences, all of us can adopt the word definitions of the Early Christians as guides for daily behavior. Said in reverse, one reason many Christians are *unspiritual* today is that they're *not* using Early Christian word definitions as a model for daily behavior.

Next, since we've agreed on our *three ground rules* (we're defining fuzzy words, using Early Christian writings for our definitions, and using those definitions as a model for daily behavior), it's time to talk more about the Early Christian letters. Today, we call those letters the *New Testament* part of the Bible. But now let's think about them a little more deeply.

The Early Christian Letters

In the Introduction to this book, I mentioned the time in my life when I studied Early Christian history around the clock for three years and read over 300 books on the subject. During those years, I studied a collection of *Early Christian letters* that were written from the middle of the First Century to the middle of the Second Century. The first letter was written in 45 AD, and the last letter was written in 156 AD.

I studied 35 of these ancient letters. Some of them were written in Israel. Others were written in Greece, Italy, and Turkey. All of them were written between 1,800 and 2,000 years ago. Most importantly, all of them were written an average of 225 years *before* the reign of Constantine. That's about six generations of Early Christians writers who lived, wrote, and died without ever hearing the name "Constantine."

The good thing about 27 of these ancient letters is that they exist today as the *New Testament* part of the Bible, and anyone can read them there. The other eight letters are little-known letters that were written outside of the *New Testament*. But they're readily available in bookstores, libraries, and online. I call these other eight letters the *little-known* letters because most Christians have never read them and don't even know they exist. These rare letters have the odd titles of *Barnabas*, *Clement*, *Didache*, *Diognetus*, *Hermas*, *Ignatius*, *Papias*, and *Polycarp*. Most Christians can't pronounce those titles today and, to tell the truth, they don't need to pronounce them or even remember them. This is the last place I'll mention these letters except in the Appendix of this book. But before we continue, it's important to know two things about these eight little-known letters:

1. First, many of the *principles* in this book came from them.

2. Second, they were well known to the Early Christians, and the Early Christians used them as *teaching tools* to help one another grow Spiritually.

Here's one last thing to remember about all 35 of the ancient Christian letters that we're using as our dictionary and our model for living. The Early Christian teachers used them to prove to small groups that they were teaching the *authentic* principles of Spiritual growth. Christian teachers had to prove to small groups that either *they* had known Jesus personally and had learned Spiritual growth from Him. Or, they had to prove that they had known another *teacher* who had known Jesus, and that they had learned the principles of Spiritual growth from that *other* teacher.[2]

Police detectives might call that an "unbroken chain of evidence." Said another way, the Early Christian teachers were careful to tell small groups *where* the principles they were teaching came from. They wanted small groups to know that the principles they were learning were the true principles of Spiritual growth. But, as years passed, all of the teachers who had *known* Jesus – and all of the teachers who had *known* teachers who had known Jesus – *died*. After that, the only way Christian teachers could prove to small groups that they were teaching the true principles of Spiritual growth was to teach from *letters* written by people who had known Jesus or people who had known people who had known Jesus.

And that's exactly what we're doing in this book. We're taking our principles of Spiritual growth from ancient Christian letters written by teachers who knew Jesus or who knew teachers who knew Jesus. The point is, we need to take our principles from sources as close to *original* Christianity as possible. Why is that so important? It's important because the Early Christian teachers didn't want *unspiritual* principles taught to small groups. They didn't want small groups to be taught wrong ideas, theories, and assumptions about Spiritual living. That's why they warned small groups to reject *impostors* who tried to teach them false theories about Spiritual life.[3]

Now – having agreed that the principles in this book came from a collection of Early Christian letters written before the reign of Constantine, let's return to the theme of the chapter: *Who are the "natural" people?* Let's start by talking about the world's most serious *troubles*.

The Most Serious Troubles

Several years ago, 2,400 of the most respected psychiatrists in the world met in San Francisco for an International Psychoanalytical Congress. The purpose of the congress was to decide what the world's most pressing *troubles* are, and to decide what to *do* about those pressing troubles. After a week of discussion, the 2,400 delegates (who included professors, authors, researchers, and specialists from every area of counseling and therapy) reached the following four conclusions about the world's troubles:

1. People are breaking more *moral* codes and having more troubles with human *relationships* today than at any other time in history.

2. These troubles are the *same* for all people everywhere, regardless of their nation, language, culture, or religion.

3. The *causes* of these troubles are: loneliness, depression, fear, hate, lust, greed, envy, selfishness, and sexual perversion.

4. The *solution* to these troubles is to have everyone on earth "lie down on a couch and let their fantasies emerge."[4]

Now, I don't know about you, but I *agree* with the findings of this elite group. I agree that people's troubles are the same the world over, and that people are having more troubles today than at any time in history. I also agree that the causes of these troubles are loneliness, depression, fear, hate, lust, greed, envy, selfishness, and sexual perversion.

But I *disagree* with the "solution" that these 2,400 psychiatrists proposed. You probably disagree with it, too. First of all, there aren't *enough* psychiatrists in the world (or psychiatric couches) to have the world's population lie down for therapy. But even if there were enough psychiatrists (and couches), I still don't think their "solution" would work. I don't think letting people's fantasies run wild is a valid cure for loneliness, depression, fear, hate, lust, greed, envy, selfishness, and sexual perversion. Do you? I think the opposite is probably true. I think that letting people's fantasies run wild is probably one of the *reasons* for the world's troubles, not one of the *cures* for it.

However, this story about these 2,400 psychiatrists brings us back to the principles of Spiritual living that we're learning. We talked earlier about the importance of finding the *cause* of a problem before trying to *solve* that problem. We said it was inefficient to fight the symptoms of a problem without knowing what was *causing* those symptoms. So let's ask ourselves this question: What's the *cause* of the loneliness, depression, fear, hate, lust, greed, envy, selfishness, and sexual perversion that the 2,400 psychiatrists analyzed? Said another way, what's *causing* the unspirituality of people all over the world?

The Non-Spiritual Person

There's an old management saying that "Recognizing a problem is half of its solution." So the beginning of Spiritual growth is to *recognize* that there's a problem of unspirituality in the world. In earlier pages, we said Early Christians didn't fit in "natural" society. We said they were strangers in the "natural" world. We said they were a royal priesthood among "natural" people. So now it's time to define the *fuzzy* word "natural." And we're going to give it the meaning that the Early Christians gave it because they had a special Greek word for "natural" people. That Greek word has three shades of meaning – but all of them are viewpoints of the same thing. The Greek adjective for *natural* can be translated to mean:

1. A *non-Spiritual* person.

    or

2. A *non-Christian*.

    or

3. A person who doesn't have the *Holy Spirit*.[5]

All three of these meanings refer to the *same* thing. A natural person is *non-Spiritual* because he or she is a *non-Christian* because he or she doesn't have the *Holy Spirit*. We're going to explain all that in detail in coming pages. But first, let's drill down deeper into what the Early Christians taught about "natural" people (non-Christians).

To begin, the Early Christians taught that natural people have two big weaknesses. First, they *can't* be Spiritual. Second, they can't even *understand* Spiritual things. The apostle Paul explained these two big weaknesses of non-Christians this way:

> "The *natural* person can't accept the things that come from the Spirit of God because they're foolishness to him or her, and he or she can't understand them because *Spiritual* things can only be *Spiritually* understood."[6]

Notice that Paul is teaching that natural people (non-Christians) are not only *non-Spiritual* – but they can't even *understand* Spiritual things. If a natural person sees, hears, or reads about something Spiritual, he or she thinks it's foolish, laughs at it, and makes jokes about it. This also implies another big question: If natural people are *non-Spiritual* and have no *understanding* of Spiritual things – then what *is* producing their thoughts and behavior? What *is* motivating them? Let's answer that puzzle now.

The Selfish Human Nature

We've now arrived at the subject of "motivators" in people. Motivators are one of the most important subjects in this book because we're discussing behavior – and behavior is produced by motivators. The word *motivator* comes from a Latin verb meaning "to move." So the word motivator refers to the inner forces that "move" us to behave during the day. Motivators are the inner drives that create our emotions that create our outer behavior during the day.

Thus, if natural people aren't being motivated by a Spiritual motivator – what *is* their motivator? The short answer is this. The motivator of natural people is their *selfish human nature*. That's why the Early Christians called them "natural" people. Non-Christians are natural people because they're being "naturally" motivated by their natural *nature*. And that's not a *good* thing.

Motivation by human nature isn't a good thing because human nature can't produce *Spiritual* behavior. The blunt truth is that human nature is self-absorbed, egotistical, conceited, vain, proud, and arrogant – and those are the motives that create the world's troubles, just as the 2,400 psychiatrists said earlier. (Notice that there's a cause-and-effect linkage here. Selfish human nature creates bad *behavior*, and bad behavior creates the world's *troubles*.)

What else but conceit and arrogance could *cause* the crime, drug abuse, divorce, child abuse, adultery, pornography, wars, drive-by shootings, and workplace massacres that we see all around us? Only the drives of the selfish human nature can explain them. Thus, the beginning of Spirituality is to accept the fact that selfish human nature is *non-Spiritual*. That's just common sense, and every religion in the world teaches it. The only difference between Christianity and the other religions of the world is that Christianity *emphasizes* the fact that human nature is *non-Spiritual* and teaches what to do about it.[7]

Now, if we spell out the linkage of cause-and-effect that's creating the world's trouble, that linkage looks like this:

1. The selfish human nature in people is an inner motivator that produces *negative* emotions in them such as lust, greed, pride, and egotism.

2. These negative emotions in people produce an outer *behavior* of drug abuse, divorce, child abuse, greed, adultery, and depression in them.

3. These negative outer behaviors in *groups* of people produce the failed economies, poverty, disease, wars, and other troubles in the world.

Of course, this non-Spiritual motivation is more evident in *some* people than in others, and it's more evident at some *times* than at others. That's because most people have a thin veneer of education, training, manners, and self-discipline pasted over their negative motivations; and that *thin veneer of civilization* is what holds society together (at least partially). This mask of civilization is what allows people to coexist and to tolerate one another to some degree. But the moment that most people are prevented from *having* something they want, or from *doing* something they want, the thin veneer of civilization drops off – and *natural* anger, pride, and ego gush forth.

Okay – thus far we've been talking about selfish human nature in simple English words. But let's pause here for our first *Greek* lesson of the book. Because as we know, the Early Christians wrote in Greek. And that requires us to define our most important Christian fuzzy words in the original Greek. Here's our first definition of a fuzzy word in the original Greek.

The Human "Flesh"

When the Early Christians wrote about the inner motivator of our selfish human nature, they called it our *flesh*.[8] Most Bible translators don't like that ugly word very much. Maybe they think it's too harsh. But whatever the reason, Bible translators usually translate the Greek word *flesh* into English in softer terms, such as: the "natural person," the "old man," or the "sinful desires." However, regardless of how we translate the word *flesh* into acceptable English, the principle is still the same: Our flesh (our human nature) is *selfish*. That's one of the most important principles in all of Christian writing. In fact, it's the cornerstone of all Early Christian teaching. So let's hit the issue head-on. The Early Christians taught that humans are *born* with a selfish nature and, because of that nature, all humans are interested only in *themselves*.

As a friend of mine used to say, people are only interested in "Old Number One." The average human is concerned primarily with his or her *own* looks, health, income, aches, pains, goals, comfort, offenses, dreams, grievances, and needs. *Not* those of other people. The truth is that people's first and main inner motivator is *flesh*, and that flesh only produces *non-Spiritual* outer behavior in people.

The problem with this great truth (and all religions teach it) is that it's difficult for people to *admit*. In fact, most people *deny* it. When pressed about their fleshy behavior, most people will say things like, "Well, I'm not really *that* bad. I know plenty of people who're meaner than I am. I make occasional mistakes, but I'm as good as the next person."

However, these thoughts are a trap. These thoughts *themselves* are selfish, and prove the principle is true. Such thoughts are a steel curtain that we pull across our mind to seal out Spiritual living. The truth is, *recognizing* our non-Spiritual behavior is the beginning of Spiritual growth. Admitting that we're *selfish* is the key to the door of Spiritual growth. And that's not a new principle. People have known that as long as there have been people. For example, over 3,000 years ago, a king of Israel named David wrote a song about selfish human nature. Here's what David sang:

> "The Lord looks down from Heaven on the sons
> and daughters of men to see if there are any of them
> who understand, any of them who seek God. But *all*
> of them have turned aside. They've *all* become evil.
> There's not *one* who does good – not even *one*."[9]

King David sang these bitter words over 3,000 years ago. Yet his words are exactly what we're talking about in this book. Flesh is *not* Spiritual. It can't even *understand* Spiritual things. So there's a deeper message in King David's song. Since we don't understand Spiritual things, when we *think* we're doing something *good*, we often aren't, since everything that's motivated by human nature is *selfish*, regardless of whether we think it is or not.

For example, people often donate to charities just to see their names in a bulletin, or on a wall, or on a plaque. People often give expensive gifts at parties just to outshine the other guests, and so forth. Even though our behavior might look "good" to outsiders, it's often actually selfish. So here's our conclusion. If we want to grow Spiritually, we can't do it by *denying* that our flesh is selfish and non-Spiritual. And that fact leads us to an important *choice*.

The Acceptance of Selfishness

As we come to the end Chapter 6, you may have a life-changing *decision* to make at this point. It's a decision that we all have to make at some time in our lives. And what we decide in this important decision sets the level at which we can grow *Spiritually* in the future. The options in this important decision are:

1. We can *accept* the Early Christian teaching that our inner human nature (our flesh) is lustful, proud, selfish, and self-centered.

2. Or we can *deny* this Early Christian teaching and cling to the worldly teaching that human nature is pure, sweet, and humble in its core.

3. Or we can *avoid* the decision and leave it to think about at some other time.

To be certain this critical decision is absolutely clear, let's look at a statement the apostle Paul made about it. In a letter to the Christian small groups in Turkey, Paul reminded them of this cornerstone teaching. Here's what he wrote about the motivation of our flesh:

> "The outer behavior produced by our inner human nature (our *flesh*) is obvious: It's sexual immorality, impurity, hatred, discord, jealousy, fits of rage, selfish ambition, dissension, envy, drunkenness, orgies, and the like."[10]

Now – who among us could deny that at least *some* of these negative traits apply to us, at least *some* of the time, in at least *some* situations? We may not be maddened ax murderers. But isn't it true that *all* of us occasionally have impure thoughts and flashes of anger? Isn't it true that *all* of us occasionally have attacks of hatred, ambition, and envy? If the answers are "Yes," then we've accepted the Early Christian teaching that our human natures are non-Spiritual, and that we're *selfish* in our most secret core.

Once we've admitted that, we're ready for the next step. We're ready to talk about the *solution* to non-Spiritual motivation. The next chapter is about that solution. The next chapter is where we start our diagrams showing exawctly how inner motivation works. But before we turn to those diagrams, let's summarize this chapter.

Summary of Chapter 6

1. All people live on one of *four* levels of Spirituality: They're either *natural* people. Or they're *infant* Christians. Or they're *growing* Christians. Or they're *mature* Christians. But everyone should strive to live on the *mature* Christian level because that's where the most healings, peace, and miracles occur.

2. The first ground rule for being Spiritual is to avoid using *fuzzy* words to discuss it. All key Christian words should be clearly defined.

3. The second ground rule for being Spiritual is to define Christian words with the original definitions given to them by Early

Christian writings *before* the reign of Constantine. (Especially the Early Christian writings in the first 150 years of Christian history.)

4. The third ground rule for being Spiritual is to use these Early Christian definitions of key Christian words as *models* for daily behavior.

5. The Spiritual principles in this book came from 35 Early Christian letters written between the middle of the First Century and the middle of the Second Century. These letters were written an average of 225 years (about six generations) before the reign of Constantine, and were written between 45 AD and 156 AD.

6. The Early Christians taught that all the world's troubles are caused by *non-Spiritual* people; and that *non-Spiritual* people are motivated by their selfish human natures (their *flesh*).

7. If we aren't living in *denial*, we must accept the principle that human flesh is *non-Spiritual*. All religions teach that, and if we accept that principle, it prepares us for Spiritual growth.

Okay – we're finished with our introductory spadework. We've discussed all of the basic ground rules and principles we need to break the ice on Spiritual living. Now we're ready to start *growing Spiritually*. That growth starts in the next chapter. Let's turn there now.

Chapter 7

THE MOTIVATIONAL DIAGRAMS

Flesh, Mind, and Spirit

In the previous chapter, we talked about a bedrock principle of Early Christian teaching. That bedrock principle is this: We have inner *motivators* within us and – more specifically – we have a *non-Spiritual* motivator within us. That non-Spiritual motivator is our selfish human nature, or our *flesh* – and it's the source of all the world's troubles. However, inner motivators are hard to *visualize*. Most people don't have a clear idea what inner motivation would look like. So the purpose of this chapter is to start a series of unique diagrams that show you visually how inner motivators work.

In this chapter, we're going to look at Diagrams 1 and 2. They illustrate the basic structure of inner motivation at the first level (the level of *non-Spiritual* motivation). Then we'll move forward in our diagrams to see Spiritual growth and finally Spiritual maturity. But we need to start with the basic model. It can be visualized in three parts. I call the three parts of human motivation *The Three Circles*.

The Three Circles

Personal motivation can be visualized as a *triangle* made up of three connected *circles*. The bottom of the triangle is open, and thus the model looks like an upside down "V." Before we look at the model, let's briefly describe its *three circles*. We've already talked about the first one. It represents our selfish human nature, or *flesh*. But let's quickly review it. Then we'll add the second and third circles to it.

The First Circle of Motivation

OUR SELFISH NATURE
(Our Flesh)

All the world's troubles are caused by the *non-Spiritual* motivator in people. The world's troubles are caused by people letting their selfish natures motivate them and create negative outer behavior in them. This negative behavior can be called "fleshy" or "carnal" behavior, and it includes every kind of crime, rudeness, adultery, cruelty, vulgarity, rage, violence, and so forth.

The Early Christians had a special Greek word for this fleshy outer behavior. That word can be translated into English as an *offense*, a *fault*, a *trespass*, or a *sin* against God and people.[1]

Of course, we don't hear the word "sin" much today. Traditional congregations seldom use it. Most people today don't stand around sipping coffee mugs and saying things like, "Well, I sinned again last night." Or, "You know, I've been sinning a lot this week."

But according to Early Christian teaching, any "natural" behavior that's powered by our inner human nature *is* sin. That's a major principle of Early Christian teaching, and it's a major key to our understanding Spirituality. Thus, the *first circle* on our diagram of human motivation represents the selfish human nature. Now let's describe the second circle.

The Second Circle of Motivation

OUR MIND
(Our Heart)

The second circle on our diagram represents our *mind*. The Early Christians talked a lot about our mind. The Greek word they used for it can be translated into English as our mind; or our understanding;

or our decision-making ability, or our will power.² Thus the Early Christians taught that our mind can *understand* things, make *decisions*, and exert *will power*. But – and this is extremely important – they taught that our mind is *Spiritually* neutral.

In other words, they taught that our mind has no *morals or ethics* of its own. Instead, it accepts without judgment whatever moral and ethical (or immoral and unethical) inner motivation that happens to be powering it. Think about that a moment. Said another way, our mind automatically produces attitudes, decisions, and behaviors that *match* whatever inner motivator is powering it – good or bad.

We could picture our mind as being like a "computer" without a "program" in it. A computer without a program just sits silently on our desk, a useless hunk of plastic and metal. But if we upload a program to it (any program, good or bad), it lights up and starts to operate on that program. The Early Christians said that's exactly the way our minds work. Our minds perform equally well on whatever inner motivator (whatever "program") is powering them.

So our minds are like the old computer saying, "*Garbage In, Garbage Out.*" Except that we could also say, "*Excellence In, Excellence Out.*" So the question we need to ask ourselves is this: What "program" is powering our minds today? Is it a "*Garbage In, Garbage Out*" program? Or is it an "*Excellence In, Excellence Out*" program?

You can guess where all this is going. We know that people's normal motivator is their *selfish human nature*. So a normal person's mind is being powered by his or her selfish nature – and that explains why most people's behavior is self-centered, vulgar, rude, and deceitful. None of us likes to hear that. But in the cold light of day, most people would admit that this Early Christian teaching is true.

Now – let's shift gears a moment to explain another important feature of our diagrams. Each of the three circles on our diagrams has a popular *synonym*. That is, each circle has an interchangeable word printed beneath it that the First Century Christians used to describe that motivator in other ways. In the case of our selfish nature, we already know that the popular synonym the Early Christians used for it is the word *flesh*.

Our *second circle* (the one representing our mind), also has a popular synonym that the Early Christian used for it. That word is *heart*. For example, when Jesus was once confronted by some angry lawyers in the city of Capernaum, He asked them: "Why do you entertain evil thoughts in your *hearts*?"[3]

Now Jesus knew that the human *heart* is only a muscle in our chest that pumps blood. He knew that our *heart* isn't really capable of "evil thoughts." He was simply using the First Century word "heart" to represent the human mind in His debate with the lawyers. And we still do that today when we say things like, "She's dear to my *heart*." What we're actually saying is, "She's dear to my *mind*." Next, let's describe our *final circle*.

The Third Circle of Motivation

OUR SPIRIT
(Our Soul)

The *third circle* on our motivational diagram is the most important one of all. It represents our *spirit*, the most amazing circle on the diagram. The Early Christians taught that all humans have an invisible *spirit* living inside them.[4] These spirits came from God; they give life to our bodies, and they return to God for judgment or rewards when we die.

Some of the most dramatic and amazing episodes in the Early Christian letters are stories about our inner *spirits*. For example, there's the wonderful story about the young daughter of Jairus (pronounced "jeye'-russ"), a ruler in the synagogue in the city of Capernaum. She was only twelve years of age when she suddenly died. Grief-stricken, Jairus ran to find Jesus and fell at His feet, begging for help. Jesus went to the dead girl's bedside, took one of her lifeless hands in His own, and said, "My child, get up." The record says that immediately the girl's *spirit returned*, and she got up and began to eat.[5]

The lesson in this story is that the little girl was dead when her spirit was *out* of her body; and then she was alive again when her spirit *returned* to her body. This episode shows that our inner *spirits* are what give us life, and that they're the *immortal* part of us that survives death.

Another touching episode about our inner *spirits* is the story of a First Century deacon in the city of Jerusalem named Steven. Steven had the call to full-time Christian service as a deacon, and in that role he delivered meals to the Christian widows of the city. However, Steven kept saying Spiritual things that angered the non-Christians of the city. So one day a mob of them picked up rocks and began to stone him. As the rocks struck him, Steven began to pray. The record says that he prayed, "Lord Jesus, receive my *spirit*." Then he sank to his knees and died.[6] This episode shows once again that when our spirits *leave* our bodies, we die. It also shows that our spirits return to *God* in heaven when they leave our bodies.

Now, like the first two circles on our diagram, our inner spirit also has a popular *synonym* that the Early Christians used to represent it. That synonym is the word *soul*. To the Early Christians, our *spirit* and our *soul* were the same thing.[7] For example, Jesus once told the story of a rich man who liked to gloat over his riches. Jesus ended the story this way: "But God said to the rich man, 'You fool! This very night your *soul* will be required of you. Then who'll get all your possessions?'"[8]

Jesus was saying that the rich man was going to die that night, and that his *spirit* was going to leave his body and return to God for its punishment or reward. But Jesus used the synonym *soul* to represent the man's inner *spirit* in the story.

Now – as we'll see in coming pages – our *spirit* (the third circle on our diagram) is the key to Christian Spirituality. It's the key to healings, peace, and miracles in our lives. With that, we're ready to see our completed diagram. Let's look at *Diagram 1* now.

Diagram 1

The Basic Model of Motivation

Here's Diagram 1 in our series. Notice that the upside down "V" is formed by the three circles we've been discussing. Also notice that each circle has its synonym shown in parentheses beneath it. The most important thing about Diagram 1 is the *black arrow* on the right side of the triangle. It's protruding from the first circle at the lower right of the diagram.

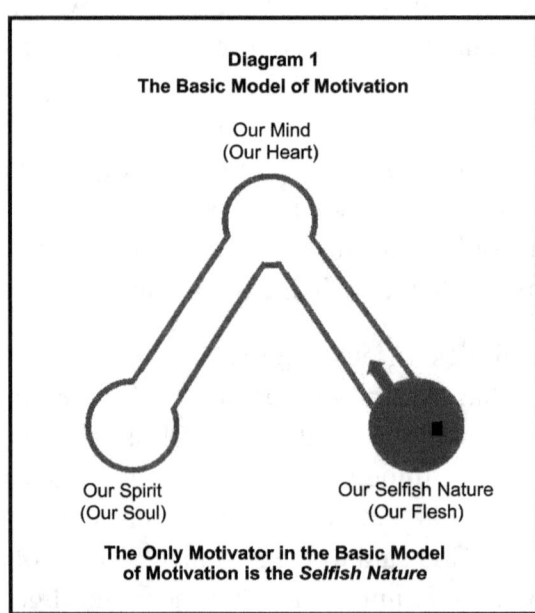

This first circle represents Our Selfish Nature (Our Flesh), and the *black arrow* indicates that the *selfish nature* in the diagram is pushing upward to motivate the *mind* at the top of the diagram.

Also note that the first circle is colored *black* because we associate the color black with *bad* things in life (things like evil, death, mourning, blackmail, black sheep, etc.), and these are exactly the kinds of things that the selfish nature produces.

Diagram 1, with its three connected circles, represents *normal* human motivation. It shows that our flesh is the *normal* motivator of our mind. But let's dig a little deeper and see the whole first level of Spirituality. Let's see a full diagram of a "natural" person. That is, a full diagram of a *non-Christian*. Here's Diagram 2.

Diagram 2

The First Level of Spirituality: The Natural Person (The Non-Christian)

Here's the *second diagram* in our series. Notice that the entire diagram is *black*. If this was a real person, his or her entire motivational system (nature, mind, and spirit) would be dominated by the motivation of the human nature. Thus, Diagram 2 is a diagram of a "natural" person. In other words, it's a diagram of a non-Christian.

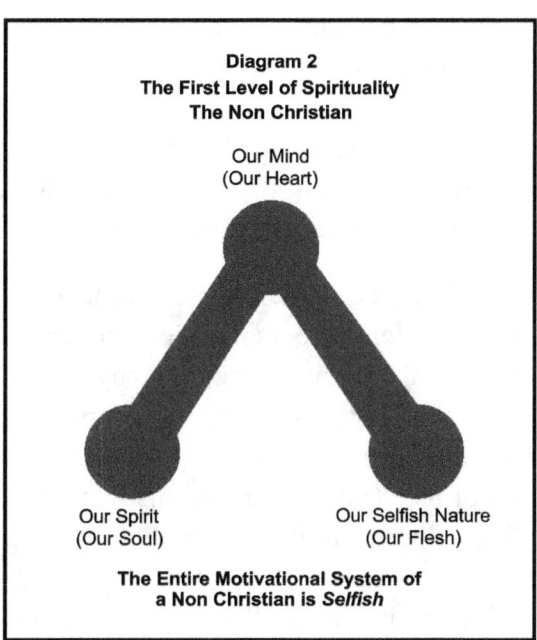

Looking at Diagram 2, we can see the problem with natural people (with non-Christians.) They only have *one* inner motivator. That one inner motivator is their *selfish human nature* (their flesh), and it's dominating their entire motivational system.

That means non-Christians can't be Spiritual and can't understand Spiritual things, even if they want to, and even if they try to. They can't be Spiritual because they don't have a *motivator* in them that can make them Spiritual. They only have *one* motivator in them; and that motivator only has the ability to make them selfish, vain, and egotistical.

Does this mean that all non-Christians are berserk jewel thieves, raving drug lords, and sinister mob bosses? Of course not. Some non-Christians are pleasant, friendly, and loving (at least to some extent, some of the time). How do we explain that? Let's repeat what we said earlier about the *thin veneer of civilization* that people have pasted over their selfish motivation.

The Thin Veneer of Civilization

We said earlier that most people have a *thin veneer of civilization* (training, education, good manners, self-discipline, and self-control) pasted over the negative behavior their selfish nature is producing. We said this thin veneer is the "glue" that holds civilized society together. Indeed, this thin veneer is what we call "being civilized." It's the only thing that makes art, science, literature, law, and government possible in natural society.

However, some people's veneer is *thinner* than others. People have different personalities, educations, etiquette training, and levels of self-discipline. To say that another way, some of us are *tamer* than others. Some of us are less prone to road rage, cursing, and rudeness than others. But all these sinful motivations are *in* all of us. They're lurking just beneath the surface, waiting to gush forth when stimulated – such as when a driver cuts us off in traffic, or when we slam our finger in a drawer, or when we break a glass of milk on the kitchen floor.

Who among us can say that we have absolutely *no* tendency to laugh at a risqué joke, or to watch a vulgar movie, or to use a swear word, or to read a vulgar book? Who among us can say that we have absolutely *no* tendency to be envious, greedy, resentful, lustful, or fearful? Most of us would admit that we have some of these tendencies in us. But *why* are they in us? The Early Christians taught that these tendencies are in us because all of us (both non-Christians and Christians) have *flesh* (selfishness) as our normal motivator – and in non-Christians, that flesh is their *only* motivator. Said another way, non-Christians don't have a *Spiritual* motivator in them. That's why in Diagram 2 the entire motivational system is all colored *black*. It's all black because there's no Spiritual motivator in non-Christians.

And – at last we now see one of the biggest reasons for becoming a *Christian*. It's to gain a *second* inner motivator that has the ability to resist the motivations of our flesh. But that brings up another question: Why *don't* non-Christians have Spiritual motivation within them? *Why* is their inner motivation Spiritually "dead"? Let's answer that incredibly important question now.

The Spiritual Deadness

As we've said, *all* people (both non-Christians and Christians) have *spirits* (souls) within them. These inner spirits give them life. These inner spirits are immortal, and they return to God for judgment or rewards when people die. But what we haven't said yet is that these inner spirits are Spiritually *dead* in their original condition at human birth. That means they're motivationally *dead*. They're motivationally dormant and passive. They don't have the ability to resist the selfishness of human nature.

This vital principle was taught consistently by the Early Christians. For example, let's quote the apostle Paul again. In a letter he wrote to the Christian small groups in the city of Ephesus in Turkey, Paul described the Spiritually *dead* spirits of non-Christians this way. He was writing to Christians at the time, but he was reminding them how they were Spiritually *dead* when they were non-Christians. Here's what Paul said to them:

> "You were *dead* in the transgressions and sins in which you used to live when you behaved in the ways of the world ... (when you were among) those who were disobedient (when you were non-Christians). All of us behaved that way at one time, gratifying the cravings of our *flesh* and following its desires and thoughts ... But because of His great love for us, God ... made us *alive* through Christ even though we were *dead* in sin."[9]

Now, notice that Paul wasn't writing this letter to the *headstones* in the Ephesus cemetery. He wasn't telling the Christians in Ephesus that they were *literally* dead before they became Christians. He was telling them that they were *Spiritually* dead before they became Christians. More specifically, he was telling them that before they became Christians their inner *spirits* had no ability to resist their selfish natures. So, as we reach the end of this chapter, we need to say it one more time: People can deny that they were born with a sinful nature. But that attitude only prevents them from becoming *Christians*. Worse, if they're already Christians, that attitude only prevents them from growing *Spiritually*. So let's close this chapter by talking about the *confession* that everyone must make at some point in his or her life.

The Confession

The word "confess" means to admit guilt for something. A *confession* is admitting that we've done something wrong. Or better yet, a confession is admitting that we're *doing* things wrong, each and every day. The confession we're talking about is admitting that we're *not* Spiritual. It's admitting that we're *not* capable of being Spiritual. It's admitting that we don't *have* the discipline and self-control to overcome our selfish nature. It's admitting that we *can't* live with peace, love, and hope without God's help.

To make this even more personal: If you'll make that confession here and now, you'll roll back the steel curtain in your mind that's been sealing off Spiritual growth. Whether you're a non-Christian or a Christian as you read these lines (and whether you attend a Christian congregation; or don't; or never have attended one), the way you respond to this confession now will determine the degree to which you grow Spiritually in the future.

Can you privately and secretly confess right now that you were born *selfish*, that your normal motivation is your *flesh*, and that you often offend both God and other people? If you can answer "Yes" to that confession, you're ready to know how our Spiritually dead spirits are *awakened*, and how they're given new supernatural *power*. But before we talk about all that, let's summarize this chapter.

Summary of Chapter 7

1. Diagram 1, shows that personal motivation can be visualized as *three circles* in the shape of a triangle with an open bottom, like an upside down "V."

2. The *first circle* (at the bottom right of the diagram) represents the inner motivation of our selfish human nature, or our flesh. It's the source of all crime, rudeness, adultery, cruelty, and rage in the world. The Early Christians called that kind of behavior *sin*, and we shouldn't be embarrassed to call it that today.

3. The *second circle* (at the top of the diagram) represents our mind, or our heart. Our mind is morally neutral and has no morals or ethics of its own. It operates on whatever inner motivator is powering it – good or bad.

4. The *third circle* (at the bottom left of the diagram) is the most important part of the triangle. It represents our inner spirit, or our soul. Our spirit is the immortal part of us that gives life to our bodies; that survives death; and that returns to God for judgment or rewards when we die. In our original condition as "natural" people (as non-Christians) our inner spirit is Spiritually *dead*. It has no ability to resist the negative drives of our selfish natures.

5. Diagram 2, which is totally *black*, illustrates the motivational problem that "natural" people (non-Christians) have. They only have *one* inner motivator – their *selfish* nature. Thus, their entire motivational system in *black*, indicating that they're motivated totally by their selfishness.

6. The key to Spiritual growth is to *confess* that we're living in the flesh. The key to Spiritual growth is to confess that we don't have the discipline to resist the drives of our selfishness; and that we need a *second* motivator in us that has the ability to resist our flesh.

And now for the Good News. Chapter 8 explains how God *awakens* our Spiritually dead inner spirits and gives us new and amazing Spiritual power. Diagram 3 in that chapter explains how people become *Christians*, and how *Spiritual growth* starts in Christians. So let's continue to the next chapter and see this Good News.

Chapter 8

THE INFANT CHRISTIAN

The Second Spiritual Level

It surprises some people to know that Jesus's original twelve disciples (Peter, John, James, Andrew, Philip, and the others) were *not* Spiritual when Jesus recruited them – and they *still* weren't Spiritual after Jesus had taught them 24/7 for three straight years. To be blunt, the twelve original disciples weren't Spiritual when Jesus traveled with them; and weren't Spiritual the night He was arrested; or the day He was executed; or the morning He rose from the dead; or the day He returned to heaven.

To say it another way, the disciples were *natural* people. They were *non-Christians*. They had only one inner motivator: their *flesh*. And their flesh produced unspiritual behavior in them the whole time they walked, talked, and ate with Jesus. Now let's not misunderstand. Jesus's disciples *were* "saints" by faith in God the Father and Jesus the Messiah. So they would have gone to heaven if they had died. But in the meantime, they were non-Christians and their daily behavior was unspiritual.

But wait a second. How do we *know* the disciples were unspiritual? We know it because of their *behavior*. As we've said, a person's *behavior* is the only evidence of how Spiritual he or she is. So let's look at the behavior of the twelve original disciples during the three years that they traveled with Jesus:

1. The whole time Jesus was teaching the disciples, they argued among themselves about which one of them was the "greatest" disciple.[1]

2. Toward the end of their training period, one of the disciples made a secret deal with Jesus's enemies to betray

Him, and then led an armed mob to Jesus's hiding place to arrest Him.[2]

3. Jesus knew He was about to be betrayed, so He asked three of His most trusted disciples to come and pray with Him for the strength and courage to face the ordeal. But instead of praying with Him, the three trusted disciples went to sleep.[3]

4. When the mob arrived to arrest Jesus, they dragged Him to the chief priest's home to be interrogated. One of Jesus's disciples followed at a distance and lingered in the courtyard to see what was going to happen. But when some of the priest's servants recognized him and accused him of being one of the disciples, he swore, cursed, and said he'd never even met Jesus.[4]

5. After Jesus was tried, executed, and buried, the disciples hid behind locked doors and wouldn't go outside for fear that they'd be recognized as Jesus's former disciples.[5]

6. Finally, when the disciples heard that Jesus had risen from the dead, one of them scoffed at the report. He rudely said that he wouldn't believe the rumor until Jesus appeared before him and proved in person that He had risen from the dead.[6]

Now, we could give more examples of the fleshy behavior by the disciples. But let's stop here and think about what these examples tell us. These are examples of *unspiritual* behavior by Jesus's most trusted and intimate disciples. He taught them for three straight years – and it had no *effect*. They never became Spiritual. How do we *explain* that? If anybody should have been Spiritual, it should have been them. But they weren't. Why not?

The disciples weren't Spiritual because they were still natural people. They were still non-Christians. They still only had *one* inner motivator, and that one motivator was their selfish nature or *flesh*. They couldn't be Spiritual, and they couldn't understand Spiritual things – even after three years of personal teaching by Jesus. They were heaven bound, but they weren't Spiritual here on earth.

All this proves something extremely important. It proves that it's impossible for *natural* people (non-Christians) to become Spiritual through teaching, studying, training, lecturing, and listening to encouraging and persuasive words. Natural people can only become Spiritual if they become *Christians*. They can only become Spiritual if they receive a *second* inner motivator that has the ability to overcome their flesh. So after Jesus was arrested, tried, and executed, His former disciples hid behind locked doors in Jerusalem. They were dejected, defeated, and disillusioned. It seemed that Jesus's plan to build a Spiritual kingdom on earth had failed, and that was the greatest *Spiritual* crisis in world history.

The Great Crisis

Despite Jesus's three years of miracles, and His teaching of thousands of people, it looked as if He had failed in part of His mission. He hadn't been able to make *Spiritual* disciples. His disciples had seen His miracles and they had heard His teachings. But they hadn't become Spiritual. Instead, they were cowering like frightened children in a closet. They were unable to experience the supernatural love, joy, peace, hope, and courage that Jesus had promised them. Of course, Jesus had known all this from the beginning. He had known that the disciples wouldn't become Spiritual – regardless of what He said or did – because the *Holy Spirit* hadn't come to earth yet to give humans the *ability* to be Spiritual.[7]

Now let's return to our story. The disciples were hiding behind locked doors in Jerusalem. It was between the time Jesus rose from the dead and the time that He returned to heaven. The record says that this was a period of 40 days. Jesus spent these 40 days appearing in person to all of His former disciples – teaching them, encouraging them, and telling them that the Kingdom of God was coming soon.[8] He appeared dozens of times to hundreds of former disciples during this period.[9]

Then as His mission on earth neared its end, Jesus made an announcement to the disciples that would change humankind forever. He appeared once more to the twelve original disciples in their hideout. They were still nervous, and some of them were planning to flee and return to Galilee to their homes, families, and jobs. But Jesus sat with them for a quiet meal, and then He made them an incredible promise. Here's what He told them:

> "Don't leave the City of Jerusalem. Instead, *wait* for the gift My Father promised you, the one you've heard me talk about. John the Baptizer baptized people in *water*. But in a few days, you'll be baptized in the *Holy Spirit* ... and when the Holy Spirit comes *in* you, you'll receive miraculous power that will make you not only My witnesses in Jerusalem ... but will make you My witnesses to the ends of the earth."[10]

This amazing statement is one of the most stunning promises ever made in recorded history. The disciples were in hiding and afraid to be seen in public. Yet Jesus was telling them that they were not only going to have the Spiritual power to come out of the house and testify about Him in the city of Jerusalem – but they were even going to have enough Spiritual power to testify about Him all over the world.

Now before we talk about the astonishing events that happened next, we need to define a fuzzy word in Jesus's amazing promise. It's one of the most important words in all of Christianity. But it's also one of the most misunderstood words in all of Christianity. Let's slow down and define the First Century word *baptism*.

The Definition of "Baptism"

In today's culture, the word *baptism* is a religious word, used mainly by the traditional Christian congregations. It normally refers to the Christian celebration of *water-baptism* and, since people don't talk about water-baptism much in daily conversation, we seldom hear the word "baptism" mentioned in public. But that wasn't true in the First Century. People *did* use the word "baptism" in daily conversation in the First Century, and it wasn't a religious word to them.

It was a word that homemakers, shopkeepers, farmers, sailors, blacksmiths, and all other people used in everyday conversation. They used it because in the First Century the word "baptism" meant to immerse something in another substance (such as vinegar, dye, oil, water, etc.), and to leave it immersed until its basic nature was changed.[11]

An example of how First Century people used the word "baptism" is the way they made pickles. They immersed *cucumbers* in vinegar, and left them until they fermented enough to change into *pickles*. Then they said that they had "baptized" the cucumbers. Another example is the way they dyed cloth. They immersed *cloth* in colored dye and left it there until it changed its *color*. Then they said that they had "baptized" the cloth. That same process was true when swordsmiths immersed hot sword *blades* in oil until they were *tempered*. After the blades were tempered, swordsmiths said that they had "baptized" the swords.

We could give many more examples of how First Century people used the word "baptized." But here's the point. When Jesus told His disciples that they were going to be *baptized* in the Holy Spirit

– and that they were going to receive supernatural power when it happened – they understood His word *baptized* in its First Century meaning. They understood that Jesus was going to return to heaven and, once there, He was going to pour out the Holy Spirit *in* them from the throne room of God, immersing them internally in Spiritual power. More, they understood that this process was going to permanently change them from *non-Spiritual* people to *Spiritual* people. They understood that in some way they didn't fully grasp, the Holy Spirit was going to soak them internally in Spiritual power, and they were going to be Spiritual ever after. For their part, all they had to do was wait in the house in Jerusalem for it to happen. And ten days later, it did.

The Miracle of Pentecost

The historic miracle that occurred ten days later wasn't a total surprise to the disciples because many years earlier, in 835 BC, a Hebrew prophet by the name of Joel had predicted it. Joel had told the people of Israel that God was going to pour out His Spirit *in* people someday, and that when He did, people would prophesy, dream Spiritual dreams, and have Spiritual visions.[12] Years later, in the First Century, another Hebrew prophet had said the same thing on the banks of the Jordan River. His name was John the Baptizer. He had told the crowds of people at the river that someone was coming soon who would *baptize* them (*immerse* them) in the "fire" of the Holy Spirit.[13]

Jesus's disciples knew about these prophets and about these amazing prophecies. So they obeyed Jesus's instructions. They stayed in the house in Jerusalem, watching, waiting, and praying. There were 120 of them, many sleeping on the flat rooftop living area. Finally the day arrived. It was 9:00 o'clock in the morning on the first day of the week. The date was May 30th in the year 30 AD. It was the morning of the annual one-day wheat harvest festival called the *Festival of Pentecost*. Peter, Andrew, John, Philip, and all the rest of Jesus's most intimate disciples were waiting. Jesus's mother, Mary, was there. So were Jesus's four half-brothers, James, Joseph, Jude, and Simon. So were His three half-sisters, together with 100 other former disciples.[14]

Even though it was only nine in the morning, the disciples had eaten breakfast, finished their chores, and were sitting in clusters praying and talking. Suddenly the miracle started. They heard a far-off sound like the roaring of an approaching tornado. The sound grew louder and closer, until it reached the house where they were huddled. Then they saw what appeared to be fire filling the house. This fire divided itself into individual flames and *settled down in* each disciple, *indwelling* him or her, and *baptizing* his or her inner spirit in supernatural power – awakening their inner spirits to Spiritual life for the first time.[15]

Next, each disciple's *mind* was temporarily filled with Spiritual power, and each began to feel the positive *emotions* that the Holy Spirit produces. So they began to rejoice and praise God. Then each disciple received a Spiritual *gift* for the first time in his or her life. All of them, including Jesus's mother, His half-brothers and half-sisters, and all the other disciples in the house, began *to speak other languages* (began to use prayer languages) that they didn't know, and that they had never spoken before.[16] We'll see in a moment why the Holy Spirit gave them that particular gift that morning, and we'll talk about Spiritual gifts in coming pages. But right now, notice that *three* different Spiritual things happened to the disciples that morning in a specific sequence:

1. First, they were *indwelled by*, and *baptized in*, the Holy Spirit's power. This permanently awakened their inner spirits to Spiritual life for the first time.

2. Second, their minds were *temporarily filled* with Spiritual power, giving them supernatural love, peace, and joy,

and erasing their fear of being seen in public and their other fleshy behavior.

3. Third, they temporarily received a *Spiritual gift* – in this case, the ability to speak other languages that they didn't know and couldn't normally speak.

All three of these experiences came from the Holy Spirit, and all three happened on the same morning at the same time. However, it's important to see that the three experiences were *separate* events. Why that's important will become clear in a moment. But to continue our record of Pentecost morning, the Holy Spirit had a specific purpose for giving the disciples the particular Spiritual gift that He gave them that morning, the gift of speaking other languages.

After all, the Spirit could have given them visions, dreams, healings, prophecies, or any of a dozen other Spiritual gifts. Or He could have given them no gift at all. But He *did* give them a gift, and it *was* the wonderful gift of speaking other languages. Why did He do that? He did it because He wanted this historic day to be the birthday of Christianity. And it was. So let's see how the Holy Spirit gave birth to an international movement in only one day.

The Birthday of Christianity

The word Pentecost (pronounced "<u>Pin</u>'-tuh-cost") comes from the Greek word for "fifty." It's the name of a wheat harvest feast that comes *fifty* days after the annual Passover Festival in Israel. The Feast of Pentecost can also be called the Feast of First Fruits – and that's meaningful too, since Pentecost is the day the first *Christians* in history were created, and since these first Christians were the "first fruits" of Jesus's ministry on earth.

Now as we said, Jesus chose the Festival of Pentecost to give birth to Christianity because He wanted to create an international movement in only one day. We'll see how He did that in a moment. But the point is that the Holy Spirit came to earth and changed the lives of 120 members of Jesus's family and former disciples forever. And that was only the beginning of the stunning event. Because at the sound of the thunderous roar of the Spirit's arrival, and at the sight of the flames filling the Jerusalem house, a large crowd of people rushed to the house and surrounded it, trying to see what was happening.

These people were in the streets because Jerusalem had thousands of *pilgrims* swarming around in it that morning. These pilgrims came from every tribe and nation on earth, and had traveled to Jerusalem to participate in the wheat festival. Hundreds of them now thronged around the house trying to see what the noise and flames meant. And then what the pilgrims heard *coming* from the house amazed them. It's important to remember that Jesus's family and disciples were from the northern province of Galilee, and that their native language was Aramaic ("air-uh-<u>may</u>'-ick"), spoken with a slurring Galilean accent. But Jesus's family and disciples weren't speaking Aramaic now.

Instead, they were declaring the wonders of God in the languages of *Arabia, Crete, Egypt, Iran, Iraq, Italy, Jordan, Turkey, Asia*, and all the other nations of the earth. They were speaking the languages that the pilgrims spoke in their own *homes*. This greatly confused the pilgrims. They knew that the people of Israel spoke Aramaic, and that the disciples in the house couldn't possibly know these foreign languages. So they began to shout back and forth to one another, asking what the strange situation meant.

The pilgrims were asking one another how people whose native language was Aramaic could speak all these foreign languages with perfect accents, pronunciation, and vocabularies. The pilgrims even began to shout to one another that maybe the disciples were "drunk."[17] (By the way, this is a classic example of how *non-Spiritual* people can't understand *Spiritual* things. After all, how can being drunk give someone the ability to speak a foreign language that he or she has never learned and has never spoken?)

At this point, the apostle Peter took over. He stepped to the edge of the rooftop and began to address the excited pilgrims in the streets. He told them that the disciples weren't *drunk* because it was only nine o'clock in the morning. Instead, Peter said, what the pilgrims were seeing and hearing was the fulfillment of *Joel's* prophecy many centuries earlier – when Joel prophesied that God would pour out His Spirit *in* people someday, and they would prophesy, dream Spiritual dreams and have Spiritual visions. Peter said that Joel's ancient prophecy was now fulfilled. Jesus had returned to heaven, had received the Holy Spirit from the Father, and had poured the Spirit out *in* the disciples in the house – causing the shocking scene that the pilgrims were now seeing and hearing. Peter ended with these thundering words:

> "Let all of Israel be assured of this! God has made this Jesus, whom all of *you* crucified, to be both Lord and Christ!"[18]

The record shows that when the pilgrims heard these words, they were cut to the quick with guilt and shame. So they began to shout to Peter and the other disciples, "But brothers, what should we do?"

Peter replied that what they should do is *repent* of their sinful behavior and ask Jesus to *forgive* them. If they did that, they would *also* be baptized in the Spirit, exactly as the 120 members of Jesus' family and former disciples had been. Peter continued by saying, "*Save* yourselves from this corrupt generation!"

And 3,000 of the pilgrims took that life-saving step. They did repent of their sins, and they did pray for Jesus to forgive them. And all 3,000 were *indwelled* by the Holy Spirit and *baptized* in the

Holy Spirit, joining the 120 members of Jesus's family and former disciples to become the first 3,120 Christians in history, making that day the *birthday* of Christianity.[19]

Now – we asked earlier why God chose the gift of speaking other languages for the Spiritual gift the disciples received that day. Now we know why. God chose that gift to attract the attention of the 3,000 pilgrims, and to cause them to join Jesus's family and former disciples as charter members of Christianity. The pilgrims *did* join, and the next morning they *returned* to their homes all over the world taking Christianity with them. Thus, in only one day Jesus had created a worldwide Spiritual movement, exactly as He had promised His disciples earlier that He would. And now, let's pause to see what the miracles of Pentecost and of Spiritual baptism mean to us today, here in the Twenty-First Century.

The Friday Night Group

Several years ago, a men's small group met in my home every Friday evening. The group consisted of a dozen members, all of whom were lifelong Christians, and all of whom held positions of authority in local Christian congregations as teachers, missionaries, elders, deacons, choir members, ushers, and so forth. One Friday evening, I asked the small group a question that I'd been thinking about all week. I asked them, "What do you think the main *difference* is between Christians and non-Christians?"

They looked at me with startled expressions. So I continued, "What if we lined up fifty *Christians* on the left side of this room, and fifty *non-Christians* on the right side of the room, and what if we compared them? Would the Christians be *different* from the non-Christians in any specific way?"

What followed was one of the most interesting discussions I've ever heard. This group of lifelong Christians and congregational authorities debated the question for over an hour and couldn't agree on an answer. The more they debated, the more they realized that *both* Christians *and* non-Christians (that includes members of other religions) could pray, worship, read the Bible, give to charities, be good neighbors, have successful careers, raise healthy families, feed the poor, and so forth.

Likewise, both Christians and non-Christians could cheat on their taxes, lie, steal, commit adultery, get divorced, and commit any other sin. Both Christians and non-Christians could even attend a Christian congregation and play an active role in it. For that matter, both could even believe in Jesus and God – because demons believe in Jesus and God, and *they* aren't Christians.[20]

So the members of the Friday night small group gave up. They couldn't agree on one specific *difference* between Christians and non-Christians. But there is one. And there's *only* one. We've been talking about it for this whole chapter. Let's turn to the apostle Paul and let him remind us of that one specific difference. Paul said that if we are Christians:

> "Our body is a temple of the Holy Spirit, who is
> *in* us, and whom we *received* from God."[21]

It's that simple. *That's* the one specific difference that the Friday night small group couldn't remember. Here are the facts. Christians are indwelled *by* the Holy Spirit, and have had their inner spirits baptized *in* the Spirit's power. That's the only difference between a Christian and a non-Christian. And notice that it's an *internal* difference. Christians have had a personal "Pentecost" that has awakened their inner spirits to serve as a second motivator within them, a motivator that has the power to overcome the evil drives of their flesh.

But none of that has happened to non-Christians. That internal difference between Christians and non-Christians is a life-saving one and a world-saving one. It started in Jerusalem on Pentecost morning on May 30th in 30 AD, and it's as real today as it was then. Here's the principle. Every Christian has had a personal "Pentecost" in his or her life. *Diagram 3* shows that personal Pentecost.

Diagram 3

The Second Spiritual Level: The Infant Christian

Here's the third diagram in our series. *Diagram 3* is a picture of a new Christian. Note that the *left* arm of the upside down "V" is now colored *white* – indicating that the Holy Spirit has *indwelled* this person and *baptized* his or her inner spirit in supernatural power. The right arm of the upside down "V" is still black – indicating that this new Christian's selfish human nature is still fully *active*. Thus, this Christian now has a *dual* motivational system. His or her inner spirit is trying to motivate him or her for *Spiritual* living. But his or her selfish human nature is still trying to motive him or her for *selfish* living.

Thus, the two inner motivators are now *competing* with one another in a "war" to control the Christian's mind.

Also notice that only a *small* portion of the Christian's mind is being influenced by Spiritual power. The small slice of *white* in his or her mind illustrates that. Sadly, most of his or her mind is *still* black.

This means that most of this Christian's mind is still dominated by the selfish nature. As a result, Diagram 3 is an image of an *infant* Christian. That is, it's an image of an *unspiritual* Christian. We read stories about unspiritual Christians in the "Christian Horror Stories" in Chapter 2. Looking at Diagram 3, we can now see the *problem* that infant Christians have: They aren't allowing enough *Spiritual* motivation to flow up from their inner spirits to empower their minds. They're still letting their selfish human natures continue to be their *primary* motivator. To be blunt, this is why *infant* Christians can be just as vain, egotistical, selfish, and sinful as non-Christians.

Infant Christians feel, think, and behave almost as if they're still *non-Christians*. Sometimes they're not even sure they *are* Christians (and neither are the people around them). But that doesn't mean infant Christians *aren't* really Christians and *aren't* going to heaven when they die. It just means infant Christians are still letting their selfish natures serve as the prime motivators of their minds while they're still here on earth.

Here's the principle. Being indwelled *by* – and being baptized *in* – the Holy Spirit is what *makes* a Christian. Christians call that being saved, redeemed, regenerated, converted, born-again, having Jesus in your heart, and many other such terms. All these terms are *synonyms* and mean the same thing. However, being saved (being Spirit-baptized) doesn't make a Christian Spiritually *mature*. When people become Christians, they become *infant* Christians, not mature Christians. All new Christians start their Spiritual journey as Spiritual babies. So let's talk more about *infant* Christians for a minute.

The Infant Christians

The Early Christians taught that when a non-Christian is saved (indwelled *by* and baptized *in* the Holy Spirit), he or she starts living on the *second* level of Spirituality – the level that the Early Christians called the "infant" level. Infant Christians are people who're indwelled by the Spirit and whose inner spirits are baptized in the Spirit, but who *aren't letting the Holy Spirit motivate them very much*. They have the potential to be Spiritual. But they're not letting it happen. Instead, they're letting their selfish natures be their prime motivator. That's why the national polls we quoted earlier show that today's average Christian is *no more Spiritual* than a non-Christian. The pollsters were interviewing *infant* Christians.

So our next question is obvious. How can an infant Christian start to *grow* Spiritually? That's the subject of our next chapter. But before we turn there, we need to emphasize the big key to Spirituality. The big key is that we must *want* to grow Spiritually. We must *want* healings, peace, and miracles in our lives. And we must want them *more* than we want our unspiritual behavior. That means one of two things as you read these lines:

1. If you're not a *Christian* yet – you need to make the decision to turn your back on unspiritual behavior. Peter told the pilgrims on Pentecost morning that they had to repent of their sins and ask Jesus to forgive them. Then you need to ask Jesus to pour out the Holy Spirit in you and baptize your inner spirit in power. That's called "getting saved" or "being born-again," and it instantly makes you an infant Christian with the potential to start living a life of supernatural healings, peace, and miracles.

2. If you're *already* a Christian – but you're not living a life of healings, peace, and miracles, you need to pray for the Holy Spirit to *fill* your mind with "Rivers of Living Water." You need to pray for Spiritual *power* to flood up from your inner spirit and *fill* your mind with supernatural peace, wisdom, and knowledge. That's called "being Spirit-filled" or "being motivated by the Spirit," and it immediately makes you a *growing* Christian who's starting to experience the *Early Christian Lifestyle*.

Now, to be sure the principles in coming pages apply to you, from this page forward we're going to assume that you *are* a Christian, and that you *are* praying to live the *Early Christian Lifestyle*. With that assumption, let's summarize this chapter and move to our chapter on Spiritual growth.

Summary of Chapter 8

1. Jesus's twelve original disciples weren't Spiritual when Jesus recruited them, and they still weren't Spiritual three years later when He left them and returned to heaven.

2. We know the original disciples weren't Spiritual because of their negative *behavior*. Their behavior was identical to that of "natural" people (non-Christians). The disciples were "saints" by faith in God and the Messiah and would have gone to heaven if they had died. But they *weren't* Spiritual in their lives on earth.

3. The reason the disciples weren't Spiritual is that they only had *one* motivator in them – their selfish human natures. So they couldn't *be* Spiritual, and they couldn't *understand* Spiritual things.

4. When Jesus appeared to the frightened disciples in their Jerusalem hideout, He promised them a *solution* to their unspiritual behavior. He promised that they were going to be *baptized* in the Spirit and were going to receive a new Spiritual *motivator* that had the ability to overcome their negative behavior.

5. The Greek word "baptize" was a household word in the First Century, not a religious word. It meant to *immerse* things (such as cloth) in other *substances* (such as dye), and leaving them there until they *changed* makeup (such as changing their color). When non-Christians are "baptized" in the Holy Spirit, the Spirit *immerses* their inner *spirits* in power and *changes* their Spiritual makeup. That process is what makes a Christian.

6. Jesus's promise of new Spiritual power for the disciples came true on the first day of the week, May 30th, in the year 30 AD, at nine o'clock in the morning. That was the morning of the annual one-day wheat festival known as the *Festival of Pentecost*. Jesus poured out the Spirit in 120 of His family members and former disciples at that moment, and three things happened to them:

    a) Their bodies were *indwelled* by the Holy Spirit and their inner spirits were *baptized* in power.

    b) Their minds were temporarily *filled* with supernatural love, joy, peace, and courage.

    c) They temporarily *expressed* a Spiritual gift (the ability to speak other languages).

7. Jesus chose the particular gift of speaking other languages for the disciples that morning because Jerusalem was filled with *pilgrims* from ever nation of the world that morning, and the result of the gift was that 3,000 of these pilgrims joined the disciples as charter members on the birthday of Christianity. The pilgrims *left* Jerusalem the next day for their *homes* worldwide, and Jesus had founded an international movement in only one day.

8. Diagram 3 is a picture of an infant Christian. It shows the *dual* motivation that all Christians have. We know it's an image of an *infant* Christian because only a tiny portion of the Christian's mind is *white*. Most of the Christian's mind is *black*. That means the Christian's motivational system is still being dominated by his or her selfish nature.

9. Being indwelled *by* – and baptized *in* – the Holy Spirit is the experience that makes a Christian. Being Spirit-baptized can also be called being saved, redeemed, converted, regenerated, born-again, having Jesus in your heart, and many other such terms. If a person is a Christian, he or she *has* been indwelled

and baptized. If a person is a non-Christian, he or she *hasn't* been indwelled and baptized.

10. Becoming a Christian means becoming an *infant* Christian. New Christians don't start as mature Christians. Spiritual growth takes time, knowledge, practice, and experience.

11. Finally, there are *two* ways people can become more Spiritual. First, if they aren't Christians, they need to become Christians and start growing Spiritually. If they're already Christians, they need to pray for the Holy Spirit to start flooding their minds with Spiritual power and start having more peace, hope, and miracles.

As we've seen, "Spirituality" is defined as the degree to which a Christian *is* (or is *not*) being motivated by the indwelling Holy Spirit. That means the key to Christianity is for all Christians to increase the extent to which they're being motivated by the inner Spirit. We call that "Spiritual growth," and that's the subject of the next chapter. Let's meet there now.

Chapter 9

THE GROWING CHRISTIAN

The Third Spiritual Level

Years ago, when researchers first began studying the ancient Christian paintings in the catacombs at Rome, they were puzzled because there seemed to be no paintings of *adults* being water-baptized. All the pictures of water-baptisms seemed to feature *children*. That made no sense to researchers, since they knew that thousands of adults had been water-baptized in ancient Rome; and they knew that the Early Christians didn't water-baptize *babies* or small *children*.

Then the researchers realized what the images were showing. The Christians being water-baptized in the catacomb pictures *were* adults. But the artists had painted them the size of *children* to indicate that they were *Spiritual* children – that they were infant Christians.[1]

In the First Century, new Christians were often called "my child," and "my son," and "my daughter," by mature Christians – even if the new Christians were actually elderly people. And these were kind and loving words, not put-downs. The terms simply acknowledged the fact that new Christians are Spiritual infants.[2]

The truth is, Spirit-baptism (being saved) only creates an infant Christian. Salvation doesn't create a mature Christian. All new Christians (then and now) start their journeys as *unspiritual* people and, sadly, some of them *stay* unspiritual. So the purpose of this chapter is to explain how Christians start growing Spiritually. The first pieces of the puzzle require us to understand how human *motivation* and *behavior* work. So let's start with those parts of the mystery.

The Principles of Behavior

We said earlier that behavior is the only evidence of *Spirituality*, and that the only evidence of a person's Spiritual *level* is the degree to which his or her behavior matches the Spirituality of the Early Christians. Thus, Spirituality isn't proved by membership in a traditional congregation, or by reading the Bible, or by listening to Christian radio. Spirituality is only proved by having the same supernatural *behavior* that the Early Christians had. But what *is* "behavior"? Let's define it now.

The Definition of "Behavior"

"Behavior" is a word that everybody uses, but few people can define. So let's define it in the simplest terms:

> *"Behavior" is a physical response to a personal situation that was triggered by an inner motivator in a person.*

The Rush Hour Traffic

For example, let's imagine that a *non-Christian* driver named "Greg" is late for work one morning, so he cuts off two *Christian* drivers in the rush hour traffic. One of these Christian drivers is named "Jack." The other is named "Jill." Jack smiles and waves at Greg, the non-Christian driver, as Greg cuts him off in the traffic. But the second Christian driver, Jill, scowls at Greg and shakes her fist at him as he cuts her off.

Thus, two different Christian drivers had two different responses to the same personal situation. In other words, they had two different *behaviors*. But what made those behaviors different? Why weren't the behaviors identical? The answer to that question is understanding the two different motivators that triggered the two different behaviors.

As we know, Christians have *two* different inner motivators. The first is their *selfish nature*, and the second is the indwelling power of the *Holy Spirit*. So to keep our traffic example simple, let's assume that Jack's behavior shows that he's a *growing* Christian who's being motivated largely by the indwelling Holy Spirit. And let's assume that Jill's behavior shows that she's an *infant* Christian being motivated largely by her flesh.

This rush hour traffic example illustrates that our Spiritual *level* as Christians is proved by our *behavior* (by our responses to personal situations), not by what we say or think. If our selfish nature is motivating our responses to a large degree, we're on the infant level as Christians. If the Holy Spirit is motivating our responses to a large degree, we're on the growing or mature levels as Christians.

The point is that non-Christians (like "Greg" in the example) need to see Christians displaying *Spiritual* behavior, not fleshy behavior. It was seeing *Spiritual* behavior by Christians that changed the world in the First Century. One of the clearest statements of that was made by the apostle Paul. He made the statement in a letter to the Christian small groups in the city Corinth in Greece. He was writing to remind them how his *behavior* had changed them when he first arrived in their city. Here's what he said about his personal behavior:

> "When I first came to you ... my words and my message were *not* in persuasive words of human wisdom, but in showing you the Holy Spirit and His *Spiritual power* – so your faith would not be based on man's wisdom, but would be based on *seeing* the power of God."[3]

Now, Paul didn't say what kind of personal behavior he *showed* the citizens of Corinth when he arrived. But it had to have been supernatural – because many of them became *Christians* as soon as Paul arrived. It's also important to see the negative lesson in Paul's letter. Paul is saying that faith can't be built on *persuasive speaking*. It can only be built on seeing the *power* of God being demonstrated. Faith is only built by *seeing* Spiritual behavior. That's one of the biggest mistakes that Christianity is making today. Its programs are based on persuasive speaking – not on demonstrations of Spiritual *behavior*.

So let's talk more about the type of behavior that *infant* Christians express, compared to the kind of behavior that growing and mature Christians express. We already know that the Early Christians taught that Christians can (and do) express two kinds of behavior during daily living. But what we haven't made clear is that they actually called these behaviors the "*Two Ways*." What's more, they held classes and taught the two behaviors to new Christians. So let's drill deeper into the *Two Ways* that all Christians can behave.

The Two Ways

One of the most poetic sentences ever written by Early Christians is also one of Christianity's most important sentences. Most people have never heard this poetic sentence because it's not in today's Bible. However, the sentence was written and spoken frequently by Early Christians, and they used it to teach new Christians the principles of Spiritual growth. Here's that poetic sentence:

> "Two Ways there are, one of *Life* and one of *Death*, and there's a great difference between the Two Ways."[4]

This sentence is the opening line of a First Century training manual that the Early Christians used to teach infant Christians how to grow Spiritually. The sentence is teaching the principle that we've been describing for several pages now. Namely, that all Christians have two inner motivators, and that those two inner motivators produce two kinds of outer behavior in Christians – one that's Spiritually *alive*, and one that's Spiritually *dead* – and that the two kinds of behavior are very *different*.

The manual's purpose was to teach infant Christians how to be Followers of The Way. That's why one of the synonyms for *The Way* was to call it "The Way of Life." To the Early Christians, the word "Life" meant behavior produced by the inner *Holy Spirit*. (The word "Death" meant behavior produced by the inner *selfish nature*.)

The words "Life" and "Death" don't have those same meanings to many Christians today. Today, many Christians are taught that the words "Life" and "Death" refer to whether or not a person is going to heaven when they die. But that avoids dealing with the issue of Christian Spiritual and unspiritual behavior while they're still on earth.[5]

Returning now to the ancient training manual we're discussing, some researchers think it was written around 60 AD in Antioch. Others think it was written around 90 AD in Ephesus. Regardless of when and where it was written, this manual is considered one of the most important First Century Christian documents ever found outside of the Bible. However, there's an even more interesting fact about the manual. Because this same "Two Ways" teaching appears again in a *second* ancient Christian training manual that was written in Second Century Egypt. This second manual was written by a different author, in a different city, in a different country, in a different century than the first manual. Yet it teaches exactly the same lesson in almost exactly the same words. Here's what the second manual says about the two kinds of Christian behavior:

> "There are ... *two powers*: that of Light and that of Darkness, and there's a great difference between the Two Ways."[6]

Notice that this second manual actually identifies "Light" and "Darkness" as being two inner *motivators* ("powers") in Christians. Also, the terms "Light" and "Darkness" are more acceptable to Christians today because they're more clearly talking about *behavior*, not heaven. Thus, in this book along with the words "Spirit" and "Flesh," we're going to use the terms "Light" and "Darkness" to represent the two *motivators* in Christians that produce their outer behavior.

Also, there's one other fact to notice about these ancient Christian training manuals. As we said, they were written by different authors, in different cities, in different countries, in different centuries. What does that tell us? It tells us that the *Two Ways* teaching was worldwide in the early centuries and that all Christians knew it. That means it should still be a worldwide teaching that all Christians know. So let's review the kinds of behaviors that the motivators of Light and Darkness produce in Christians. Let's start with the positive view, and see what type of behavior the motivator of *Light* produces in Christians.

The Motivator of Light

The word "Light" was a symbol of *God* to the Early Christians, and so it was also a symbol of the Spiritual *power* that the indwelling Holy Spirit gives Christians.[7] Light symbolized an inner motivation of purity, joy, and knowledge in Christians.[8] Probably the best description of the motivator of Light was written by Paul. Here's how Paul described the kind of behavior that the inner motivator of Light (the indwelling Holy Spirit) produces in Christians:

> "What the indwelling *Holy Spirit* (the motivator of Light) produces in Christians is an outer behavior of love, joy, peace, patience, kindness, goodness, faithfulness, gentleness, and self-control."[9]

This supernatural outer behavior – produced by the motivator of Light – revolutionized the world in the First Century. It was so important that the Early Christians mentioned it in *nine* different letters of the *New Testament*.[10] (Many Christians today call the behavior of Light the "fruit of the Spirit" because the *King James Version* of the Bible used the word "fruit" when it was published in England in 1611.)

But now let's look at the opposite side of Christian motivation. Let's take the negative view, and see what type of behavior the motivator of *Darkness* produces in Christians.

The Motivator of Darkness

The word "Darkness" was a symbol of *fleshy* behavior to the Early Christians, and so it was also a symbol of the selfish *power* of flesh (of selfish human nature) in Christians. Here's how Paul described the kind of behavior that the inner motivator of Darkness produces in Christians:

> "The behavior produced by the *flesh* (the motivator of Darkness) is obvious. It's adultery, fornication, lust, shamelessness, idolatry, drug abuse, hatred, strife, excessive excitement, rage, excessive ambition, division, envy, murder, intoxication, carousing, and all other such conduct."[11]

Thus, it was this Dark motivator in Christians that produced the "Christian Horror Stories" we saw in Chapter 2. That's why the Early Christians used special synonyms for the behavior produced by the flesh – synonyms such as: *The Way of Wickedness*, *The Way of Sinners*, *The Way of the Black One*, and other such evil terms. Christians who allow their inner motivator of Darkness (their flesh) to produce their behavior are *sinning* – even though they're Christians.

Said another way, the motivator of Darkness makes Christians feel, think, and act as if they were *non-Christians*. This means that Christians who express Dark behavior (fleshy, selfish behavior) are Spiritual infants. And if an ancient Christian artist painted their portrait on a catacomb wall, he would paint them the size of *children*.

And now a glaring question confronts us. *What* can an infant Christian do about his or her Dark motivation? *How* can infant Christians subdue the Darkness within them, and start growing Spiritually? It's time to talk about the glorious and amazing experience called *Spirit-filling*.

The Experience of Spirit-Filling

Before Jesus returned to heaven, He promised His disciples that a day was coming when they would receive a miraculous new inner *motivator* that would change their lives. Jesus made that promise in the temple courts on the last day of the Festival of Tabernacles in late October of 29 AD. The temple was overflowing with celebrating people at the time, and Jesus and His disciples were there too, even though the temple guards were searching for Him to arrest Him. Regardless of the danger, Jesus stood in the crowd and made this amazing promise:

> "He or she who believes in me, as the Scriptures have said, will have *Rivers of Living Water* flowing up from within him or her. (He was referring to the Holy Spirit here, whom those who believed in Him

would receive on the Day of Pentecost, since up to that time the Holy Spirit had not yet been given.)"[12]

Notice that the apostle John, who wrote the record of the event, took pains to explain in parentheses what Jesus's promise meant. John wanted readers to understand that the "Living Water" Jesus promised was the inner *motivation* of the indwelling Holy Spirit. But John also wanted readers to remember that at that time (October, 29 AD), the Holy Spirit had *not* yet been poured out in people to give birth to Christianity. (The promise came true seven months later, on Pentecost morning, May 30th, in 30 AD.)

Water is one of the Christian symbols for the Holy Spirit. So the meaning of Jesus's promise is clear: After being indwelled by the Holy Spirit and becoming Christians, the next step in Spiritual growth is to be *motivated* by "rivers" of supernatural "water" flooding up from the indwelling Holy Spirit. Another term for this is "being Spirit-filled." The Early Christians used many synonyms for the process of Spirit-filling. They also called it *behaving in the Spirit; being full of Light; being children of Light; walking in the Light*, and other such terms.

The apostle Paul proved the importance of being *Spirit-filled* when he wrote one of the most provocative sentences Christians ever wrote. In a letter addressed to the Christian small groups in the city of Ephesus, Paul simply commanded them to:

"Be filled with the Spirit!"[13]

Two things are noteworthy about this bold statement. First, it's written in the Greek *command* tense. We don't have that tense in English. But in First Century Greek, it was the tense that army officers used to issue orders to their troops. That means Paul's statement wasn't a suggestion, a recommendation, or a hint for Christians. It was an *order* for Christians.

Second, the fact that Paul had to issue his command reveals a tragic truth: *All* Christians aren't *always* Spirit-filled. If *all* Christians *were* always Spirit-filled, Paul wouldn't have had to issue his command. Tragically, all Christians weren't Spirit-filled in Paul's day; and all Christians aren't Spirit-filled in our day. That explains why Christianity is losing influence nationally and why people are dropping out of Christianity nationwide.

To summarize: Being "motivated" by the Spirit means having some percentage of our mind influenced by the Holy Spirit's power for some period of time. Being "filled" with the Spirit means having *most* of our mind (the majority of it) influenced by the Holy Spirit for *most* of the time. That gives us two tests for Spiritual motivation, not just one:

1. The first test is how *much* of a Christian's mind is being influenced by the Spirit?

2. The second test is how *long* does that influence last?

Paul's command for Christians to be Spirit-filled also raises another important question. Is it really *possible* for all Christians to be Spirit-filled? To answer that question, all we need to do is remember what happened to the 3,120 family members, former disciples, and foreign pilgrims on Pentecost morning in Jerusalem. That was the morning Jesus's promise of Spirit-baptism came true. The apostle Luke, who wrote the record of the event, wrote:

"*All* of them were filled with the Holy Spirit."[14]

This means that Jesus's mother, Jesus's four half-brothers, Jesus's three half-sisters; along Peter, John, Andrew, Philip, and all the other original disciples; along with 100 other former disciples; along with 3,000 foreign pilgrims (each a different age, gender, educational level, occupation, and background), were *all filled with the Spirit* that day. Best of all, this same supernatural process of

Spirit-filling has continued down through the centuries and is still available to us today. That proves that *all* Christians can be Spirit-filled. And it also highlights our *goal* as Christians.

The Christian Goal

Increasing the Holy Spirit's influence over our minds until we're habitually *Spirit-filled* is the primary goal of all Christians. Everything that Christians are supposed to have, be, and do comes from being habitually Spirit-filled. That's the message of this book, and that's the purpose of Christian life on earth. So let's state that goal again:

> *The goal of all Christians is to be motivated by the Holy Spirit more often, and for longer periods of time, until they become habitually Spirit-filled.*

We're going to explain how to reach that goal next. But before we do, let's slow down a moment to define the fuzzy word "Spiritual."

The Definition of "Spiritual"

We've been using the word "Spiritual" for many pages now without *defining* it, and that's not a good thing. Authors should never leave a key word of their theme undefined. But I did that on purpose. I wanted us to discuss *motivation, behavior,* and the differences between *Spiritual* motivation and *fleshy* motivation first. The reason is that it's only after understanding those vital principles that we can fully understand the fuzzy word "Spiritual."

The sad truth is that today the word "Spiritual" is so fuzzy that it's virtually meaningless. Everybody means everything by it. People use the word "Spiritual" to describe sunsets, trees, whales, crystals, salads, and almost anything else. So, as always, let's go back to the original First Century Greek to see what the Early Christians meant by the word "Spiritual."

The apostle Paul was the first Christian writer to use the Greek adjective *Pneumatikos* ("new-mah-tea-<u>cahss</u>'"). And that's the word that we translate today as "Spiritual." Paul used it 19 years *after* the Day of Pentecost.[15] That's extremely important because it tells us that the word "Spiritual" wasn't known or used until *after* Pentecost morning when the Spirit came to earth to indwell humans. The non-Christian religions of the day didn't use it; and the non-Christian writers of the day didn't use it. This means the word "Spiritual" is a uniquely *Christian* word. Said another way, people couldn't *be* Spiritual until *after* Pentecost when Christianity was founded. Think about that a moment. Being "Spiritual" is an exclusively Christian experience.

The truth is that the word "Spiritual" comes from the word "Spirit" – referring to the *Holy Spirit*, the third Person of the Trinity. That means the word Spiritual refers to *God*, and out of respect for Him I always *capitalize* the word Spiritual.[16] Used correctly, the word Spiritual only refers to the motivation of the Spirit in Christians. But now let's be even more specific:

> *The word "Spiritual" refers to the supernatural behavior, gifts, and experiences produced in Christians by the indwelling Holy Spirit. It refers to the Spirit's inner motivation – the flow of the Rivers of Living Water in Christians that produce a supernatural lifestyle in them.*

This definition means that sunsets, trees, whales, crystals, and salads can't be Spiritual because they aren't supernatural *behavior* flowing out of Christians from the Holy Spirit. The Early Christians never used the word *Pneumatikos* to refer to sunsets, trees, whales, crystals, or salads. They only used it to refer to the indwelling power of the Holy Spirit. Earthly things can touch us emotionally, and sometimes can even point us to God, since He created them. But it's wrong to call earthly things "Spiritual."

As we said, being *Spiritual* happens on a "sliding scale" in Christians, and the two tests of it are how *much* and how *long* a Christian lets the Holy Spirit motivate him or her. Infant Christians don't let the Spirit motivate them very much for very long – so they're not Spiritual. Mature Christians let the Spirit motivate them a lot for a long time, so they *are* Spiritual.

All this brings up one final question. *Why* is the Holy Spirit named "Holy"? Why isn't He just named "The Spirit"? The answer is so important that it can't be overstated. The Holy Spirit is named "Holy" because His role on earth is to produce *holiness* in Christians. That's why Jesus poured Him out *in* the disciples on Pentecost morning – to make them *holy* Christians. Let's say it again: Christians are supposed to be *holy*. That's God's perfect will for them.

The Greek word "holy" refers to a person who's *separated* from sin; who's *devoted* to God, and who's set *apart* for God's purposes – in short, a person who's *holy*. A holy person is one whose behavior is ethical, moral, pure, and satisfying to God on His throne in heaven. That's why all Christians are correctly called "saints," as we'll discuss in later pages. It's because they're separated from worldly evil and live holy lives.[17] But let's go even deeper. Let's talk about the *part* of a Christian's body that's motivated by the Spirit. Let's talk about a Christian's *mind*.

The Christian Mind

When God's Rivers of Living Water flow up within us and give us the supernatural experience of being Spirit-filled, which *part* of our body do the Living Waters *fill*? We already know the answer.

But it's still profound. Our *mind* is the part of our body that the Holy Spirit floods with Light, Life, and supernatural power. On our motivational diagrams, the *second circle* (at the top of the diagram) represents our mind. And we said our mind has the ability to understand things, to make decisions, and to exert will power.

But we also said that our mind is morally neutral. It has no built-in values, morals, and ethics of its own. It produces behavior by operating on whatever moral (or immoral) *motivator* is powering it – and normally that's our *flesh*. Then how does the Holy Spirit *overcome* our fleshy motivation? Here are the instructions the apostle Paul gave the small groups in the cities of Rome and Ephesus. Here's how he said Christians can fill their minds with the power of the Holy Spirit:

> "*Push back* your sinful nature (your fleshy motivator). *Don't* conform any longer to your previous behavior – the one that was corrupted by deceitful cravings. Instead, be transformed by *letting* the Holy Spirit (your Spiritual motivator) renew your mind. *Let* the Holy Spirit create your new self, the one designed to be like God in true righteousness and holiness, the one that'll help you find God's perfect will for your life."[18]

This dramatic advice by Paul is even more striking when we realize the meanings of some of the Greek words he used. He's telling Christians to be assertive, to be active, and to consciously decide to let the Holy Spirit motivate them. He's telling Christians that *they* control how much and how long they're Spirit-filled. Notice the words *push back*; *don't*; *letting*, and *let* in Paul's instructions. These are action words. They tell us that Christians themselves are in control of their *own* Spirit-filling. Spirit-filling doesn't just hit Christians as they stroll in the mall. It happens to Christians who actively pray for it and seek it. We're going to talk more about

Spiritual hunger in the next chapter. But now we're ready to see an image of a Christian who's *growing Spiritually*. It's Diagram 4.

Diagram 4

The Third Spiritual Level: The Growing Christian

This is our *fourth diagram.* Notice that the *white* color on the left arm of the diagram now flows deeply into the top circle – the one representing the *mind*. Half of the mind is now the color *white*. This indicates that half of this Christian's mind is being motivated by the Holy Spirit – the motivator of Light. In other words, this Christian is *half* Spiritual.

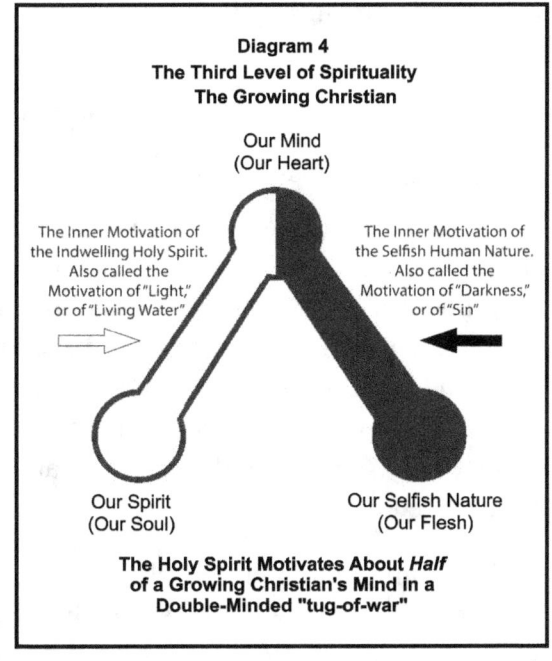

Also notice that the black color on the right arm of the diagram has been pushed half way out of the Christian's mind. Thus, the motivation of his or her flesh – the motivator of Darkness – is greatly diminished. Thus, Diagram 4 is the image of a *growing* Christian, a Christian at level three of Spiritual growth.

But as we'll see in the next chapter, these motivational levels aren't necessarily *permanent*. The motivation of the Spirit ebbs and floods in a Christian's mind during the day like the ocean's tides. Christians who're growing in the Spirit are *more* Spiritual some days, and *less* Spiritual other days, depending on which motivator is winning the "tug-of-war" between Spirit and flesh in their mind.

Growing Christians have "mountaintop experiences" some days, and "valley experiences" other days. Why? Because the Spirit and the flesh are struggling for supremacy in a daily "war." Also notice the *descriptions* on the left and right sides of Diagram 4. These descriptions explain the *Two Ways* of Christian motivation. Finally, Diagram 4 raises our next logical question: What *makes* the Holy Spirit flood up and motivate a Christian's mind? Let's talk about the *process* of Spirit-filling next.

The Process of Spirit-Filling

The *process* of Spirit-filling is simple, easy, and normal for all Christians. How do we know that? We know that because many of the Early Christians were socially powerless slaves, women, children, and the elderly. Many were illiterate, and most had simple careers as shepherds, farmers, soldiers, carpenters, traders, and fisher folk. The point is, most Early Christians were everyday people with simple backgrounds. Because of that, being Spirit-filled *had* to be simple, easy, and normal – or the Early Christians *couldn't* have experienced it.

More importantly, the Early Christians were *not* taught how to be Spirit-filled by teaching the way that we do it today: with classes, textbooks, videos, and homework. They learned to be Spirit-filled through *experience*. Think of it this way. On the Day of Pentecost, the first 3,120 Christians learned how to be Spirit-filled in a few minutes without *any* teaching at all. They just *experienced* it right where they were standing in Jerusalem. However, they *wanted* to be Spirit-filled. They *expected* to be Spirit-filled. And they *asked* to be Spirit-filled. We still learn Spirit-filling the same way. We have to *want* it. We have to *expect* it. And we have to *ask* for it. That's the whole process.

Think about the 3,000 pilgrims who became new Christians on Pentecost morning. They left town the *next* day (Pentecost was a one-day festival), and *returned* to their homes in other lands. But think about this. When they arrived back in those distant lands, who *taught* them how to be Spirit-filled as a daily lifestyle? After all, they had only had one *day* of Christian experience. The answer to the riddle is extremely important. The answer is: The *Holy Spirit* taught them.

One of the Holy Spirit's most important roles on earth is *teaching* Christians. Think about the millions of Early Christians who never *saw* one of the training manuals we discussed earlier. The truth is that those manuals were rare and priceless. They were painstakingly written on papyrus scrolls and were hand-carried by special couriers to be read aloud to the small groups in major cities like Corinth, Ephesus, and Rome. But what about the Christians in the remote towns, small fishing villages, and camps in the open countryside? *They* never saw the manuals. So who taught *them*?

The *Holy Spirit* taught them. Let's repeat the principle, since we're going to talk about it more in the next chapter. The rule is this: The *Holy Spirit* is fully capable of teaching all Christians how to be Spirit-filled. He doesn't need pastors, priests, and professors helping Him. He doesn't need textbooks, tablets, and tests helping Him. All He needs is Christians who want to be Spirit-filled, who expect to be Spirit-filled, and who pray to be Spirit-filled.

The Prayer for Spirit-Filling

A friend of mine used to say, "What you *think* about all day is what you *worship*." He was right. That's also a clue to how to be Spirit-filled. All we need to do is *think* about the Holy Spirit during the day and *pray* to Him during the day. A man once asked me what "words" he needed to pray to be Spirit-filled. I told him that he only needed *four* words. He looked surprised and asked what the four words were. I said the words are: *"Fill me, Holy Spirit."*

In my own case, as soon as I open my eyes each morning, I roll out of bed onto my knees beside my bed and pray those four words. Then I pray for the people and the tasks I'll be facing that day, and I ask the Holy Spirit to teach me, encourage me, and help me with those tasks. Then as often as I can during the day, I repeat the simple four-word prayer: *"Fill me, Holy Spirit."* That's all there is to the process of being Spirit-filled. After that, the most important thing about Spirit-filling is the result of it. So let's talk about the *result* of Spirit-filling next.

The Result of Spirit-Filling

The *result* of full Spiritual motivation (Spirit-filling) is obvious from everything we've said. Spiritual motivation increases our *positive* behavior. And it decreases our *negative* behavior. It increases our love, joy, peace, patience, and healings. And it decreases our anger, lust, greed, fear, and doubt. The percentage of these two opposing behaviors is the test of how much we're being influenced by the Holy Spirit.

Said another way, *all* Christians are motivated to some greater or lesser degree by the Holy Spirit because *all* Christians are indwelled by him. Thus, all Christians have supernatural love, joy, peace, patience, and healings to some greater or lesser extent. But as we've said, all Christians aren't Spirit-filled. All Christians' minds aren't influenced in the majority by supernatural love, joy, peace, patience, and healings.

As we said earlier, observing a Christian's daily behavior is the only way to tell the degree to which he or she is being motivated by the Spirit. We only need to observe the degree of *holiness* in a Christian's behavior (the degree of supernatural love, joy, and peace) to know how much he or she is being motivated by the Spirit. And by the way, some Christians wonder whether being Spirit-filled is a "dramatic" experience. So as we near the end of the chapter, let's talk about the *drama* of Spirit-filling.

The Dramatics of Spirit-Filling

To begin, let's remember that God's purpose in filling Christians with the Holy Spirit is to make them supernaturally *loving, patient, kind, and gentle* – and those aren't especially dramatic behaviors. The truth about Spirit-filling is that it's not usually filled with *drama* – and it wasn't designed to be. God designed Spirit-filling to be personal, pleasant, and peaceful. He designed it to give Christians strength, discipline, courage, wisdom, and everything helpful and good.

That means the amount of drama in Spirit-filling comes from the *drama* (if any) of the situation in which it's happening. For example, my first experience with Spirit-filling was fairly dramatic because it happened in a *dramatic* situation. As I mentioned in the Introduction to this book, I've been a Christian since childhood, but I had never heard the term "Spirit-filling." (Or if I *had* heard it, it hadn't stuck in my mind.) So I was 32 years of age before I experienced my first Spirit-filling.

It happened in a New York City hotel room. I was the executive vice president and a director of a corporation that was failing financially at the time due to an unexpected stock market crash, and I was distressed, frustrated, and worried. One afternoon, after a particularly stressful conference, I knelt in my hotel room and called out to God for the first time since I was a teenager. And to my surprise (because I didn't know what Spirit-filling was), a profound sense of peace and power came over me, and the Holy Spirit began to supernaturally teach me.

In those days I kept a small travel Bible in my luggage, but seldom took the time read it. However, there on my knees in my hotel room, the Holy Spirit prompted me to get that little travel Bible out of my luggage and to open it. I unzipped it, and it fell open to a certain Old Testament passage. Then for about two hours, the Holy Spirit used that Old Testament passage to teach me *what* was happening in my life – *why* it was happening – and *what* the result was going to be.

That was my first experience with Spirit-filling, and I didn't know what it was or what to call it. But the words in the Bible seemed to shimmer and rise up off the page as the Holy Spirit taught me. When He finished with the teaching and the profound sense of His presence subsided somewhat, I got up, checked out of the hotel, and caught a flight home. But I was never the same. My life, my career, my finances, and even the city in which I lived all changed in following weeks. Everything the Holy Spirit taught me in the hotel room came true, and I was a different person afterwards.

But here's the question. Was my Spirit-filling *dramatic*? It depends on how we define "dramatic." My experience was personal, pleasant, and peaceful. It was warm, wonderful, and worthwhile. But I don't know that it was "dramatic." I was alone in a quiet hotel room with no other noise or disturbance. I cried a lot, and I hadn't cried since childhood. My life was also changed forever in a couple of hours. But on the other hand, the experience wasn't filled with theatrical type action and emotion. So I'm not sure we should call it "dramatic."

I've had many such Spirit-filling experiences since that time. And all of them have been consoling, comforting, and courage-building. I think that means being Spirit-filled may, or may not, be "dramatic" depending on how we define "dramatic." However, Spirit-filling always changes us for the better. So let's close by seeing one of the most important principles in this chapter. It's this:

The Holy Spirit is the greatest Gentleman in the universe. He never interrupts when we're talking about something else or doing something else. He works by invitation only.

That means *we* (not the Holy Spirit) are in control of our own Spiritual motivation and our own Spirit-filling. If we ignore the Holy Spirit during the day, we won't have much Spiritual motivation. If we seek Him during the day, we'll have Spiritual motivation. All we need to do is want to be Spirit-filled, expect to be Spirit-filled, and to pray, "Fill me, Holy Spirit."

And now, to be sure that the coming pages apply to you personally, let's assume from this point that you're praying to be Spirit-filled; that you're committed to being Spirit-filled, and that you're praying for more and deeper Spirit-filling. With that agreed, let's summarize this chapter.

Summary of Chapter 9

1. "Behavior" is *a response to a situation.* More completely, behavior is *a physical response to a personal situation that was triggered by an inner motivator in a person.* Thus, the evidence of a Christian's Spiritual level is found in his or her *behavior.* Are his or her responses to daily situations positive, or negative? The more *positive* they are, the more Spirit-filled he or she is.

2. A Christian's daily behavior is supposed to be so *Spiritual* that it attracts non-Christians to Christianity and makes them to want to be Christians too.

3. Spiritual growth doesn't come from *listening* to wise and persuasive human words. It comes from *seeing* Spiritual behavior being demonstrated.

4. The ancient teaching of the "Two Ways" of Christian motivation is so important that it's taught in *nine* different books of the *New Testament*. It was also taught in Early Christian training manuals and letters outside of today's Bible.

5. "The Way of Light" is a lifestyle in which the inner *Holy Spirit* produces a behavior of supernatural love, joy, healings, peace, and miracles in Christians. Thus, "The Way of Light" is a synonym for being Spiritually motivated, or for living the *Early Christian Lifestyle*.

6. "The Way of Darkness" is a lifestyle in which the inner *flesh* produces a behavior of hate, anger, trouble, stress, and turmoil in Christians. Thus, "The Way of Darkness" is a synonym for being motivated by the flesh, or for living a *non-Christian* lifestyle.

7. Jesus called the inner motivation of the Holy Spirit "Rivers of Living Water" that flow up in a Christian's mind and influence his or her behavior for holiness.

8. Being *Spirit-filled* is the Christian goal, and all Christians are commanded to seek it.

9. The word "Spiritual" refers to *supernatural behavior, gifts, and experiences* being produced in Christians by the indwelling Holy Spirit. The word comes from the Greek word for "Spirit," referring to the Holy Spirit, third Person of the Trinity. Thus, the word "Spiritual" should always be capitalized out of respect for God.

10. The Holy Spirit is named "Holy" because one of His roles is to produce *holiness* (pure and clean behavior) in Christians.

11. When the Holy Spirit motivates a Christian, the part of his or her body that the Spirit influences is the Christian's *mind*.

12. Christians are in control of their own Spirit-filling and Spiritual growth at all times.

13. Diagram 4 illustrates the motivational system of a *growing* Christian. All Christians have *two* inner motivators in them – Light and Darkness (Spirit and flesh) – and these two motivators are at "war" for control of a Christian's mind.

14. Being Spirit-filled is simple, easy, and natural. The best way to learn it is by experiencing it.

15. To be Spirit-filled, all Christians need to do is want it, seek it, and pray four simple words during the day: "Fill me, Holy Spirit."

16. Being Spirit-filled often isn't "dramatic." Instead, Spirit-filling is personal, pleasant, and peaceful because the Holy Spirit's role is to be personal, pleasant, and peaceful with Christians.

17. The Holy Spirit is the greatest Gentleman in the universe. He never interrupts while we're talking about something else or doing something else.

In the next chapter, we're going to continue our discussion of Spiritual motivation, Spiritual growth, and Spirit-filling. In that chapter, we're going to talk about how to grow to Spiritual maturity by forming the new habit of being Sprit-filled throughout the day.

Chapter 10

THE MATURE CHRISTIAN

The Fourth Spiritual Level

We said in the previous chapter that the goal of a Christian is to be *Spirit-filled*. We said Spirit-filling is the only way Christians can be different from non-Christians, and that everything a Christian is supposed to *have*, *be*, and *do* comes from being Spirit-filled. Finally, we said Spirit-filling is easy, and every Christian can experience it – regardless of age, gender, health, education, race, finances, or any other variable. So in this chapter, let's build on those principles and talk about how Spirit-filling relates to *Spiritual maturity*. Let's open with a story that shows the main requirement for becoming a mature Christian.

The Stranger at the Luncheon

Several months after I was Spirit-filled for the first time in my New York hotel room, my doorbell rang about 2:00 o'clock one afternoon. I opened the front door and was surprised to see a close friend, Dwayne Evans (not his real name), standing on the steps. Dwayne was a deacon in the traditional Christian congregation that we attended, and he and I often met during the week to plan Sunday school lessons, covered dish meals, and other such traditional events.

But this time was different. As soon as I saw Dwayne through the glass of my storm door, I knew something unusual had happened. His eyes were wide and he had an excited look on his face. I unlocked the storm door and said, "Dwayne, what are you doing here? Were we supposed to meet today?"

"No," he almost shouted, "but you won't believe it! You just won't believe it!"

"Won't believe what," I said. "What has happened?"

"I just met the most amazing man I ever met," he answered, "and he told me the most incredible thing I ever heard. We talked about it for over an hour!"

"Talked about *what* for over an hour?" I asked. "What did the man *say*?"

"He told me that all the miracles in *Acts* are still available today," Dwayne replied, referring to the book of *Acts* in the Bible. "He said that angels, healings, and all the other miracles in *Acts* still happen today!"

"But that's impossible," I said. "Who *was* the man?"

"I can't explain everything here on the steps," Dwayne said. "Get your coat and Bible. Let's go for coffee and I'll tell you the whole story."

We drove to a nearby coffee shop, found a quiet table, and ordered two cups of coffee. Then we talked, read verses in *Acts*, and sipped coffee, until 5:00 that afternoon. Dwayne said his adventure had started at noon that day when he was introduced to a stranger at a business luncheon. After lunch, he and the stranger had walked to their cars together, chatting as they went. Dwayne had casually asked where the man "went to church," and the stranger had replied that he didn't "go to church." He said he worshiped in a small group in a home.

That led to a discussion of small groups, and that's when the man told Dwayne that every Spiritual experience that had happened to the Early Christians still happened today. The man said that the healings, prophecies, visions, and all the other supernatural events recorded in *Acts* still happened today in the small group that he attended. Dwayne said such a thing was *impossible* because miracles ended in the First Century. (Dwayne and I had been taught that in our traditional congregation.)

The stranger had smiled and asked politely what Bible *verse* said that. Dwayne unlocked his car, got out his Bible, opened it on the hood of his car, and started trying to find a verse that said miracles ended in the First Century. But he couldn't find one. The more he looked, the more he realized that there was no such verse. Eventually, the stranger shook Dwayne's hand and said, "May God richly bless your Spiritual search." Then he drove away. That's when Dwayne rushed to my house to tell me what had happened.

So Dwayne and I sat in the coffee shop for three hours, reading passages in *Acts* and trying to understand what the stranger had said. Finally it was time for dinner. Dwayne drove me home and pulled in my driveway. He turned off the engine and sat silently for a moment, staring out the windshield. Then he asked softly, "What do you think we should do?"

"I think we should pray," I answered. "If what that man said is true, I want it. I want the same healings, angels, miracles, and everything else that the Early Christians had."

"Me too," Dwayne said quietly. "Let's pray for it now."

With that, Dwayne laid his head on the steering wheel and closed his eyes. So I leaned forward, folded my hands against the dashboard, and closed my eyes too. Then we both said simple prayers. I don't remember our words now, but we prayed something like this:

> "Lord, we don't know if the things that man told Dwayne are true or not. We don't know if First Century miracles still happen today. But if they do, we want them. We want everything Christians had in the book of *Acts*, and we're asking You for them right now. Amen."

Dwayne drove away and I went in my house for dinner. I didn't know it then, but my life was about to change again – this time even more completely than it had changed when I was Spirit-filled in my New York hotel room. And by the way, I still didn't know what had *happened* to me in New York. The experience hadn't been repeated and no one had explained it to me. I still hadn't heard the words "Spirit-filled" spoken by anyone. So I had assumed that my New York experience was some kind of once-in-a-lifetime "mountaintop experience" that would never be repeated. However, in the days following my prayer with Dwayne in the driveway, I was introduced to a whole new world of Spiritual experiences that I had never known existed.

In a matter of weeks, I met other Christians who were as Spiritually hungry as I was. And they showed me new books to read, new meetings to attend, and other people I should meet. I was introduced to a man in a nearby town who had a small group meeting in his home. He was a retired military officer and a self-taught Bible scholar. He befriended me, and we sat on his patio for hours as he talked me through the *New Testament*, explaining how the Early Christians had lived, gathered, and worshiped.

Though I was a lifelong Christian, I'd never heard any of the things this man showed me. Those sessions on his patio were my first baby steps toward what eventually became my own three-year study of Early Christianity that I mentioned in the Introduction. I also attended this man's small group meeting several times, and that's where I first saw Spirit-guided worship – with visions, prophecies, healings, and other First Century type supernatural experiences.

Within a year, Dwayne and I had both started small groups in our own homes, and we were both having Early Christian experiences ourselves. I still didn't know what was happening to me, and I still didn't know the right words to describe it. But I stumbled on in blind faith, seeking deeper experiences with God, and trying to live an *Early Christian Lifestyle* myself. My Spiritual hunger gradually paid off, and before long I was having Spiritual experiences the likes of which I had previously only read about in the pages of the Bible.

But let's stop a minute. I opened this chapter with the true story of "The Stranger at the Luncheon" to illustrate the kind of Spiritual *hunger* that's required for Christians to reach Spiritual maturity. So now it's time to look at our fifth diagram. It's an image of *Spiritual maturity*.

Diagram 5

THE MATURE CHRISTIAN

Here's the *fifth diagram* in our series. It shows the fourth and final level of Spirituality. It's our *Spiritual Maturity* diagram. The color *white* on the left arm of the diagram extends almost all the way across the top circle of the diagram that represents the *mind*. About three-quarters of this Christian's mind is now white, indicating that a large portion of his or her mind is being influenced by the Holy Spirit. The Holy Spirit is flooding this Christian's mind with Living Water to a level of Spirit-filling – and beyond – giving 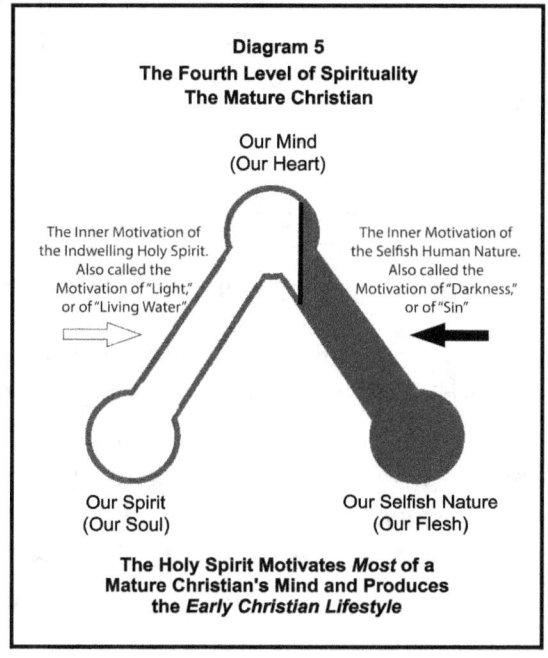 this Christian many supernatural abilities, thoughts, decisions, and experiences.

Also note that the *black* color on the right arm of the diagram, the arm that represents the motivator of Darkness (our flesh), is being pushed almost completely out of this Christian's mind. This indicates that the tyranny of his or her flesh is almost completely suppressed. We're assuming that this Christian is *habitually* Spirit-filled, and thus this filling will remain at this average level all day (though it will ebb and flood slightly as circumstances change).

Thus, Diagram 5 is a diagram of a Spiritually mature Christian. It's a diagram of a Christian who's made a *habit* of being *Spirit-filled*. Said another way, it's a diagram of a Christian who has made a habit of being fully motivated by the Spirit. If this diagram was a real Christian, he or she would be living the *Early Christian Lifestyle* of healings, peace, miracles, guidance, and other wonderful supernatural experiences.

Next, to sharpen our understanding of Spiritual maturity, let's look at *six tips* for tapping into its supernatural power personally. Here's our first tip for Spiritual maturity: It's the need to individually *seek* it.

The First Tip for Spiritual Maturity

Seek Spiritual Maturity

We've already talked about this first tip for Spiritual maturity because we talked about what Dwayne and I did that afternoon in my driveway – we sincerely prayed for it. But it's important to know that *seeking* Spiritual maturity is taught in both the *Old* and *New Testaments*, and both of them teach that the *more* of God's power we seek, the *more* of God's power we find. The opposite is also true. The *less* of God's power we seek, the *less* of God's power we find.[1]

For example, Jesus taught that if we "hungered and thirsted" for righteousness (if we hungered and thirsted for Spirit-filling) we *would* be filled.² In one of His most tender and dramatic teachings, Jesus illustrated how God responds to our Spiritual seeking. Jesus said that everyone who *asks* the Father for Spiritual things *will* receive them. He said that if a child asked its father for an *egg*, the father wouldn't give the child a *scorpion*. Likewise, Jesus said that if human fathers are that giving to their own children:

> "How much more will your Father in heaven give the *Holy Spirit* to those who ask Him?"[3]

This was a popular teaching in small groups during my early years of Spiritual growth, and it's still one of my favorite teachings today. This verse encourages all people to *seek* the four supernatural experiences that every human should have. Let's review the four experiences that everyone should seek.

The Four Supernatural Experiences

Here are the four supernatural experiences that all people should seek. Everyone should seek:

1. To be *indwelled* by the Holy Spirit and to have his or her inner spirit *baptized* in the Spirit, thus becoming a Christian.

2. To have Spiritual *behavior* (the "fruit" of the Spirit), thus expressing supernatural love, joy, peace, patience, kindness, etc., as a lifestyle.

3. To have Spiritual *gifts*, thus expressing supernatural healings, visions, wisdom, prophecies, and knowledge, etc., as a lifestyle.

4. To be habitually *filled* with the Spirit, thus having his or her Spiritual gifts and Spiritual experiences always expressed with supernatural love, joy, peace, patience, kindness, etc.

Now, assuming that we're obeying this first tip, and that we're *seeking* Spiritual Maturity, let's now see our second tip – the need to be open to *new* experiences.

The Second Tip for Spiritual Maturity

Be Open to New Experiences

Our second tip is related to the first one. If we're going to *seek* Spiritual maturity, we also need to be open to *new* experiences. As we said earlier, the Holy Spirit is the greatest Gentleman in the universe and He never overrides our personal will power. He only gives us things by "invitation." When I prayed in the driveway with Dwayne that afternoon, I "sent" the Holy Spirit an "invitation" for all the new supernatural things He could give me. And He "accepted" my invitation by giving them to me.

I was open to browsing in new bookstores, meeting new Christians, visiting new small groups, attending new breakfast groups, lunch groups, and dinner groups – but most of all – I was open to new Spiritual behavior, gifts, and experiences. And day by day, week by week, month by month, I gradually experienced deeper and deeper Spiritual behaviors, gifts, and experiences. That's the power of openness to new experiences.

Now let's shift gears and see our third tip. It's a rough one, since it concerns fighting the *war* that all Christians have with their selfish human natures.

The Third Tip for Spiritual Maturity

Fight the Inner War With Vigor

Some Christians don't realize it, but they have an inner *war* raging within them. This inner war is the reason Spiritual maturity is rare, and it's the reason that even mature Christians occasionally feel flashes of anger, vengeance, and lust. In the previous chapter, Diagram 4 was a picture of a *growing* Christian whose mind was *half* white and *half* black. Diagram 4 was an image of a double-minded Christian who was motivated half by the indwelling Holy Spirit, and half by his or her selfish nature. But there were two things about Diagram 4 that we didn't mention in the previous chapter. First, we didn't mention the *viciousness* of the war between the two motivators; and second, we didn't mention that the war is *permanent*.

Let's repeat that. All Christians have a vicious war within them (even mature Christians), and that war is permanent. It lasts a lifetime. It never stops. The differences are that *mature* Christians usually win the war. *Growing* Christians win it about half the time. And *infant* Christians usually lose it. We see a real-life example of this vicious, permanent war illustrated in the life of the apostle Paul.

The apostle Paul was one of the most educated, intelligent, and Spiritual Christians who ever lived. He wrote over half of the *New Testament*. He traveled the world and introduced Christianity to many nations and cities. And yet he was honest enough to confess that *he* had a vicious and permanent problem with inner Darkness. Here's what Paul said about his personal war with the flesh:

> "I know that nothing good dwells in me – that is, in my *flesh*. I want to do what's right, but I *don't*. The good things I want to do, those I *don't* do. But the bad things I don't want to do, those are the very things that I *do*. Now, if I do bad things that I don't really want to do, it's not me doing them. It's *sin* dwelling in me that's doing them."[4]

Now notice that Paul is verifying all the principles we've been talking about. He's verifying that he has an inner motivator of *flesh*; and he's verifying that this motivator is viciously and permanently producing *sinful* behavior in him. So let's stop and think about that a second. Paul was a First Century Christian teacher, prophet, and apostle. He wrote over half of the *New Testament*. He was loved and respected in cities and nations far and wide. And yet he still had a problem with sinful behavior.

That says it all. That proves that every Christian on earth has the same inner war. Of course, Paul explained in later verses that because of everything Jesus had done for him, he delighted in God's righteous law, and God's righteous law always rescued him. But even with all that, Paul admitted that in his *flesh*, he would always be, "A slave to the law of *sin*."[5]

We also need to know that Paul wasn't the only First Century teacher to write about the inner war that Christians have. James, one of Jesus's half-brothers, wrote about it too.[6] But it was the apostle Peter who explained how Christians can *win* the war, and why Christians *must* win it. Here's what Peter said:

> "Beloved, I urge you, as strangers and pilgrims in this world, to suppress the unspiritual desires (of your *flesh*) that *war* against your inner *spirit*. Instead, have such good behavior among the non-Christians that even if they falsely accuse you of doing evil things, they'll still see your ethical and moral behavior and will glorify God for it."[7]

Peter is reminding us that one reason we're Christians is to display so much Spiritual behavior that we *attract* non-Christians to Christianity. But Peter is also reminding us that the responsibility for suppressing our flesh rests squarely with *us*. More, we should never underestimate the negative power of flesh. Peter proved that when he used the Greek word "war" in these verses. The First Century Greek word Peter that used refers to fighting with the *violence of a soldier in combat*.[8]

Can you imagine that? Our flesh is fighting to be our prime motivator with the violence of a soldier in the heat of battle. *That's* why Christians struggle with (and sometimes succumb to) occasional fits of rage, lust, greed, and revenge. Let's see a final Early Christian statement about the viciousness of this war. It's one of the most chilling statements in Early Christian writing. It was written by an elder named Quadratus ("quah-<u>drat</u>'-toos") in the city of Athens, Greece. Quadratus described the war with our flesh this way:

> "Our flesh, though suffering no wrong from our spirit, yet *hates* our spirit and makes *war* on it – because our spirit hinders our flesh from indulging in its sinful passions."[9]

That's it in a nutshell, and nothing could be clearer. Our flesh is totally dedicated to producing anger, greed, and graft in us – and it *hates* our inner spirit because our inner spirit is empowered by the Holy Spirit to resist its evil ways. The good news is that we Christians *can* win the war – if we ask the Holy Spirit to fight it for us. All we need to do is pray continually to be Spirit-filled, and the war is won.

Now let's go to our next tip. As we've mentioned several times, even at the mature level, the Holy Spirit's motivation inside Christians ebbs and floods like the ocean's tides. That being true, how do we know *when* we're Spirit-filled? More, how do we know when we're *habitually* Spirit-filled? The answers to these questions are in our next three tips. Let's continue on to see tip four. It's the *51 percent rule*.

The Fourth Tip for Spiritual Maturity

The 51 Percent Rule

Most Christians realize that the Holy Spirit's power within them isn't passive and still. They sense during the day that the Spirit's power is flooding up in them at times; then ebbing back at times. Then flooding up again; then ebbing back again. This ebbing and flooding of the Spirit's power happens because the Holy Spirit rises and falls in us during the day to meet the needs of our changing situations. Some situations require courage. Others require disciple. Others require love, and so on.

Thus, Spirit-filling is *situational* to some extent. The Holy Spirit fills us with as much power as we need for specific situations at specific times. But we need a more precise way to *measure* Spirit-filling than just knowing how it works. So we can use the *51 percent rule*. In many areas of life – such as chemistry, stock ownership, boards of directors, and other such technical and legal situations – people rely on the 51 percent rule.

For example, 51 percent of a chemical in a mixture often gives that mixture its name. Or 51 percent stock ownership in a corporation gives control of that corporation. Or a 51 percent approving vote on a board of directors passes a resolution, and so forth. We could cite many examples. But the point is that this rule can also be used to measure Christian Spirit-filling. When the Holy Spirit is motivating *51 percent* or more of a Christian's mind, he or she is *Spirit-filled*. When the Spirit is motivating *less* than 51 percent of a Christian's mind, he or she is being influenced by the Spirit to some degree, but he or she *isn't* Spirit-filled.

The truth is that there's a big difference between being Spirit-*influenced* and being Spirit-*filled*. All Christians are Spirit-*influenced* to some extent, since all Christians are indwelled by the Spirit. But to qualify as being Spirit-*filled*, a Christian's mind must be motivated a minimum of 51 percent by the power of the Spirit – just as we saw in Diagram 5 in this chapter.

Now, still talking about the 51 percent rule, there's still a piece of the maturity puzzle missing. It's the *time requirement* that defines maturity. Let's see that time factor now.

The Time Requirement

Assuming that we're still talking about Christians whose minds are *51 percent* or more filled with the Spirit (as shown in Diagram 5), let's now consider another principle. Let's say that a Christian named "Jill" is Spirit-filled an average of *one* hour a day. A Christian named "Jim" is Spirit-filled an average of *six* hours a day. And a Christian named "Jack" is Spirit-filled an average of *sixteen* hours a day. All three Christians are Spirit-filled. But which one of them is Spiritually *mature*?

Can we agree that "Jack" is the Spiritually *mature* person in the group? Why? Because he's Spirit-filled more than *51 percent* of his waking hours. "Jill" and "Jim" are Spirit-filled *less* than 51 percent of their waking hours. Thus, Spiritual maturity is not only defined by being *Spirit-filled*. It's also defined as having the habit of being Spirit-filled *most* of the day. And "Jack" was the only Spirit-filled Christian who met that second application of the 51 percent rule.

Summary: To fully understand Spiritual maturity, it's necessary to use the *51 percent rule* in two ways, not just one. A Christian's mind must be *motivated* 51 percent or more by the Holy Spirit. But then that motivation must *continue* for 51 percent or more of a Christian's waking hours. And to be fair, when we're using these two applications of the rule, we should only measure *averages* of behavior with it. That's our fifth tip.

The Fifth Tip for Spiritual Maturity

Measure Only Average Behavior

In the same way that tides, sunlight, and seasons have *cycles*, the motivation of the Holy Spirit in us has *cycles* too. Spiritual motivation flows in peaks and valleys in us depending on how much Spirituality we need in given situations during the day. We don't need much Spiritual motivation when we're asleep. But we need a whole bunch of it when a coworker offends us on the job. So Spiritual power ebbs and floods during the 24-hour day, based on whether we're sleeping, eating, praying, worshiping, working, or dozens of other typical situations. But let's slow down a minute. How do we know this is *true*? How do we know Spiritual power *really* ebbs and floods in us during the day?

We know it's true because the Greek word for "filled" that the Early Christians used means to be *temporarily* "filled" as situations need it. For instance, when Jesus's 120 family members and former disciples were "filled" with the Spirit on Pentecost morning, the Greek verb used in the written record of the event meant that they were *temporarily* filled for that time and that event. It didn't mean that they were permanently filled forever.[10]

Let's say that a different way. Whether a person is an *infant*, or a *growing*, or a *mature* Christian, the Holy Spirit ebbs and floods in him or her at *that* level. This ebb and flood of the Spirit happens at a low level in infant Christians; it happens at a medium level in growing Christians, and it happens at a high level in a mature Christian. But it happens in all three. We could visualize the principle this way. If you had a radio tuned to a far off station that was fading in and out as you listened to it, you'd barely hear the station if the radio volume was *low*. You'd hear it better if the volume was *medium*. And you'd hear it best if the volume was *high*. But – at all three settings – the sound would still fade in and out in a cycle. That's how the Holy Spirit works at all three levels of Spirituality.

Returning to our theme, since Spirit-filling is cyclical at all levels of Spirituality, it makes sense to use the *law of averages* to measure it. To do that, we "dismiss" a Christian's *highest* Spirituality during the week; and we "dismiss" a Christian's *lowest* Spirituality during the week. Instead, we estimate a Christian's *average* Spirituality during the week. Said another way, it's not what we do on "mountaintop" days; and it's not what we do on "valley" days. It's what we do on *average* days that counts.

Finally, here's our sixth and final tip for Spiritual maturity. It's the need to be habitually Spirit-filled at the mature level.

The Sixth Tip for Spiritual Maturity

Be Habitually Spirit-Filled

As we've seen, all Christians are influenced to some degree by the Holy Spirit because all Christians are indwelled by Him. The trouble is, Christians get comfortable at whatever level of Spiritual influence they're on, and that level becomes their *habit*. They get comfortable at a certain level (often the *infant* level), and that level becomes their daily lifestyle.

As we said earlier, millions of Christians are living habitually at the *infant* level of Spiritual motivation. That's why national polls show the average Christian is no more Spiritual than a non-Christian. Of course, some Christians have a habit of living at the *growth* level and that's good. But that's still not enough. God wants all Christians to have a habit of living at the *mature* level. Why does He want that? He wants that because that's the best level for Christians, and for their families, and for their friends and coworkers, and for any non-Christians who're watching them.

Scientists say it takes a minimum of *three weeks* (21 days) to develop a weak new habit. After that, the weak new habit grows stronger each day until eventually it's locked in for life. That means for Christians to form a new habit of being Spiritually mature, they must pray for *three weeks* for their minds to be motivated 51 percent or more by the Spirit for 51 percent or more of their waking hours. That takes discipline, courage, and faith. That's also why First Century Christians were called "disciples." Let's talk about *disciples* now.

The Definition of "Disciples"

The First Century Greek word for *disciple* means a person who's a learner, a student, or a trainee.[11] Thus, it makes perfect sense to call Christians disciples. When the Holy Spirit indwells a non-Christian and makes a Christian out of him or her, the Spirit isn't creating a *mature* Christian. He's creating an *infant* Christian. After that, it's up to that Christian to exert enough discipline and dedication to grow to Spiritual maturity. This means that Christians are learners, students, and trainees who're learning to be mature Followers of The Way. They're learning to live the *Early Christian Lifestyle*. It's God's will for Christians to be disciples and for them to grow to maturity. Here's what Paul said about God's mandate for Christians to reach Spiritual maturity:

> "Christ Himself gave us (the full-time servants of apostles, prophets, teachers, etc.) to equip His people – so the Body of Christ may be built up until we *all* reach unity in the faith and in the knowledge of the Son of God, and become Spiritually *mature*, attaining the whole measure of the *fullness* of Christ. Then we'll no longer be Spiritual infants."[12]

These verses prove that it's God's will for Christians to be Spiritually mature and, more than that, for Christians to attain such a high level of Spirit-filling that they reach the *fullness* of Christ. Think about what that means. But it was Peter who described our discipleship the most clearly. Here's what Peter said about God's mandate for us to seek maturity:

> "Make every effort to *complete* your faith with goodness; and goodness with knowledge; and knowledge with self-control; and self-control with perseverance; and perseverance with godliness; and godliness with brotherly kindness; and brotherly kindness

with love. Because if you possess these qualities in *increasing measure*, they'll keep you from being ineffective and unproductive in your knowledge of our Lord Jesus Christ."[13]

Notice that Peter puts full responsibility for Spiritual growth on Christians *themselves*. Also notice that by using the term "increasing measure," Peter is making it clear that Spiritual growth is *progressive* over time. There's no such thing as "instant" maturity, or "instant" perfection, or "instant" sanctification. Logically, Spiritual growth is gradual over time, and it requires prayer, dedication, supernatural experiences, and socializing in a small group of like-minded Christians.

Also, as long as we're talking about Spiritual growth being gradual, let's talk about another connected issue. It's this. Is there a "sign" that Christians are Spirit-filled? "Yes," there is. But it's not the one that many Christians think it is. Let's talk about the *sign* of Spirit-filling next.

The "Sign" of Spirit-Filling

In upcoming chapters, we're going to discuss three different supernatural activities that the indwelling Holy Spirit expresses through Christians. These three supernatural activities are independent of one another. They aren't connected, and they operate separately. The three activities are:

1. *Spiritual behavior.* Also called the "fruit" of the Spirit, this includes the supernatural traits of love, joy, peace, and patience, etc., that the Holy Spirit produces in Christians. If these traits are 51 percent or more of a Christian's behavior, he or she is Spirit-filled. If they are 51 percent of a Christian's waking hours, he or she is Spiritually mature. Thus, Spiritual behavior is the

sign of Spirit-filling and maturity. But that behavior can be expressed *without* Spiritual gifts or Spiritual experiences because the three work independently. Summary: Spiritual behavior (fruit) is the *sign*, and the *only* sign, that a Christian is Spirit-filled or mature.

2. *Spiritual gifts*. These are the supernatural healings, visions, prophecies, etc., that the Holy Spirit produces in Christians. They are temporarily dispensed by the Spirit as He alone decides. The gifts can be expressed *without* Spiritual behavior or Spiritual experiences because the three work independently. Summary: *Spiritual gifts* are a sign that a person is a Christian. They are *not* a sign that a Christian is either Spirit-filled or Spiritually mature because *infant* Christians can express Spiritual gifts and can have Spiritual experiences.[14]

3. *Spiritual experiences*. These are supernatural answers to prayer, miraculous rescues from danger, appearances by angels, etc., that the Holy Spirit produces for Christians. They are temporarily dispensed by the Spirit as He alone decides. The Spiritual experiences can be produced *without* Spiritual behavior or Spiritual gifts because the three work independently. Summary: *Spiritual experiences* are a sign that a person is a Christian. But they are *not* a sign that a Christian is either Spirit-filled or Spiritually mature because *infant* Christians can express Spiritual gifts and can have Spiritual experiences.

Summary: All three of these supernatural activities prove that a person is indwelled by the Holy Spirit and is a *Christian*. But only one of them (Spiritual behavior) is the *sign* that a Christian is Spirit-filled or mature. Sadly, some of today's traditional congregations innocently teach their members that expressing *Spiritual gifts* is the "sign" a Christian is Spirit-filled. But we know that can't be true because *infant* Christians can express Spiritual gifts. The apostle Paul proved that in his first letter to the small groups at Corinth. But the worst thing about teaching that gifts are the "sign" of Spirit-filling is that it harms Christianity. It harms Christianity because it encourages *infant* Christians to express gifts in the *flesh*, and that turns off both other Christians and any non-Christians who see it.

Finally, as this chapter draws to a close, let's talk about one more issue. It's related to what we just finished discussing – the problem of infant Christians expressing gifts in the flesh. Let's close by talking about *excessive fleshy emotions*.

The Excessive Fleshy Emotions

We said earlier that Spirit-filling isn't necessarily dramatic, and that mature Christians seldom display theatrical and dramatic emotions. We said the Holy Spirit is the greatest Gentleman in the universe, and that His role is to make Christians loving, peaceful, gentle, and patient. However, we also know that Christians have two sources of emotion in them, and that one of those sources is the flesh – which usually is *not* loving, peaceful, gentle, and patient.

Indeed, Christians behaving in the flesh can be as loud, unruly, embarrassing, frightening, and inappropriate as non-Christians. That being true, imagine what would happen if a whole congregation built its worship services on expressing *excessive fleshy emotions*.

The word "excessive" means anything that's beyond what's normal, justifiable, or desirable. And in my travels over the years, I've visited congregations where the members shouted, wailed, swayed, and danced in the aisles during worship, and where the music was so loud that it hurt my ears. Those things were excessive fleshy emotions. Jesus explained this principle when He was teaching a member of the Jewish ruling council named Nicodemus ("nick-uh-<u>dee</u>'-mus") how to be Spiritual. Jesus gave Nicodemus this rule for being Spiritual. Jesus said:

> "Everything produced by the flesh is *flesh*. And everything produced by the Holy Spirit is *Spirit*."[15]

Jesus was saying that *fleshy* emotions and *Spiritual* emotions are two different things. He was saying that the flesh can't produce *Spiritual* emotions, and that the Holy Spirit can't produce *fleshy* emotions. Jesus was saying that Spiritual emotions are always respectful, gentle, considerate, polite, and uplifting; and that fleshy emotions are always disruptive, divisive, embarrassing, harsh, and loud – and that's how we tell the difference between the two.

Sadly, some Christians today aren't aware of Jesus's teaching, and don't understand the difference between fleshy emotions and Spiritual emotions. Some Christians have even been taught that *fleshy* emotions *are* "Spiritual." But that can't be true, since Spiritual emotions are always gentle, peaceful, loving, and polite – and wailing, dancing in the aisles, and playing music so loud that it hurts people's ears *isn't* gentle, peaceful, loving, and polite.

And now we've reached the end of the chapter. But we haven't reached the end of the true stories and the life-changing principles. Next, we're going to talk more about Spiritual behavior, gifts, and experiences. We're also going to talk more about small groups, Spiritual worship, and living the *Early Christian Lifestyle* in today's world. Some of our most interesting pages lie just ahead. But I'd like to close with another quote from the apostle Paul. It sums up everything we've said to this point, and it's my prayer for you as we end this chapter. After the prayer, we'll summarize the chapter and move on.

> "Don't you know that *you* yourselves are God's temple, and that God's Spirit dwells *in* you? For that

reason, I bow my knees to the Father and pray that out of His glorious riches, He'll strengthen you with Spiritual power through the Holy Spirit's indwelling of your inner being, and that Christ will dwell *fully* in your mind."[16]

Summary of Chapter 10

1. The Christian goal is to be habitually Spirit-filled. That's the only way Christians can be different from non-Christians.

2. Spirit-filling is easy and every Christian can experience it, regardless of age, gender, health, education, race, finances, or any other variable.

3. The habit of *seeking* Spiritual maturity is taught in both the *Old* and *New Testaments* of the Bible, and both teach that the *more* of God's power we seek, the *more* of God's power we will find.

4. Diagram 5 is a diagram of a Spiritually mature Christian. It's a diagram of a Christian who's made a habit of letting the indwelling Holy Spirit motivate 51 percent or more of his or her mind, for 51 percent or more of his or her waking hours.

5. The four supernatural experiences that every person needs are: To be baptized in the Holy Spirit and become a Christian; to express Spiritual behavior; to express Spiritual gifts, and to make Spirit-filling a habit.

6. The six tips for reaching Spiritual maturity are: To seek it; to be open to new experiences; to fight the inner war with vigor; to use the 51 percent rule; to measure only average behavior, and to be habitually Spirit-filled.

7. The Holy Spirit is the greatest Gentleman in the universe and never overrides our will power. Thus, to grow Spiritually we must be open to new Spiritual experiences.

8. Christians have an internal tug-of-war within themselves between Spirit and flesh. But they can win that war if they focus on the Holy Spirit and ask Him to fight it for them.

9. The Holy Spirit's power in Christians is not passive and still. It's cyclical and floods up and ebbs back in response to the needs of the day. Thus, we use the *51 percent rule* to tell when a Christian is Spirit-filled: When 51 percent or more of a Christian's mind is being motivated by the Spirit, he or she is Spirit-filled. If less than 51 percent of a Christian's mind is being motivated by the Spirit, he or she is being *influenced* by the Spirit to some degree, but he or she is not Spirit-filled.

10. When measuring Spiritual maturity: We not only measure whether a Christian's mind is 51 percent or more Spirit-filled, but we also measure whether he or she is Spirit-filled 51 percent or more of his or her waking hours.

11. Christians quickly become comfortable at whatever Spiritual level they're on (often the *infant* level) and that becomes their habitual lifestyle. This means that the key to Spiritual maturity is making Spirit-filling a *habit*. It takes three weeks to develop a new habit, so Christians must focus on Spirit-filling for at least three weeks to make it a habit.

12. A *disciple* is a person who's a learner, student, or trainee. Christians are disciples because they're learning to live the *Early Christian Lifestyle*.

13. The indwelling Holy Spirit expresses three different supernatural activities through Christians, and they work independently of one another. The three activities are:

a) Spiritual behavior (the "fruit" of the Spirit).

b) Spiritual gifts.

c) Spiritual experiences.

These all prove that a person is indwelled by the Spirit and is a *Christian*. But only one of these is a sign that a Christian is Spirit-filled or mature. That sign is Spiritual behavior (fruit) when it is 51 percent or more of a Christian's behavior, and when it lasts for 51 percent or more of his or her waking hours.

14. Jesus taught that human flesh produces fleshy emotions and behavior; and that the Holy Spirit produces Spiritual emotions and behavior. More, the flesh can't produce Spiritual behavior, and the Spirit can't produce fleshy behavior. So worship services that are embarrassing, frightening, rude, loud, and inappropriate are expressing excessive fleshy emotions, not Spiritual emotions.

PART III

The Early Christian Lifestyle

Chapter 11

THE SPIRITUAL BEHAVIOR

The "Fruit" of the Spirit

As we've seen, Christianity isn't about believing Christian doctrines (although that can be helpful). And it's not about attending a Christian congregation (although that can be helpful too). Instead, it's about living a *special lifestyle* – having a special *behavior* – whether or not we believe various doctrines or attend a certain congregation. The rock bottom truth is that Christianity is the process of being *motivated* by the Holy Spirit: doing what He prompts us to do, and going where He prompts us to go. God expects us to live a Spirit-guided life regardless of anything else. We know that's true because Jesus taught it in a riddle. Here's that *riddle*.

The Riddle of the Vineyard

During one of His many debates with the chief priests and elders in Israel, Jesus challenged them with a *riddle*. His riddle proves how important it is for Christians to live a *lifestyle* that pleases God, regardless of what they personally think or say. Jesus told the priests and elders that once upon a time there was a father who owned a vineyard and who had two sons that worked in the vineyard.

One day the father asked the first son to go to work in the vineyard. But the son said "No," and refused to go. Then later, the son changed his mind and *did* go to work in the vineyard.

Meanwhile, the father asked the second son to go do the needed work in the vineyard. And the second son said that "Yes," he'd go. Then later, he changed his mind too, and he *didn't* go to work in the vineyard.

Then Jesus challenged the priests and elders with this riddle: *Which of the two sons did their father's will?* After discussing it, the priests and elders replied that it was the *first* son, the one who said "No" at first, but then did the work in the vineyard anyway. And that was the correct answer.[1]

Now – what did Jesus's riddle mean, and how does it apply to Christians today? Jesus was teaching the priests and elders the same principle of *Spiritual behavior* that we've been talking about in this book. He was teaching them that *behavior* is more important than what we think or say. Today, many Christians "intellectualize" Christianity by hearing sermons about it, reading books about it, watching videos about it, and talking about it in coffee shops. But many of them don't have much *Spiritual behavior*. Christianity is a "mind game" or "head trip" to them.

And of course, sermons, books, videos, and coffee shops all have a place. But Jesus taught in "The Riddle of the Vineyard" that our heavenly Father wants us to accept His guidance and learn how to have Spiritual behavior. He wants that because the more Spiritual *behavior* we have, the more Spiritual *knowledge* we have. We don't understand Spiritual things first, and then have Spiritual behavior. That's the Christian lifestyle backwards. Think about it. The more *Spiritual behavior, gifts, and experiences* we have – the more knowledge we have about Spirituality. Sermons, books, videos, and coffee shops can't give us that knowledge. Spiritual knowledge only comes from Spiritual living. That means Christians need to focus and learn Spiritual living. To continue that learning, let's analyze one of the most popular but misunderstood *synonyms* for Spiritual behavior.

The Definition of "Fruit"

One reason Christians don't have much Spiritual behavior today is that they've heard the fuzzy word "fruit" too often. The word "fruit" makes them think of apples and oranges, but it usually doesn't make them thing about Spiritual behavior. So let's define the *synonym* "fruit," and talk about where it came from.

The phrase "the 'fruit' of the Spirit" comes from the 400-year old *King James Version* of the Bible, published in England in 1611. The KJV was published by a committee of English priests working under an archbishop working under King James of England.[2] The priests translated the original Hebrew and Greek manuscripts of the Bible into the *Elizabethan English* of their day – and that's why the KJV is full of language like, "thou doest" and "thee knowest," etc.

The KJV is one of the most popular versions of the Bible in history, and over half of all Christians still read it to this day. But one unintended consequence of that is that many KJV Elizabethan phrases have crept into present day translations of the Bible (such as the *New International Version*), and that confuses Christians, since we don't speak Elizabethan English today.

A good example of this problem is the phrase "the *fruit* of the Spirit." In previous pages, we talked about the apostle Paul's teaching on the behavior that the Holy Spirit produces in us – but we discussed it using contemporary English. Let's return to that teaching now. However, this time let's use the KJV translation from 1611 England. Here's how the KJV translated Paul's words:

> "The *fruit* of the Spirit (in us) is love, joy, peace, longsuffering, gentleness, goodness, faith, meekness, and temperance."[3]

The word "fruit" in these verses is the *Elizabethan* translation and that makes it fuzzy. Paul isn't writing about the "fruit" we buy at a farmer's roadside stand during the summer. He's writing about the *Spiritual behavior* the Holy Spirit creates in us. But when Christians read the word "fruit" today, they may not realize that

Paul means *motivation and behavior*. Thus, better translations of the Elizabethan word "fruit" in contemporary English might be:

> "The Holy Spirit *produces* (in us) love, joy peace ..." Or, "The *produce* of the Holy Spirit (in us) is love, joy, peace ..." Or, "The *motivation* of the Holy Spirit (in us) is love, joy peace ..." Or, "The *result* of the Holy Spirit (in us) is love, joy, peace ..."

These translations of the fuzzy word "fruit" make it clear that Paul isn't talking about apples and oranges. He's talking about the motivation of the Holy Spirit and the supernatural behavior it produces in us. That's why I always put the word "fruit" in parentheses, and I also try to use it as seldom as possible. I always try to use the translations we just illustrated.

But there's still another problem with how we translate these verses from Paul. In addition to the Elizabethan word "fruit" being fuzzy, many Christians have also been taught that Paul's list of *nine* behaviors in the verses is the complete list of the *Spiritual behaviors* that the Holy Spirit produces in us. But that's not true. There are many additional Spiritual behaviors listed in the *New Testament*. So let's look at a list of 20 of them. Table 1 is that list, and it shows the chapters and verses where the behaviors are found in the Bible.

Table 1
The List of Spiritual Behaviors
(List of The "Fruit" of the Spirit)

Galatians 5:22 –	Second Corinthians 6:7 –
1. Love 2. Joy 3. Peace 4. Patience 5. Kindness 6. Goodness 7. Faithfulness	15. Truthfulness 16. Righteousness
Galatians 5:23 – 8. Gentleness 9. Self-Control	**Second Peter 1:5 –** 17. Knowledge
Romans 15:13 – 10. Hope	**Second Peter 1:6 –** 18. Perseverance
Colossians 1:11 – 11. Endurance	**Second Peter 1:7 –** 19. Godliness
Ephesians 4:2 – 12. Humbleness	**Philippians 1:9 –** 20. Insight
Second Corinthians 6:6 – 13. Purity 14. Understanding	

Now – the thing to remember is that this list shows the *personality* of the Holy Spirit. His personality is one of supernatural love, joy, peace, patience, and the rest of the traits in this table. That means when a Christian is motivated by the Holy Spirit, his or her personality also becomes one of supernatural love, joy, peace, patience, and the rest of these traits. That's how the Early Christians turned the world upside down Spiritually in only 70 years. Non-Christians saw these wonderful Christian behaviors on display in the shops, streets, and fields, and they wanted those traits too. So they became Christians to get the traits, and that's how Christianity spread around the world. This principle is so important that we need to consider the *motivational linkage* that creates the *special behavior* that we call Christianity.

The Motivational Linkage

Let's summarize the cause-and-effect linkage that creates behavior: First, the two *motivators* in Christians (the Holy Spirit and the flesh) create either positive or negative *emotions* in them. These emotions create either positive or negative *behavior* in them. These behaviors create either positive or negative *habits* in them. And these habits create either positive or negative *lifestyles* in them. We can diagram the linkage this way:

1. Motivators ➔ 2. Emotions ➔ 3. Behaviors ➔ 4. Habits ➔ 5. Lifestyles

This linkage means that *all* Christians either have a predominately positive or a predominately negative lifestyle – depending on which inner motivator is influencing them the *most*. Christian lifestyles are similar to the "garbage in, garbage out" rule in computer programming. If bad information is the *input* to a system, bad information will be the *output* of the system. That's a computer programming law.

But that same law is true in Christian motivation. If selfish emotions are the *input* to a Christian's motivational system, a *selfish* lifestyle will be the output of his or her system. And by the way, since we've only mentioned "emotions" briefly in the book, let's take a moment to think about the difference between *Spiritual* emotions and *fleshy* emotions.

The Spiritual vs. Fleshy Emotions

The word "emotion" is from the same Latin root as the word "motivator," and the two words are closely related. Emotions are the internal feelings (sensations, stimulations) that motivators use to produce our behavior. For example, if our *fleshy* motivator produces an emotion of anger in us – that emotion will generate an outer behavior of anger (such as road rage). Conversely, if the indwelling Holy Spirit produces a *Spiritual* emotion like peace in us – that emotion will generate an outer behavior of peace (such as peace during a serious illness).

But as we've said, many Christians don't realize they have a "tug-of-war" inside them between these positive and negative emotions. Worse, they don't realize that the *negative* emotions are often winning that war. In the previous chapter, we talked about congregations where the attendees shout, wail, sway, dance in the aisles, and play deafening music during services. We said those services are a result of *excessive fleshy emotions*, so they're an example of negative emotions winning the tug-of-war in today's Christians.

Now, how do we *know* those kinds of Christian services are the result of *fleshy* emotions? We know it from reading Table 1 above. Table 1 shows that the behaviors the Holy Spirit produces in us result from emotions of peace, gentleness, humility, purity, Godliness, kindness, respectfulness, consideration, politeness, and all things uplifting. Think about those positive emotions a moment.

However, the behaviors that the negative emotions of the *flesh* produce in us are the opposite. They're selfish, embarrassing, confusing, egotistical, out of control, disruptive, and divisive. So – which type behavior best describes the loud and confusing services we just mentioned? Don't we agree that such loud and confusing services are the product of *fleshy* emotions, not the product of Spiritual emotions?

These differences in behavior remind us of another subject we discussed earlier. We said that *Spiritual behavior* is the *sign* that a Christian is Spirit-filled. Said another way, the behaviors listed in Table 1 above are the *sign* that a Christian is Spirit-filled. As an example of this sign that a Christian is Spirit-filled, let's close with another true story. It's the true story of the *fire pit*.

The Fire Pit

I was once visiting a Christian family who was camping in a campground near my home. The husband was a Spirit-filled Christian, and we were sitting in camp chairs beside a *fire pit* that he had built from loose stones around the campsite.

We were sipping coffee from tin mugs, and talking about Christians we knew and miracles we'd seen. Unexpectedly, the logs in the fire pit shifted with a shower of sparks, and one of the fire pit's stones came loose and rolled across the ground toward the husband's feet. Without realizing what he was doing, he unconsciously reached down with his bare hand and picked up the stone to put it back in the fire pit. What he didn't realize was that the stone was smoking hot from the fire. What happened next is a good example of the *sign* of a Spirit-filled Christian.

As the husband picked up the stone, he instantly realized that it was hot, and he immediately dropped it without making a sound or saying a word. Then he started to rub his fingertips with his thumb the way people do when they have something sticky on their fingers. He was completely relaxed and calm the whole time. His face showed no anger, pain, or stress. Instead, he started saying softly to himself, "Thank you, Jesus. Bless you, Jesus. Praise you, Jesus."

Then with the toe of his boot, he pushed the hot stone back into its place in the fire pit, took another sip of coffee, and continued our conversation as if nothing had happened. And to him, nothing *had* happened. He never mentioned the hot stone, and his hand wasn't burned. His unconscious response to the hot stone was the sign of a Spirit-filled Christian. The sign of a Spirit-filled Christian is supernatural behavior in everyday life.

The fire pit story shows how the *Rivers of Living Water* that Jesus promised us flood up when we need them and give us supernatural behavior that surpasses human understanding. And by the way – can you imagine what a *non-Christian* might have said and done if he or she had picked up a hot stone the way this Christian did? With that, let's summarize this chapter.

Summary of Chapter 11

1. Christianity isn't about believing doctrines or attending Christian congregations, although those things can be helpful. Christianity is about living the *Early Christian Lifestyle* of Spiritual behavior, gifts, and experiences.

2. In the "Riddle of the Vineyard," Jesus taught that accepting the Spiritual guidance of our heavenly Father and learning Spiritual behavior is more important than anything else we think, do, or say.

3. The word "fruit" (as in "the 'fruit' of the Spirit") is a fuzzy word. It comes from the *King James Version* translation of the Bible and is an *Elizabethan English* word. It's a synonym for the supernatural behavior that's motivated by the indwelling Holy Spirit. Better translations of the original Greek would be: the *product* of the Spirit ... the *result* of the Spirit ... or what the Spirit *produces* in us.

4. The word "emotion" comes from the same Latin root as the word "motivator," and the two are related. *Emotions* are the inner feelings that motivators use to produce our *behavior*.

5. The motivational linkage that produces behavior is:

    Motivators ➜ Emotions ➜ Behaviors ➜ Habits ➜ Lifestyles.

    The motivator that *dominates* in a Christian (flesh or Spirit) is the one that produces his or her daily lifestyle. If *fleshy* emotions dominate, a Christian has a daily lifestyle like a non-Christian. If the *Spirit's* emotions dominate, a Christian has a daily lifestyle of supernatural love, joy, peace, and patience.

6. Many Christians have been taught that Paul's list of *nine* behaviors in *Galatians* is the complete list of the behaviors the Holy Spirit produces in Christians. But there are more Spiritual behaviors listed in the *New Testament*. *Twenty* of them are listed in Table 1 in this chapter.

7. Spiritual behavior (the "fruit" of the Spirit) is the *sign* of a Spirit-filled Christian.

8. The story of "The Fire Pit" shows the kind of Spiritual behavior the Holy Spirit produces in Spirit-filled Christians, and that behavior is the *sign* of Spirit-filling. The fire pit story shows how the *Rivers of Living Water* that Jesus promised us flood up in times of need and give us supernatural behavior to cope with life.

We've now come a long way toward understanding the *Early Christian Lifestyle*. But the picture isn't complete yet. There are still two more vitally important aspects of that Christian lifestyle that we haven't yet discussed. So next, let's talk about a side of Christian life that's often misused and misunderstood today. Let's talk about *Spiritual gifts*.

Chapter 12

THE SPIRITUAL GIFTS

The Hospital Room

Recently my wife, Joanna, and I heard that a Christian man we knew was in the hospital with serious medical problems. I'll call him "Charles." We went to visit Charles, and when we arrived at his room, his wife and several of his relatives were there. They gathered around us as we entered and began to introduce themselves and shake hands.

As this was happening, I glanced in the direction of Charles's bed and was shocked at what I saw. Charles lay flat on his back with a sheet pulled up tightly around his neck. His face was waxy and his eyes were glassy. He saw me looking at him and tried to speak, but he could only groan. He had every appearance of a person who was extremely ill and perhaps even dying.

Without thinking about it or even realizing what I was doing, I instantly obeyed a strong inner impulse. I turned away from the chattering group and stepped quickly to Charles's bedside. I pulled back his sheet, took one of his limp hands in my mine, and began to pray for him quietly under my breath.

Within seconds, something wonderful happened. Charles's eyes suddenly cleared. Color flooded his cheeks and his voice returned. He sat up, pushed back the sheet, and began to smile at the group in the room and to join in their chatter. I stepped away from his bed and rejoined the group at the door, making no comment and – to this day – I don't think anyone else in the room realized what happened during those seconds. I don't even think Charles realized what happened. But the hospital released him two days later and he returned home to his family.

I opened this chapter with the story of Charles because our theme in this chapter is *Spiritual gifts*. Charles's story is an example of the gifts of healings – and his story shows how important Spiritual gifts are to all Christians, past, present, and future. The truth is, we can't cope with life on this troubled planet without them. So let's begin our discussion by talking about where the Spiritual gifts come from. Let's talk about their *source*.

The Source of Spiritual Gifts

As we know from earlier pages, when people are indwelled by the Holy Spirit and their inner spirits are immersed in supernatural power, the Holy Spirit becomes a second *motivator* within them that produces Spiritual outer behavior in them. But what we didn't say in earlier pages is that the indwelling Spirit is *also* the source of the Spiritual gifts in Christians. This means that, since all Christians are indwelled by the Spirit, all Christians have all the Spiritual gifts within them at all times, ready to be expressed when, where, and how the Holy Spirit chooses.

It's important to emphasize that Spiritual gifts originate *only* from the indwelling Holy Spirit. They don't originate from us humans. They're not human talents, skills, or abilities, and they can't be produced by human nerves, brains, and bones. They're supernatural acts of God. That's why the First Century Christians called them "gifts of grace." The Spiritual gifts are miracles that the Holy Spirit freely grants us because of our heavenly Father's mercy, generosity, forgiveness, and grace.[1] So let's dig deeper into the *details* of the gifts.

The Details of Spiritual Gifts

The first *detail* we need to know is that all Christians have *one* permanent gift from the Spirit that they're supposed to use to help other Christians. I call that our "full-time" gift. The apostle Paul explains our full-time gift this way:

> "Each Christian has his or her own *personal* gift from God. One of you has one kind of gift, and one of you has another ... but the Holy Spirit Himself produces the gifts, and He dispenses them (allocates them) to Christians as He alone decides."[2]

Notice that the important thing about our full-time gifts is that God wants us to use them to *help* (to *serve*) other Christians. The root purpose of the gifts is to strengthen, encourage, and comfort other Christians, both as individuals and as small groups. It's interesting that the word *gift* comes from a Greek root verb that means "to be happy." So God's plan is for the gifts to make us *happy*. That's one reason Paul said:

> "Don't neglect the gift within you ... *fan the flames* of the Spiritual gift that God gave you."[3]

But it was the apostle Peter who explained God's plan for our full-time gifts the best. Here's what Peter said about our full-time gifts:

> "Each of you should *use* whatever Spiritual gift he or she has received from God to *serve one another* as good stewards, faithfully administering God's grace in all of its forms."[4]

So both Paul and Peter said the purpose of our full-time gifts is to *help* other Christians. Serving other Christians with our personal gift isn't an optional idea or an interesting suggestion. It's a mandate from God. And for good reason, since our gifts are *supernatural* abilities that let us help other Christians in ways we couldn't help them with our *human* talents, skills, and abilities. That means if *we* don't express our full-time gift, we're shortchanging other

Christians. And if *they* don't express their full-time gift, they're shortchanging us. But the best news of all is that, in addition to our full-time gift, the Spirit also expresses the other gifts through us temporarily as needed. I call those our "part-time" gifts.

For example, I don't have the full-time gifts of healings. My full-time gift is a different one. Despite that, several times over the years the Holy Spirit has expressed the gifts of healings through me temporarily in wonderful and amazing ways – as He did in Charles's hospital room in the earlier story. In fact, over the years the Spirit has temporarily expressed many of the Spiritual gifts through me at least once, and some of them several times. I've also seen Christian friends express many part-time gifts as needed in small group situations. Of course, it only makes sense for the Spirit to express *both* full-time and part-time gifts through us. Think about it this way. What would happen if a small group of Christians was meeting, and one of the participants needed healing – but nobody in the room had the full-time gifts of healings? How would the Holy Spirit solve that problem?

He'd solve it by doing the obvious thing. He'd choose another Christian in the group and temporarily express the gifts of healings through him or her. That's exactly what happened in Charles's hospital room. When I walked through the door, the Holy Spirit chose me as a temporary conduit for the gifts of healings for Charles. Why did the Spirit choose me? Only He knows. My best guess is that because He had used me to express the part-time gifts of healings in the past, He knew I'd respond to His inner prompt as I entered the room.

The point to remember is that the *full-time* gifts and the *part-time* gifts are two different things, and that the Holy Spirit expresses both of them through us. We also need to remember that the Spirit expresses the Spiritual gifts *through* Christians, *for* Christians. The gifts exist only so Christians can "serve one another," as Peter said.

Peter also said that we Christians are "a chosen people," "a royal priesthood," "a holy nation," and "God's special possession."[5] As a result, it's only logical for the Spiritual gifts to be unique and exclusive benefits for *Christians* only.

On the other hand, there *are* occasions when the Holy Spirit expresses a Spiritual gift through Christians for the benefit of *non-Christians*. There are examples of that in the Early Christian letters.[6] We saw one earlier when the 120 members of Jesus's family and former disciples expressed the gift of prayer languages for the benefit of the *non-Christian* pilgrims in the streets on Pentecost morning.

But let's be clear. The primary purpose of the gifts is so *Christians* can help *Christians*. The Spiritual gifts are intended as a tool for Christians to energize, motivate, heal, and teach one another through the Holy Spirit's power – especially in small groups, as we'll see in coming pages. Now, let's pause here to summarize what we've said about Spiritual gifts thus far. Here are five *principles* about them.

The Five Principles of Spiritual Gifts

1. The Spiritual gifts are supernatural and miraculous, and they only come from the indwelling Holy Spirit within Christians.

2. The Spiritual gifts are not human talents, skills, or abilities.

3. All Christians have all of the gifts within them at all times, ready to be dispensed (allotted, or used) when, where, and how the Holy Spirit chooses.

4. All Christians have one full-time gift for the purpose of helping other Christians. In addition, the Holy Spirit

expresses the other gifts through all Christians part-time as needed.

5. The Holy Spirit occasionally uses the gifts for the benefit of non-Christians (as He did on Pentecost morning), but that is rare, because the primary purpose of the gifts is so *Christians* can help *Christians*.

Next, it's important to know that there's no rank order (no priority levels, or degrees of importance) among the gifts. All the gifts are equal. That's true because all the gifts come from the Holy Spirit, and all of them are designed to meet the needs of Christians. That makes them equal in value.[7] For instance, if one Christian is healed of a sickness, and another Christian has a vision telling him or her to accept a promotion at work – which of the gifts was the most important?

And the answer is: *neither* of the gifts was the most important. They were equally important. Why? Because two different Christians had two different needs, and those needs were equal in importance to the two Christians involved. So here's the guideline Paul gave us for using our gifts:

> "Earnestly desire the *most serviceable* gifts (the most useful, or the most helpful gifts)."[8]

When Paul said this, he wasn't saying that some gifts are *more* important than others. (Or for that matter, that some gifts are *less* important than others.) He was saying that Christians should desire the gifts that *best meet the needs* of the other Christians in their small group. However, all that still leaves one big question unanswered: How does a Christian *discover* his or her full-time gift?

The Discovery of Full-Time Gifts

Let's start by talking about how Christians *don't* discover their full-time gift. They don't discover it by using one of the online or paper "gift tests" that some traditional congregations use these days. Such tests aren't accurate, and that shouldn't surprise us. After all, how could a "test" designed by humans predict which part-time gifts the Holy Spirit will use to help what future Christians, with what future needs, in what future small groups, at what future times and places? Humans can't predict that. That would make humans as smart as the Holy Spirit.

The truth is that these online and paper tests don't differentiate between *full-time* and *part-time* gifts – probably because the test-makers don't know there *is* a difference. So they lump all the gifts together in one test without indicating which is which. That invalidates the test. Another problem with such tests is that they include *human* talents, skills, and abilities in the tests as "gifts." For example, many tests include things like singing, dancing, writing, drawing, painting, playing musical instruments, and so on, as "gifts" of the Spirit. But they're not. Those are *human* talents, skills, and abilities. That's why Paul and Peter didn't list singing, dancing, writing, drawing, painting, and playing musical instruments in the *New Testament* as Spiritual gifts.

So instead of using one of the online or paper tests, a better way for Christians to discover their full-time gift is the way the Early Christians discovered theirs: by *experiencing* their gift while participating in a small group. After all, the Holy Spirit *wants* us to know our full-time gifts. He's not keeping them a secret. Thus, to use the military term, we can discover our full-time gift "in the field," worshiping with a small group of like-minded, Spirit-filled Christians. That's how I discovered mine. And that's how I've seen dozens of other Christians discover theirs. Here's a true story that illustrates that principle.

The Shy Young Mother

Once, during refreshments after worship in a small group, a shy young Christian mother (let's call her "Janice") said to me, "You know, it's funny, but I felt like I was supposed to say something during worship today. But I didn't."

"You didn't?" I replied. "But why didn't you, Janice? You should've *said* whatever it was."

"Well," she said, "I just had this strong feeling that I was supposed to say something. But I was too embarrassed to say it."

"Look, Janice," I said. "Promise me something. The next time you get that feeling during worship, promise me that you'll speak up and say whatever it is."

She hesitated a moment and then responded, "Well, okay. If you think it's all right, then I will."

And so she did. During worship a couple of weeks later, a lull came in the singing and praying, and suddenly Janice began to speak softly. She gave the group a beautiful message of encouragement that touched and inspired everyone in the room. She had discovered her full-time gift. It was the gift of *encouraging*.

By the way, there's also a hidden lesson in Janice's story. It's this: If Janice hadn't been worshiping in a small group of Spirit-filled, like-minded Christians that morning, she might never have discovered her full-time gift. If she'd been sitting in a traditional congregational service that day, what are the chances she would have discovered her Spiritual gift? Slim to none, don't you think?

But now let's dig even deeper into the gifts. Let's talk about where the gifts fit the overall pattern of the supernatural events that all Christians are meant to enjoy. In other words, what's the relationship between the Spiritual gifts and Spirit-baptism; and Spiritual behavior; and Spirit-filling; and Spiritual experiences? Which comes first? Where do the others fit? Let's look at the *sequence* of the basic Spiritual events.

The Sequence of Spiritual Events

When Christianity was founded on Pentecost morning in the First Century, the 120 family members and former disciples of Jesus were the first humans to experience the indwelling power of the Holy Spirit. And they experienced it in a *sequence* of five supernatural events. Here's that sequence of events, as recorded in the second chapter of the book of *Acts*:

1. Event #1: The 120 family members and former disciples were *indwelled* by the Holy Spirit, and their inner spirits were *baptized* in the Spirit and awakened to Spiritual life. This made them Christians and gave them the potential to experience the next four supernatural events in the sequence.

2. Event #2: The 120 family members and former disciples received the ability to temporarily express *Spiritual behavior* (supernatural love, joy, peace, patience, etc.). This came second in the sequence because Spiritual behavior can only be expressed after people have been indwelled and baptized in the Spirit (in Event #1).

3. Event #3: The 120 family members and former disciples were temporarily *Spirit-filled*. The indwelling Holy Spirit surged up and filled their minds, becoming the main motivator of their behavior. This came third in the sequence because Spirit-filling can only happen after Christians are expressing Spiritual behavior (in Event #2).

4. Event #4: The 120 family members and former disciples temporarily expressed a *Spiritual gift*. In this case, it was the gift of prayer languages to attract non-Christians to Christianity. This came fourth in the sequence because the Spiritual gifts are intended to be used by Christians who are expressing Spiritual behavior at the time – and in fact, by Christians who are Spirit-filled at the time (in Event #3).

5. Event #5: The 120 family members and former disciples temporarily had a *Spiritual experience*. They experienced the miracle of seeing the 3,000 pilgrims join Christianity and then return to their homes in distant lands to launch worldwide Christianity in only one day. This came fifth in the sequence because the pilgrims could not have been attracted to Christianity unless the disciples expressed the Spiritual gift of speaking other languages (in Event #4).

Now, this was the sequence of the five basic Spiritual events on Pentecost morning. Today, they don't always happen in this exact sequence. Except for one thing. The *first* supernatural event must *always* be indwelling and Spirit-baptism (in Event #1). Why? Because the other four supernatural events come from *it*. Without it, nothing else can happen.

Also remember that these five supernatural events are separate and independent. They can all happen at the *same* time (as they did on Pentecost morning), or they can happen at *different* times, as they often do today. In other words, after Spirit-baptism (Event #1) – which is the baseline event – the other events can happen in any sequence, at any time. But the five experiences *should* always happen in the Pentecost sequence if possible, since that's how they were *designed* to happen. Let's review the Pentecost sequence and see why it's the *best* one.

The Best Sequence for the Experiences

God's plan for the Spiritual gifts is that they're intended to *help* other Christians. But more importantly, they're intended to help other Christians in *loving* ways. It's a turn-off to both Christians and non-Christians to see the Spiritual gifts used with *fleshy* behavior. That's what the infant Christians were doing at Corinth, and that's why Paul criticized them.[9] So the sequence of the five experiences as they happened on Pentecost morning is the *best* one because it prevents the gifts from being used in the flesh. Let's review the sequence to see that:

1. Event #1: *Spirit-baptism*. This comes *first* because it's the baseline event that makes a Christian and makes the other events possible.

2. Event #2: *Spiritual behavior*. This comes *second* because it comes *from* Spirit-baptism and because it's the proof that a person is a Christian, and that he or she is growing Spiritually.

3. Event #3: *Spirit-filling*. This comes *third* because it comes *from* Spiritual behavior – *Spirit-filling* is being filled with Spiritual behavior.

4. Event #4: *Spiritual gifts*. These came *fourth* on Pentecost morning because the gifts are intended to be used with *loving* behavior – they're intended to be used by *Spirit-filled* Christians. Infant Christians can and do use Spiritual gifts in the flesh. But that gives Christianity a bad image and Paul condemned it.

5. Event #5: *Spiritual experiences*. These came *fifth* on Pentecost morning because it was the first morning of Christianity and this was the logical place for them in the first sequence of Spiritual events in Christian history.

Today, Spiritual experiences can happen at any time because answers to prayer, rescues from danger, angelic appearances, and so on, are needed by Christians in all times and in all places.

With this background under our belts, we're now ready to look at a complete *list* of the Christian Spiritual gifts. Here it is.

The List of Spiritual Gifts

There are two reasons why we haven't looked at a *list* of the Spiritual gifts until now. First, I'm not sure an accurate list is possible. Second, I'm not sure a list is helpful. Our frame of reference in this book is that we want to do things the way the Early Christians did – and they simply *experienced* the gifts, whether or not they could name them or define them. Think about it this way. The Holy Spirit can express a gift through a Christian regardless of whether he or she knows what it is or can explain it. After all, the Spiritual gifts are supernatural and are coming from the throne room of heaven. So it's not surprising if we don't understand them.

A good example is the episode in Charles's hospital room in our earlier story. I don't know exactly what happened in Charles's room that day. I know it was some kind of supernatural *healing*. But even that's a puzzle since, in the original Greek, this gift is called the "*gifts of healings*." Both words are *plural*, indicating that God does many kinds of healings for many kinds of Christians in many kinds of ways.[10] So, precisely what *kind* of a healing did God give Charles's that day? I don't know. And it probably doesn't matter, since Charles got out of bed and went home.

To summarize: I think Christians should simply *experience* the gifts, instead of trying to name them and define them. Intellectualizing the gifts impedes their use. Even professional researchers aren't sure how many gifts there are; or what their names are; or what they do.

However, we do know that the Old Testament prophet, Joel, mentioned two gifts in his prophecy about the Day of Pentecost.[11] And we know that Paul mentioned 18 gifts in his letters. So we know that there are at least 20 gifts we can identify in the pages of the Bible.[12]

So here's our list of those 20 gifts, showing where each is mentioned in the Bible. We've deleted *duplications*; and we've omitted the six *calls* to Christian service, since they're calls and not Spiritual gifts. Here's the list.

Table 2

The List of Spiritual Gifts

Joel 2:28	
1. Dreams.	*Seeing prophetic and Spiritual images while asleep.*
2. Visions.	*Seeing prophetic and Spiritual images while awake.*
Romans 12:6-8	
3. Serving.	*Deacon type work – cooking, serving, etc., for other Christians.*
4. Teaching.	*Spiritually instructing, guiding, and training other Christians.*
5. Encouraging.	*Consoling, comforting, and praying for other Christians.*

6. Giving.	*Giving clothes, food, money, time, and shelter to Christians.*
7. Protecting-Guarding.	*Elder type work – often mistranslated "leading" or "ruling."*
8. Mercy.	*Having compassion and a prayer burden for afflicted Christians.*
First Corinthians 12:8-10	
9. Words of Wisdom.	*Having wise insight, judgment, and decisiveness in matters.*
10. Words of Knowledge.	*Sensing the facts, the truth, and the meaning of situations.*
11. Faith.	*Having supernatural trust, assurance, and personal belief.*
12. Healings.	*Includes every kind of physical, emotional, and mental healing.*
13. Miracles.	*Having supernatural control over physical conditions.*
14. Discerning evil spirits.	*Recognizing and resisting satanic and demonic influences.*
15. Translating prayer languages.*	*Translating prayer languages for a group to build its strength.*

First Corinthians 12:28	
16. Helping.	*Aiding poor, sick, disadvantaged, or handicapped Christians.*
17. Guiding-Steering.	*Setting new courses for groups – often mistranslated "governing" or "administrating."*
First Corinthians 14:3-4	
18. Prophesying.	*Foretelling events and expressing divine revelations.*
19. Using prayer languages (praying in the Spirit) – privately.*	*Using prayer languages privately to build personal strength.*
First Corinthians 14:27	
20. Using prayer languages (praying in the Spirit) – publicly.*	*Expressing a message in prayer languages in a group to build group strength. Must be translated by the speaker or by another Christian in the group who has the gift of translating.*

* *"Using prayer languages" means speaking some of the world's 7,000 languages that the speaker (or translator) doesn't personally know. This gift is private, and is only used publicly if a translator is present. Paul said this gift is a form of prayer – so it can be called praying in the Spirit," and "using prayer languages." But in the literal Greek it's called "speaking other languages."*

As we said, some researchers might add gifts to this list, and some might subtract gifts from the list. That doesn't bother me. I want the Holy Spirit to express as *many* gifts through me as He wants to express – whether or not I know what they are. Like everything else in Christianity, our ability to express gifts improves with time and experience. For instance, if I hadn't already experienced Spiritual gifts for several years before I walked into Charles's hospital room that day, I might not have responded to the Spirit's prompting and Charles might not have been healed.

Now – it's helpful here to slow down and think more specifically about *one* of the 20 Spiritual gifts. This gift is unusual because it can be used *three* different ways. It's also the only gift that Christians control. And because of that, it's also the most misused of the gifts. It's the first gift ever given to Christians, and it's the most common gift worldwide. We're talking about the gift of *speaking other languages*. It can also be called "using prayer languages" or "praying in the Spirit." Let's pause to think about this gift's multiple uses, and about its uses and misuses.

The Use of Prayer Languages

The Spiritual gift of *prayer languages* (praying in the Spirit, speaking other languages) is different from the other gifts because God designed it for Christians to use three different ways:

1. It can be used *privately* to build up personal Spiritual strength.

2. It can be used *publicly* to build up group Spiritual strength. (But a Christian with the gift of translating must be present; or the speaker himself or herself must translate the message.)

3. It can be used *publicly* (with or without a translator) to attract non-Christians to Christianity. It was used that way on Pentecost morning. But this use of the gift is rare.

Now, since the gift of prayer languages is so flexible, it's almost as if Christians have "two" full-time gifts in them. Their "first" full-time gift is the one God gave them for helping *other* Christians (healings, prophecies, encouraging, etc.). Their "second" full-time gift is one God gave them to help *themselves* – their prayer languages. The unusual thing about this "second" full-time gift is that Christians have full control over it. Prayer languages are the *only* gift that Christians can personally start and stop at will.

When a Christian uses this gift, his or her inner *spirit* prays directly to *God* in one of the world's 7,000 different languages. The Christian using the gift doesn't know which language is being used or what the words mean. That's because prayer languages bypass the human mind and go directly to God. (The apostle Paul confirms these facts in *First Corinthians*, chapter 14, verse 14.)

However, instead of trying to explain this gift further, let me just tell the story of how I discovered it personally. The first time I saw the gift, it was used by a pastor's wife. The second time I saw the gift, it was in a dream. Let me tell those stories.

The Pastor's Wife

I said previously that during the weeks following my driveway prayer when I asked God for everything the Early Christians had, I read books, met people, and went to meetings that I thought might help me understand how miracles happen in today's world. I followed every lead that might help, and it was during that time of searching that I heard about a retired pastor who was rumored to know how miracles happen today. (Let's call him "Rev. Setter.") So

I phoned Rev. Setter for an appointment, and arrived on his doorstep one afternoon under my umbrella in a rainstorm.

Rev. Setter led me to his den, put away my damp umbrella, and listened as I explained that I was there to find out how Early Christian miracles still happen today. We settled down in comfortable chairs with cups of coffee, and Setter began telling me about his career as a pastor. About that time, the front door opened, and his wife returned from a trip to the supermarket. She was wearing a damp raincoat and carrying two wet bags of groceries. As Setter continued talking about his career, his wife quietly put away her groceries, hung up her wet raincoat, and slipped into the den where we were talking. Without a word, she sat down on a sofa near me.

As the reverend continued chatting about his life and travels, I realized that his wife on the sofa was whispering something quietly. This attracted my attention, and I glanced in her direction. She was sitting with her head bowed and her eyes closed, and seemed to be whispering tenderly. Then I realized she wasn't whispering at all. She was speaking softly in a foreign language that I didn't recognize. I didn't understand it then, but I was seeing the Spiritual gift of prayer languages for the first time.

The remarkable thing about it was my reaction. In a way that I didn't understand until later, I recognized deep inside myself what she was *saying*. A feeling of pleasure spread over me, and I thought, *How nice of her to pray that for me*!

Of course, I had no conscious idea what she was praying. But deep inside, my spirit understood her message. Meanwhile, the reverend continued chatting. He made no comment about his wife, so neither did I. In due time, my appointment with the Setters was over. He glanced at his watch and stood up. He hadn't told me anything about miracles. The rain had stopped, and his wife had stopped praying. So I thanked them for their warm hospitality and left – pleased and happy – but with no understanding of what I had seen.

Rev. Setter had apparently been satisfied to let his wife's prayer languages answer my question about miracles in today's world, and to let the Holy Spirit guide my next steps. And soon, the Holy Spirit did exactly that.

The Grand Canyon Dream

Several nights after my appointment with Rev. Setter, I had a Spiritual dream. In the dream, I was standing on the rim of a canyon that resembled the Grand Canyon. It was sunrise, and I was facing the huge orange ball of the rising sun over the canyon. The rocks and walls were glowing in brilliant shades of yellow and orange. I was wearing a long robe and standing with my arms raised in praise. And – like Rev. Setter's wife – I was praying fluently in a language that I didn't recognize.

Then in the middle of my dream, the alarm clock on my bedside table went off. I awoke with a jerk and, as I sat up to turn off the alarm, I realized that one of the foreign words I'd been praying in the dream had frozen in my mind as the clock sounded. I've never forgotten that word. It sounded like "*kapeesh*." In the years since then, I've been told that there's an Italian word that sounds like that. So maybe I was praying in Italian in the dream. Regardless, my dream was comforting, peaceful, and encouraging – but I had no idea what it meant. I didn't know the Holy Spirit was preparing me for my own gift of prayer languages, and that they would be one of the most rewarding experiences of my life.

The Miracle in the Den

About two weeks after my Grand Canyon dream, I was home alone one Saturday morning. I was sitting in my favorite den chair in my bathrobe, reading a book that all the small groups in my area were reading at the time. The book was about a pastor in California who had discovered his gift of prayer languages, and who had written a book about how much it increased his faith. I was on a page in the book that told the story of a Christian woman named "Mary." Mary was sitting with a group of Christian friends in front of a fireplace in a California beach house on a chilly fall night.

The group was talking about the gift of prayer languages, and they were telling one other how they had discovered their gift and how much it meant to them. But Mary hadn't used the gift yet, so she didn't have anything to tell. After a while, she quietly excused herself and walked out onto a deck that overlooked the moonlit sea. She wondered if she'd ever use the gift, and so she started to pray about it. As she gazed at the moonlit ocean, she told the Holy Spirit that she wanted the gift too, and she wanted the Spiritual strength and faith from it that she could see in her Christian friends at the fireplace.

Suddenly, the clear thought came to her mind that she should simply *try* to use the gift. So, standing alone on the deck, she spoke a sound, making sure she wasn't speaking in English. To her surprise, she spoke a foreign-sounding word. So she tried again, and this time she spoke foreign-sounding words for several minutes.

She found that she could start and stop at will, and could speak fluently and without difficulty each time she tried. Feeling a sense of deep satisfaction, she reentered the house and joined the group at the fireplace. They glanced up as she returned, so she gave them a big smile and said, "Now I have the gift, too. I've never been so happy or felt so good. It's wonderful."

After reading about Mary's experience, I put the book in my lap and thought about what Mary had done. I thought, *I wonder if that's all there is to it? I wonder if all I have to do is just speak out loud, making sure I'm not speaking English?*

After thinking for a few minutes, I decided to try. I purposefully made a sound, being sure not to speak an English word. To my surprise, I made a foreign sound. I stopped and thought, *Whoa, was that the gift?*

I sat thinking for a minute. Then I made another foreign sound. Paused, then another. Paused, then another. The words were there each time I tried. They started when I started, and they stopped when I stopped. I had complete control over them, and could speak fluently and effortlessly each time I tried. The experience was calm, peaceful, pleasant, and encouraging.

Since that morning in my den, I've learned a lot about the private gift of prayer languages, and I still use them every day. I've learned that they're a form of *prayer* (that's why Christians call them "prayer languages," and that's why Paul called them "praying in the Spirit"). I've also learned that prayer languages keep me Spiritually strong. As we said earlier, the miraculous thing about them is that our inner *spirit* is praying directly to *God*, bypassing our human mind with messages we don't understand, but messages that give us comfort and hope. That's logical, because our human mind has no idea what we should be praying about each day.

The apostle Paul wrote more about the gift of prayer languages than he did any other gift. He said he used the gift more than other Christians, and that he wanted all other Christians to use it. Here's how Paul explained it:

> "Any Christian who uses the gift of prayer languages isn't speaking to humans. He or she is speaking directly to *God*. Indeed, no one else can understand, since he or she is uttering mysteries from his or her *inner spirit* ... a Christian who uses this gift *edifies* himself or herself ... so I'd like *every* one of you to use it ... when I express the gift, my inner

spirit is praying ... and I thank God that I can use the gift more than all of you."[13]

Notice that Paul says that prayer languages "edify" us. That's important. In the original Greek, Paul is saying that prayer languages help Christians *grow Spiritually*. The Greek word for "edifies" means the gift *builds* up Christians in wisdom, grace, holiness, and blessedness.[14] That's amazing. It's also something all Christians need.

In the years since my experience in the den, I've followed Paul's advice, and I express the gift daily, often whispering prayer languages under my breath as I work or do chores. But another benefit of gift is that it sometimes acts as a "gateway" gift for Christians. It *prepares* them for expressing the other Spiritual gifts. That's exactly what happened to me. Soon after I began using prayer languages, I also began to experience the other gifts. So prayer languages make us more receptive to visions, prophecies, healings, dreams, and all the other gifts. I've known dozens of Christians who used their gift of prayer languages first; and then soon afterward begin expressing other gifts.

Now – it's interesting that the Early Christians set rules for using prayer languages. Paul said the gift should only be used in *private* because using it in public confuses and upsets other people.[15] As we've said, the gift is only used in *public* when the Holy Spirit has a message for a group – but even then, it's only used if the speaker can translate the message, or if another Christian is present with the gift of translating prayer language messages.

The problem with this gift is that prayer languages have been *misused* worldwide in the past 120 years, and that has confused millions of Christians. Some of today's congregations break the rules that the Early Christians set for the gift and (exactly as Paul warned) that has caused great pain in Christianity. So before we close this chapter, let's honestly discuss some of the misunderstandings about this gift.

The Misunderstandings

It's tragic that the very first Spiritual gift that God gave Christians, and the one that is used the most by Christians worldwide, is also the gift that's the most misunderstood. These misunderstandings originated with the Pentecostal movement that was founded by the students of Charles Fox Parham's Bethel Gospel School in Topeka, Kansas in January of 1901.[16]

The inexperienced and confused students at the school had several misunderstandings about the gift, and then years later those misunderstandings were passed on to all the other Christian denominations when the Charismatic movement was founded by Dennis Bennett at St. Mark's Episcopal Church in Van Nuys, California in April of 1960.[17]

So let's slow down now and be as open and factual about these misunderstandings as we can. Here are some of the most frequent of the misunderstandings:

1. *Private Prayer Languages Are Misnamed.* When God gave the gift of prayer languages to Christians on Pentecost morning, its Greek name was *laleo heteros glossa*. Properly translated, those words mean, *"to speak other languages."*[18] The apostle Paul taught that this gift can also be called "using prayer languages" or "praying in the Spirit." Sadly, like the phrase the "fruit of the Spirit," the priests in England who translated the *King James Version* in 1611 translated these Greek words into Elizabethan English as, *"to speak in other tongues."* They did that because people in their time called languages "tongues." The problem is that present day Bibles

(such as the *New International Version*) continue to use that unfortunate term, and many congregations still teach their members to call the gift "*speaking in tongues*" – which makes it sound strange, otherworldly, and weird, and makes many Christians avoid it.

2. *Private Prayer Languages Are Not For Public Use.* The personal gift of prayer languages is for private Spiritual growth only.[19] The gift is not supposed to be used in *public* because that makes other people think the speaker is deranged.[20] The only exception is those rare occasions when the Spirit uses the gift to give a *public* message to a group to help its members grow. But the Spirit only does that if the speaker can translate the message; or if another Christian is present who can translate it.[21] An example of the gift being used in *public* is Pentecost morning, when the Spirit used it to attract the *non-Christian* pilgrims to Christianity.[22] But today, some congregations still teach their members that the gift can be used in *public* during worship, prayer meetings, socials, etc. – with the result that Paul warned us about. Some people think they're "insane."[23]

3. *Private Prayer Languages Are Not For Fleshy Use.* Infant Christians can use prayer languages the same way that growing and mature Christians can use them. But God designed the gift for private, personal Spiritual growth. So if infant Christians mistakenly use the gift in *public* with fleshy emotions (loudness, boldness, aggressiveness, etc.), it offends other people and makes them avoid the gift themselves, missing the benefits it could give them.

4. *Private Prayer Languages Are Not a "Second" Experience.* The students at the Bethel Gospel School thought they

were having a "second" Spiritual experience when they started using prayer languages. They thought that because Charles Parham had taught them about a special "end-times experience" he had learned about in a Christian commune the previous summer. Thus, his students didn't know that *all* Christians have *all* the gifts the moment they're saved. So when they began using prayer languages in the school, they thought they were having Parham's special "end times experience" that people supposedly received "second" after salvation. The students began teaching that as a new doctrine, and today, many congregations still teach that being Spirit-baptized is a "second" experience that comes after salvation, and that prayer languages are the "sign" that a Christian has received this "second" experience.

5. *Spirit-Baptism And Spirit-Filling Are Not the Same Thing.* Because of their confusion over having a "second" experience, the students at the Bethel Gospel School also misunderstood Spirit-filling. They thought being *baptized* in the Spirit and being *filled* with the Spirit are the *same* thing. They didn't realize that all Christians are Spirit-baptized (saved), but not all Christians are Spirit-filled (having minds motivated 51 percent or more by the Spirit). Today, many congregations still teach that being Spirit-baptized and being Spirit-filled are the same thing.

6. *Prayer Languages Are Not a "Sign" Of Spirit-Filling.* Finally, as mentioned in the clauses above, the students at the Bethel Gospel School misunderstood the *sequence* of three basic Christian events: 1) Spirit-baptism (being saved); 2) Spirit-filling (having a mind flooded with power from Spiritual growth); and 3) using prayer languages (which all Christians can do at any time). The students thought these basic events were a special

"second" package that Christians can "receive" after salvation – and that prayer languages are the "sign" that Christians have "received" this package. But none of that is true. As we know, Spirit-baptism is just another name for being *saved*, so all Christians are Spirit-baptized. And being *saved* (Spirit-baptized) is being indwelled by the Holy Spirit (the source of the Spiritual gifts). So all Christians have all the gifts, including prayer languages, the moment they're *saved* (even if they're not expressing them at the time). Thus, these misunderstandings are making a mountain out of a mole hill. They're much ado about nothing. They're telling Christians that they need to have their salvation experience all over again as a "second" experience. The confusion that has caused in Christianity for the past 120 years can't be calculated.

But now let's put aside these misunderstandings that were started by the students at the Bethel Gospel School in 1901, and let's close the chapter on a positive and upbeat note. The Spiritual gifts are from *God*, and they're *good* for all Christians. Their purpose is to make Christians *happy* and to help them *grow* Spiritually. All Christians *can*, and *should*, express the gifts. Christians are commanded to "eagerly desire" the gifts, and to "stir up" the gifts in themselves because that's "the way of love." Christians are cautioned not to argue over the gifts, but to cherish them and to use them as channels of blessing for themselves and others. I try to do these things in my life, and I pray that you're doing them in your life too. So with that agreed, let's summarize the chapter.

Summary of Chapter 12

1. The Spiritual gifts are supernatural and come from the indwelling Holy Spirit in Christians. They are not human talents, abilities, or skills. All Christians have

all the gifts in them, ready to be expressed as the Spirit chooses. Each Christian has one full-time gift to help other Christians. Then the Spirit expresses the part-time gifts temporarily through Christians as needed.

2. Expressing gifts is a sign that a person is a *Christian* (that he or she is indwelled by the Holy Spirit and is Spirit-baptized). Expressing gifts is not a sign that a Christian is Spirit-filled because *infant* Christians can express gifts, and they're not Spirit-filled.

3. The gifts are expressed *through* Christians, *for* Christians. Their purpose is for Christians to be able to help other Christians. Only on rare occasions does the Spirit use Spiritual gifts for the benefit of non-Christians as He did on Pentecost morning.

4. There is no rank order among the gifts. They are equal in importance because the Spirit uses all of them to meet all of the needs of all Christians.

5. The best way for Christians to discover their full-time gift is by worshiping in a small group of like-minded, Spirit-filled Christians.

6. The best way to learn to express Spiritual gifts is not to hear about them or read about them. It's to *experience* them in everyday life.

7. One of the gifts – prayer languages – is unique because God designed it for individual Christians to help themselves personally and privately.

8. Prayer languages have been misunderstood for the past 120 years, and that has caused much pain in Christianity.

These misunderstandings originated when the students at Charles Parham's Bethel Gospel School in Topeka, Kansas founded the Pentecostal Movement in 1901. Then these misunderstandings were passed on to all the other Christian denominations when the Charismatic Movement was founded at St. Mark's Episcopal Church in Van Nuys, California in 1960.

Now, before we go, let's make one final point. From this page forward, let's assume that *you* are either expressing Spiritual gifts now, or that you're earnestly praying to start expressing them. That way, the rest of the principles in this book will apply to you as we discuss small groups, Spiritual worship, and all the rest of the new things we're going to discuss. Let's move on to Chapter 13 now.

Chapter 13

THE SPIRITUAL EXPERIENCES

The Young Man at Breakfast

One morning, my phone rang just as I was preparing a late breakfast. I answered it, and heard the voice of a young Christian man whom I knew slightly. He said he had an urgent question to ask me. He said he was calling from a pay phone near my house, and that he'd like to drop by immediately to ask me his urgent question. I agreed, and ten minutes later he was seated at my breakfast table as I ate (he had already had breakfast). He was fidgety, so I told him to go ahead and ask his question, since I could see he was anxious to ask it.

He sat up straighter in his chair and blurted out, "What would you do if tomorrow's news said an ancient scroll had been found in Israel proving Jesus never existed and that Christianity was a hoax?" He leaned forward in his chair, anticipating my answer.

Without looking up from my eggs I replied, "I'd believe in Jesus and Christianity anyway."

He was dumbfounded. "You'd believe in Jesus and Christianity *anyway*?" he said in a loud and incredulous tone. "But *why!*"

"Because they're real," I said. "Jesus does exist, and Christianity isn't a hoax."

"But," he argued, "how do you *know* that? How can you be so sure?"

"I'm sure because I've *experienced* Jesus and Christianity," I said. "I've experienced love, joy, peace, healings, visions, prophecies, angels, miraculous answers to prayer, and all the other wonderful things that Christians experience. So it doesn't matter to me what the news says or what they find in Israel. I know for a fact that Jesus is alive and that Christianity is real."

We talked some more, had prayer, and the young man left with a thoughtful look on his face.

Now, the point of this story is that we humans tend to believe what we've *experienced*. And the reverse is also true. We tend not to believe what we *haven't* experienced. That's why it's so important for Christians to *experience* the supernatural behavior, gifts, and experiences of the Holy Spirit as often as possible, as much as possible. Books, classes, lectures, videos, and PowerPoints all have their place. But the Early Christians didn't *have* those things. All they had was personal *experience* with the Spirit's power. Yet their faith held firm in the face of cruel kings, occupying armies, tortures, and mass executions.

Earlier, we quoted one of the apostle Paul's letters to the small groups in the city of Corinth. Let's review that quote now, since it describes the principle we're discussing here. Paul's letter confirms that deep Christian faith only comes from *experiencing* the supernatural power of the Holy Spirit. Here are Paul's words again:

> "When I came to you ... my words and my message were *not* in the persuasive words of human wisdom – but in *showing* you the Holy Spirit and His Spiritual *power*, so that your faith would not be based on man's wisdom, but would be based on the *power* of God."[1]

The Greek noun for "faith" that Paul used in this quote means confidence, conviction, belief, and trust in something – specifically in God, Jesus, and the Holy Spirit.[2] Paul is saying that when he arrived in the city of Corinth, he didn't use wise and persuasive human words to lead the Corinthian people to faith in God. He led them to faith by *showing* them the power of the Holy Spirit.

So now we've discovered another priceless Spiritual principle: The Holy Spirit teaches Christians and builds their faith by showing them supernatural experiences. That's what I was trying to tell the young man at my breakfast table in the earlier story. Christian faith is built by experiencing the supernatural. Such supernatural experiences happen through three different activities of the Holy Spirit. We've already talked about these *activities*. But let's refresh our memory now.

The Three Activities of the Spirit

Here are the three *activities* the Holy Spirit uses to build our Christian faith. He builds our faith through:

1. *Spiritual Behavior* (also called "the Fruit of the Spirit"). This is personal behavior of *supernatural* love, joy, peace, patience, kindness, goodness, and faithfulness, etc. This behavior is supernatural because human nature can't produce it. It's only produced by the indwelling power of the Holy Spirit. Seeing it personally builds a Christian's faith.

2. *Spiritual Gifts*. These are *supernatural* healings, dreams, visions, prophecies, miracles, etc., that the indwelling power of the Holy Spirit produces in Christians. These gifts are supernatural and can't be produced by human nature. Seeing these gifts personally builds a Christian's faith.

3. *Spiritual Experiences*. These are *supernatural* angelic visitations, miraculous answers to prayer, supernatural rescues from danger, etc., that the Holy Spirit arranges for Christians. These experiences are supernatural and can't be produced by human means. Seeing them personally builds a Christian's faith.

As we've seen, the Holy Spirit uses Spiritual behavior, Spiritual gifts, and Spiritual experiences to build our Christian faith. We've talked about the first two of these in previous chapters, and so the theme of this chapter is how the Spirit uses *Spiritual experiences* (physical situations) to build our faith. As our first example, let's tell the *crucifix* story.

The Crucifix

Several weeks after I returned home from being Spirit-filled for the first time in my New York hotel room, I was confused about something. Having grown up in a traditional congregation, my parents had taught me to pray to our heavenly Father. So I had never prayed to *Jesus*. However, after returning from New York, I found myself thinking about Jesus a lot. I also noticed that my Christian friends often prayed to *Him*, instead of to the Father. So I began to wonder to whom I should pray – should I continue to pray to the Father? Or should I start praying to Jesus, too?

As it happened, there was a public park near my office that had acres of trees and walking trails. So one day during my lunch break, I left my office and went to this park. I walked alone down one of its trails, until I came to a stone bridge with a stream running under it. I stopped on this bridge, looked up at the sky, and began to pray to the heavenly Father. I told Him that I had been taught to pray to *Him* as a child, but now I was wondering if I should also pray to His Son, Jesus.

By the way, I use a lot of *hand gestures* when I talk, and I was using them in this prayer. Unconsciously, I was holding out my left hand as I prayed, and I was tapping my left palm with my right index finger.

"God," I said, tapping my left palm, "I need to know if I should pray to *Jesus*. I'm asking You for a definite and clear answer. I'm asking you for an answer that's so definite and so clear that I can see it and feel it and know that it's really from You."

I continued praying along these lines until I felt better, then I returned to my office and dismissed the incident from my mind. The next morning, as I walked down the street toward my office from the parking garage where I kept my car, I met a coworker on the sidewalk. This coworker was a Greek-American Christian whose grandparents had come from the old country. As we greeted one another on the sidewalk, I noticed that he had his right fist clinched in his pants pocket, as if he was gripping something tightly. That seemed a little odd, but I thought nothing of it at the moment.

Soon, we stopped on the curb to wait for a traffic light, and my coworker said, "Uh, I don't know why I did it, but I did something for you last night."

"You did something for me last night?" I asked in surprise.

"Uh, yeah," he said, "I went up in the attic and opened my grandmother's old suitcase from Greece. I don't know why I did it," he stammered. "I, uh, just had to, that's all."

"I don't know what you mean," I said. "What does your grandmother's suitcase have to do with me?"

He didn't say anything else. Instead, he jerked his clinched fist out of his pocket, thrust it toward me, and said loudly, "Here!"

As it happened, I was holding a briefcase in my right hand, so I instinctively held my left hand out toward him, palm up. He opened his fingers and a beautiful sterling silver antique Greek *crucifix* dropped into my left hand.

The figure of Christ on the crucifix landed face up in my palm, facing me. I found myself staring at the sterling silver face of *Jesus*

– on the very spot in my left palm where I had tapped the day before in the park with my right index finger.

I had never held a crucifix before, so for a few seconds didn't realize what was happening. Then a feeling of peace and warmth flowed over me and I realized the truth. In less than twenty-four hours, the heavenly Father had answered my prayer exactly as I had requested. He'd answered it in a way that was so definite and so clear that I could see it and feel it and know it was really from Him. He had used a *physical experience* to build my faith.

The Holy Spirit's Lessons

The point of this story is that when the Holy Spirit teaches us something – and especially when He does it through a *physical experience* – it changes us in ways that human lessons can't change us. For one thing, we don't forget the Spirit's lessons like we do human lessons. I can pick up a book that I read just three or four years ago, and I won't recognize parts of it today. But I can describe supernatural lessons that the Holy Spirit gave me thirty or forty years ago in full detail today.

That's the power of Spiritual teaching. It transcends time and space. And so we've discovered yet another valuable Spiritual principle: The *more* supernatural experiences we have directly from the Holy Spirit, the *more* faith we have as Christians. Sadly, the opposite is also true. The *less* supernatural experiences we have from the Spirit, the *less* faith we have.

That's why *mature* Christians have more faith than *infant* Christians. That's also why the Early Christians were called "a Spiritual house," "a holy priesthood," "a holy nation," and "foreigners and exiles" among natural people.[3] All Christians are different from other people. But Spiritually mature Christians are *really* different from other people.

The Holy Spirit's lessons are also never boring, repetitious, or predictable. (This'll be significant in our chapter on Spiritual worship.) His teachings are always full of surprises, unexpected twists, and unusual joys. For example, God has a sense of humor. We caught a glimpse of that when He answered my prayer in the park by dropping a *crucifix* in the palm of my hand the next morning. The truth is, God has all of the emotions that we humans have – except that His emotions are always holy, righteous, and pure.

In the Preface and Introduction of this book, I said that our theme was going to be showing you how to live the *same* Spiritual lifestyle that the Early Christians lived. I call that living the *Early Christian Lifestyle*. In this chapter, we've discovered a big part of that theme. Namely, that you and your loved ones can grow in faith quicker by having more *physical experiences* with the Holy Spirit. Let's reinforce that principle with a quick fictitious example that illustrates how supernatural *experiences* strengthen our faith.

The Angels in the Coffee Shop

Here's your exam. Answer the following questions truthfully:

1. Which would *increase* your faith the most? Reading a book about angels – or meeting an angel?

2. Which would *increase* your faith the most? Hearing a lecture on supernatural healing – or being supernaturally healed?

Can we agree that *experiences* increase our faith more than just *reading* or *hearing* about them? Exploring that principle, let's consider a fictitious example. Imagine that you're sitting in a coffee shop with two Christian friends. One is named "Roger," the other is named "Millie." Millie puts her coffee cup down and calmly announces that she saw an *angel* in her bedroom last night.

Roger, who is an *infant* Christian, chuckles and says, "Oh, I doubt that. You had a hallucination because angels aren't real."

Now, if you weren't too sure about angels yourself, Millie's statement might confuse you. You might even side with Roger and join with his chuckles. However, if you had been in the hospital recently and had seen an angel in your hospital room *yourself*, you'd probably ignore Roger's chuckles and say something like, "That's wonderful, Millie. Because when I was in the hospital I saw an angel, too. Tell me about your angel, and I'll tell you about mine."

See the difference that real life *experiences* make? You and Millie have *seen* angels. Roger hasn't. So you and Millie have more *faith* in angels than Roger does. That's one of the reasons Jesus performed so many miracles during His time on earth. It built people's faith. That's also one of the reasons the Early Christians continued having miracles after Jesus returned to heaven. And it's also one of the reasons miracles continue among Christians today. It builds our faith.

Jesus promised that He would send the Holy Spirit back from heaven to *teach* us everything we need to know about living a Spiritual life, and to *remind* us of everything He taught while He was on earth.[4] That promise has never been withdrawn. It's still in full force and effect today. The Early Christians said it this way:

"Jesus is the *same* yesterday, today, and forever."[5]

The problem with the Holy Spirit's marvelous supernatural lessons is that we have to be *open* to them. Let's talk about that *openness* for a moment.

The Openness to Spiritual Lessons

The Holy Spirit knows us a lot better than we know ourselves. That means *He's* the only one who can choose which supernatural teachings, miracles, signs, gifts, and physical experiences we need to strengthen our faith. In turn, that means we need to trust Him completely. We need to be completely *open* to everything He wants to teach us. Earlier, I told the story of how Dwayne and I prayed in my driveway and asked God to give us everything that the Early Christians had. We were *open* to everything God wanted to give us.

But now let's look at that prayer backwards. What if Dwayne and I *hadn't* been open to everything God wanted to give us? What if Dwayne and I had made a list of the Spiritual things we *wanted* – and the Spiritual things we *didn't* want? And what if we had prayed in the driveway something like this:

> "Now, God, here's the thing. We *want* You to give us healings. But we *don't* want to see an angel. We *want* prophecies, but we *don't* want visions. We *want* dreams, but we *don't* want gifts of mercy, etc."

Wouldn't that have been absurd? I'm incredibly glad we *didn't* pray that way. If we *had* prayed that way, I'd have missed countless fantastically beautiful supernatural experiences over the years, and my faith wouldn't be one tenth of what it is today.

So as we come to the end of this chapter, let's pause to check our progress. We've said that the *test* of a Christian's Spiritual level is the degree to which he or she is living the *Early Christian Lifestyle*. We've said the test of living the *Early Christian Lifestyle* is the degree to which we're letting the Holy Spirit express Spiritual behavior, Spiritual gifts, and Spiritual experiences through us. Now it's time to tie all those pieces together. Now it's time to talk specifically about how to *live* the "Early Christian Lifestyle" in today's world. In the next chapter, we're going to talk about socializing and worshiping in Christian small groups. And to keep those lessons applicable, let's assume now that *you* and your loved ones are *open* to every experience that God wants to give you. Now let's summarize and close.

Summary of Chapter 13

1. The three activities of the Spirit that give Christians supernatural experiences are:

    a) Spiritual behavior.

    b) Spiritual gifts.

    c) Spiritual experiences.

2. Humans tend to believe what they've *experienced*; and to not to believe what they *haven't* experienced. That means Christians need to express supernatural behavior, gifts, and experiences as much as possible, as often as possible.

3. The Holy Spirit teaches Christians most often by internal revelations. But He can also use outer physical experiences (such as objects, people, and situations) to teach us.

4. The *more* supernatural experiences we have from the Holy Spirit, the *more* our faith grows. And the *fewer* supernatural experiences we have, the *less* our faith grows.

5. The Holy Spirit's lessons are never boring, repetitious, or predictable. They're full of surprises, unexpected twists, and unusual joys.

6. Christians need to be *open* to everything God wants to give them. The Holy Spirit is the only one who knows what kinds of supernatural experiences, teachings, miracles, signs, gifts, and wonders each Christian needs to build his or her faith.

Next, it's time to discuss one of the most vitally important subjects in this book. It's time to talk about positive peer pressure and power of socializing in Christian small groups. Using everything that we've learned thus far, it's time to see why relaxed, informal, Christian small groups are so desperately important to us all.

The next chapter is the crown jewel of the book. It combines everything we've said about the *Early Christian Lifestyle*, traditional congregations, Spiritual behavior, Spiritual gifts, and Spiritual experiences. Small groups have been the front line in the war between flesh and Spirit since Pentecost morning. Small groups have been the battlefield of the Spiritual war since the birthday of Christianity. So let's turn to Chapter 14, and start learning about small groups.

Chapter 14

THE SMALL GROUPS

Holograms, Hosts, and Outlaws

Earlier, we said it's important to have a hunger for the deeper Spiritual life; and that it's important to seek new experiences to feed that hunger. We said the Holy Spirit reveals Himself through Spiritual behavior, gifts, and experiences, and that we need to be open to those revelations of His supernatural power. However, there's one thing we haven't mentioned yet. We haven't mentioned how hard it is to do all those things *alone*. It's true that a Christian could grow Spiritually all alone on an uninhabited island if he or she had to – but it wouldn't be easy.

I wasn't alone in my driveway when I prayed for God to give me everything the First Century Christians had. My friend, Dwayne, was sitting in the car beside me praying the same prayer. We'd spent the afternoon together reading the book of *Acts*, and we'd spontaneously parked in my driveway to pray. And by the way – does that kind of behavior sound familiar? It should. Because that's the *Early Christian Lifestyle* that we're talking about. That's the kind of informal, relaxed, supportive small group behavior that the original Christians had when Christianity was founded. Dwayne and I had lived it that afternoon without knowing it. We didn't know anything about the *Early Christian Lifestyle* then, and we didn't realize until months later what had happened to us that afternoon.

But here's the point. Christians grow Spiritually faster and deeper when they gather in informal, relaxed, supportive small groups and openly express Spiritual behavior, gifts, and experiences. So now let's pick up some loose threads from earlier chapters and see even more clearly why Early Christian type *small groups* are so important.

The Early Christian Small Groups

Many Christians don't realize that the original Christians didn't gather in big groups in big buildings and watch big programs the way Christians do today. Instead, for the first three centuries of Christian history (about the first eight generations of Christians), all Christians gathered in *small groups* in private homes. That makes sense when you think about it. Meeting in small groups in private homes is quicker, easier, safer, cheaper, more confidential, more convenient, and more intimate than meeting in big groups in big buildings.

Of course, big buildings were *available* to the Early Christians if they'd wanted to rent, borrow, or build them. But they didn't. Why didn't they? After all, they'd all been members of non-Christian temples and shrines before they became Christians, so they were very familiar big buildings. The answer to that question is simple, yet profound. The Early Christians gathered in small groups in private homes because that's the *best way to grow Spiritually*.

Here are the facts about small groups from Early Christian history. Small groups are mentioned 30 different times in 10 different books of the *New Testament*, and 12 different ancient cities are mentioned as having Christian small groups in them. Those cities include Antioch, Capernaum, Colossae, Corinth, Ephesus, Jerusalem, Laodicea, Miletus, Philippi, Rome, Thessalonica, and Troas, and that's not an exhaustive list. Those are just the cities that are mentioned in the *New Testament*. There were thousands of small groups in every city and nation of the world that weren't mentioned in the pages of the *New Testament*.

Archaeological digs and museums prove that's true. For example, in Rome's museums there are ancient property records that list by name 25 different Early Christian small groups that met in private homes in the city of Rome. (Of course, there were hundreds more small groups in Rome, but most of Rome's property records were destroyed over the centuries and only these 25 records survived.) In addition, archaeological digs have unearthed physical evidence of Early Christian home meetings in the ancient cities of Aqaba, Capernaum, Damascus, Megiddo, Rome, Salamis, and others. So we know for a fact that the Early Christians gathered in small groups in private homes during the first three centuries of Christian History.

However, it was the apostle Paul who documented Early Christian small groups the most. For instance, he devoted an entire chapter of one of his letters to Christian small groups, and to mentioning the names of some of the hosts and participants in those groups.[1] Paul opened that chapter by mentioning a small group that met in a private home nine miles outside of Corinth, Greece; and by mentioning a Christian woman named Phoebe who'd been a participant in that group. Then he mentioned "all the groups of the Gentiles" (all the small groups of non-Jewish Christians). He went on to mention a group in the home of Priscilla and Aquila in Rome; and then small groups hosted by Aristobulus and Narcissus, and then "all the groups of Christ" (all the Christian small groups in the area). Next, he referred to a small group hosted by a man named Gaius, and then throughout the chapter, Paul mentions the names of Christians who participated in various small groups, including Andronicus, Junias, Amplias, Urbanus, and others.[2]

Here's the point. From the amount of ink that Paul used writing about small groups, we realize that small groups meeting in private homes were tightly woven into the tapestry of the Early Christian culture. But now a word of caution. Here's where we pick up a loose thread from an earlier chapter. Let's slow down here to be honest about the misuse of the English word "church" in the *New Testament*. The truth is that Paul did *not* write about "churches" in his letters. He wrote about *small groups* in his letters. Let's discuss that flawed translation.

The Misuse of the Word "Church"

Previously, we said that the corrupt Fourth Century Roman emperor, Constantine, built a city called "New Rome" in the Eastern Empire, and that he invented the word "church" in that city 300 years *after* Christianity was founded. And also 300 years *after* the Early Christians developed their culture of meeting in small groups. We said Constantine's word "church" migrated across the world over the centuries, drifting through several countries and several languages, until it ended up in England, where it was improperly used in 1611 by the committee of priests who translated the *King James Version* of the Bible. Then, because of the KJV Bible's worldwide popularity in the centuries following 1611, Constantine's word "church" is now accepted by all Christians, who use it without conscious thought.

But – as we've said several times – the word "church" is a *non-Christian* word that shouldn't be used by Christians without conscious thought everywhere. Constantine's word "church" was invented to refer to *religious buildings*, such as the temples of the sun god (of which Constantine was the high priest). Thus, if today's Christians use the word "church" at all, they should only use it to refer to *religious buildings*. (For example, Christians today might say things like, "That building over there is the First Community *Church*.")

However, the Constantinian word "church" should never be used to refer to Christian *people*, or to *gatherings* of Christian people. When today's Christian leaders say things from the pulpit like, "Good morning, *church*!" The people should sit silently, since *buildings* can't speak. Or, when leaders say things like, "We're really having *church* tonight, aren't we!" The people should look confused, because how do you "have" a *building*? Or, most lamentable of all, when leaders *capitalize* the word "Church" in their writings (identifying it as a proper noun and a one-of-a-kind entity), they're using a *non-Christian* word to refer to Christian people or Christian gatherings in a non-historical way.

To solve that problem personally, I try to never use the word *church*, either verbally or in writing. Instead, I try to use words like "small group," "group," "congregation," "home group," "gathering," and "people," etc., when talking about Christians or Christian gatherings. Why do I do that? I do it because the correct translation of the First Century Greek word that refers to Early Christians and Early Christian gatherings is the simple English word, *group*.[3]

Here's an example. In the chapter Paul wrote about the small groups in Rome, today's English Bibles have Paul saying: "Greet Priscilla and Aquila (and) the *church* that meets in their house."[4]

But since the word "church" didn't *exist* when Paul penned those words, it shouldn't be used to translate them. Instead, using the correct Greek translation we mentioned above, here's how Paul's words should be translated: "Greet Priscilla and Aquila (and) the *group* that meets in their house."

Now, time out. How do we *know* Paul's letter should be translated that way? Without being too technical, we know it because the Greek word Paul used in that sentence is the noun *ekklesia* (pronounced "eh-clay-<u>see</u>'-uh"). That was the word the First Century Christians always used to refer to their home meetings, and it translates as *group* or *gathering*. They didn't use the Constantinian word "church" because it didn't exist in their day.

So let's say it again. There never was an early "church"; or a First Century "church"; or a primitive "church," or anything else called a "church" before the Fourth Century. Yet history books continue to use the word *church* on almost every page – never stopping to think that it's a non-Christian word, and that by using it they're keeping Christians focused on the care and maintenance of *buildings* instead of on small groups and Spiritual growth.

Summary: In this book, we'll try to only use the terms *group ... gathering ... small group ... home group ... congregation ...* and related terms to describe Christian people and Christian gatherings. Our hope is that this'll help readers stay focused on small groups and Spiritual growth, instead of on the institutional structure that Constantine created.

Now, let's continue with our theme: Early Christian small groups. By the end of the Third Century, there were millions of Christians worldwide gathering in thousands of small groups in hundreds of villages, towns, and cities. So let's discuss how these small groups met and why they met. To start that discussion, let's explain the effects of *positive peer pressure*.

The Positive Peer Pressure

A friend of mine used to say, "There's no pressure like peer pressure." He was right. Except that he didn't mention that there are *two* kinds of peer pressure, not just one. There's *positive* peer pressure. And there's *negative* peer pressure. Both are equally influential. For example, people become drug addicts, commit murder, commit suicide, join street gangs, rob convenience stores, and do scores of other ungodly things – all because *negative* peer pressure is being applied to them. Sadly, humans are hypersensitive to what other people think about them, and they'll do *anything* to be accepted by their social group.

Thus, the term "peer pressure" refers to the *social pressure* that's applied to people by their family, friends, and coworkers – all of whom want them to act like those families, friends, and coworkers *want* them to act. That means the question isn't *whether* Christians have peer pressure. They do. The real question is: What *kind* of peer pressure do Christians have? Is it positive? Or is it negative? To be more specific, as a reader of this book, what kind of peer pressure do *you* have? Are your peers pressuring you to be a Spiritually mature

Christian? Are they pressuring you to be an infant Christian? Are they pressuring you not to be a Christian at all?

We know from the Christian "horror stories" in Chapter 2, that many Christians today are Spiritual *infants*. That tells us two tragic things. First, these infant Christians are probably applying peer pressure to their friends, family, and coworkers to become infant Christians *too*. Second, their friends, family, and coworkers are probably returning the favor by applying peer pressure on them to *remain* infant Christians. And so the carousel of peer group pressure turns and turns in people's lives.

One thing is obvious. Christians who're trapped in negative peer pressure have a tough decision to make. I once had an aunt who would say, "Birds of a feather flock together." She meant that we need to *avoid* people who're applying negative peer pressure to us; and we need to *seek* people who will apply positive peer pressure to us. That's one reason the Early Christians met in small groups in homes. That was a way for them to avoid the negative peer pressure of the non-Christian world.

This makes so much sense that we shouldn't need to say it. But we do. Because millions of Christians today are caught in the *negative* peer pressure trap, and don't know how to get out of it. Happily, the theme of this chapter is that they *can* get out of it, and that they *must* get out of it. The apostle Paul told us why. Here's what he said:

> "Don't have *unequal* fellowship with people of *weak* faith. After all, what do Righteousness and Wickedness have in common? How can Light participate with Darkness? You're the temple of the living God, and God said, 'I will dwell in them and walk in them, and I will be their God, and they will be My people.' Therefore, '*Come out from among them and be separate*,' says the Lord."[5]

That's crystal clear, isn't it? Christians aren't supposed to socialize with people of "weak faith." And it's important to realize that the word Paul used in this passage – the one translated "weak faith" – has *two* meanings. First, it can mean an *infant* Christian who has weak faith. Or second, it can mean a *non-Christian* who doesn't have faith at all.[6]

Regardless of which way we translate Paul's word, the principle is clear: Christians who want to grow Spiritually *can't* do it under negative peer pressure from people who *don't* want them to grow. It's that simple. That means changing peer groups from *negative* to *positive* is one of the biggest challenges all Christians face. Let's face it. It's hard to break old habits. But the choice is obvious. We can spend most of our time socializing with infant Christians and non-Christians. Or we can spend most of our time socializing with growing Christians and mature Christians. God commanded us to do the *latter*. So to obey Him, we need to pray as often as we think about it, *"God, give me Spiritual peers."*

Of course, praying for Spiritual peers doesn't mean we'll never be in the presence of infant Christians or non-Christians. We probably have family members, friends, and coworkers who're infant Christians or non-Christians. More, our daily routines probably force us to socialize with them. We can't help that. But we *can* limit the amount of negative peer pressure they apply to us. How can we do that? We can fight the problem from the opposite end. In other words, we can neutralize *negative* peer pressure by overcoming it with *positive* peer pressure. To do that, we need to find one or more other Christians who're as hungry for Spiritual growth as we are – and then start socializing with that other Christian (or those other Christians) by forming an Early Christian style small group with them. Let's repeat that for emphasis:

> *The key to Spiritual growth is to find one or more other Christians who're also seeking Spiritual*

growth; and to start socializing as much as possible with that other Christian (or Christians) by forming an Early Christian style small group with them.

To summarize: The Early Christians applied positive peer pressure to one another by spending as much time as possible with other Christians who were like-minded and hungry for Spiritual growth. And they spent as *little* time as possible with infant Christians and non-Christians. That principle hasn't changed since the First Century. It still works the same way today as it worked then.

However, another problem Christians have today is that they misapply, misunderstand, and mistranslate the term "small group." In other words, the phrase "small group" is *fuzzy*. So let's define the phrase *small group* next.

The Definition of a "Small Group"

One of the best books ever written on *small groups* was written by a Harvard professor by the name of Dr. George C. Homans.[7] His book, *The Human Group*, is a classic that's still used to teach teambuilding in university classes. While writing his book, Homans researched small groups in many settings. He studied them in factories, street gangs, south pacific islands, and many other places. What he discovered is that the principles of small groups are the *same* worldwide – regardless of where a small group is located, and regardless of what kind of people form it.

This means that, although Homans didn't mention *Christians* in his book, the principles he discovered apply to Christian small groups the same way they apply to any other small group and – even more interestingly – the principles Homans discovered are the very same ones that the Early Christians used to form their small groups.

Most simply put: Homans discovered that a small group is a gathering of people who're *socializing in a participative organizational structure*. And if we apply that structure to Christianity, many Christians today who say they're "in small groups" actually *aren't*. That tells us why the small group programs attempted by many congregations so often fail. The "small groups" they formed weren't *really* small groups.

Now, using the Homans research, there are *five* parts a social structure must have to qualify as a true small group. Looked at in reverse, any social structure that fails one or more of these *five* parts isn't a true small group. Here are the *five* parts of a true small group.

The Five Parts of a Small Group

1. **Group Size**. The same *two* to *twelve* like-minded participants must always meet. Small groups start with two people and end at about twelve people (because the structure starts to break down at about a dozen people.) However, since most groups have visitors, children, and absenteeism, a small group's practical size can be *fifteen* to about *twenty* participants.

2. **Face-to-Face Interaction**. Each participant must have *face-to-face* interaction with each of the others. Interaction is 60 percent body language, so participants must be able to have face-to-face interaction. Internet techniques (smart phones, Facebook, etc.) have a place – but small groups can only be sustained long term by *face-to-face* interaction.

3. **Two-Way Interaction**. Interaction must be *two-way*. True interaction is a *dialog*. Each participant must have two-way interaction with each of the others. Teaching

and lectures have a place – but small groups can only be sustained long term by *two-way* interaction.

4. **Frequent Interaction**. Interaction must be *frequent*. Relationships develop through frequent interaction. Small groups are a "family" structure that requires daily meeting if possible; and weekly meeting at a minimum. Occasional meetings have a place – but small groups can only be sustained long term by *frequent* interaction.

5. **Extended Interaction**. Interaction must be over an *extended* period. Relationships develop with time. It takes weeks for a small group to bond. Then bonding grows tighter the longer the participants meet. Random meetings have a place – but small groups can only be sustained long term by *extended* interaction.

As we can see from the five Homans parts, a true small group is a specific organizational structure similar to a typical *family*. That's why the apostle Paul often used the word "household" when writing about small groups. Early Christian small groups were often built around two or three *families* gathering in one home. Indeed, Paul's word "household" in the Greek can even be translated, *home*, *house*, or *family*.[8] But now – before continuing – since we're talking about *Christian* small groups in this chapter, we must add a *sixth* part to the Homans tests.

The Sixth Part of a Small Group

As we said earlier, Professor Homans didn't mention Christians in his book. His research was for non-Christian readers, so he didn't add a *Spiritual* part to his research. That means we must add a *sixth* part before we can tell if a small group is a *Christian* group or not. Here's that sixth part.

6. **Spiritual Interaction**. Interaction must be *Spiritual*. The purpose of Christian small groups is for the participants to interact with one another using Spiritual behavior, gifts, and experiences. Spiritual interaction is what makes Christian small groups different from non-Christian small groups. Watching videos, reading books, and listening to lectures all have a place – but Christian small groups can only be sustained long term by *Spiritual* interaction.

Summary: The true Christian small group structure has *six* unique parts that promote God's purposes on earth. The true Christian small group structure is *participative*, and its structure allows the Holy Spirit to truly and freely teach, guide, heal, and mold participants in ways that no other type of structure can do.

But now let's dive deeper into small groups. There are *three* basic types of small groups, and all three use the *same* six-part structure we just discussed. The only difference between them is that each plays a different role in the *Early Christian Lifestyle*. Here are the three *types* of small groups.

The Three Types of Small Groups

1. **Social Groups**. "Social" means Christian friendship and companionship. That can include chatting in coffee shops; or meeting for breakfast; or for prayer; or to share testimonies; or for covered dish meals; or it can include picnics; sports; games; birthday parties; weddings; or just sitting and talking. Social groups can be *Spiritual* to some extent, but their Spirituality is limited by the group's attention to the activity (the meal, game, or entertainment, etc.). Social groups can include prayer and other religious behaviors – but their *main* purpose is "fellowship."

2. **Teaching Groups**. "Teaching" means giving Christians new skills and knowledge through educational materials and methods. That can include Bible studies; seminars; retreats; conferences; videos; books; Sunday school, and all other learning experiences. Teaching groups can be *Spiritual* to some extent, but their Spirituality is limited by the group's attention to the activity (the book, video, or lecture, etc.). Teaching groups can include prayer and other religious behaviors – but their *main* purpose is "discipleship."

3. **Worship Groups**. "Worship" means honoring, adoring, and loving God. That can include singing to Him, praising Him, praying to Him, and expressing Spiritual behavior, gifts, and experiences, as well as the ceremonies of the Lord's supper and water-baptism. Worship small groups are the most *Spiritual* groups because their Spirituality is *not* limited by other activities – their only purpose is "praise and worship."

The Changing of Group Types

Small groups can *change* types as needed. They can drift in and out of the three small group types to satisfy the changing needs of the participants. A *social* group can change into a *teaching* group when the social is over. A *teaching* group can change into a *social* group when the teaching is over. A *worship* group can change into a *social* group after the worship is over. A *social* group can change into a *worship* group when the social is over, and so on.

However, a small group is only *one* of the three types at a given point in time, based on the group's majority *behavior* at that time. For example, if a group's majority behavior is *social* at a given point in time, their group is a *social* group at that time – even if they think it's something else or say it's something else. The test is: What are the participants *doing*? Socializing? Teaching? Worshiping?

As we said, *worship* groups are the most Spiritual types because they generate Spiritual behavior, gifts, and experiences with the fewest distractions. So let's talk how that happens.

The Spirituality of Worship Groups

Worship type small groups are unique compared to social and teaching groups in two key ways:

1. First, a worship group doesn't have a human *leader* or human *agenda*. The Holy Spirit guides the group and prompts the worship experiences.

2. Second, a worship group lets participants *truly and freely* express Spiritual behavior, gifts, and experiences.

Of course, social and teaching groups are valuable and important, and all Christians should participate in them. But the unique and specific purpose of a worship group is praise and worship. (After all, it's hard to sing praises while eating pizza, and it's hard to prophesy while watching a video.) Yet sadly, in Christianity today, social and teaching type small groups are often the *only* ones Christians attend – if they attend any small groups at all. That means Christians need to make a special effort to participate in all *three* kinds of groups, but with their emphasis on *worship* groups.

Accordingly, from this point forward, we're going to focus on worship type small groups. That's the type group today's Christians understand the least, and the type they attend the least. With that agreed, let's talk about why the participants in small group worship need to be *like-minded*.

The Like-Mindedness

We've already said that small group participants need to be *like-minded*. Like-mindedness isn't totally necessary in social and teaching groups. But it's totally necessary in worship groups. After all, a few bored participants aren't fatal to a social or a teaching group. But bored participants are the kiss of death in a worship group.

Now, what *is* it that the participants in a worship group need to be like-minded *about*? They need to be like-minded about the *true and free* expression of Spiritual fruit, gifts, and experiences in worship. Said another way, they need to be unified in the willingness to be *Spiritual* in worship. That's not required in social and teaching groups. But it *is* in worship groups.

How can worship groups be sure they have like-mindedness? The solution is in the formation of the group. The founding participants of a worship group must be like-minded about *Spiritual* worship. If they aren't fully committed to truly and freely expressing Spiritual behavior, gifts, and experiences, the group will soon flounder. Connected to that, an even bigger problem in worship groups is the issue of *guidance*. Let's talk about that thorny subject next.

The Guidance of a Small Group

One of the most important things about small group worship is the decision about *guidance*. In other words, who *is* (and who *isn't*) going to guide the group? Jesus made one of His most amazing promises when He told His disciples that *He* was going to be personally *present* during their small group worship. Many Christians today don't realize that Jesus made that promise. But He did. Here's what He told His disciples (and all future Christians) before He returned to heaven:

> "If two of you *agree* (are *like-minded*) on earth about anything you ask, it'll be done by My Father in heaven. Because where two or three Christians gather in My Name, *I am there in the midst of them.*"⁹

This is an astonishing promise. But notice that it's *conditional*. Jesus said He would be present in small groups (and that their prayers would be answered) *if* they like-minded in what they asked for. He also said the participants in small groups (especially worship type small groups) had to be Spirit-filled because He said the participants had to meet "in My name."

That last principle needs explaining. In the First Century, if a person did something in another person's "name," they were doing it with that other person's full ability and authority. And the only time Christians have the full ability and authority of Jesus is when they're *Spirit-filled*. So Jesus was promising His disciples (and all future Christians) that He'd be in their midst during small group worship *if* they were like-minded and *if* they were Spirit-filled.

That's a supernatural miracle. But here's why it happens. Jesus and the Holy Spirit are *both* part of the Trinity of God. That's why in some verses of the New Testament the Holy Spirit is called the "Spirit of *Christ*," and the "Spirit of *Jesus*."¹⁰ Jesus is present every place the Holy Spirit is present – and the Holy Spirit is present every place Jesus is present. So if the Holy Spirit is present in small group worship, Jesus is present in it, too.

All of this brings us right back to the decision about *guidance* in small group worship. If Jesus and the Holy Spirit are *present* in small group worship – shouldn't *they* be allowed to guide that small group worship? The answer is obviously, "Yes." But in today's Christianity they often *aren't* allowed to guide it.

They're usually aren't allowed to guide it because in today's Christianity most small groups have a *human* leader. That human leader may be a pastor, elder, deacon, Sunday school teacher, song leader, or some other authority figure; or it may be the host of the group; or it may be an outspoken and domineering participant in the group. Regardless of who it is, if a *human* is leading a small group's worship – Jesus and the Holy Spirit *aren't* guiding it. That's tragic, because Jesus and the Holy Spirit should be guiding it. How do we know that? We know that because all Christians are part of the *Body of Christ*.

The Body of Christ

When small groups of like-minded, Spirit-filled Christians gather for worship, they form a small unit of the *Body of Christ*. God's plan for Christian small groups is for them to be small units of His *Body* on earth, and for them to do the things that He would do if He was still walking the earth as a man. Paul described that stunning principle this way:

> "Jesus is the Head of the Body, the *group* (all Christians) ... (and) God placed all things under His feet, and appointed Him Head of everything in the *group*, which is His Body."[11]

Notice in Paul's words that the *Body* of Jesus and the Christian *group* are the same thing. They're synonyms for one another. The Christian group is the Body of Christ, and the Body of Christ is the Christian group. So when a small group meets for any purpose (social, teaching, or worship), they become a *unit* of Jesus's Body on earth; and they're supposed to do the things that Jesus would do if He was here. Except for one thing. Small groups can only experience the power of Jesus in the degree to which they let Him *guide* their group. Jesus is the *Head* (the superior, the headmaster) of everything in His *Body* – and that includes being the *Head* of worship type small groups while they're worshiping.

This is why I try to never use the terms "leader" and "leadership" when I'm talking about small group worship. I try to use the terms "guide" and "guidance." Because in today's world, the words "leader" and "leadership" are emotionally-charged terms that imply a *human leader* who's physically and mentally in command of a group (usually in a dictatorial way), in the sense of a factory foreman or an army sergeant. But that's *not* the kind of "leadership" we want in small group worship. We want a *Spiritual guide*. And that Spiritual guide is Jesus, acting through the indwelling power of the Holy Spirit in the group's participants.

After all, Jesus and the Holy Spirit can only guide a group if it gives them *permission* to do so. And even if a group gives them permission, they can only guide that group by expressing Spiritual behavior, gifts, and experiences in the group's participants.[12] This last principle introduces us to the biggest *mistake* that today's Christians make when they try to set up a worship type small group.

The Biggest Mistake in Small Groups

The Hologram Story

Some years ago, I was visiting a laboratory in a Midwest aerospace company, when I noticed a man at a workbench adjusting some lights and mirrors. So I stopped to watch him. He saw me watching and asked, "Have you ever seen a hologram?" (He pronounced it "holl'-uh-gram," rhyming with the word Hollywood.)

"No," I said, "I've never even heard of one."

"Then let me show you one," he said. With that, he picked up a large piece of black plastic that looked like a photographic negative and handed it to me. "Hold this up to the light and tell me what you see," he said.

I took the piece of plastic, held it up to a light, and saw the image of a jet fighter plane. "Why, I see a jet fighter," I answered.

"Exactly," he replied. "Now watch this." He took a pair of scissors and snipped off a tiny corner of the big negative. He clamped this in a pair of locking tweezers and handed the tweezers to me. "Okay," he said, "hold this up to the light and tell me what you see."

I took the snippet in the tweezers, held it up to the light, and saw the *same* jet fighter. "Wow," I said, "I still see the jet fighter!"

"Precisely," he said. "In a hologram, you can see the whole picture in the smallest piece."

I've never forgotten that experience in that lab, and here's how the *hologram* principle applies to small groups. The biggest mistake traditional congregations make today when they set up small groups is this: They set them up as *mini-congregations*. They snip off a tiny piece of the parent congregation, move it into someone's home, and call it "a small group." Then they operate the snippet the same way they operate the parent congregation. They have a *human* leader in charge of it. (Usually a pastor, associate pastor, deacon, elder, or some other authority figure from the parent congregation.)

Next, they give this leader an approved *agenda* outlining everything that's going to happen in the small group. Then they give the leader an approved list of *songs* from an approved hymn *book*. Then they give the leader an approved lesson *plan* from an approved *textbook* or *video*. Then they give the leader a list of *announcements* to be made each week about upcoming events in the parent congregation. Finally, they give the leader a *basket* to pass around to collect an *offering* for the parent congregation. And so it goes. You get the idea. But that isn't a small group. That's a hologram of the parent congregation. That's a *mini-congregation*.

This kind of structure is bad enough for social and teaching type small groups – but it's deadly in worship type small groups. There are two tragic results in such holographic small groups:

1. First, the Holy Spirit doesn't *guide* them very much because He never overrides our human will.

2. Second, the participants in holographic small groups continue to think and act like *traditional* Christians, and little Early Christian type Spiritual worship occurs.

It helps to remember that traditional congregations today have their roots in the institution that Constantine established in the Fourth Century – and that institution had a *formal, rigid, ceremonial, legalistic, large group, spectator* type structure.

In contrast, the Early Christians had an *informal, relaxed, non-ceremonial, non-legalistic, small group, participator* type structure.

Guess which of these two structures generates the most Spiritual worship? Isn't the answer easy? Christian history, common sense, and personal experience all reveal that the Early Christian *participator* type structure wins hands down.

Next, since we're talking about the structure of small group worship, let's see the role that the *host* plays in small group worship.

The Hosts in Small Groups

The host (and/or hostess) who provides a home for a small group has more authority and influence on a group than we might realize. After all, it's the *host's* parking space, home, furniture, time, energy, etc., that the group is using free of charge. A group's participants are literally visitors in a host's home. Thus, participants tend to be polite, patience, and tolerant with almost anything a host says or does. That's normal. Except for one thing. Hosts can quickly become the *unelected* human leaders of groups without the groups consciously realizing it.

If the hosts of small groups are outspoken and opinionated, they can cripple Spiritual worship and, in severe cases, can cause groups to disband. Said another way, only like-minded, Spirit-filled participants should be participants in worship type small groups, and that goes *double* for the host. He or she needs to be one of the most *Spiritual* participants in the group. And if he or she isn't one of the most *Spiritual* participants in the group, he or she should pray about continuing as the host.

Hosts in worship type small groups can't have hidden agendas; can't promote personal political and religious beliefs; can't practice personal leadership skills; and can't feed personal loneliness or neediness. They can be logical and organized, and they can do things like keeping email lists of the participants, controlling the temperature in the home, keeping pets locked up, directing parking, and so forth. But they can't control worship. That's the Holy Spirit's turf.

Now, as we reach the end of the chapter, we need to think about one final important question. It's this. If Early Christian worship groups were so powerful and so amazing – what *happened* to them? Where did they go? Let's close by talking about *Emperor Theodosius*.

The Outlawing of Small Groups

You may have wondered what ever *happened* to the worship type small groups that were the key to Christianity's success in the first three centuries of Christian history. What *happened* to the miraculous small groups that Christians enjoyed for the first 300 years of Christianity? We already know that Constantine started dismantling Christianity in the early Fourth Century; and we already know that he did incredible damage. But it was a *later* Fourth Century emperor who came 40 years after Constantine who did the most harm of all.

His name was *Flavius Theodosius Augustus* – Theodosius for short (pronounced "theo-doe'-see-us"). Like the other Roman emperors who followed Constantine, Theodosius continued the process of destroying Early Christianity. And one of the most disastrous things he did was to pass a law called the *Lex Fidei* (pronounced "lex fee'-day"). In Latin, that means the *Law of Faith*. This decree outlawed *small groups* in the empire. It said that people who gathered in small groups (instead of in government approved basilicas, temples, and shrines) were now "heretics" and subject to arrest, torture, and imprisonment.[13]

At that point in history, Christian small group worship (and its amazing Spirituality) died out. And to this day, Christian Spirituality has never fully recovered. In other words, at the end of the Fourth Century, about 350 years (about nine generations) *after* Christianity was founded, a Roman emperor legally ended the informal, relaxed, non-ceremonial, non-legalistic, participator type small group worship that Christians had enjoyed since Pentecost morning.

Now – can the wonderful First Century style of Christian worship still be experienced today? The answer is, "Of course." From all that we've said to this point in the book, it's clear that the *Early Christian Lifestyle* can still be lived today, including Spiritual small group worship. All it takes is like-minded, Spirit-filled Christians who want it, seek it, and expect it.

To that end, let's assume that *you've* found one or more other Christians who're as hungry for Spiritual growth as you are; and who're willing to form an Early Christian style small worship group with you. What happens next? What do the participants do when an Early Christian style small worship group meets? We're going to discuss that in the next chapter. But before we do, let's summarize this chapter.

Summary of Chapter 14

1. The "Early Christian Lifestyle" that we're talking about in this book includes an informal, relaxed, non-rigid, non-ceremonial, non-legalistic, participator type small group worship. The Early Christians worshiped that way for the first three centuries of Early Christian history, and Christians can worship that way today.

2. The Early Christians worshiped in small groups in private homes because that's the quickest, easiest, safest, cheapest, most confidential, convenient, and intimate way to worship – and also because it's the fastest way to grow Spiritually.

3. Christians grow Spiritually the fastest when they truly and freely express Spiritual behavior, gifts, and experiences in a small group setting.

4. Small groups are mentioned 30 different times in 10 different books of the New Testament, and 12 different ancient cities are mentioned as having Christian small groups in them. Also, the surviving property records of ancient Rome list by name 25 different Early Christian small groups that met in the city (the other records have been lost). Finally, archaeological digs have unearthed physical evidence of Early Christian small groups in the ancient cities of Aqaba, Capernaum, Damascus, Megiddo, Rome, Salamis, among others. We know from all this evidence that small groups were the way that the Early Christians met and worshiped before Constantine came to power in the Fourth Century.

5. The most accurate translation of the Early Christian Greek noun for a small group is the word *group* – not the word "church." When Paul wrote about the small group in Priscilla's and Aquila's house, he wrote in Greek, "Greet the *group* that meets

in their house." He didn't say, "Greet the *church* that meets in their house."

6. There were thousands of Early Christian small group home gatherings worldwide in hundreds of villages, towns, and cities; and they were the "engines" that "generated" the Spiritual power of early Christianity.

7. There are two kinds of peer pressure: *positive* peer pressure and *negative* peer pressure. Both are equally influential. The best way to fight negative peer pressure is to neutralize it with positive peer pressure. That can be done by finding at least one other Christian who's hungry for Spiritual growth and then socializing with that other Christian in the six-part Early Christian small group format.

8. A "small group" is defined as a gathering of Christians who're socializing with a specific six-part organizational structure. The six parts of that small group structure are:

   a) The same two to twelve like-minded Christians must interact.

   b) Their interactions must be face-to-face.

   c) Their interactions must be two-way.

   d) Their interactions must be frequent.

   e) Their interactions must be over an extended period of time.

   f) Their interactions must permit Spiritual behavior, gifts, and experiences to be expressed during worship.

9. The three types of small groups are:

    a) Social Types.

    b) Teaching Types.

    c) Worship Types.

10. The types of small groups (social, teaching, and worship) can change as a meeting's needs change. But at any point in time, groups can be identified as one of the three basic types by the majority behavior of the participants at the time.

11. The *worship* type small group creates the most Spirituality in participants because it doesn't have a human leader, and because it permits the true and free expression of Spiritual behavior, gifts, and experiences.

12. Like-mindedness is required in small group worship. It's important (but not required) in social and teaching small groups. Participants in a worship type small group must be like-minded about expressing Spiritual behavior, gifts, and experiences in their worship.

13. Jesus promised He would be personally *present* during small group worship when the participants were like-minded and Spirit-filled. But that also means that Jesus, through the indwelling power of the Holy Spirit, must be allowed to *guide* small group worship.

14. Christians are the *Body* of Christ, and Jesus is the *Head* of His Body (of all Christians everywhere). Thus, when a worship type small group gathers, it's a small *unit* of Jesus's Body and, as a group, it has many of the same supernatural powers that Jesus has.

15. The words "leader" and "leadership" are emotionally-loaded words in today's world that imply a person who's physically in command of a small group – often in a dictatorial way. The words "guide" and "guidance" are better for Christian small groups, since Jesus is their Head and guides them via the indwelling power of the Spirit.

16. The biggest mistake today's traditional congregations make when they form small groups is that they set them up as *mini-congregations* and operate them like the parent congregation – with a human leader, prepared lessons, prepared agendas, prepared music, and so forth. This is deadly to *worship* type small groups, since they need true and free expression of Spiritual behavior, gifts, and experiences.

17. The *host* of a worship style small group can become the *unelected* leader of the group if he or she is outspoken and opinionated. That means the host of a small group (especially the host of a worship style small group) must be chosen carefully and should be one of the most *Spiritual* participants in the group.

18. Theodosius, a Fourth Century Roman emperor who lived 40 years after Constantine died, did great harm to early Christianity. He passed a law called the *Lex Fidei* that made small groups illegal and that made participants of small groups "heretics." Christian small groups – and Christian Spirituality – faded greatly at that point in history.

Okay – it's time to take the next step in understanding small group worship. It's time to talk about one of the most interesting and exciting experiences any Christian can have: *Spirit-guided* worship. Turn to Chapter 15, and let's talk about how the Early Christians worshiped – and how we can worship the same way today.

Chapter 15

THE SPIRITUAL WORSHIP

Mistakes, Choices, and Puppies

We said earlier that Christians could grow Spiritually all alone on deserted islands if they had to – but that it'd be difficult. Now we know *why* it'd be difficult. Christians were designed by God to gather in small groups and to do what Jesus would do if He was still walking the earth. Christians were meant to form small units of the Body of Christ and be "the fullness of Him" in the world.[1]

More than that, we Christians were meant to serve one another with behaviors, gifts, and experiences of the Spirit. And we can't do that alone either. That also requires gathering in small groups for socializing, teaching, and worship. Finally, we know that negative peer pressure can overwhelm Christians who're all alone in non-Christian families or careers, and being participants in small groups can neutralize that threat too. All of this being true, we now see why small groups are such a necessary part of the Christian experience. And as a quick review, we defined a small worship group this way:

> *Two or more of the same like-minded Christians who gather frequently, face-to-face, with two-way interaction, over an extended period time, with an open expression of Spiritual behavior, gifts, and experiences.*

But now let's be even more specific. Let's talk about *how* Christians gather for small group worship and what *happens* when they do. And to be certain the principles apply to you and your family, we're going to assume from this point on that you're either a participant in a small worship group now; or that you're praying to form one; or that you're praying to find one to join.

So this chapter is about what to *do* (and *not* to do) when you and your small group gather for Spiritual worship. Let's start by dealing with the two biggest mistakes that small group worshipers make. We've already talked about the first one, but let's glance at it again. It's the mistake of creating holographic *mini-congregations*.

The *Mini-Congregation* Mistake

We said previously that one of the biggest mistakes Christians make when they form a small group for worship is that they form it as a "hologram" of a traditional congregation. We said a hologram is a laser image in which the whole image can be seen in its smallest part. Thus, if a small group is created as a hologram of a traditional congregation, it's created as a *mini-congregation*. It has the same attitudes, rituals, and controls that a traditional congregation has. It has a *human* leader, a *preplanned* order of service, *preplanned* music, and *preplanned* everything else. It usually even has a pastor, associate pastor, elder, deacon, or some other authority figure present to supervise.

But – as we know – the mini-congregation structure is the kiss of Spiritual death in small group worship. Why? Because Spirit-guided worship doesn't *have* a human leader, a human order of service, humanly selected music, or human supervision. It's *Spirit-guided*. The Holy Spirit prompts the participants when to pray, sing, and express Spiritual gifts. It's true, of course, that several basic decisions need to be made for a small group to gather efficiently and effectively. However, these decisions should only create the bare bones of the gathering. Let's look at those five bare-bones choices now.

The Five Small Group Decisions

1. Decide a *place* to meet.

2. Decide a *day* or *evening* to meet.

3. Decide a time to *start*.

4. Decide a time to *end*.

5. Decide whether *snacks* or *refreshments* are to be shared; and if they are, who'll be responsible for them, and who'll clean up afterwards.

That's it. Nothing else needs be decided. Nothing about the *worship* itself should be discussed because tampering with the worship itself can *grieve* the Holy Spirit.[2] Another reason for limiting decision-making to these five points is that we Christians don't *know* what the Holy Spirit wants to do in worship. We don't know if He wants to heal someone; or have an angel visit the group; and which participants He wants to give a vision, a teaching, a song, a prophecy, a word of knowledge, or a word of wisdom. Why don't we know these things? There's an *Old Testament* Scripture that tells us why. Here's what God thinks about human understanding:

> "'*My* thoughts are not your thoughts, and your ways are not *My* ways,' says the Lord. 'For as the heavens are higher than the earth, so *My* ways are higher than your ways, and *My* thoughts are higher than your thoughts.'"[3]

What could be clearer? We humans are clueless. We have no *idea* what the Holy Spirit wants to do in worship. And to be totally honest, that's part of the joy and excitement of Spiritual worship. Spiritual worship is filled with surprises and unexpected pleasures that human-planned worship could never match. Or looked at in reverse, that's why human-planned worship is often disappointing. The human planning canceled out the amazing and surprising things that the Holy Spirit had wanted to do during worship.

What we're talking about is the issue of "leadership" in worship. The most honest question a small worship group can ask is: Who's going to oversee our worship? Is it going to be a *human*? Or is it going to be the *Holy Spirit*? That's a desperately serious decision. Let me tell a story that shows how deeply imbedded the confusion is over "leadership" in today's Christianity.

The Man Who Wanted a Pastor

I was once participating in small group worship in a Christian friend's home, and we were just settling down to start worship when the doorbell rang. I happened to be sitting near the front door, and the host gestured for me to answer the bell. I stood up and opened the door, and a neatly dressed man was standing on the steps. He had a big smile on his face and was holding a Bible in his hand.

I said, "Good morning," pushing the door open wide for him. "May I help you?"

"Yes," he replied. "Is this where the Christians are meeting? A friend told me about your group, and I thought I'd worship with you today."

"Yes, this is the place," I answered. "Come in and make yourself at home. We're just about to start."

He stepped into the entry foyer and asked politely, "Are you the pastor?"

"No," I replied. "We don't have a pastor."

He paused and glanced at me. "You don't have a pastor? Then who's your elder?"

"Well, we don't have an elder, either," I said. "We're just a group of Christians who gather to worship God and love one another."

His eyes narrowed and a frown spread over his features. "You don't have either a pastor *or* an elder?" he asked with an edge in his voice. "Then who keeps *order* in your group?"

"Oh," I answered. "The Holy Spirit keeps order. He guides us."

"Yes," he snapped, "I know about the Holy Spirit. But you need a pastor or elder to keep *order* in your group!"

"Well, actually we *don't*," I explained. "The Spirit guides us and we've never had any disorder."

The man stared at me a moment. Then he shook his head in disbelief, jerked open the front door, and went down the front steps muttering, "That's absurd! I'd never go to a meeting that didn't have a pastor or elder to keep order!"

He drove away and we never saw him again.

What's the lesson in this story? The lesson is that most Christians today have either grown up in traditional congregations, or at least they've been exposed to traditional congregations through books, movies, and TV, or by attending weddings, funerals, Christmas services, Easter services, musical concerts, and other events in traditional congregations. And because of that, most Christians think traditional congregational services *are* Christian worship.

In other words, they think Christian worship *is* what they see in traditional services. It never occurs to them that *Spirit-guided* worship is possible. They can't imagine a Christian event that doesn't have a pastor, priest, bishop, elder, deacon, choir leader, Sunday school teacher, Bible study leader, youth leader, choir leader, bus driver, or janitor in charge of it – telling the people where to sit, and when to stand, sing, pray, and pay.

We could call it a culture-conflict, a values-clash, a habits-collision, or some other big term. But whatever we call it, it's a massive blind spot in today's Christianity that's so huge we can't over-emphasize it. Here's something that many Christians have never thought about:

The Holy Spirit is perfectly capable of guiding small group worship – if we'll let Him do it.

That was true when Christianity was founded in Jerusalem in the First Century. And twenty centuries later, it's still true today in your own town or city. Previously, we discussed an amazing promise that Jesus made to all Christians before He returned to heaven. Let's repeat that promise and remember the lesson in it. Here's what Jesus promised:

"If two (or more) of you agree on earth about anything you ask, it'll be done by My Father in heaven. Because where two or three Christians gather in My Name, *I am there in the midst of them.*"[4]

We've asked this question before, but now let's ask it again: If Jesus and the Holy Spirit are *present* in small group worship, shouldn't they be allowed to *guide* that worship? We've said the answer is "Yes," and since that's true, it introduces the second big mistake small groups make in worship. This second mistake is related to the first mistake (forming holograms of traditional congregations), but this second one adds a new twist. It's the mistake of having *preconceived notions*.

The Preconceived Notions Mistake

The mini-congregation mistake is an *organizational* mistake. This second mistake is an *attitudinal* mistake. It's the habit many Christians have of arriving for worship with *preconceived notions* about it. In other words, they arrive knowing what's going to happen during worship and, worse of all, being comfortable with knowing what's going to happen during worship.

Said another way, whether they're attending a traditional congregation or a small group, if Christians have worship that's *preplanned* for them by other humans, all they have to do is sit and watch it as passive spectators. Their only involvement is obeying the human instructions they've been given and to daydream between action steps. But such preconceived notions take away the surprises, the freshness, the newness, the humor, and the other unexpected and supernatural things that occur when the *Holy Spirit* guides worship.

That freshness and newness is why the Early Christians worshiped in Spirit-guided small groups. And it's why today we should worship in small groups structured like the Early Christian structured them. That's the only way we can avoid the straight jacket of human preplanning. It's the only way we can let the Holy Spirit out of the locked closet that Constantine put Him in during the Fourth Century. For years I've used this motto with small group worshipers:

*Never come to small group worship with a preconceived notion about what's going to happe*n there.

Compare that kind of open-mindedness to how today's congregational Christians are conditioned to "worship." As they enter their building, they're handed a "bulletin" with a preplanned "order of service" printed on it. The bulletin tells them minute-by-minute what's going to happen during the "service." They know before they sit down who's going to *pray*, who's going to *speak*, who's going to make *announcements*, who's going to play *music*, who's going to read *Scripture*, and when they'll be asked to stand, sit, sing, listen, pray, pay, and leave.

But that kind of preplanned human worship leaves an important question unanswered: Where does the *Holy Spirit* fit in? When does *He* get to say something or do something? We already know the Holy Spirit never overrides human will power. So when people preplan small group worship, they cancel everything the Spirit wanted to do. Said another way, the reason we have small group worship is to *avoid* preconceived notions. Here's the principle:

*The more we preconceive and preplan worship,
the less Spiritual that worship will be.*

That says it all. That's the reason for small group worship. That's what lets the Holy Spirit out of His musty locked closet.

The Key to the Spirit's Closet

Thus, avoiding preconceived notions means that the "key" to Spirit-guided small group worship is to ... *have* no key. Participants in small group worship must come to gatherings with no idea about what's going to happen. They need to arrive with no agenda in mind – except the desire to see the miracle of the Holy Spirit guiding their worship. The "key" to small group worship is simply true and free worship. So now we need to stop and define the fuzzy word *worship*.

The Definition of the Word "Worship"

As usual, let's go to the First Century Christian letters to define the fuzzy word *worship*. In the First Century, the word for "worship" was a surprising term that bears little resemblance to what people call worship today. The First Century term for *worship* came from the Greek root meaning a *dog*, and it meant to kiss the master's face and lie at his feet like a loving pet.

What does that kind of worship look like in real life? It looks like this: The Early Christians worshiped on their *knees* much of the time, and often they worshiped *prone* on their faces on the floor. We see an example of that in the *New Testament* where the 24 elders fall on their *faces* before God.[5]

Worship the way the Early Christians did it is total submission to, and complete reverence for, God. If you've ever had a pet dog, you know what we're talking about. Your dog wanted to be near you. He went where you went, nuzzled you, whined for your attention, and ignored everybody but you. That's an image Early Christians worship. We may not understand the depth of that kind of true and free worship until we get to heaven. But we do know it's *different* from what people call "worship" today.

I remember one night several years ago when I dreamed a Spiritual dream. In that dream I was worshiping God – and when I awoke the next morning, I was lying prone on the floor beside my bed. I don't know how I got there, except that I must have gotten out of bed and prostrated myself before God during my dream.

Worship the way that Early Christians did it is *that* kind of reverence and submission. And that brings us back to the theme of this chapter: Who's going to orchestrate our small group worship? Are humans going to *lead* it? Or is the Holy Spirit going to *guide* it? We already know Jesus is the Head of the Christian group worldwide, and so He has every moral, legal, ethical, and Spiritual right to guide all Christian worship at all times and in all places.[6]

But exactly *how* do we let Him do that? How do we let Jesus activate the indwelling power of the Holy Spirit in a group's participants to generate Spiritual worship? The Early Christians gave us two principles for the process. They're the principles of *truth* and *freedom* in worship. Let's see them next.

The Two Principles of Spirit-Guided Worship

The first principle that the Early Christians gave us for worship is that it must be *true* worship. Here's what the apostle John said about true worship:

> "Real worshipers will worship the Father in Spirit and in *truth*, for they're the kind of worshipers the Father seeks. God is a Spirit, and real worshipers must worship Him in Spirit and in *truth*."[7]

In the original Greek, the word "truth" that John used means *real and factual* worship. It means worship that *actually and factually* does express the Spiritual behavior, gifts, and experiences during worship that satisfy our duty to God.[8]

The second principle the Early Christians gave us for worship is that it must be *free*. Here's what the apostle Paul said about free worship:

> "The Lord is the Spirit – and where the Spirit of the Lord is, there is *freedom*."[9]

In the original Greek, the word "freedom" that Paul used means to worship without human agendas, schedules, plans, and rituals. It means to worship without human legalism and control.

So, if we put these two powerful principles together, we see that God intends for Christians to worship Him *with* a true and free expression of supernatural behavior, gifts, and experiences; and *without* a false and rigid human control. What does that kind of worship look like? Let's now see the *specifics* of Spirit-guided worship.

The Specifics of Spirit-Guided Worship

To be *specific*, Spirit-guided worship is supernatural from start to finish. It begins with the Holy Spirit and ends with the Holy Spirit. Spirit-guided worship happens when the Holy Spirit expresses Himself through the participants of a small group. Spirit-guided worship happens when small group worshipers participate in the supernatural.

That means Spirit-guided worship is always surprising. It's always spontaneous. It's filled with supernatural behavior, gifts, and experiences that heal, encourage, and teach the worshipers. Spirit-guided worship is sharing supernatural emotions that strengthen and uplift the worshipers. Spirit-guided worship is a nearness to God that's so profound the worshipers feel like "pets" lying contentedly at the Master's feet.

But we need more details. We need to see exactly what Spirit-guided worship *looks* like. What actually *happens*? Here's how the apostle Paul described Spirit-guided small group worship:

> "When you gather together (*for worship*), be filled with the Spirit: speaking to one another with praise choruses, hymns, and songs from the Spirit. Sing and make music in your mind to the Lord! Each one of you (*every one of you*) will have in mind (*from the indwelling Holy Spirit*) a hymn; or will have in mind a teaching from the Spirit; or will have in mind a revelation from the Spirit; or will have a message in a prayer language. But whatever you do, in word or in deed, do it all in the Name of the Lord Jesus, giving thanks to God the Father, so that your small group can *grow* in wisdom, grace, virtue, and holiness."[10]

That's an amazing picture of Early Christian worship. And notice that it stands on two strong pillars. Both pillars must be fully expressed, and both come from the indwelling Holy Spirit in the worshipers. The pillars are an expression of the *Rivers of Living Water* that Jesus promised all Christians. Here are the two pillars of Spirit-guided worship.

The Two Pillars of Spirit-Guided Worship

1. The first pillar of Spirit-guided worship is the true and free expression of Spiritual *behavior* (the "fruit" of the Spirit) by the small group worshipers. All worshipers must express supernatural love, joy, peace, patience, kindness, goodness, faithfulness, gentleness, self-control, etc., as the Holy Spirit guides.

2. The second pillar of Spirit-guided worship is the true and free expression of Spiritual *gifts* by the small group worshipers. All worshipers must express supernatural visions, teachings, words of wisdom, words of knowledge, healings, miracles, prophecies, messages in prayer languages, translating messages in prayer languages, etc., as the Holy Spirit guides.

Of course, Paul's description of Spirit-guided worship above was written by a *First Century* Christian. So what does Spirit-guided worship look like today? Is it similar to what Paul described? Let's see an *example* in today's world.

The Example of Spirit-Guided Worship

Before we see our *example*, a word of caution. We said earlier that Christians should never come to worship with preconceived notions about what's going to happen. We said true and free worship is participative, surprising, and spontaneous. Because of these principles, no two Spirit-guided worship sessions are exactly alike. The Holy Spirit never does exactly the same thing in exactly the same way. Under His guidance, some worship is mostly singing. Some is mostly teaching. Some is mostly testimonies; or prayer; or visions, or healings, or other gifts. Sometimes it's mostly a holy quietness. But most frequently, it's a mixture of all these things and more.

Therefore, since the Holy Spirit guides each worship session differently, it's not possible to give a "typical" example of Spirit-guided worship. Instead, let's create a *generic snapshot* of it. But (and this is important) let's base our snapshot on a small group that's made up of Spiritually mature Christians. Let's base it on a group that worships with a true and free flow of Spiritual fruit, gifts, and experiences.

The Snapshot at the "Smiths"

With that agreed, let's now visit the fictitious "Smith" family as they host a Spirit-guided small worship group in their home. And since small groups don't have *names*, the participants in the group refer to their group by the host's name. For example, they say things like, "I worship at the Smiths." And "My group meets at the Smiths." And "We're going to the Smiths tonight." And "Wasn't worship wonderful at the Smiths last week!" So with that, let's visit the "Smiths" house, and see how they worship in the Spirit. Here we go.

The Spirit-Guided Worship at the "Smiths"

As the time for worship approaches, the participants begin arriving at the "Smith's" home. Much hugging, cheek-kissing, hand-shaking, and shoulder-patting goes on as the participants gather, since they're expressing Spiritual behavior (supernatural love, joy, peace, etc.); and since they're anticipating what the Holy Spirit is going to do during worship.

As the participants enter, they gather in a room where they can all sit in loose order facing one another on couches, armchairs, folding chairs, and so on. Participants of all ages and both genders sit together. Some sit on the floor or on stools. Everyone talks, laughs, jokes, hugs, and puts away coats and handbags as they settle down.

Some of the participants may carry dishes of food to the kitchen if the group plans a meal or refreshments after worship.

As the time for worship to start draws near, the room grows quieter. Laughing and joking start to fade away. Some participants close their eyes, a smile on their faces, hands resting comfortably in their laps or on their Bibles. Here and there participants may start to hum softly. A stillness gradually settles over the room like a warm blanket being spread over the group. This feeling of stillness and peace means the Holy Spirit is ready to start guiding the worship.

The first thing that often happens is that one of the participants starts to *sing*. He or she does that because a melody is clear in his or her mind – meaning the song is being prompted by the Holy Spirit. The other participants join in and sing along. After a verse or two, the participants sense that the song is over, and the singing automatically stops. But within seconds, another worshiper starts another song, and the group joins in again. The singing is relaxed and informal. There's no pressure to do anything but enjoy the singing. Some participants sit with their eyes closed and just listen. Others hum. Others keep time with a foot or by tapping a finger.

Participants who don't know the words will soon learn them, and meanwhile they hum or mouth the words. There is no sheet music. There are no song books. There are no instruments. The participants don't miss these, and don't notice if anyone is off-key or not singing. The group's entire focus is on God and on worshiping Him. The singing is interspersed with scattered prayers and participants whispering, "Thank you Jesus … bless you Jesus … praise you Jesus." There are also scattered moments of silence ("holy hushes") that last a few seconds, and then the next song or prayer begins.

As worship continues, a *oneness* in the Spirit develops that can't be understood in human terms. Some of the participants start to sense what the Holy Spirit is going to do *next* – and some even sense what some of the other participants are *thinking*. For example, a participant might start a song and, as he or she does, other participants might chuckle aloud as they join in. These other participants did this because they had *sensed* this participant was going to start this song, and when the participant *did*, they couldn't hold back a happy chuckle.

At times, a more experienced participant might encourage a less experienced participant by asking something like, "Alice, aren't you thinking about song x-y-z? Why don't you go ahead and start it for us." At this, Alice starts the song. Or a more experienced participant might ask, "Jerry, is the Spirit reminding you of a Bible verse? Why don't you read it for us?" At this, Jerry quotes a Bible verse or opens his Bible and reads one.

This *oneness* is possible because the participants are so filled with the Spirit that their thoughts have become supernaturally unified. Also, as we saw in the apostle Paul's description of Spirit-guided worship earlier, the participants aren't limited to songs and Bible verses. Spiritual gifts of all kinds are expressed by the participants, including visions, teachings, healings, revelations, prophecies, words of knowledge, words of encouragement, and all the rest.

The Holy Spirit expresses these gifts through the participants as conduits of His power. He knows what needs each participant has, and He knows what needs the whole group has. So He uses the gifts of the Spirit in the same relaxed, informal way that the singing and Bible readings were expressed.

For example, a participant named "John" might say in a peaceful and relaxed way, with his eyes closed and a smile on his face, "I don't know why, but God seems to be saying that we should pray for somebody's *job* tonight. Does anyone else have that impression?"

At this, a participant named "Harry" might speak out and say, "John, I think that's me. I might lose my job this week and I need prayer." The group might stop here and pray for Harry. Or John might quietly speak a prophecy and say, "No, Harry, I think God's saying that you *won't* lose your job this week and that you can stop worrying." (The group may rejoice at their next meeting when Harry tells them that he did in fact keep his job.)

And so it goes. Many kinds of supernatural behavior, gifts, and experiences are expressed as worship continues. Some participants have *joint* experiences in which several of them receive different parts of a vision, and each describes the part of the vision that he or she sees. Or some participants receive different parts of a teaching, and each tells the part of the teaching that he or she has been given. Or several participants might read parts of a connected Bible teaching.

But eventually, a time comes when the worship begins to *lighten*. It's as if the warm blanket over the group is being gently *lifted*. This means that the Holy Spirit is bringing the worship to an end. (The Spirit always honors the start times and end times set by the group.)

As this feeling spreads around the room, participants start to open their eyes, smile at one another, and chuckle with happiness. They might glance around the room and nod to one another in satisfaction. Some might wipe away tears. Others may pat one another's arms or shoulders in pleasure. Soon participants start to stand up and move around the room, and the Spirit-guided worship session is over.

Next, if the group has planned to share a meal or refreshments after worship, the participants may move to a kitchen, dining room, patio, or other dining area. If the group doesn't plan to share a meal or refreshments, the participants will probably relax and chat in the worship room. Either way, the group usually engages in a time of *afterglow* before leaving the "Smith's" home – and this afterglow is important.

But before we talk about afterglow, let's pause to ask some bold and honest questions. How do we *know* that the Early Christians *really* worshiped the way the "Smiths" worship? Does the way the "Smiths" worship *really* match the way the Early Christian worshiped?

The Record of Spirit-Guided Worship

The apostle Paul wrote the most about Spirit-guided worship, and even he didn't say much about it. He apparently assumed that his readers were *already* participants in Spirit-guided worship and didn't need him to say much about it. However, we can piece together a clear statement about Spirit-guided worship by splicing words from three of Paul's letters. Using those excerpts, here's how Paul described Spirit-guided worship in the First Century:

> "When you gather together (*for worship*), be filled with the Spirit: speaking to one another with praise choruses, hymns, and songs from the Spirit. Sing and make music in your mind to the Lord! Each one of you (*every one of you*) will have in mind (*from the indwelling Holy Spirit*) a hymn; or will have in mind a teaching from the Spirit; or will have in mind a revelation from the Spirit; or will have a message in a prayer language. But whatever you do, in word or in deed, do it all in the Name of the Lord Jesus, giving thanks to God the Father, so that your small group can *grow* in wisdom, grace, virtue, and holiness."[11]

Now – did you notice that these are the *same* words we saw earlier in the chapter? Yet notice how closely they match the generic snapshot of worship at the "Smiths" that we just described. Aren't the two descriptions almost *identical*? This proves that Spirit-guided worship hasn't changed over the centuries. It's still the same today as it was with the Early Christians. That same worship is still available today to any Christian who wants it. Now let's return to the time of *afterglow* after worship.

The Afterglow After Worship

The word *afterglow* refers to that comfortable feeling we have after an especially satisfying experience. It's the feeling we have when we've read the last page of a good book. Or when we put down our fork after a delicious meal. Or when we wave goodbye to friends after a pleasant visit. Afterglow is a time after worship when participants discuss with pleasure the wonderful things that happened during that worship. Afterglow can be over a meal or refreshments, or it can be in the same room where the worship took place.

Afterglow is a time of reliving the worship – talking about the visions, prophecies, healings, and other experiences that occurred. It's also a time for questions, answers, and discussion. We saw an example of it earlier with the story of "Janice." That was the story of the shy young Christian mother who was prompted by the Spirit to express the Spiritual gift of *encouraging*, but had been too embarrassed to obey. It was during *afterglow* that she confided in me and that I urged her to express her gift the next time she was prompted. Thus, afterglow is a time of debriefing, reinforcement, and teaching that helps the participants grow (especially infant Christians and the children in the group).

But eventually even the afterglow winds down, and worship at the "Smiths" comes to an end. The participants begrudgingly start collecting their belongings to leave. They genuinely don't want to go, but they're also cheerful, happy, satisfied, and eagerly looking forward to the next worship session. And until that next session, they'll continue to think about the *results* of this session.

The Results of Spirit-Guided Worship

What are the *results* of Spirit-guided worship? In my experience, Spirit-guided worship changes a Christian's life forever. It did mine. And I know other Christians whose lives were permanently changed by participating in small group worship. I remember something a man said to me once about it. I had asked him how he liked Spirit-guided worship in his small group. He had looked at me with a steady gaze for a moment and then said, "Nothing I've ever *seen*, *done*, or *had* gives me the peace that Spirit-guided worship gives me."

That was beautiful. But the apostle Paul said it even better. Speaking to us down through the centuries, Paul gave us this law for worship. If we follow Paul's law, we can have the same power, glory, and majesty in worship that Christians had in his day. Here's Paul's law:

> "We worship by the *Spirit* of God, and we put no confidence in *human* effort."[12]

As we come to the end of the chapter, let me tell a story that shows the *results* of Spirit-guided worship. It's the story of the puppy in the sun.

The Puppy in the Sun

I was talking to a Christian man once who had never experienced Spirit-guided worship. I was telling him what happens during Spiritual worship and how wonderful it is – when he interrupted me with an interesting question.

He said, "I understand what you're saying. But when worship is over and you're back in the daily grind, how do you feel *then*?"

That made me stop and think. Then an image formed in my mind. It came from my childhood summers on my grandfather's farm. My grandfather kept hunting dogs in those days, and one summer a female dog had given birth to a litter of puppies while I was on the farm.

On this particular afternoon, I had visited the dog's pen after the puppies had finished nursing, and I saw a sight that was now clear in my mind. After nursing, one of the puppies had rolled over on its back in the warm sun. Its little belly was stretched tight with warm milk, and its paws were relaxed in midair. It was completely satisfied. It needed nothing else and wanted nothing else. It was at peace with its mother, with the other puppies, and with the world. It was a perfect picture of peace, contentment, and well-being.

So I looked at the man and said, "I can tell you exactly how I feel after Spirit-guided worship is over and I'm back in the daily grind. I feel like a puppy full of warm milk and sleeping on its back in the warm sun."

Christianity was successful in the early centuries because it was *powered* by the Spirituality of small groups. And Christianity is struggling today because it's *not* powered by the Spirituality of small groups. Most Christians today don't participate in Spirit-guided small group worship. But they should. Let me tell one last story that tells us why.

The Young Woman's Question

Several years ago, Spirit-guided worship was over and we were enjoying afterglow, when a young woman asked a wonderful question. She was so filled with the Spirit that her face glowed, and she asked the group, "I wonder why people wait until they die to experience heaven? Why don't they experience some of it here on earth?"

My sentiments exactly. That's why we're talking about Spirit-guided worship. It's a glimpse of heaven on earth. So in our next chapter we're going talk more about Spirit-guided worship and about how to live a Spirit-filled life. Before we do, let's summarize this chapter.

Summary of Chapter 15

1. The first big mistake Christians make when they form small groups is that they form them as "holograms" of traditional congregations. They form them *as mini-congregations* with the same attitudes, rituals, and controls of traditional congregations. That cancels true and free worship the way the Early Christians did it.

2. The second big mistake that Christians make when they form small groups is that they expect everything to be preplanned for them by humans. They have *preconceived notions* about what's going to happen. Instead, the motto of small group worship is: *Never come to small group worship with a preconceived notion about what's going to happen there.*

3. Preplanning cancels Spirit-guided worship because the Holy Spirit doesn't override human will power: *The more we preconceive and preplan worship, the less Spiritual that worship will be.*

4. True and free Spirit-guided small group worship is based on this foundational principle: *The Holy Spirit is perfectly capable of guiding small group worship – if we'll let Him do it.*

5. The big question for all Christians is: Who's going to orchestrate their worship? Are humans going to *lead* it? Or is the Holy Spirit going to *guide* it? Jesus is Head of the Body of Christ worldwide and so – using the indwelling power of the Holy Spirit in Christians – He should be allowed to guide the worship of all of the small groups in His Body.

6. Christians think traditional congregational worship *is* Christian worship. It doesn't occur to them that *Spirit-guided* worship is possible.

7. Spirit-guided worship must be *true* humble submission and adoration of God.

8. Spirit-guided worship must be *free* without legalism, rituals, and controls.

9. Only five basic decisions should be made when planning small group worship:

    a) Decide a *place* to meet.

    b) Decide a *day* or *evening* to meet.

    c) Decide a time to *start*.

    d) Decide a time to *end*.

    e) Decide whether *snacks* or *refreshments* will be shared; and if they are, who'll be responsible for them, and who'll clean up afterwards.

10. In Spirit-guided worship, the Holy Spirit expresses Himself through the participants of a small group with Spiritual behavior, gifts, and experiences that heal, encourage, and teach the participants of a small group.

11. True and free Spiritual worship stands on two powerful supernatural pillars:

    a) The full expression of Spiritual *behavior* (Spiritual "fruit") by the participants.

    b) The full expression of Spiritual *gifts* by the participants.

12. Sometimes Spirit-guided worship is mostly singing; other times it's mostly teaching; or mostly testimonies; or mostly prayers; or mostly visions; or mostly healings, or mostly peaceful quietness. But most frequently it's a mixture of these and more.

13. The First Century Greek word for "worship" comes from the Greek root word for a *dog*. It means to kiss the Master's face and lie at His feet like a loving pet. That's why the Early Christians worshiped on their knees much of the time, and often they worshiped prone on their faces.

14. The apostle Paul briefly described Spirit-guided worship this way:

> "When you gather together (*for worship*), be filled with the Spirit: speaking to one another with praise choruses, hymns, and songs from the Spirit. Sing and make music in your mind to the Lord! Each one of you (*every one of you*) will have in mind (*from the indwelling Holy Spirit*) a hymn; or will have in mind a teaching from the Spirit; or will have in mind a revelation from the Spirit; or will have a message in a prayer language. But whatever you do, in word or in deed, do it all in the Name of the Lord Jesus, giving thanks to God the Father, so that your small group can *grow* in wisdom, grace, virtue, and holiness."

15. There's no typical example of Spirit-guided worship. The Holy Spirit is always spontaneous and unpredictable. However, this chapter gave a generic snapshot of what Spirit-guided small group worship often looks like.

16. Afterglow is a time following worship during which the participants discuss what happened during the worship session. It's

often done over refreshments or a meal, and it's a time of reinforcement and learning that's important to infant Christians and to children.

17. The most important aspect of small group Spirit-guided worship is the *result* it has on participants. Many Christian's lives are permanently changed by Spirit-guided worship.

18. The apostle Paul gave this principle of Christian worship for all future Christians: "We worship by the *Spirit* of God, and we put no confidence in *human* effort."

In the next chapter, we're going to talk more about how individual Christians and Christian small groups can live the *Early Christian Lifestyle* in today's world. We're also going to talk about how traditional congregations can form *para-groups* that support and reinforce the Spiritual growth of their congregation. Let's turn to that chapter and start implementing all that we've learned so far.

Chapter 16

THE CHRISTIAN LIFE TODAY

Habits, Styles, and Saints

The title of this book is *Saving Christianity*, and in previous pages we talked about the problems that Christians face today. We talked about the millions of Christians who're dropping out of traditional congregations each year; and the thousands of traditional buildings that are being abandoned for lack of attendance; and the hundreds of pastors, priests, choir leaders, musicians, and other Christian employees who're leaving to take secular jobs; and how Christians are no longer a meaningful influence on society because so many of them are no more Spiritual than non-Christians.

We also talked about *why* these things are happening. We said Christianity is faltering because today's traditional congregations don't satisfy people's Spiritual needs – and we said that's true because the Roman emperors dismantled *Spiritual* Christianity in the Fourth Century. They did that by outlawing small groups and forcing Christians to start meeting as spectators in big programs in big buildings shaped like courthouses. We said that was the start of institutional Christianity, and we said during the past 1,700 years that institutional Christianity became today's traditional congregations.

That was the bad news. The good news is that we also said what to *do* about these problems. We said that the most logical solution is to return to some of the habits that made Christians Spiritual before the Roman emperors destroyed original Christianity. We called that "living the *Early Christian Lifestyle*." That solution can make Christians today as Spiritual as Christians were before the Roman emperors took over. So the purpose of this last chapter is to talk in greater detail about how to live the *Early Christian Lifestyle*. Let's start by seeing the *Master Principle* for living it.

The Master Principle

In earlier pages, we described the *Early Christian Lifestyle* in detail. We've diagrammed it and told stories about Christians who're living it. We described how it works, where it works, and when it works. So now it's time for practical application. Now it's time to implement that lifestyle. In the Preface of this book I said, "If we *do* what they did, we'll *have* what they had." That was a reference to the *Master Principle*. Now let's see it fully stated. Here it is:

If we DO everything Spiritual that the Early Christians did – and if we DON'T do anything unspiritual that they didn't do – we'll live the same supernatural lifestyle that they lived.

Read the principle again and think about what it's telling us. It's telling us that to live the supernatural lifestyle that the Early Christians lived, we need to change our personal behavior in two specific ways:

1. First, we need to start *doing* everything *Spiritual* (everything motivated by the Holy Spirit) that the Early Christians did.

2. Second, we need to *stop* doing everything *fleshy* (everything motivated by the selfish nature) that the Early Christians didn't do.

If we do both of these First Century behaviors, we'll have the same love, joy, peace, patience, miracles, and hope that the Early Christians had. Of course, the key to living these two behaviors is to be *Spirit-filled* – to have 51 percent or more of our mind flooded with the indwelling supernatural power of the Holy Spirit. Those are the "Rivers of Living Water" that Jesus promised Christians before He returned to heaven.

But now let's shift gears and talk about a *big* problem that we haven't mentioned yet in the book. We already know that our flesh doesn't let itself be pushed out of our minds without a fight. We already know there's a war between Spirit and flesh in us, and that our flesh is trying desperately to win that war. But none of that is the worst of it.

The big problem we haven't mentioned yet is that our flesh has *outside* help in its war against the Spirit. We need to talk about *the other* enemy that we face – one who's in an evil alliance with our flesh. His name is *Satan*.

The Kingdom of Satan

There's an old advertising rule that says never spend time and money advertising your competition. That's why companies don't show competitive products in their ads. That's also why I don't talk much about *Satan*. I don't like to spend time and money advertising the enemy. But we need to talk about him here in the last chapter. Here's why. One of Christianity's least understood – and least discussed – failures is that many Christians today don't believe in *Satan*.

I often say that the biggest trick Satan ever played on Christians was teaching them that he's not *real*. That accomplished two things for him. First, it leaves Christians with nobody to blame for their troubles but *God*. Second, it keeps Christians from *resisting* Satan because they don't think he's there to resist.

So let's clear the air. Let's be deathbed honest. Satan and his army of demons are *real*, and their mission on earth is to steal from Christians; to hurt Christians; and to destroy everything Christians try to do.[1] Think about those facts before reading on.

The Early Christian writers, such as John and Paul, boldly and openly taught about Satan. They called him the Devil; the Great

Dragon; the Old Serpent, and the Evil One.[2] The apostle John called him a Liar; the Father of Liars; a Murderer; the Accuser of Christians, and the Deceiver of the World.[3] Think about how much power those sinister titles give Satan. But the apostle Paul went even further. He called Satan the *god of this world*.[4]

That means, as far as our physical surroundings are concerned, we're living in *Satan's* kingdom – not God's. That explains why Christians have so much trouble. It's not God who's tempting them, discouraging them, robbing them, and making them miserable. It's Satan.

For that reason, it's wrong when a baby dies for Christians to say, "God, why did you take our baby?" Because God *didn't* take the baby. *Satan* did. Or when there's a car wreck, it's wrong for Christians to say, "If that's the kind of God you are, I don't want anything else to do with you!" But God *isn't* that kind of God. *Satan* is. Or when Christians take out an insurance policy, it's wrong for that policy to say tornadoes, earthquakes, and hurricanes are "acts of God." Because they're *not*. They're acts of *Satan*.

Summary: If we Christians are going to live like Early Christians in today's world, we need to be clear about which supernatural person is *for* us – and which supernatural person is *against* us. I used to have a friend who always said, "I give God all the *credit* and none of the *blame*." That's what all Christians need to be doing.

We also need to start doing something else. We also need to start aggressively *fighting* Satan. James, one of Jesus's half-brothers, told us how. He said the first thing we need to do is submit ourselves fully to God. Second, we need to start "resisting" Satan. The Greek word "resist" that James used means to *oppose* Satan, to *stand up to* him. James said if we do these things, Satan will "disappear" and leave us alone.[5]

Thus, one of the most important questions a Christian can ask is this: Exactly *how* do we oppose Satan? *How* do we stand up to him? The answer is inside us. It's not outside us in the physical world. We've been saying that for many pages. But let's tell a story now that puts the principle in a new light. Let's tell the story of the *white dog*.

The White Dog

Many years ago, someone told me this story. It's supposed to be based on a true incident.[6] I don't remember who told me the story, but it goes like this: A young missionary graduated from seminary and was assigned to work in a remote village of a third world country. Arriving at the village, the young missionary decided that the first thing he needed to do was get help from the most *Spiritual* person in the village.

The villagers told him that the *chief* was the most Spiritual person in the village, so the young missionary went to the chief's hut to ask for advice. After introductions, the missionary said, "Chief, everyone tells me that you're the most *Spiritual* person in the village. So let me ask you a question. How did you get so Spiritual?"

The chief was silent several minutes. Then he replied in a grave tone, "I have two big dogs inside me. One is white. The other is black. And they fight all day until one of them wins." Then the chief sat silently staring into space.

The young missionary was shocked. "Mercy!" he said. "I never heard such a thing! Which dog wins?"

The chief answered solemnly, "The one I *feed* the most."

The *white dog* in this story represents the inner motivation of the *Holy Spirit* within us. And the *black dog* represents the inner motivation of our *selfish nature* within us. All Christians want the

Holy Spirit (the "White Dog") to win their daily war with our flesh. All Christians want to be Spirit-filled, not flesh-filled.

But the story leaves one important question unanswered. How do we *feed* the White Dog? How do we increase Spiritual motivation and decrease fleshy motivation? Happily, the *Early Christian Lifestyle* we're discussing in this book does both things at once. That's how we *feed* the "White Dog" and *starve* the "black dog." So, as we continue our practical application, let's see four *habits* that enable us to live like First Century Christians.

The Four Habits of Early Christian Living

The *Early Christian Lifestyle* did three things for Christians in the First Century, and we need those three things today. Here's what that Early Christian living offers:

1. It increases Spiritual behavior.

2. It decreases fleshy behavior.

3. It resists Satan's influence.

Now, how does the *Early Christian Lifestyle* do these things? It does them because it's composed of four connected habits. Let's list the four *habits*, then talk about each one in turn. If we're going to live like First Century Christians, we must habitually:

1. Be Spirit-filled. That lets us *express* supernatural love, joy, peace, patience, and kindness, etc., in daily life.

2. Express Spiritual gifts *while* we're Spirit-filled. That lets us express Spiritual gifts *with* love, joy, peace, patience, kindness, etc., in daily life.

3. Shun evil. That lets us *avoid* Satan's temptations in daily life.

4. Be in a small group. That lets us grow *Spiritually* in daily life.

Now let's discuss each of these habits, starting with the habit of being *Spirit-filled*.

Christian Lifestyle Habit #1

The Habit of Being Spirit-Filled

Christianity is unique among the world's other 4,000 religions because it's built on a foundation of its members being *Spirit-filled*. No other religion is built on that foundation. That makes being Spirit-filled the most important habit that a Christian can have. If God only allowed us to have one of the four habits on our list, the one we should ask for is Spirit-filling. Why? Because *without* it, the other three habits are futile. Said another way, trying to express Spiritual gifts; and trying to shun evil; and trying to participate in a small group are futile if we're in the flesh.

Now since we discussed Spirit-filling in chapters 9 and 10, there's no need to repeat those discussions here. However, one thing we do need to remember is that the Early Christians called Spirit-filling by many different synonyms. Among other things, they called it: *being full of the Spirit; living according to the Spirit; behaving in the Spirit; being filled with the Spirit; and letting the word of Christ dwell in us richly.*

That fact proves that Spirit-filling was important to them. Another way we know it was important to them is that apostle Paul commanded us to "Be filled with the Spirit!" in the Greek *command* tense. That's why we said the goal of all Christians should be to pray as often as possible, "Fill me, Holy Spirit."

Being Spirit-filled is the hallmark of a *Spiritual* Christian. And being habitually Spirit-filled is the hallmark of a *mature* Christian.

All of Christianity's problems that we've talked about in this book stem from one root cause: Christians aren't *Spirit-filled*. Said in reverse, if more Christians were Spirit-filled, Christianity wouldn't have the problems it has today. Let's see an amusing but true image of that problem next.

The Gas Logs

My friend, Rev. John D. Shields, uses this image to explain how Spirit-filling works. He says that non-Christians are like the *gas logs* that many families have in their fireplaces. When a non-Christian is indwelled by the Holy Spirit and becomes a Christian, the indwelling Spirit becomes a "pilot light" inside him or her. So as an infant Christian, he or she has a tiny "flame" of Spiritual power burning inside – but it's not a blazing fire. Then, when a Christian prays to be *Spirit-filled*, the "pilot light" of the Holy Spirit ignites the "logs" of his or her mind, and his or her behavior blazes brightly with supernatural love, joy, peace, patience, and kindness.

I like that analogy. But several questions still remain: What makes the "pilot light" of the Holy Spirit *ignite* the "logs" of our mind? What *makes* us Spirit-filled? Also, how do we *know* when we're Spirit-filled?

How to be Spirit-Filled

Let's not make it too hard. To be Spirit-filled, all we need to do is to know it's *possible*; to know we *want* it; and then to *pray* to get it. Spirit-filling has to be that simple for two reasons:

1. First, many of the Early Christians were children, women, slaves, elderly, and other socially powerless people. Many couldn't even read or write. Yet *they* lived Spirit-filled lives. So Spirit-filling must be *simple* or the Early Christians couldn't have done it.

2. Second, Jesus promised that everyone who prays for Spirit-filling *will* be filled. We saw His promise earlier, but let's repeat it. Jesus said that if a child asks its father for an egg, the father won't give the child a scorpion, and so, "How much more will your Father in heaven give the *Holy Spirit* to those who ask Him?"[6]

Thus, every Christian who honestly and sincerely prays to be Spirit-filled *will* be Spirit-filled. If you're not praying daily to be Spirit-filled, please start it today.

How to Know You're Spirit-Filled

Our second question is even more interesting. We asked: How do we *know* when we're Spirit-filled? To answer our second question, we need to remember that Spirit-filling is a *special kind of behavior*. In chapter 9, we defined "behavior" as:

A physical response to a personal situation that was triggered by an inner motivator in a person.

In the case of Spirit-filling, the motivator we're talking about is the Holy Spirit within Christians; and the physical response we're talking about is an outer behavior of supernatural love, joy, peace, patience, and kindness. We saw an example of a Spirit-filled Christian response in chapter 11, with the "Fire Pit" story. We saw in that story the wonderful truth that when Christians are Spirit-filled, their supernatural responses are often automatic and unconscious.

Like the Spirit-filled Christian at the campsite in the "Fire Pit" story, we may not be fully aware of our supernatural behavior. We can have Spirit-filled responses to situations and not realize we're doing it. After all, the Holy Spirit is the greatest Gentleman in the universe. He's always loving, kind, and gentle. So when we're Spirit-filled, we have that *same* behavioral profile. We're loving, kind, and gentle too – even if it's an unconscious reflex.

Summary: The test of how much we're Spirit-filled is how *Spiritual* our responses are to daily situations. Are our responses loving, kind, and gentle? Are they hateful, unkind, and gruff? Are they somewhere in between?

Here's our final exam: If we slam a drawer on our finger – or if we break a glass of milk on the kitchen floor – what's our *automatic, unconscious* response? Do we smile, chuckle, and take care of the problem? Or do we frown, moan, and utter a swear word? If we're stuck in traffic, do we pray and hum a hymn? Or do we glare at the other drivers and curse them under our breath? If our superior asks us to work late, do we smile and say, "Sure." Or do we frown, sigh, and think, *Why me? I worked late last week! Why don't they ever ask somebody else?*

And ... if we failed that final exam, we need to start praying more consistently. Every time we think about it during the day, we need to close our eyes and pray, "Fill me, Holy Spirit."

Now let's turn to our second habit for Early Christian living. It's the habit of expressing *Spiritual gifts*.

Christian Lifestyle Habit #2

The Habit of Expressing Spiritual Gifts

Our second habit for Early Christian living is the habit of expressing *Spiritual gifts*. We talked about Spiritual gifts (visions, prophecies, healings, helps, encouraging, etc.) in chapter 12, so we won't repeat those facts. But we do need to remember that Spiritual gifts are extremely important to all Christians because they're the "tools" the Holy Spirit uses to guide, heal, and encourage us – personally and in small groups.

This means that every Christian needs to be ready, willing, and able to express Spiritual gifts every day and – more importantly – to express them while being *Spirit-filled*. As we know, the gifts should *only* be expressed with love, peace, patience, kindness. We said in chapter 12 that all Christians are commanded to "stir up" their gifts to *serve* other Christians. However, that service must *always* be done gift-wrapped in the "fruit" of the Spirit.

Another wonderful thing about expressing the gifts while we're *Spirit-filled* is that they're often "automatic" when we're *Spirit-filled*. Sometimes we're not aware we're expressing a gift when we're Spirit-filled. We saw an example of that in chapter 12, with "The Healing in the Hospital Room" story. When I drove to the hospital to visit "Charles" that day, I knew that when the visit was over I would pray for him, since I always pray for patients at the end of hospital visits. But I had no idea that the moment I entered his room God would express the part-time gifts of healings through me. My behavior was an unconscious Spiritual response, and I didn't even realize until later what I had done.

The point is, the *Holy Spirit* decides when and where we'll express gifts. We don't have to make the decisions. We don't have to sit at our breakfast table and make a list of when and where we'll express gifts that day. We *couldn't* do that anyway. Because we don't know what Christians we'll meet that day and what needs they'll have. Only the Holy Spirit knows those things.

But here's another wonderful fact to remember. Sometimes our gifts are meant for our own *private* benefit. For example, we can have a vision that reveals something about our personal life that only *we* are meant to know. I remember a case that happened to me three or four years ago. I was sitting on the side of the bed in a hotel room putting on my shoes. And as I was sitting with a shoe in my hand, the Holy Spirit gave me a beautiful vision telling me something about my life that He wanted me to know. I got up, went to my laptop, and made notes about the vision while it was happening. Those notes still inspire me today. But that Spiritual gift was meant only for me. I didn't receive it in a small group, and nobody else ever knew I received it.

Another example of a Spiritual gift that's meant only for our benefit is our personal, private gift of prayer languages. They're the only Spiritual gift that we control. All Christians have this gift within them at all times, and its only purpose is to increase their faith. So let's pause to talk about the private uses of personal *prayer languages*.

The Uses of Prayer Languages

The private gift of *prayer languages* is usually not the first Spiritual gift that Christians express. Nor is it a "sign" that Christians are Spirit-filled. Nor is it a "sign" that Christians are mature. Nor is it more important than any other gift. Nor is it a requirement for being saved. In fact, the gift of prayer languages only has one purpose: to build our faith.

As we've said, private, personal prayer languages are the only gift over which Christians have full control. They can start the gift and stop the gift anytime they want. Some Christians start using their prayer languages as children. And sadly, some Christians never start using them at all. So let's be careful in the next few paragraphs and be as honest about the subject as we can.

As explained in Chapter 12, I was fortunate with my own discovery of prayer languages. The first time I saw the gift, it was used in a gentle, tender, loving way by a pastor's wife sitting near me in a den. Because of that, the gift didn't bother me at all. I wasn't offended or confused by it. And to the contrary, I was touched by it, and the experience helped prepare me for my own experience a few days later.

But tragically, not every Christian is introduced to this amazing gift in a gentle, tender, loving way. Some Christians are exposed to it by Christians who're using it in the *flesh*, sometimes publicly, and sometimes with wailing, swaying, and dancing in the aisles. Worse, some Christians are exposed to the gift by *fleshy* Christians confronting them boldly and asking them whether they've received "tongues," and telling them that if they haven't, they "don't have the Spirit."

Such bold aggressiveness is impolite, inappropriate, and false. The most appalling thing about it is that it confuses Christians – with the result that they avoid the gift afterwards, losing the faith-building power that the gift could have given them.

But let's forgive and forget. Let's dismiss those negatives now, and turn instead to the *positives*. Let's turn to the surprising *benefits* that private, personal prayer languages give us.

The Benefits of Prayer Languages

At some point in their lives, many Christians wonder whether they really *are* Christians. They wonder whether they really *do* have an inner Spirit. And whether the Holy Spirit really *has* indwelled them. And whether their inner spirit has really *is* Spiritually awakened. And whether they really *do* have Spiritual gifts. Here's what these Christians are asking:

1. Do I *really* have an inner spirit?

2. Has the Holy Spirit *really* indwelled me and immersed my inner spirit in Spiritual power?

3. Has my inner spirit *really* been awakened to new Spiritual life as a second inner motivator within me?

4. Do I *really* have Spiritual gifts in me?

Now, how could the average Christian be expected to answer such deep questions? Happily, that's one of the benefits of personal prayer languages. That's one of the reasons prayer languages have such faith-building power. But – how do prayer languages give us those answers? The apostle Paul told us how. We quoted his teaching chapter 12. But let's review it now. Here's what Paul taught the Christian small groups in Corinth about the gift of personal prayer languages:

> "Christians who express the gift of *personal prayer languages* aren't speaking to other Christians. They're speaking to God, and their *inner spirits* are telling God intimate secrets that other people aren't meant to know. This *strengthens* Christians Spiritually. However, they don't understand what their *inner spirits* are telling God, because their inner spirits are bypassing their minds and speaking directly to God."[8]

As you can see, this teaching confirms all four of the questions we just asked. It confirms that we *do* have inner spirits. It confirms that we *have* been indwelled, and that our inner spirits *have* been baptized in power. It confirms that our inner spirits *are* awakened, and *are* acting as inner motivators. And it confirms that we *do* have Spiritual gifts within us because we're *using* one when we use our prayer languages.

These revelations are a supernatural miracle. But there's more. Paul told the Christian small groups in Rome that, due to the weakness of our human mind, we often don't *know* what to pray for. When that happens, the indwelling Holy Spirit intercedes for us with another miracle. He lets our inner spirit pray *directly* to God with all the prayers we didn't know how to pray. And He does that by using prayer languages, since they *bypass* our conscious minds.[9]

After all, our inner spirit doesn't have vocal cords, so it must use ours. It also must bypass our weak human mind – since our mind would *filter and distort* what our inner spirit was trying to pray to God. In addition, our spirit prays directly to God in some of the *7,000 languages* on earth that we don't personally know. That prevents us from knowing what our inner spirit is praying, and we can't filter and distort the prayer. (I've known Christians who spoke seven or eight languages fluently – but who never recognized what they were saying in their prayer languages.) These facts tell us that prayer languages are necessary for Christians. So let's talk about how Christians can start *using* them if they're not already doing so.

The Habit of Prayer Languages

The most common mistake Christians make when they start *using* their prayer languages is that they expect the languages to just "burst out" of them without any effort on their part. They sit silently and prayerfully, waiting for the languages to start. And when the languages *don't* start, they're disappointed, feel guilty, and stop trying. But waiting for the languages to burst out is illogical. None of us started speaking *English* that way. When we started speaking English as babies, we wanted to communicate with our parents, and so we activated our vocal cords and started trying to speak to them.

That same thing is true of prayer languages. We want to speak directly to God, and so we activate our vocal cords and start trying to speak to Him. We don't know what the "sounds" we're making mean. We just know they give us comfort and that we enjoy making them. But that was true of learning English too. When we were babies, we didn't know what our English "sounds" meant either.

Now – specifically *how* do we start using our prayer languages? As we know, the Holy Spirit doesn't overrides human will power, so we must *want* to use them; we must *decide* to use them, and then we must exert will power and *try* to use them. In chapter 12, I described my own first experience with prayer languages. I was sitting alone in my den in my bathrobe reading a book when I used them for the first time. I've known other Christians who used their prayer languages for the first time while driving their car. And while taking a shower. And while sitting on a dock. And while hiking in the woods. I even knew a choir leader who used his prayer languages for the first time by singing them.

So using prayer languages doesn't have to be in a church building, and a pastor, priest, elder, deacon, bishop, or other authority figure doesn't have to be present. Prayer languages are a calm, quiet, personal experience that can be used any time, any place, by any Christian.

But still – exactly *how* do we activate our vocal cords and start making sounds that aren't English sounds? Think about this. What if you wanted to mimic "speaking a foreign language." What would you do? Or what if you wanted to simulate "talking to a Slovakian." What would you do?

You'd activate your vocal cords and start making "sounds" (unknown words). But you'd make sure the sounds you were making weren't *English* sounds. That's how you start prayer languages. Without being shy, you just start making sounds. And immediately you get some surprises. You discover that the sounds you're making continue as long as you continue. They start when you start. They stop when you stop. You have no idea what they mean, but you can tell from the inflections, pauses, and rhythm that you're speaking real Spiritual messages directly to God in some of the earth's 7,000 languages.

And by the way, that's what the scientific studies have found over the years. Scientific studies have found that prayer languages really *are* languages. Languages from Arab dialects to Zulu dialects have been identified in laboratories when Christians used their prayer languages under test conditions.[10]

So let's close this section with two final questions: Can *all* Christians use their prayer languages? And *should* all Christians use their prayer languages? Let's once again let the apostle Paul give the answers. Here's what Paul said to the Christian small groups in Corinth:

"I want you *all* to speak in prayer languages."[11]

Next, continuing with our practical application, let's turn to the *third* way Christians can live with Spiritual power on a daily basis. This third habit helps us stop feeding the black dog and helps us avoid temptations during the day. It's the Early Christian habit of *shunning evil*.

Christian Lifestyle Habit #3

The Habit of Shunning Evil

Christians need a special *mindset* if they're going to stop "feeding the black dog," and if they're going to avoid Satan's seductive temptations. That special mindset is "automatic" if Christians are Spirit-filled. But whether or not they're Spirit-filled, *all* Christians need to have this mindset every day, even if they must activate it "manually" because they're infant or growing Christians. That special mindset is called *shunning evil*.

The word "shun" means to avoid something; to stay away from it; to abhor it. So the Early Christians had a two-word *motto* in their conversations and letters. They also used it when they met or left one another on the street. That motto was, "Shun Evil!" Early Christians didn't say, "Goodbye" the way we do today. They waved to one another and said, "*Shun Evil!*"

Other translations of the original Greek for this phrase can mean to *turn away* from evil, or to *avoid* evil.[12] The word "evil" means behavior that's morally or ethically wrong, or that's wicked, injurious, destructive, or harmful to Christians and other people.[13] Thus, this third habit is a habit of avoiding everything immoral, unethical, and wicked. That's our first line of defense against Satan and our flesh (which Satan likes to use as a tool against us).[14]

Christians are bombarded every minute of the day with the temptation to watch vulgar movies, TV, and Internet programs; to read lewd books and magazines; and to listen to risqué music, jokes, and conversations. Coworkers and friends are doing these things, and that negative peer pressure often *desensitizes* Christians until they're not aware of the vulgarity and sexual innuendos in their own thoughts, words, and deeds.

Exactly how does shunning work? It works best when Christians are Spirit-filled. Shunning is "automatic" when Christians are Spirit-filled. Spirit-filled Christians *can't* be rude, crude, vulgar, and fleshy – because the Holy Spirit *isn't* rude, crude, vulgar, or fleshy, and Spirit-filled Christians are filled with Him. The problem is that all Christians *aren't* Spirit-filled. So it's important for all Christians to start immediately forming the habit of shunning evil in all its forms and shapes.

Here's what to do. Shunning is a process of minute by minute, hour by hour, day by day *decision-making*. It's the choice of what radio stations we listen to in our car. It's the choice of what TV programs and websites we watch. It's the choice of what movies we attend. It's the choice of what books and magazines we read. And it's the choice of the friends and coworkers with whom we socialize. Here's the key question: Are our choices the ones the *Holy Spirit* wants us to make? Or, are our choices the ones that *Satan* and our *flesh* want us to make?

How can we tell the difference? We can tell the difference because the Holy Spirit always chooses friends, coworkers, hobbies, and entertainments that are *noble, pure, lovely, admirable, and worthy of praise*.[15] Satan and our flesh always choose the opposite. They always choose friends, coworkers, hobbies, and entertainments that are vulgar, pornographic, and filled with lowbrow humor, bathroom jokes, swearing, and sexual innuendo.

Happily, there *are* Christian radio stations, movies, TV programs, websites, books, magazines, friends, and coworkers available if we take the time and effort to look for them. But here's the principle: Most Christians would be shocked if someone invited them to a *Satanic* worship service. Yet many Christians happily patronize Satan-inspired radio, TV, movies, books, magazines, and websites.

Summary: Shunning is difficult at first. It takes courage and disciple to change old habits. But the Early Christians did it. That's why they were called "saints." And that's why today's Christians are supposed to be called *saints* too. Let's talk about that principle next.

The Christian Saints

We haven't said anything yet about the fact that all Christians were called "saints" in the early centuries. We don't hear much about Christians being *saints* today. But in Early Christian history, the word "saint" wasn't a special institutional title given to special dead Christians as a special honor. In First Century Greek, the word means *holy one*, and in the First Century the word referred to any Christian who was living a daily lifestyle that was pure, clean, modest, chaste, and separated from evil.[16]

Thus, all Christians (past, present, and future) are *saints*, and are supposed to be acting like it. Said another way, the word "saint" is a generic term for all Christians. That's why the apostle Paul opened many of his letters with the words, "To the *saints* at Rome …" (or at Ephesus, or whatever city he was writing).[17] Paul wasn't writing to *dead* Christians. He was writing to the *live* Christians in those cities. His assumption was that they were all living pure, clean, modest, chaste, lives that were separated from evil.

Of course, all of them *weren't* living that way. And all Christians *aren't* living that way today. But all Christians *should* live that way. And all Christians *can* live that way if they have the proper encouragement and stimulation. Well, where can Christians find that kind of encouragement and stimulation in today's world? That question opens the door to our final habit. Our last habit is one that gives Christians the strength to be saints. It's the habit of *small group worship*.

Christian Lifestyle Habit #4

The Habit of Small Group Worship

There are many old slogans to the effect that, "There's strength in numbers" ... "a cord of many strands can't be broken" ... "united we stand, divided we fall," and so on. These old slogans are true. They mean that a group has more power and influence than one person all *alone* has. The Early Christians understood that, and that's why they focused on *small group* worship. However, the Early Christians also understood that large, formal groups dissipate Spiritual power, and they wanted to retain Spiritual power. So they focused on *small, informal* groups from two to about a dozen or more participants.

In chapter 14, we discussed Christian small groups in detail. So in this chapter we'll only say that Christians can't live the *Early Christian Lifestyle* in all of its power and beauty without joining (or forming) a small worship group with the six-part structure that we discussed in chapter 14. That means regardless of whether you attend a traditional congregation; or whether you're a dropout from one; or whether you've never attended one – small group worship is still necessary for you to live a saintly lifestyle.

In other words, you need to find at least one other Christian who's like-minded about living a Spirit-filled life, and start meeting with that other Christian (or those other Christians) as often as possible – daily if that's feasible – and weekly at a minimum. That other Christian may be a coworker; a family member; a friend; or a member of a local Christian congregation. But if you're going to succeed, your meetings must be organized in the six-part Early Christian structure. As we saw in chapter 14, the most common organizational structure in Christianity today is the large, formal, *spectator* structure.

Less common (it's actually rare) is the small, informal, *participator* structure that the Early Christians used. The difference between the two is important. The *Early Christian Lifestyle* we're describing in this book *can't* be lived without the power of the six-part Early Christian group structure. But – *how* can you participate in a small group if you can't find one to join? Again, let's not make it too hard. You can easily form your own. Here's a true story that proves it.

The Car in the Parking Lot

I once knew two Christians who worked in a large office building and whose cars were parked outside the building. They decided that they wanted to form a small worship group, so instead of eating in the company cafeteria each day and talking business, they started bringing baggie lunches to work and spending their lunch hour in one of their cars: singing, praying, reading Scripture, and expressing gifts as the Spirit guided.

Thus, though there were only two of them, and though they only met in a car, their meetings fulfilled all six parts of the true small group structure. Their story also proves that small group worship can be simple, quick, and easy. It doesn't have to be hard, slow, and complicated. Also, as you might guess, after a few weeks of meeting in their car, the Spiritual impact the two Christians had began to simulate the other Christians in the building, and eventually their small group grew to about 15 participants meeting in a private room of the building.

That story also reminds us of yet another principle of living the Early Christian life. We haven't talked about this principle either, but here it is now: There's a special supernatural unity among Christians who're living with the four habits we're describing. The Early Christians called that special unity "fellowship." Let's talk about the supernatural unity of true Christian *fellowship* next.

The Supernatural Fellowship

The Early Christians had a special Greek word for the supernatural unity that exists between Spirit-filled Christians when they're together. In the Greek, that special word can be translated simply as *fellowship*. The problem with the English translation "fellowship" is that it's been watered down so much today that it's become trivial. For example, many Christians today think "fellowship" means a covered dish meal in the "fellowship hall" of a congregational building.

But to the Early Christians, "fellowship" meant a supernatural experience. The Greek word they used was *koinonia* ("coin-oh-knee'-ah"). To them, *koinonia* meant a miraculous experience of love, oneness, and caring between two or more Christians that only exists when they're Spirit-filled. It's another Christian principle that has to be experienced to be understood.

In the Introduction to this book, I told the story of a non-Christian who lived in Second Century Rome. He was watching a group of Early Christians behaving in the streets with amazement, and he turned to his friends and said:

"Look at them! They love one another almost before they know one another!"

That's what supernatural fellowship (and supernatural unity) looks like. People see it. People are amazed by it. People comment on it. And people want it. Jesus prophesied about that special fellowship before His crucifixion. At His last meal with His disciples, He predicted it with this prophecy:

> "By *this* all people will know that you're my disciples: If you have *love* for one another."[18]

True Christian fellowship consists of two or more Christians sharing a supernatural level of unity in a tangible, physical way. To understand that, it's important to know that the word "love" in Jesus's prophecy was a unique word. It wasn't used by any of the other religions in Jesus's day. In the original Greek, it meant a powerful *Spiritual* unity that only Christians can experience – and that unity is the foundation of Christian *fellowship*.[19] Real fellowship is Spiritual, and only Spiritual Christians can experience it.[20]

But let's go deeper. There's an old analogy about the supernatural Christian fellowship in a small group. It's called the *wagon wheel* analogy. Let's see it next.

The "Wagon Wheel" Analogy

Imagine an old-fashioned *wagon wheel* on a pioneer covered wagon. Imagine that the *rim* of the wheel represents a Christian small group. Then imagine that the *spokes* of the wheel represent the individual Christians in the group. Finally, imagine that the *hub* of the wheel represents the Holy Spirit.

Now, if you've ever noticed, the spokes of a wheel always slant *inward*. That is, as they move away from the rim and toward the hub, they get *closer* together. So here's the analogy: As the Christians in a small group become more and more Spiritual, they move closer and closer to the Holy Spirit. But at the same time, they're also moving closer and closer to one another.

Thus, the more Spiritual the Christians in a small group become, the more *unified* their fellowship becomes. Said another way, you can tell how Spiritual a Christian small group is by how warm, loving, caring, and physical their *unity* is. A few paragraphs back, we saw an example of that supernatural unity when we quoted the story of the non-Christian in Second Century Rome who said of the Christians in the street, "Look at them! They love one another almost before they know one another!"

That non-Christian was seeing real Christian unity (real Christian fellowship) being acted out on the streets of Rome. So here's the principle: When two or more Spirit-filled Christians meet – even if they're complete strangers – they sense one another's Spirituality and they have immediate supernatural unity. Let's illustrate that with the story of the "Holiday Inn Breakfast Hug."

The Holiday Inn Breakfast Hug

Once, when I was a management consultant, a client booked me in a Holiday Inn in upper New York state, and I checked in late one night. It was my first visit to this client's company because our contract had been negotiated over the phone. The vice president with whom I had negotiated had given me the description of a manager I was supposed to meet for breakfast the next morning, and that manager was going to be my contact during the contract.

So the next morning I rode down the elevator, walked to the breakfast room, and looked around. Soon I saw a man matching the description I had been given. He was sitting alone at a table, sipping coffee.

I approached this man's table and said, "Excuse me, are you Joe Adams?" (Not his real name.) He smiled and said he was. We shook hands and I pulled up a chair. As I poured myself a cup of coffee, "Joe" opened a black notebook and began to explain the day's plans and appointments. Nothing at all was said about religion, and we were focused entirely on the consulting project.

But after a minute or two, Joe's eyes widened. A look of pleasure spread over his face. He put down his coffee cup with a clatter and said in a surprised voice, "Why, you're a Christian, aren't you!"

"Yes, praise God," I answered, "I am."

Instantly and without conscious thought, we both jumped to our feet and began to embrace, laugh, and pound one another on the back. Tears came to our eyes and joy flooded over us. For several seconds we were unaware of our surroundings and of the curious eyes staring at us from other tables. After a minute or two, we regained our composure and sat down, wiping our eyes and laughing. As we continued breakfast, I learned that Joe was a Spirit-filled Christian who had a small worship group in his home every week. In the following months, I got to know Joe and his group well, and we had many wonderful hours of Spiritual fellowship together while I consulted with his company.

That kind of supernatural fellowship isn't unusual, and it shouldn't be. I could give a dozen examples of the same thing happening to me over the years in airports, hotels, restaurants, elevators, and other unexpected places. The lesson is this: There's a unity among Spirit-filled Christians that the Early Christians called *fellowship*. And that unity hasn't changed over the centuries. It's as real today as it was in the First Century. Spirit-filled Christians still recognize one another immediately, and still love one another unashamedly. In the original Greek, the word *koinonia*, loosely translated "fellowship," actually means to *participate* in the lives of other Christians by sharing behavior, gifts, and experiences with them Spiritually; and sharing time, talent, and treasure with them physically.[21]

That's why I always refer to the members of small groups as "participants." I do that because small group members are more than *spectators*. They're *participators* in one another's lives – both Spiritually and physically. I've known small groups that shared gardens, hobbies, sports, vacations, shopping trips, picnics, and about everything else with one another – in addition to being unified in their Spirit-filled worship sessions each week.

Summary: The four Christian Lifestyle habits we've discussed (being Spirit-filled; expressing Spiritual gifts; shunning evil, and worshiping in small groups) are the true Christian *culture*. They're the culture that Christians lived in the early centuries, and they're the culture that Christians can – and should – be living today.

But there's still one last part of small group meetings that we haven't covered. It's an important part, yet few Christians know anything about it. It's the surprising subject of full-time Christian *servants*.

The Full-Time Servants

As we near the end of the chapter, let's complete our practical application by talking about the fact that some Christians in every generation are *called* by the Holy Spirit to be full-time *servants* to the small groups in their areas. Some are even called to be full-time servants to Christian small groups worldwide.

However, these calls from the Spirit aren't status symbols or socially powerful roles. In the original Greek, the word "servant" refers to people who're table waiters, personal attendants, people who run errands, and all people who serve the public at the sacrifice of their own time, comfort, and pleasure.[22]

Also in the original Greek, the word "calls" refers to a set of supernatural roles in the Christian culture. There are *six* of these Spiritual servantships, and they were created by the Holy Spirit when Christianity was founded. Let's list these six calls. Then let's talk about them briefly. Here are the six supernatural calls to full-time Christian service:

1. Apostles.

2. Deacons.

3. Elders.

4. Evangelists.

5. Prophets.

6. Teachers.[23]

These six calls are still active today, and are still being administered by the Holy Spirit. They've never been revoked or withdrawn.[24] The problem is that their meanings were confused, diluted, and changed into status symbols by the Roman emperors in the Fourth Century. So today, the calls can only be seen in their confused and diluted forms, if they can be seen at all.

A good way to understand how these calls originally worked is to consider the apostle Paul's calls. We could consider Peter, or John, or Luke, or any of the other New Testament servants – since all of them had full-time calls to Christian service. But Paul was unique because he had a *triple* call. He had the calls of a prophet, a teacher, and an apostle as he traveled among the Christian small groups worldwide.

The fact that Paul had triple calls helps explain His incredible Spirituality. He's one of the best-known Christian servants in world history and wrote over half of the New Testament, as well as single-handedly spreading Christianity over much of the world. So let's use Paul as an example of how the Holy Spirit *calls* a Christian to full-time servantship.

As we read the record of one of Paul's calls, we need to remember that Paul's Jewish name was "Saul." So when the Bible is referring to Paul doing things among Jews, he's called "Saul," and that's his name in this passage. Here's what the record says about Paul's call to full-time servantship as an *apostle*:

> "In the Christian group at Antioch, Turkey there were *prophets* and *teachers*. Among them were Barnabas ... and *Saul* (Paul). While the group was serving the Lord and fasting, the Holy Spirit said, 'Set apart for me Barnabas and *Saul* for the work to which I've *called* them.' So, after the group had fasted and prayed, the group laid hands on the two and sent them off. The two, being sent by the Holy Spirit (as new *apostles*), went to the seaport of Seleucia and sailed for Cyprus."[25]

Notice several important principles in this fascinating record. Paul was *already* a prophet and a teacher when he received his third call to be an apostle. (We don't know when he received his first two calls.) This episode also shows that it's the *Holy Spirit* who calls Christians to full-time service (not other humans or institutions). This incident also reveals that local Christians on the ground who know the Christian must *recognize and approve* of his or her call. (Not societies, denominations, or institutions.) Finally, this record shows that it's the *Holy Spirit* who guides and directs the work of His servants. (Not human superiors.) Said another way, the calls to Christian service are *supernatural* from start to finish. Looked at in reverse, if a Christian truly has a call from the Holy Spirit, the local Christians on the scene recognize that, and the servant is openly guided by the supernatural power of the Holy Spirit.

Now – we know that all Christians have Spiritual gifts. But not all Christians have a supernatural call to full-time service. Also, like the Spiritual gifts, there's no rank order or hierarchical structure to the calls. The calls are equal in importance to the small groups who're receiving the benefits. Finally, some of the job titles used by today's traditional congregations (job titles such as "deacon," "elder," and "teacher," etc.) *sound* as if they might be some of the six supernatural calls from the Holy Spirit. But the actual *tasks* that these titles represent today are only diluted simulations of the original First Century calls.

For example, today's "missionaries" are simulations of First Century *apostles*. Today's "deacons" are simulations of First Century *deacons*. Today's "pastors" and "priests" are simulations of First Century *elders*. Billy Graham would be today's version of a First Century *evangelist*. And some of today's radio and TV "Bible teachers" are today's versions of First Century *teachers*. (Interestingly, we don't seem to have many Christians today filling the role of First Century *prophets*.)

What's also confusing is that today's traditional congregations have added dozens of new job titles to the original First Century list. Today's congregations have also added a hierarchical structure to their job titles that didn't exist in the First Century. Thus, today's congregations have youth pastors, associate pastors, visitation pastors, senior pastors, archdeacons, chaplains, district superintendents, bishops, archbishops, cardinals, and many other job titles that the Holy Spirit didn't create in the First Century.

It'd take another chapter (and maybe another book) to describe how these six supernatural calls to full-time Christian service worked in the First Century, and how they can – and should – still work today. For instance, as we know, every Christian family in the early centuries either hosted a small group in their home, or they attended one in a neighbor's home. So everyone in a Christian community knew where the small groups were meeting, and who was meeting in those small groups. Said another way, everybody knew everybody, so everybody knew everybody's qualifications. That made it easy for the full-time servant Christians to accept their calls, and to move quietly and confidently among the small groups to fulfill their duties.

But Christianity isn't structured that way today. Today it's divided into hundreds of highly compartmentalized and competitive denominations – and true small groups are rare to non-existent in today's society. Because of that, the supernatural calls to Christian servantship aren't understood, practiced, or appreciated now the way they were in the early centuries. But they *could* be, and *should* be. And perhaps someday they *will* be.

Now let's turn to our final issue: How can Early Christian living the way we've discussed it in this book be *applied* in today's Christianity? To answer that, let's talk about the *challenge* that today's pastors, priests, bishops, district superintendents, and other leaders face.

The Challenge to Today's Leaders

It's easy to see the *challenge* that today's Christian leaders face. Many are overworked, tired, discouraged, and confused. Attendance and income are *decreasing* in many congregations, and complaints and unrest are *increasing*. That's why many pastors, priests, and other leaders are leaving Christian work for secular jobs.

But on the other hand, national surveys show that 52 percent of the adult population is *still* affiliated with a Christian congregation – meaning that millions of people are still interested in Christianity and are still seeking Spiritual help. This means that if a pastor, priest, or other leader *wants* to stay on the job, and *wants* to work in a congregation that's growing in attendance, income, and Spirituality – there's still a chance to make that happen.

So specifically *what* should a pastor, priest, or other leader do? Once again, let's not make it hard. In chapter 6, we said that

"Recognizing a problem is half of its solution." And after reading this book, all pastors, priests, and other leaders see the *problem*: Christianity is declining. They also see the *cause*: Large, formal spectator-type worship *isn't* effective. They also see the *solution*: Small, informal, participator-type worship *is* effective.

The obvious implication is that we should *link* the two types of worship together without creating more confusion, frustration, or decline in our congregations. How can we do that? Let's close this chapter by talking about the *para-groups solution*.

The Para-Groups Solution

In First Century Greek, the word *para* refers to something that's beside you; or near you; or working parallel to you.[26] Thus, "para-groups" are systems in which one group operates beside, near, or parallel to, another group – so the two groups can interact, but aren't physically connected and continue to operate independently. In other words, the two groups cooperate and support one another – but in practical matters they operate separately.

That means a traditional congregation (let's call it the *first* group) can create a set of small groups (let's call them the *second* group) that operate parallel to it – yet they don't interfere with it, or vice versa. How would such a set of para-groups work? Here are ten *guidelines* for how traditional congregations can implement para-groups.

The Guidelines for Para-Groups

To implement the para-groups solution in a congregation, the following ten *guidelines* should be followed:

1. The creating of para-groups should be approved by the head pastor or priest, and also by the majority of the other congregational leaders.

2. The creating of para-groups should be approved by the majority of the congregation.

3. To gain these approvals, there should be open discussions of para-groups over a period of time – using books, classes, seminars, and videos, etc., followed by business meetings and congregational votes as required.

4. The goal of the para-groups should be for their participants to adopt the *Early Christian Lifestyle* as a way of life.

5. Participation in the para-groups should be voluntary. Participants should not be *assigned* to groups, and the Holy Spirit should be allowed to work out the details with each participant. Likewise, congregational members should have the freedom *not* to participate in para-groups if they choose not to participate.

6. The para-groups must be formed in the six-part Early Christian style described in chapter 14. They can't be formed as "holograms" of the parent congregation; and they must be completely free of supervision and control by the parent congregation.

7. The para-groups should be formed around host families and should meet in private homes where possible.

8. Pastors, priests, elders, deacons, bishops, and other congregational leaders must not participate in the para-groups as control figures who're present to supervise and keep order. Instead, leaders should participate as coequal participants in the para-groups, or not at all.

9. The participants in the para-groups must be open to expressing Spiritual behavior, Spiritual gifts, and Spiritual experiences.

10. Strife, resistance, and negative comments by some congregational members can be expected in the para-groups solution because *unspirituality* in congregations is the reason para-groups are needed in the first place. But such resistance must not be allowed to stop the solution – and obeying these guidelines can minimize such trouble.

Next, before we make some closing comments, let's summarize Chapter 16.

Summary of Chapter 16

1. In discussing the *Early Christian Lifestyle* we said, "If we do what they *did*, we'll have what they *had*." That was a reference to the Master Principle for Christian living. Fully stated, the Master Principle says:

   If we DO everything Spiritual that the Early Christians did – and if we DON'T do anything unspiritual that they didn't do – we'll live the same supernatural lifestyle that they lived.

2. The biggest trick Satan has played on Christians is telling them he's not *real*. But he *is* real, and his mission is to steal from Christians; to hurt Christians; and to destroy everything Christians try to do. But if Christians "resist" him (oppose him, stand up to him), Satan will flee.

3. In the "White Dog" story, the *white dog* represents the inner motivation of the Holy Spirit in Christians; and the *black dog* represents the inner motivation of the selfish nature. Every Christian wants the White Dog (the Holy Spirit) to win the inner war with the flesh, and the best way to make that happen is to "stop *feeding* the black dog."

4. Living the *Early Christian Lifestyle* is the best way to resist Satan and to avoid "feeding the black dog."

5. To live the *Early Christian Lifestyle*, Christians must:

   a) Be habitually Spirit-filled.

   b) Habitually express Spiritual gifts.

   c) Habitually shun evil.

   d) Be habitually active in a small worship group.

6. The purpose of the Spiritual gift of personal, private prayer languages is to build up a Christian's faith. Prayer languages are the only gift over which Christians have full control. The problem is that some Christians have been turned off by seeing other Christians use the gift in the *flesh*. However, we Christians must forgive and forget these negatives, and focus on the *positive* benefits that the gift gives us.

7. Shunning evil is "automatic" when a Christian is Spirit-filled. But since many Christians *aren't* Spirit-filled, all Christians need to "manually" implement the habit. Shunning evil means to avoid friends, coworkers, hobbies, and forms of entertainment that involve vulgarity, pornography, lowbrow humor, bathroom jokes, swearing, or sexual innuendo.

8. All Christians are *saints*. In the original Greek, the word means *holy ones* – referring to Spirit-filled Christians who aren't vulgar, rude, or crude. The word "saints" is a generic term for all Christians, and all Christians are expected to live lives that are separated from evil.

9. Spirit-filled Christians enjoy a supernatural unity called *fellowship*. This supernatural fellowship occurs when two or more Christians experience Spiritual *oneness*. Today, the word

"fellowship" has been watered down until it often only means a covered dish meal in a "fellowship hall." But true supernatural fellowship is one of the most precious benefits of being a Christian.

10. In the "Wagon Wheel" analogy of a *small group*, the rim of the wheel represents the small group. The spokes of the wheel represent the individual Christians in the group. And the hub of the wheel represents the Holy Spirit. As Christians move closer to the Holy Spirit (the hub) by becoming more Spiritual, they also move closer to one another. Thus, the more Spiritual a small group becomes, the more supernaturally unified its participants are.

11. There are six supernatural *calls* to be full-time Christian *servants*. They were created by the Holy Spirit when Christianity was founded, and they're still active today. The six calls are: apostle; deacon; elder; evangelist; prophet, and teacher. The calls were greatly diluted by the Roman emperors in the Fourth Century, and today those diluted versions can still be seen in the job titles of today's traditional congregations.

12. The challenge to today's Christian pastors, priests, and other leaders is that many of them are overworked, tired, discouraged, and confused. That explains why so many are leaving for secular jobs. But the majority of the population is still affiliated with a Christian congregation, and is still looking for Spiritual help. So there's hope for pastors, priests, and other leaders who want congregations that are growing in attendance, income, and Spiritually.

13. The solution for today's declining congregations is to create *para-groups*. The Greek word *para* refers to something that operates beside something else, or that's parallel to something else. So, a traditional congregation can create a set of small

groups that operate parallel to it, and the two groups can mutually support one another without interfering with one another. Ten *guidelines* for the para-groups solution are:

a) The para-groups must be approved by all congregational authorities.

b) The para-groups must be approved by the majority of the congregation.

c) There must be open discussion of the para-groups over time, with books and classes, etc., followed by meetings and votes as required.

d) The goal of para-groups is for their participants to adopt the *Early Christian Lifestyle* and to live Spirit-filled lives.

e) Participation in the para-groups must be voluntary. Participants must not be assigned, and members must be free to join whatever group they want, or not to participate at all if they want.

f) The para-groups must be formed as six-part Early Christian style small groups, and they must not be "holograms" of the parent congregation.

g) The para-groups should be formed around host families meeting in private homes where possible.

h) The congregational authorities must not participate in the para-groups as command and control figures, but as coequal participants.

i) The participants in the para-groups must be open to expressing Spiritual behavior, Spiritual gifts, and Spiritual experiences.

j) Strife and negative comments are to be expected in the congregation because *unspirituality* exists. But resistance must not stop the para-groups, and following these guidelines can minimize such troubles.

And now, some closing comments about all that we've said in this book.

The Glimpses of Heaven

In chapter 15, I told the story of the young woman who asked our group why people always wait until they die to experience heaven. She wanted to know why people don't experience some of heaven now, while they're still on earth.

I wrote this book in answer to that young woman's question. I wrote it to explain why Christians *aren't* glimpsing heaven; and how they can *start* glimpsing it. The Early Christians saw bits of heaven every day, and it gave them the Spirituality to turn the world upside down in 70 years.

So what *happened* to that amazing Spirituality? Where did it go? Nothing happened to it and it didn't go anywhere. It's available today just like it was in the First Century. Except that Christians aren't *experiencing* much of it these days – for all the reasons we've discussed in this book.

When I was young, there was a popular myth to the effect that people only used 10 percent of their *brainpower*. You've probably heard that old myth too. In recent years, lab tests have proved it to be false.[26] But I sometimes say that Christians only use 10 percent of their *Spiritual* power, and I suspect you agree after reading this book.

Christian Spirituality hasn't changed since Pentecost morning. The only thing that has changed is the way we *experience* it (or *don't* experience it) today. The informal, participator style small group worship of the early centuries is virtually extinct today. And in its place, we have the formal, spectator style large group worship of today's congregations.

But that doesn't have to stop us. If you and I want the same peace, patience, and miracles that the Early Christians had – we can have them. All we need to do is start living the way the Early Christians lived. As we've said, "If we *do* what they did, we'll *have* what they had."

The *Early Christian Lifestyle* that we've described in these pages is a glimpse of heaven on earth. The stories in these pages prove it. Starting with the story of "The Children Who Wanted a Dog" in the Preface, and going through the "Fire Pit" story and all the others, we've shown page by page that original Christianity is a *new way of living*. That's what the Early Christians called it, and that's what it is.[27] Christians who want Spiritual growth today (who want healings, peace, and miracles) simply need to return to the basics of Early Christian living.

What if it was *true* that we only use 10 percent of our Spiritual power? And what if we increased that power to 20 percent? Or 30 percent? Or 50 percent? How would our lives change? Would we see more visions? Would more angels minister to us? Would we have more healings? Would we have more answers to prayer?

The answers are "Yes."

How do I know that? I know it because all those things have happened to me, my friends, and the participants of small groups I've known. So as we come to the end of this book, I want *you* to experience those things too. I want *you* to have glimpses of heaven too. How can you do that? Just follow the plan spelled out in these pages. Find at least one other person who's as like-minded about living a Spirit-filled life as you are, and start worshiping with that person. Start developing the "Four Habits of Early Christian Living." And then give the Holy Spirit the time and freedom to work. Before long, you'll know what glimpsing heaven is like too.

So now our time together is over. But some shining day we'll meet again in our Father's heaven. Until that day, there's no better way to say goodbye than to say it with the prayer that Jude, one of Jesus's four half-brothers, prayed twenty centuries ago. Let's pray his prayer together as a close for this book:

> "To Him who is able to keep you from stumbling, and to present you before His glorious presence without fault and with great joy – to the only God, our Savior, be glory, majesty, power, and authority through Jesus Christ our Lord, before all ages, now, and forevermore. Amen."[29]

Appendix

Glossary

51 PERCENT RULE. A rule that says that when 51 percent (or more) of a Christian's mind is being motivated by the Holy Spirit, he or she is considered Spirit-filled. When this condition is a habit, a Christians is considered Spiritually mature.

AFTERGLOW. A time of relaxation and discussion (usually over refreshments or a meal) after small group worship.

APOSTLES. One of the six calls to full-time Christian service. The word "apostles" is from the Greek word *apostolos* ("uh-pah'-stuh-lahss"), referring to Christians who are sent out as messengers. Jesus sent out over 100 apostles, including both males and females. The role of apostles is to travel to areas where non-Christians live, to convert them to Christianity and start small groups with them.

ARAMAIC LANGUAGE. Aramaic ("air-uh-may'-ick") is a Semitic language spoken in daily conversation by Jews in the First Century. Jesus and His disciples, being from the province of Galilee, spoke Aramaic with a slurring accent that identified them as being from the Lake Galilee area. However, the disciples wrote in Greek, the national language of Israel at the time, and most of them also knew some Latin and Hebrew.

BAPTISM IN THE HOLY SPIRIT. The English word "baptism" is from the Greek noun *baptisma* ("bop'-teas-mah"), a household word in the First Century that meant to immerse something in another substance (water, oil, vinegar, etc.) until it was saturated and its basic nature was changed. An example would be immersing cucumbers in vinegar until they changed into pickles. In religious terms, being indwelled by the Holy Spirit and having one's inner spirit baptized (immersed) is the experience that creates a Christian. It can also be called: being saved, redeemed, converted, regenerated, born-again, and other such terms. It happened for the first time in history in Jerusalem, Israel at nine o'clock in the morning on The Lord's Day (the first day of the week), on May 30th, in the year 30 AD, the time and date that Christianity was founded. When a non-Christian is Spirit-baptized, his or her inner spirit is awakened to Spiritual life to act as a new motivator within him or her to counteract the negative drives of his or her selfish human nature.

BASILICA. The word "basilica" ("buh-sill'-uh-cuh") means a *royal court*, and is the Latin word for a First Century Roman courthouse. Basilicas were used in ancient Rome for royal events, military and government events, and for trials, executions, and funerals. Common people tended to avoid them. The Emperor Constantine built the first Christian "church" buildings ever built. He built them in Fourth Century Rome, and he chose the *basilica* design for them to intimidate the Early Christians and to suppress the free and informal Spiritual lifestyle that they had been living.

BEHAVIOR. "Behavior" is an outer response to a personal situation that is caused by an inner motivator. The Greek word for "behavior" is *peripateo* ("perri-pah-tay'-oh"). It literally means "to walk," but figuratively it means to conduct oneself a certain way or to act a special way. The Early Christians were recognized for their pure and holy behavior.

BEHAVING IN THE SPIRIT. To respond to daily situations while being motivated by the Holy Spirit.

BEHAVING IN DARKNESS. To respond to daily situations while being motivated by the selfish human nature (or by flesh).

BIBLE. An ancient collection of 66 manuscripts written by 40 different authors in three different languages on three different continents over a period of 1600 years. The word "Bible" comes from the Latin word *biblia* and the Greek word *biblos*, meaning a "book." Today's Bible is divided into the Old Testament and the New Testament. In the First Century, the Old Testament was a set of Greek scrolls kept in the Jewish synagogues and not readily available to the people.

These are the "Scriptures" that Jesus and His disciples often quoted. After Christianity was founded, the New Testament was written in the form of Greek scrolls by the Early Christians.

BODY OF CHRIST. The worldwide Christian group. All Christians are individual parts of the Body of Christ; all Christian small groups are small units of the Body of Christ; and Jesus is the Head (the leader, or guide) of all individual Christians and all small groups of Christians. Christians are commanded to do all the things that Jesus would do if He was still walking the earth.

BORN-AGAIN. One of several synonyms for being baptized in the Holy Spirit and becoming a Christian. The Greek phrase is *gennao anothen* ("geh-nah'-oh ahn'-oh-thin"), means "born from above," or "born from a higher place," referring to the Holy Spirit coming down from heaven to indwell a non-Christian and make him or her a Christian.

CALLS TO CHRISTIAN SERVICE. The Holy Spirit issues six supernatural calls to full-time service to certain selected Christians. The calls are: apostle; deacon; elder; evangelist; prophet, and teacher. Some Christians receive multiple calls. For example, Paul had triple calls as a teacher, prophet, and apostle. Today's institutional denominations use some of these words as job titles today, but the tasks they represent are not the same supernatural tasks that they were in the First Century.

CATACOMBS. The "catacombs" are underground Christian burial cemeteries in Rome, Italy. The word comes from the Latin word, *catacumbae*, an area outside of Rome where about 40 underground burial tunnels have been discovered that extend for miles under the earth. The tunnels were begun in the late First Century when Roman law forbade burial inside the city. The local soil is *tufo*, a soft volcanic dirt that is easy to dig and that hardens to stone when exposed to the air. The tunnels were not used for worship or for hiding places, but were simply underground tombs. They are valuable today for the Early Christian paintings, sculptures, carvings, and art objects found in them, since these reveal how the Early Christians thought, worked, and lived.

CHARISMATIC MOVEMENT. The Charismatic movement was founded by an Episcopal priest named Dennis J. Bennett in St. Mark's Episcopal Church in Van Nuys, California in April, 1960. Bennett announced from the pulpit that he had "received a personal Pentecost with the gift of speaking other languages," and an immediate uproar broke out in the congregation. Bennett resigned, his story made national headlines, and the Charismatic movement was born. Afterwards, Bennett traveled, spoke, and wrote books about his experiences for the rest of his life. The Charismatic movement was a form of Pentecostalism that invaded the mainline denominations, and in many ways it was an underground movement. Its biggest mistake was adopting the Pentecostal doctrines that Spiritual gifts are a "second" experience that comes "after" salvation; and that the Spiritual gift of speaking other languages is the "sign" that a Christian is Spirit-filled or Spiritually mature, since infant (immature) Christians can express the gift.

CHRISTIAN. A "Christian" is a person who has been indwelled by the Holy Spirit and has had his or her inner spirit baptized (immersed, saturated) by the Holy Spirit and Spiritually awakened to serve as a second motivator within him or her. Non-Christians have not had this experience, so Spirit-baptism is the difference between a Christian and a non-Christian. The word "Christian" was not the original term for Spirit-baptized people, who were originally known as *Followers of The Way*. The term "Christian" is an insult started by the non-Christians in Antioch, Turkey in 61 AD. Today, the word "Christian" is problematic since, as a religious title, it masks the fact that Spirit-baptized people should be known by their pure and Spiritual lifestyles.

CHRISTIAN SYMBOLS. The earliest known Christian symbols that have ever been found were found in the catacombs of Rome, and date from the late First Century. A few of these early symbols are a: fish; anchor; shepherd; lamb; boat; sparrow; dove; peacock; olive branch, and various Greek letters used as abbreviations for Christian ideas. Today's Christian cross, a symbol of the world's most horrible execution device, was not an original Christian symbol and was not found in the catacombs. It originated with the Roman Emperor Constantine in the Fourth Century.

CHRISTIANITY. A term for worldwide Christians, or the Body of Christ worldwide.

CHURCH. The non-Christian word "church" refers to any public building being used for any religious purpose by any religion, including the non-Christian religions. "Church" buildings, and the word "church," originated with the Roman emperor Constantine in the Fourth Century. He built the first "church" buildings, designed in the *basilica* (courthouse) style, and gave them the name "churches." Before the Fourth Century, Christians met in small groups in private homes and referred to these small groups as an *ekklesia* ("eh-clay-see'-uh"), the Greek word for a "group." Thus, the word "church," if it is used at all, should only be used to indicate a *building*, not Christians as people, or gatherings of Christian people.

CLERGY. The "clergy" (referring to pastors, priests, bishops, etc.) was founded by the Roman emperor Constantine in the Fourth Century. The word is from the Latin word *clerici*, the Latin word for *clerks*. Constantine founded the "clergy" when he founded institutional Christianity. He divided Early Christians into the "clergy" and the "laity," and then subdivided the "clergy" into deacons, priests, bishops, archbishops, cardinals, and many other job titles.

CONSTANTINE. A Fourth Century Roman emperor named *Flavius Valerius Constantinus*, called "Constantine" for short, the founder of institutional Christianity. He was an illegitimate child, an orphan, and was raised as a vicious combat soldier in the Roman army. He eventually became a power-mad dictator who murdered his own wife and son, as well as many relatives and political opponents. He was not a Christian, and was a priest in the sun god religion. He built the first "church" buildings in history and coined the word "churches" for them. His negative impact on Christianity was so immense that original Spiritual Christianity never fully recovered. Constantine has been whitewashed in history books, and is called "the first Christian emperor," and the "emperor who saved Christianity," etc. Because of that whitewashing, few Christians today know who he really was and what he really did.

DAY OF PENTECOST. "Pentecost" ("pin'-tuh-cost") is the name of an annual one-day wheat harvest festival that was held in Jerusalem, Israel on May the 30th, in the year 30 AD, the day Christianity was founded. Thus, May 30th each year is the *birthday* of Christianity. The Festival of Pentecost is celebrated fifty days after the Feast of the Passover in Israel. (The word "pentecost" comes from the Greek phrase *pentekoste hemera*, meaning "fifty days.") In 30 AD, the festival fell on the first day of the week, and at 9:00 o'clock that morning Jesus poured out the Holy Spirit from heaven in 120 of his disciples who were waiting for it in a house in Jerusalem. That was the founding of Christianity and was the first time the Holy Spirit had indwelled people, baptized their inner spirits with power, and awakened their inner spirits to Spiritual life as second inner motivators. Later that day, 3,000 festival pilgrims from all over the world were also baptized in the Spirit and made into Christians; after which they returned to their home countries, and worldwide Christianity was founded.

DEACONS. One of the six calls to full-time Christian service. The word "deacon" is from the Greek word *diakonos* ("dee-ah'-cuh-nahss"), which literally means "servants," in the sense of table waiters. Figuratively, the word refers to Christians who serve other Christians. So the work of a deacon is to care for needy Christians

– distributing money, food, and water to them and providing shelter for them.

DENOMINATION. The word "denomination" refers to a division in Christianity. It is from the Latin word, *denominare*, meaning to give something a name and to set it apart as something special, or something that is one-of-a-kind. Today's denominations are "named divisions" in Christianity. They originated during the Middle Ages when a group of protesting priests (Martin Luther, John Calvin, and others) resigned from the Roman Catholic Denomination – founded by Constantine in the Fourth Century – and then continued subdividing into smaller and smaller groups through doctrinal debates.

"DICTIONARY" FOR CHRISTIAN WORDS. The "dictionary" for the original meanings of today's Christian words is the set of surviving ancient letters written by the original Christians in the First and Second Centuries, since they best understood original Christian principles. There are 35 of these ancient Christian letters written between 45 AD and 156 AD. They were written in Greek, and 27 of them are readily available in the New Testament portion of the Bible. The other eight letters are available in bookstores, libraries, and online. Today, all Christian words should take their meanings from these ancient letters. Thus, Christian words that are *not* in these 35 ancient Christian letters should not be used. (For example, such words as "church," "denomination," "clergy," and "laity" are not in the ancient Christian letters.)

DISCIPLE. A "disciple" is a learner, student, or trainee. The word is from the Greek word *mathetes* ("mah-thay-tace'"). In the First Century, a disciple was a person being trained by a mentor. Jesus called His followers disciples, and after Christianity was founded, the term was applied to all Christians because all Christians are being trained in Spirituality by the Holy Spirit.

DIVISION. The word "division" (as in a "division" in a Christian group) is from the Greek word *schisma* ("cease'-mah"), meaning a faction, clique, schism, or split in a Christian group. The Early Christians condemned divisions in Christian groups as a sign of Spiritual immaturity.

DOCTRINAL DEBATE. "Doctrinal debate" (*do-you-believe-what-I-believe arguments*) is the source of most Christian divisiveness and the root of today's denominations. The Early Christians condemned doctrinal debate as a sign of Spiritual immaturity.

EARLY CHRISTIAN LIFESTYLE. The lifestyle of the original Christians – the original Followers of The Way – that was based on the habits of being Spirit-filled; expressing Spiritual gifts; shunning evil, and worshiping with Spirit-guided worship in like-minded, Spirit-filled small groups. This mode of Early Christian living can still be lived today by Christians who understand it and seek it.

ELDERS. One of the six calls to full-time Christian service issued by the Holy Spirit. The term "elders" is confusing today because there were *three* Greek words that referred to the "elders" of the First Century. However, all three referred to the same people in the same position. They merely describe it from three different viewpoints. The first word, *presbuteros* ("pres-boo'-teh-rahss"), described elders as *old men* because they were wise and Spiritually mature older men. The second word, *episkopos* ("eh-peas'-coh-pahss"), described elders as *guardians* because they were gatekeepers who guarded the small groups from "wolves" (false teachers). The third word, *poimen* ("poy-main'"), described elders as *herdsmen* or *shepherds*, because they were caretakers who cared for the physical and Spiritual needs of the small groups. Thus, "elders" were *one* position of servants who worked in co-equal teams among the small groups of their area. That is important because today's denominations often divide eldership into two or three different levels of "pastors," "priests," "bishops," and other job titles, creating unnecessary hierarchies. Indeed, entire separate denominations have been named after some of these words. The best proof that these three Greek words all refer to *one* position is in *First Peter*, chapter 5, verses 1-2, where Peter uses all three Greek words in one Scripture while discussing the position of "elder." The two verses need to be read in the original Greek to see all three words clearly. Finally, today's term, "pastors," did not exist in First Century Christianity. The word "pastors" was coined by the translators of the *King James Version* of the Bible in England in 1611 to translate the word *poimen* (shepherds, or herdsmen) in *Ephesians*, chapter 4, verse 11, into Elizabethan English. They did that to justify the role of institutional "pastors" in the Anglican denomination.

EMOTIONS. "Emotions" are a key to understanding the Christian lifestyle. Christians are motivated primarily by the *negative* emotions of their selfish natures; or primarily by the *positive* emotions of the indwelling Holy Spirit.

EVANGELISTS. One of the six calls to full-time Christian service issued by the Holy Spirit. The word "evangelists" is from the Greek *euaggelistes* ("you-ahn-gay-lee-<u>stayss</u>'"), meaning a person who comes with good news. Evangelists work among the small groups in an area to tell non-Christians the good news of Christianity and to convert them to Christianity.

EVIL. The word "evil" is from the Greek word *kakos* ("cah-<u>cahss</u>'"), referring to things that are morally and ethically bad, injurious, and destructive, to both Christians and non-Christians. The Early Christians taught that *evil* is produced not only by people's selfish human natures, but also by Satan and his demons, who use people's selfish natures as tools against them.

EXPERIENCE. Humans tend to believe what they have *experienced*, and to disbelieve what they have *not* experienced. For that reason, one key to Spiritual growth is that Christians must be open to, and to seek after, new Spiritual experiences with the Holy Spirit.

FAITH. The word "faith" comes from the word *pistis* ("<u>pis</u>'-tiss"), meaning to be persuaded or convinced of something, especially to be persuaded that God, Christ, and the Holy Spirit are real. The Early Christians taught that Christian faith is built by experiencing new and different supernatural experiences with the Holy Spirit.

FELLOWSHIP. The word "fellowship" is from the Greek word *koinonia* ("coin-oh-<u>knee</u>'-ah"), meaning to share Spiritual behavior, gifts, and experiences with other Christians, as well as sharing time, talent, and treasure with them. True fellowship is a supernatural *unity* of people that only occurs when Christians are Spirit-filled.

FLESH. The word "flesh" is from the Greek word *sarx* ("<u>sarx</u>'"), meaning "flesh" in the sense of the motivations of the selfish human nature in people. Flesh is the inner motivation to be proud, angry, selfish, critical, vulgar, slanderous, lustful, hateful, cruel, argumentative, fearful, and stubborn in both Christians and non-Christians.

FOLLOWER OF THE WAY. The phrase "Follower of The Way" is from the Greek phrase *kata hodos*, meaning to have a special or unusual behavior or lifestyle. "Followers of The Way" was the original name for Christians, indicating that they were a special people motivated by the Holy Spirit. Over 30 years after the movement was founded by Jesus in Jerusalem, the non-Christian citizens of the City of Antioch in Turkey began mocking the Followers of The Way by jeering at them, "*Christiani! Christiani!*" This jeer stuck, and eventually Followers of The Way became known worldwide as "Christians."

"FRUIT" OF THE SPIRIT. (See "Result of the Spirit")

GIFTS OF THE SPIRIT. The phrase "gifts of the Spirit" is from the Greek words, *charisma Pneuma*, meaning a divine favor from the Holy Spirit. The word *charisma* ("<u>harr</u>'-is-muh") comes from a Greek root meaning to be happy. The word *Pneuma* ("new'-mah") refers to the Holy Spirit. A Spiritual gift is a miraculous ability graciously expressed through a Christian by the indwelling Holy Spirit. Its purpose is to bring happiness and positive results to the Christian through whom it is expressed, and to the Christians receiving its benefits. There are an estimated 20 different gifts of the Spirit mentioned in the Old and New Testaments.

GOAL OF CHRISTIANS. The Early Christians taught that the goal of all Christians is to be habitually Spirit-filled – that is, to be Spiritually mature.

GREEK LANGUAGE. Alexander the Great of Greece conquered Israel in 332 BC, and made the Koine' Greek of his day the national language of Israel. Jesus's disciples wrote in Greek, and so the New Testament was written in Greek. That can be problematic today, since institutional translators have at times distorted the original meanings of some of the New Testament's Greek words to make them fit today's denominational doctrines. Koine' Greek is extinct today, and is nothing like the modern Greek spoken in the nation of Greece.

GROWING CHRISTIAN. A "growing Christian" is one who is pursuing the goal of being habitually Spirit-filled. A growing Christian's mind is a battleground between the motivation of his or her selfish nature and the motivation of the indwelling Holy Spirit.

HABIT. A repetitive behavior that is often unconscious. It takes 21 days to create a weak new habit. After 21 days, the new habit grows stronger each passing day. Christians are commanded to make Spirit-filling a daily habit.

HEALINGS. One of the best known and interesting of the Spiritual gifts the Holy Spirit expresses through Christians. The phrase "gifts of healings" is from the Greek words *charismata iamaton* ("cuh-ris'-muh-tuh i-am'-uh-toun"). Both words are plural, indicating that there are many different illnesses from many different causes, but that the Holy Spirit can heal them all.

HEART. The word "heart" is from the Greek word *kardia* ("car-dee'-ah"), literally meaning the human heart, but it is also a synonym for the human mind in Christian writing.

HOLY. The word "holy" is from the Greek word *hagios* ("hog'-ee-ahss"), meaning something or someone who is pure, chaste, modest, clean, and free from fault. *Hagios* can also be translated "saint."

HOLY SPIRIT. The term "Holy Spirit" is from the Greek words *Hagios Pneuma* ("hog'-ee-ahss new'-mah"), referring to the Third Person of the Trinity. Before Jesus returned to heaven, He promised that the Holy Spirit would come to earth and indwell people and make them Holy. That promise was fulfilled at 9:00 o'clock in the morning, on May 30th, in the year 30 AD, the morning of the annual one-day wheat festival known as the "Feast of Pentecost." Jesus poured out the Holy Spirit from heaven that morning in 3,120 family members, former disciples, and festival pilgrims, indwelling them and baptizing (immersing) their inner spirits in Spiritual Power. This event was the founding of (the birthday of) the Spiritual movement that today we know as Christianity; and being indwelled by and motivated by the Holy Spirit is the difference between a Christian and a non-Christian.

INFANT CHRISTIAN. An "infant" or "immature" Christian is one who is letting his or her selfish human nature be the main inner motivator of his or her outer behavior. Many Christians today are infants, which is why polls show that the average Christian today is no more Spiritual than a non-Christian.

JESUS. Also named Jesus the Christ, Jesus our Lord, Jesus the Son of God, Jesus the Messiah, and Jesus the second Person of the Trinity (as well as many other names). Jesus founded the Spiritual movement that today we call "Christianity" in Jerusalem, Israel at 9:00 o'clock in the morning on The Lord's Day (the first day of the week), on May 30th, in the year 30 AD. That was the morning of the annual one-day wheat harvest Festival of Pentecost, and

Jesus poured out the Holy Spirit from heaven and Spirit-baptized (immersed) the inner spirits of 120 of his family and former disciples, awakening their inner spirits to Spiritual life as new motivators within them. Later that day, 3,000 pilgrims in the streets were also Spirit-baptized, after which they left for their home countries, launching worldwide Christianity with 3,120 charter members.

LAITY. The word "laity" is from the Latin word *laici*, referring to non-professional, non-priestly people – that is, people who are not members of the "clergy." The Roman emperor Constantine divided Christianity into a "laity" and a "clergy" (*clerici*) in the Fourth Century, and Christianity is still divided into a laity and a clergy today.

LIFESTYLE. A "lifestyle" is a habitual way of behaving or living. The Early Christian lifestyle was a pure and Spiritual lifestyle called Following The Way. It was a lifestyle of peace, healings, miracles, and angels that changed the world Spiritually in only 70 years.

MASTER PRINCIPLE. A principle of Spiritual growth that says: *If we DO everything Spiritual that the Early Christians did – and if we DON'T do anything unspiritual that they didn't do – we'll live the same supernatural lifestyle that they lived.*

MATURE CHRISTIAN. A "mature" Christian is one who has made a habit of being Spirit-filled – meaning that the Holy Spirit is habitually motivating 51 percent (or more) of his or her mind.

MIND. The word "mind" is from the Greek word *nous* ("noose'") meaning the human mind. The Early Christians taught that the mind has three main abilities: It can understand things; make decisions, and exert will power. But they taught that it has no morals or ethics of its own. It simply responds to the inner motivators (good or bad) that motivate it.

MODEL FOR SPIRITUALITY. The model for Christian Spirituality today is the lifestyle that the Early Christians lived during the first three centuries of Christian history. Their habitual Spiritual behavior is the pattern for human Spirituality in every century. Today, the test of "Spirituality" for any Christian or Christian activity is how closely that Christian or activity matches the behavior of the Early Christians. Their model can also be called the *Early Christian Lifestyle* or Early Christian living.

MOTIVATION. The word "motivation" is from the Latin word *motus*, meaning "to move." So motivation refers to the inner motivators that move people to respond either positively or negatively to life's situations. That is, motivation is what creates human behavior. Non-Christians only have one inner motivator – their selfish human natures. Christians, who are indwelled by the Holy Spirit, have two inner motivators (their selfish human natures and the indwelling power of the Holy Spirit) that compete in an internal "war" for the domination of their behavior.

MOTIVATION OF DARKNESS. "Darkness" is a synonym for the inner motivation of the selfish human nature, or flesh, in people, both Christians and non-Christians.

MOTIVATION OF LIGHT. "Light" is a synonym for the inner motivation of the indwelling Holy Spirit in Christians. Non-Christians do not have this motivation.

MOTIVATOR. The word "motivator" is closely related to the words "motive" and "motivation," and is from the Latin word *motus*, meaning "to move." A motivator is an inner force that moves people to respond either positively or negatively to a situation. Non-Christians have one motivator: their human nature, which produces negative responses to situations. Christians have two motivators: their human nature; and then the indwelling Holy Spirit, which produces positive responses to situations. These two motivators struggle internally to dominate a Christian's behavior.

NATURAL PERSON. This is the term the Early Christians used

to refer to non-Christians. The word "natural" is from the Greek word *psuchikos* ("sue-hee-cahss'"), meaning a "natural person," or an unspiritual person, or a person who does not have the Holy Spirit. Thus, *psuchikos* refers to non-Christians because they are motivated completely by their inner flesh, or their "natural" desires.

NEW TESTAMENT. Twenty-seven Early Christian letters (or "books") that were inspired by the Holy Spirit and written in the Greek language between 45 AD and 90 AD. The purpose of the letters was to record the history of Jesus and the founding of Christianity, and to give advice and instructions to the Early Christian small groups.

OLD TESTAMENT. Thirty-nine ancient books inspired by the Holy Spirit and written by ancient Israelite authors in the Hebrew language between 1,450 BC and 400 BC. The purpose of these books was to record the history, poems, and prophecies of the Israelite people and their relationship to God.

PARA-GROUPS. The para-groups solution is a set of Spirit-filled Christian small groups that operate "beside" a parent congregation to support it Spiritually, but not to interfere with it operationally, or vice versa. The word "para" is from the Greek word *para* ("puh-rah'"), meaning something that works or operates beside, near, or parallel to, something else.

PAUL. Paul is one of the best known First Century Christian apostles, prophets, and teachers. He wrote over half of the New Testament and single-handedly spread Christianity around the world. He was Jewish, and his Jewish name was "Saul." But his Greek and Roman name was "Paul." He was from the tribe of Benjamin, and was a Roman citizen. He was born in Tarsus, Turkey in 1 AD. Later he moved to Jerusalem, Israel to complete his education. He also learned the trade of tent making. Eventually he became an educated, intelligent, and devout Pharisee, and a vicious persecutor of Christians until he himself became a Christian through a Spiritual experience while traveling from Jerusalem to Damascus. Paul had triple calls from the Holy Spirit as a prophet, teacher, and apostle. He was eventually imprisoned in Rome, Italy and was beheaded on the Ostian Highway, June 29, 67 AD by the Roman emperor Nero. Paul's remains lie under the altar of a basilica on the Ostian Highway outside of Rome. A marble slab covers his grave, placed there by Constantine in the Fourth Century. It has the Latin inscription: *Paulo Apostolo Mart*. This means, "Paul, the Martyred Apostle."

PEER PRESSURE. Peer group pressure is one of the most powerful influences on humans, and its influence is almost always negative. However, a Spirit-filled Christian small group can create positive peer group pressure on a Christian and produce Spiritual growth in him or her.

PENTECOSTAL MOVEMENT. The Pentecostal movement was founded by Charles Fox Parham in Topeka, Kansas in 1901 at his "Bethel Gospel School." The school only had 34 students and operated less than a year. On the night of December 31, 1900, the students held a New Year's Eve prayer service, and Parham prayed for them "to receive the end-times baptism" he had been teaching them, and that he had learned in a Christian commune in Shiloh, Maine the previous summer. During this service the students began expressing the personal and private Spiritual gift of speaking other languages, and the Pentecostal movement was born. Parham closed the school the spring of 1901 and went on the road as an itinerate preacher. His travels led to the "Azusa Street Revival" in Los Angeles in April, 1906; and by 1914, Pentecostal denominations were springing up across the country. The Spiritual gifts that Parham's students expressed at the school were valid. But their understanding of the gifts was innocently mistaken in several ways: Spiritual gifts are not a "second" experience that comes "after" salvation; and Spiritual gifts are not a "sign" that a Christian is either Spirit-filled or Spiritually mature.

PETER. Peter is one of the best known First Century Christian apostles and elders. He was one of Jesus's original 12 disciples, and later was a respected and long time elder in the small groups at Jerusalem. He was born as a Jew in the village of Bethsaida on the eastern shore of Lake Galilee; but later moved to Capernaum on the north-central shore. Peter's Jewish name was Simon bar Jona (meaning Simon, son of Jonas). Jesus later changed his name to "Peter," a Greek name that means a small stone. So Peter is known by several names in the New Testament. He is called "Peter," "Simon-Peter," and "Cephas" (Aramaic for Peter). The ruins of Peter's home still stand in ancient Capernaum today. About 60 AD, Peter traveled to Rome, where he visited Paul in prison. He was then arrested during the Christian persecution by the Roman emperor Nero during July, 64 AD. And later, on October 13, 64 AD, Nero had him crucified upside down in the circus (the race track) on the west side of the Tiber River at the foot of Vatican Hill. Peter's body was buried by the soldiers in an unmarked grave in a Roman graveyard on the slope of the hill, and for years his grave was a secret pilgrimage site for Christians. In the Fourth Century, the Roman emperor Constantine built a basilica over Peter's grave, and today his bones (which have been scientifically identified) lie in a small mausoleum 30 feet beneath the floor of *St. Peter's Basilica* in St. Peter's Square in Rome. Also, the prison in which Peter was held, and the chains which held him, can still be seen in Rome.

PROPHETS. One of the six calls to full-time Christian service issued by the Holy Spirit. The word "prophets" is from the Greek word *prophetes* ("prah-faye'-tace"), meaning persons who speak messages from God. The original Greek word means "to say before," "to foretell," or "to predict." Thus, prophets reveal things that are going to happen before they actually occur.

RESULT OF THE SPIRIT. The term the *result* of the Spirit (or the "fruit" of the Spirit) is from the Greek phrase *karpos tou Pneuma* ("car-pahss' touw' new'-mah"), referring to the effect of – or the result of – or the product of – being motivated internally by the Holy Spirit. The result of Spiritual motivation is the *positive* emotions of love, joy, peace, patience, gentleness, kindness, and a dozen more such positive emotions, which in turn become outer behaviors. Some Christians call these behaviors the "fruit" of the Spirit because the *King James Version* of the Bible translated the Greek word *karpos* that way in England in 1611.

SAINT. A synonym for a Christian, more specifically, a synonym for a Spiritual Christian. The word "saint" is from the Greek word *hagios* ("hog'-ee-ahss"), meaning "holy one."

SAVED. A synonym for being baptized in the Holy Spirit and becoming a Christian. The word "saved" is from the Greek word *sozo* ("sowed'-zoh"), meaning to rescue someone from destruction. (Also see "Born-Again.")

SHUN EVIL. An Early Christian motto used in conversation and letters. The Greek words can be translated: *Avoid evil*! Or *Stay away from evil*! Christians are mandated to avoid all forms of profanity, lewdness, vulgarity, pornography, rudeness, crudity, sexual innuendo, and everything risqué or off-color.

SIN. A synonym for unspiritual or negative behavior. The word "sin" is from the Greek word *hamartia* ("hah-mar-tea'-ah"), meaning a fault, failure, or guilty deed. So sin is any thought, word, or deed that is motivated by the selfish human nature (flesh) and/or inspired or stimulated by Satan.

SOUL. A synonym for the inner spirit in humans. The word "soul" is from the Greek word *psuche* ("sue-hay'"), meaning the invisible, immortal part of humans that gives them life on earth, and that at death returns to God for judgment or rewards.

SMALL GROUPS. The Early Christians met informally in small groups in private homes for the first three centuries of Christian history (about the first eight generations of Early Christians). The groups were usually built around one or two families, with friends, neighbors, and visitors joining in. Group sizes ranged from two to a dozen or more people. Worship in these groups was guided by the Holy Spirit, and the groups were the key to the Spirituality of the Early Christians. Tragically, the Roman emperors in the Fourth Century outlawed small groups and forced Christians to start attending large programs in large groups in large buildings designed like courthouses. Today, Early Christian style small groups can still be formed by like-minded Spirit-filled Christians who have the goal of growing Spiritually together.

SMALL GROUP PARTS. A true Christian small group has six parts: Two to twelve or more like-minded and Spirit-filled Christians must gather; the interactions must be face-to-face; the interactions must be two-way; the gatherings must be frequent; the gatherings must be over an extended period of time, and the gatherings must allow the Spiritual behavior, gifts, and experiences to be expressed.

SMALL GROUP TYPES. The three types of Christian small groups are: Social; teaching; and worship. The worship type group is the most Spiritual. In practice, small groups can change types during the same meeting as needs change. For example, a *worship* group can change to a *social* group when worship is over and refreshments are served.

SPEAKING OTHER LANGUAGES. One of the most frequent and beneficial of the Spiritual gifts. (Also known as using prayer languages, and praying in the Spirit.) The name of this gift comes from the Greek words *laleo heteros glossa* ("lah-lay'-oh hea'-tuh-rahss glow'-suh"), which translate as, "to speak other languages," and means to speak fluently in languages other than any a Christian can normally speak. This gift was expressed for the first time by 120 of Jesus's family members and former disciples on Pentecost morning in Jerusalem on May 30th, in 30 AD. The gift is expressed today by Christians in two ways: *privately and personally* to edify themselves; and *publicly* to edify groups. When the latter happens, either the speaker or another Christian must translate the message. In England in 1611, the translators of the *King James Version* Bible mistakenly translated the words *laleo heteros glossa* to read, "to speak with other tongues." That is problematic for today's Christians, since those odd Medieval words make the gift seem strange and something to be avoided. The gift of prayer languages should always be expressed while Christians are Spirit-filled, so that it is expressed with love, peace, patience, and kindness.

SPIRIT. The word for the inner human "spirit" (lower case) is the word *pneuma* ("new'-mah," lower case), meaning "spirit" and referring to the invisible, immortal spirit within humans. It is also known as the soul. The spirit came from God, is created in God's image, gives life to humans, and returns to God at death for judgment or rewards. In non-Christians, the inner spirit is spiritually dead and has no ability to motivate the person for good behavior. When a non-Christian is baptized in the Holy Spirit and becomes a Christian, his or her inner spirit is awakened to Spiritual life and becomes a new second inner motivator that produces Spiritual behavior.

SPIRIT-FILLED. The term "Spirit-filled" is from the Greek words *Pneuma pimplemi* ("new'-mah pim'-play-me"), meaning to be temporarily filled for a specific purpose. A Christian is Spirit-filled when the Holy Spirit is motivating 51 percent (or more) of his or her mind, producing love, joy, peace, and patience in his or her outer behavior. When this condition becomes a habit, the Christian is considered Spiritually mature.

SPIRITUAL. The word "Spiritual" (capitalized) is from the Greek word *Pneumatikos* ("new-mah-tea-cahss'"), meaning "Spiritual," and referring to the motivation of the Holy Spirit within Christians. The word originates from the Greek *Pneuma*, referring to the Holy Spirit, part of the Trinity of God, and so it is capitalized. The word Spiritual appears in Early Christian writing only *after* the Day of Pentecost, since humans could not *be* Spiritual until Christianity was founded.

SPIRITUAL GROWTH. The process of positive behavioral change in which Christians are motivated more and more by the Holy Spirit for longer and longer periods of time, with the goal of being habitually Spirit-filled. All Christians are originally "infants," and are motivated mostly by their flesh when first indwelled. They remain infants until they earnestly seek Spiritual growth.

SPIRITUAL HUNGER. The Holy Spirit never overrides human will power. Thus, Christians remain infants and continue to be dominated by their selfish human natures until they become hungry enough to aggressively seek Spiritual growth.

SPIRITUAL UNDERSTANDING. Spiritual matters can only be *Spiritually* understood. Thus, non-Christians cannot understand Spiritual matters at all; and Christians can only understand Spiritual matters to the extent that they are motivated by the indwelling Holy Spirit. Thus, Spirit-filled Christians have the most Spiritual understanding of all. The apostle Paul stated this principle in *First Corinthians*, chapter 2, verses 14-15.

TEACHER. One of the six calls to full-time Christian service. The word "teacher" is from the Greek word *didaskalos* ("di-dah'-scuh-lahss"), meaning to hold discussions with people and to instruct them in a discussion format.

THE LORD'S DAY. The Early Christians called the first day of the week "The Lord's Day" because it is the day that Jesus rose from the dead, and also the day that the Holy Spirit came down from heaven on Pentecost morning to establish Christianity. In the Fourth Century, the Roman emperor Constantine renamed The Lord's Day the "*Venerable Day of the Sun*," meaning the day to worship the Roman sun god. Over the centuries this phrase was shorted to today's term, "Sunday."

THE LORD'S SUPPER. A symbolic ceremony in which Christians eat a piece of bread (sometimes unleavened) and drink a sip of wine (sometimes a fruit juice substitute) to demonstrate to friends and family that they are Christians and are grateful for what Jesus has done for them. Today the ceremony is also called "communion," the "eucharist," or "mass" by various denominations. Jesus started this ceremony following His last meal with His disciples before He was arrested, and thus the name, *The Lord's Supper*. The ceremony is not a requirement to be saved, and bread and wine have no Spiritual effect. However, for Christians who want to voluntarily participate in the ceremony, it can be a moving experience.

THE WAY. The Early Christians were originally known as "Followers of The Way" because of their Spiritual lifestyle. The words "The Way" are from the Greek phrase *kata hodos* ("cuh-<u>tah</u>' haa-<u>dahss</u>'"), meaning to have a special or unusual behavior or lifestyle. Later, the non-Christians in the city of Antioch, Turkey renamed the Followers of The Way "Christians."

TWO WAYS. The Early Christians taught that all Christians can have *two* different outer behaviors because they have *two* different inner *motivators* within them. The first outer behavior can be a positive one of "Light" (one of purity and Spirituality) motivated by the indwelling Holy Spirit. The second outer behavior can be a negative one of Darkness (one of impurity and unspirituality) motivated by the inner selfish nature. These two inner motivators in Christians are at constant "war" with one another to dominate a Christian's outer behavior.

UNKNOWN LETTERS. A collection of First and Second Century Christian letters that were not included in today's New Testament, but were considered inspired by the Early Christians. These include the letters of: *Barnabas, Clement, Didache, Diognetus, Hermas, Ignatius, Papias,* and *Polycarp,* all written between 90 AD and 156 AD. The unknown letters are very useful to fill in missing facts on how the Early Christians, lived, thought, worked, and died.

VISION. One of the Spiritual gifts expressed through Christians by the Holy Spirit. The word "vision" is from the Greek word *horama* ("har'-um-ah"), meaning a scene that is supernaturally granted by God, or a supernatural spectacle seen with the eyes, and sometimes in a dream.

WATER-BAPTISM. A symbolic ceremony in which Christians immerse themselves in water to demonstrate to friends and family that they have been indwelled by the Holy Spirit, and that their inner spirits baptized (immersed) in the power of the Holy Spirit. In the First Century, only adults and older children were water-baptized, since they are the only ones who can make an informed decision to become a Christian. Water-baptism is not a requirement to be saved, and water has no Spiritual effect. However, for Christians who want to voluntarily participate in the ceremony, it can be a moving experience.

WAGON WHEEL ANALOGY. An analogy of how a Christian *fellowship* works. The rim of the wheel represents the small group. The spokes of the wheel represent the individual Christians in the group. The hub of the wheel represents the Holy Spirit. Since the spokes of a wheel draw closer together as they move from the rim to the hub, as Christians become more Spiritual by moving closer to the Holy Spirit, they also become closer together. The principle is that a Spirit-filled small group has a supernatural *oneness* that no other group can match.

WHITE DOG / BLACK DOG. A traditional story about Christian Spiritual growth. The story concerns a village chieftain who tells a young missionary that the key to Spirituality is to "feed the white dog" (the indwelling Holy Spirit), instead of "feeding the black dog" (the selfish human nature).

WILL POWER. Will power is one of the three abilities of the human mind, and the indwelling Holy Spirit never overrules it. Thus,

Christians must consciously yield to the indwelling Holy Spirit to have Spiritual behavior, gifts, and experiences.

WORSHIP. The Greek word for Christian "worship" comes from the Greek word *proskuneo* ("prahss-coo-nay'-oh"), referring to a "dog" in the sense of a loving pet kissing its master's face and lying at its master's feet. True and free Christian worship is therefore an attitude of total submission and reverence toward God while being guided by the indwelling Holy Spirit, usually during Spirit-filled small group worship.

Early Christian Letters

(In Chronological Order)

1. "JAMES." (45 AD) A letter written by the Christian apostle James, addressed to worldwide Christians. James, one of Jesus's younger half-brothers, wrote the letter from Jerusalem, Israel. This is the earliest known Christian letter ever discovered.

2. "GALATIANS." (49 AD) A letter written by the Christian apostle, prophet, and teacher, Paul, and addressed to the Christians in the province of Galatia, Turkey. Paul wrote the letter from Antioch, Turkey. This is the first letter known written by Paul. He was not one of Jesus's original twelve disciples, so he never met Jesus physically. However, Paul had an incredible supernatural experience while traveling on the road to Damascus, Syria, during which he met Jesus in a vision. Afterwards, he became a Christian and one of early Christianity's leading apostles, prophets, and teachers who wrote over half of the New Testament letters.

3. "MARK." (50 AD) A record of the life of Jesus written by John Mark, one of the original twelve apostles, and addressed to non-Jewish and Roman Christians worldwide. John Mark was the son of a wealthy Jewish mother who lived in Jerusalem, and was a close friend of the apostles Paul, Peter, and Barnabas. John Mark wrote this record from Jerusalem, Israel.

4. "FIRST THESSALONIANS." (51 AD) A letter written by the Christian apostle, prophet, and teacher, Paul, and addressed to the Christians in the port city of Thessalonica, Greece. Paul wrote the letter from Corinth, Greece.

5. "SECOND THESSALONIANS." (51 AD) A letter written by the Christian apostle, prophet, and teacher, Paul, and addressed to the Christians in the port city of Thessalonica, Greece. Paul wrote the letter from Corinth, Greece.

6. "FIRST CORINTHIANS." (56 AD) A letter written by the Christian apostle, prophet, and teacher, Paul, and addressed to the Christians in the port city of Corinth, Greece. Paul wrote the letter from Ephesus, Turkey.

7. "SECOND CORINTHIANS." (57 AD) A letter written by the Christian apostle, prophet, and teacher, Paul, and addressed to the Christians in the port city of Corinth, Greece. Paul wrote the letter from Macedonia, Greece.

8. "ROMANS." (58 AD) A letter written by the Christian apostle, prophet, and teacher, Paul, and addressed to the Christians in Rome, Italy. Paul wrote the letter from the port city of Corinth, Greece.

9. "MATTHEW." (60 AD) A record of the life of Jesus written by Matthew, one of the original twelve apostles, and addressed to Jewish Christians worldwide. Matthew had been a tax collector for the occupying Roman government of Israel, and had been hated by his fellow Jews. He gave up tax collecting to follow Jesus, and later became an apostle. Matthew wrote this record from Jerusalem, Israel.

10. "LUKE." (60 AD) A record of the life of Jesus written by the apostle Luke. (Known as Dr. *Loukas* in Greek, and Dr. *Lucas* in Latin.) Luke was a medical doctor and was not one of the original twelve apostles, so he never physically met Jesus. This letter was addressed to non-Jewish Christians worldwide. Luke himself was Greek, and was the only non-Jew to write part of the New Testament. Luke was a close friend of the apostle Paul, and was with Paul when he was executed in Rome. Luke wrote this record from Caesarea, Israel. Later, Luke also wrote the record called "Acts."

11. "EPHESIANS." (61 AD) A letter written by the Christian apostle, prophet, and teacher, Paul, and addressed to the Christians in Ephesus, Turkey. Paul wrote the letter from prison in Rome, Italy.

12. "PHILIPPIANS." (61 AD) A letter written by the Christian apostle, prophet, and teacher, Paul, and addressed to the Christians in Philippi, Greece. Paul wrote the letter from prison in Rome, Italy.

13. "COLOSSIANS." (61 AD) A letter written by the Christian apostle, prophet, and teacher, Paul, and addressed to the Christians in Colossae, Turkey. Paul wrote the letter from prison in Rome, Italy.

14. "ACTS." (61 AD) A historical record of early Christianity written by the Christian apostle and medical doctor, Luke. (Known as Dr. *Loukas'* in Greek, and Dr. *Lucas* in Latin.) Luke was a medical doctor, and was not one of Jesus's twelve original disciples so he never physically met Jesus. The letter was addressed to worldwide Christians, and Luke wrote it from Rome, Italy while visiting the apostle Paul in prison. Luke was a close friend of the apostle Paul, and was with Paul when he was executed in Rome. Luke also wrote the earlier record of Jesus's life called the gospel of "Luke."

15. "PHILEMON." (61 AD, "phi-lee'-mon.") A letter written by the Christian apostle, prophet, and teacher, Paul, and addressed to a Christian named Philemon, who was a Christian slave owner living in Colossae, Turkey. Paul wrote the letter from prison in Rome, Italy.

16. "FIRST TIMOTHY." (63 AD) A letter written by the Christian apostle, prophet, and teacher, Paul, and addressed to a Christian evangelist named Timothy in Ephesus, Turkey. Paul had been temporarily released from prison at this time, and wrote this letter from Macedonia, Greece.

17. "FIRST PETER." (63 AD) A letter written by the Christian apostle and elder, Peter, and addressed to worldwide Christians. Peter was one of Jesus's original twelve disciples. He was from Bethsaida, Israel, a small fishing village on the shores of Lake Galilee, and he owned a prosperous fishing business with four of Jesus's other original disciples – Andrew, James, John, and Philip. Peter wrote this letter from Rome, Italy, where he was visiting Paul in prison, and teaching in the busy Christian community in Rome.

18. "SECOND PETER." (64 AD) A letter written by the Christian apostle and elder, Peter, and addressed to worldwide Christians. Peter wrote this letter from Rome, Italy. It is Peter's last known letter because he was arrested in a citywide persecution of Christians started by the Roman Emperor Nero in July, 64 AD. Nero had crucified Peter upside down in a racetrack in western Rome on October 14, 64 AD. Peter was buried in an unmarked grave in a cemetery on the slopes of Vatican Hill. His grave eventually became a pilgrimage site for Christians and, in the Fourth Century, the Roman Emperor Constantine bought the cemetery and built a basilica (a large church building) over Peter's grave. That basilica still stands in Rome today, known as "St. Peter's Basilica." Peter's gave is still accessible to the public by special appointment from the Vatican. It is thirty feet below the floor level of the basilica.

19. "TITUS." (65 AD) A letter written by the Christian apostle, prophet, and teacher, Paul, and addressed to a Christian elder named Titus in Crete, Greece. Paul wrote the letter from Macedonia, Greece.

20. "SECOND TIMOTHY." (66 AD) A letter written by the Christian apostle, prophet, and teacher, Paul, and addressed to a Christian evangelist named Timothy in Ephesus, Turkey. Paul had been arrested for the second time at this point, and wrote this letter from prison in Rome, Italy where he was about to be executed. This is Paul's last known letter. He was martyred by the Emperor Nero outside of Rome on June 29, 67 AD. Paul was beheaded in

a meadow near the third milestone of the Ostian Highway in southeast Rome. The place where he was beheaded is now the site of the Tre Fontane monastery. Paul was buried nearby in the family cemetery of a local Christian family. Then, in the Fourth Century, the Roman Emperor Constantine bought the cemetery, and built a basilica (a large church building) over Paul's grave. That basilica stands in Rome today, and Paul's tomb can be viewed by the public.

21. "HEBREWS." (68 AD) A letter written by an unknown Christian apostle, and addressed to the Jewish Christians in Italy. Where the letter was written is also unknown. Some researchers claim that the apostle Paul wrote this letter. However, since Paul was beheaded in Rome a year before this letter was written, that is doubtful.

22. "JUDE." (70 AD) A letter written by the Christian apostle Jude, one of Jesus's younger half-brothers, and addressed to worldwide Christians. Jude wrote the letter from Jerusalem, Israel.

23. "JOHN." (70 AD) A record of the life of Jesus written by the Christian apostle John, and addressed to worldwide Christians. John was one of Jesus's original twelve disciples and was from Bethsaida, Israel, a small fishing village on the shores of Lake Galilee. His well-to-do parents were named Zebedee and Salome and they owned a fishing business. John was called "a son of thunder" because of his father's emotional personality. John wrote this record from Jerusalem, Israel.

24. "FIRST JOHN." (90 AD) A letter written by the Christian apostle John, and addressed to the Christians in Asia Minor. John wrote the letter from Ephesus, Turkey.

25. "SECOND JOHN." (90 AD) A letter written by the Christian apostle John, and addressed to an unnamed Christian woman and her children. John wrote the letter from Ephesus, Turkey.

26. "THIRD JOHN." (90 AD) A letter written by the Christian apostle John, and addressed to a Christian elder somewhere in Asia Minor. John wrote the letter from Ephesus, Turkey.

27. "REVELATION." (90 AD) A vision written down by the Christian apostle John, and addressed to worldwide Christians. John wrote the Revelation one Lord's Day morning (one Sunday morning), deep in a cave on the Greek island of Patmos, where he was living in exile. John was Spirit-filled at the

time – and Jesus visited him in the cave and gave him a wondrous vision, which he copied down. That vision is now known as the book of Revelation in the New Testament.

28. "DIDACHE." (90 AD, "<u>did</u>'-uh-key.") A first century Christian training manual written by an unknown early Christian teacher, and addressed to worldwide Christians. The document is also known as *The Teaching of the Twelve Apostles,* and some researchers think the apostle Paul helped write it in Antioch, Syria, in 60 AD. Other researchers think it was written by a group of unknown authors in Ephesus, Turkey, in 90 AD. The document was lost for centuries and was discovered in a monastery in Istanbul, Turkey, in 1883. Many researchers think this is one of the most important early Christian documents ever found.

29. "CLEMENT." (95 AD, "<u>clem</u>'-ent.") A letter written by the Christian elder Clement, and addressed to the Christians at Corinth, Greece. Clement wrote the letter from Rome, Italy. He knew the apostles Paul and Peter personally, and may have also known some of the other early apostles. Some researchers think Clement helped the apostle Paul write some of Paul's letters when he was in prison in Rome. Clement's letter was important to the early Christians, and it was read aloud in Christian groups as late as 170 AD.

30. "IGNATIUS." (112 AD, "ig-<u>nay</u>'-shush.") A collection of seven letters written by the Christian elder, Ignatius, from Antioch, Syria, and addressed to the Christian home groups in Ephesus, Magnesia, Tralles, Philadelphia, Rome, and Smyrna. Ignatius had known the apostles Paul, Peter, and Barnabas personally. He wrote these letters while being taken under arrest to Rome, Italy, where he was executed by being thrown to wild animals.

31. "BARNABAS." (120 AD, "<u>barn</u>'-uh-bus.") A Christian training manual written by an unknown Christian apostle (not the Barnabas who traveled with Paul). It was addressed to worldwide Christians. This letter was important to the early Christians and was considered inspired by the Holy Spirit. However, in later years it was not included in the New Testament.

32. "DIOGNETUS." (125 AD, "die-ahg-<u>knee</u>'-tuhss.") A letter written by the Christian elder, Quadratus ("quah-<u>drat</u>'-toos"), from Athens, Greece, and addressed to the Roman Emperor, Hadrian, in Rome, Italy. This is one of the most beautiful and detailed early Christian letters ever written. Some scholars believe Quadratus presented this letter in person to Emperor Hadrian when Hadrian visited Athens in 125 AD. The letter's purpose was to convert Emperor Hadrian to Christianity, but no one knows if the letter succeeded.

33. "PAPIAS." (130 AD, "pah'-pea-us.") A teaching written by the Christian elder, Papias, from Hierapolis, Turkey, and addressed to worldwide Christians. Papias had known the apostle John personally, and had also been friends with the elder Polycarp. Papias wanted to record all the teachings of Jesus's twelve original apostles – and he filled five books with the teachings. Tragically, most of his writing has been lost in history, and only the portions known today as "Papias" have survived.

34. "HERMAS." (140 AD, "hair'-mis.") A teaching written by the Christian elder, Hermas, from Rome, Italy, and addressed to worldwide Christians. Hermas was a freed Jewish slave who later became a Christian elder and lived on a farm outside of Rome. This document is also known as *The Shepherd* by some researchers, and is thought to have been written over a period of years, starting about 90 AD. It is still considered inspired by the Holy Spirit by many Christians, and it is still read and revered by some of today's Christian denominations.

35. "POLYCARP." (156 AD, "polly'-carp.") A letter written by the Christian elder, Marcion ("mar'-see-un"), in Smyrna, Turkey, and addressed to the Christians in Philomelium, Turkey. The subject of the letter is the execution of another elder at Smyrna named Polycarp, who was friends with the apostle John, and the elders Ignatius and Papias. Polycarp's death gives the document its popular name, *Polycarp*. This is the earliest known letter describing a Christian martyrdom.

Notes

Introduction

1. James A. Kleist, ed. *Ancient Christian Writers* (New York, NY: The Paulist Press, 1948), p. 210, adapted from Minucius Felix's *Octavia* 9:2.

Chapter 1

1. The "fish" symbol is very old in human history, and was used by non-Christians before Christianity was founded. However, the Early Christians adopted it immediately, and today it is a purely Christian symbol. The first five disciples that Jesus recruited were Andrew, Peter, James, John, and Philip. All five were professional fishermen on Lake Galilee. These five disciples had obviously seen, and perhaps even used, the "fish" symbol before they became disciples, so it was a natural symbol for them to adopt. Jesus recruited these disciples in *John*, chapter 1, verses 35 through 42; and *Mark*, chapter 1, verses 14 through 20. The Greek word for fish is *ichthus* (pronounced "eh-<u>thoos</u>'"), and Jesus gave the symbol its new Christian meaning. He did this in *Matthew*, chapter 4, verse 19; and *Mark*, chapter 1, verse 17, when He said to His fishermen disciples, "Come, follow Me, and I will make you *fishers of men*." Jesus was saying that the "fish" represented *non-Christians* who needed to be converted, and that His disciples now represented "fishermen." These meanings can be clearly seen in carvings and paintings on the catacomb walls in Rome today, where Christians are depicted in boats pulling in loads of "fish" (non-Christians), and where Jesus is depicted as an anchor with sharpened flukes with "fish" (non-Christians) being hooked on them. Also, this original "fish" symbol is depicted as a complete fish, with head, tail, eye, scales, etc. The simple "fish" of two curved lines that one sees on cars today is a later symbol that dates from the Middle Ages. These meanings are verified in such references as: W. E. Vine, *An Expository Dictionary of New Testament Words: Volume II* (Old Tappan, NJ: Fleming H. Revell Company, 1940), p. 105; James Strong, *The Exhaustive Concordance of the Bible* (Nashville, TN: Abingdon Press, 1890), p. 38; William F. Arndt and F. Wilbur Gingrich, *A Greek-English Lexicon of the New Testament and Other Early Christian Literature* (Chicago, IL: The University of Chicago Press, 1957), p. 385; and A. R. Fausset, *Fausset's Bible Dictionary* (Grand Rapids, MI: Zondervan Publishing House, 1963), pp. 232-233; and in https://en.wikipedia.org/wiki/Ichthys (July 30, 2012).

2. Tim Dowley, ed. *Eerdman's Handbook to the History of Christianity* (Berkhamsted, Herts, England: Lion Publishing Company, 1977), p. 2 of the Introduction by Robert D. Lander.

3. Adapted from *First Peter*, chapter 2, verses 9 through 11.

4. Adapted from *Acts*, chapter 24, verses 1 through 24.

5. The Greek word for "Way" is *hodos* (pronounced "hah-dahss'"). Depending on the context, it can refer to a literal path, road, or journey. Figuratively, it refers to a special way of thinking and acting, such as a special course of conduct, a special lifestyle, or a special type of behavior. This meaning is verified in such reference books as: *An Expository Dictionary of New Testament Words: Volume II*, pp. 339-340; *The Exhaustive Concordance of the Bible*, p. 51; and *A Greek-English Lexicon of the New Testament and Other Early Christian Literature*, pp. 556-557.

6. Jean Comby, *How To Read Church History: Volume 1* (New York, NY: The Crossroad Publishing Company, 1985) p. 36, as adapted from *Tertullian's Apology*, chapters 37, 39, 42.

7. Adapted from *Diognetus*, chapter 5, verses 1 through 9, in *Ancient Christian Writers* (New York, NY: The Paulist Press, 1948), pp. 138-139.

8. Adapted from *Ephesians*, chapter 1, verse 1; and *First Peter*, chapter 2, verses 9 through 11.

9. Adapted from *Romans*, chapter 3, verse 17; *Second Peter*, chapter 2, verse 2; *John*, chapter 14, verse 6; *Second Peter*, chapter 2, verse 21, and *Acts*, chapter 18, verses 25 and 26.

10. Adapted from *Acts*, chapter 11, verse 26. The history of the word "Christian" is confirmed in reference works such as *An Expository Dictionary of New Testament Words: Volume I*, p. 191; Everett F. Harrison, ed. *Baker's Dictionary of Theology* (Grand Rapids, MI: Baker Book House, 1960), p. 114, and A. R. Fausett, *Fausett's Bible Dictionary* (Grand Rapids, MI: Zondervan Publishing House, 1963), p. 126.

Chapter 2

1. *Questions And Answers About Americans' Religion*, The Gallup Organization, http://www.gallup.com/poll/103459/questions-answers-about-americans-religion.aspx?version=print (September 15, 2012). The 91 percent population figure is based on the year 1948. *America Becoming Less Christian, Survey Finds*, CNN Living, http://articles.cnn.com/2009-03-09/living/us.religion.less.christian_1_american-religious-identification-survey-christian-nation-evangelical?_s=PM:LIVING (September 15, 2012).

2. Drew Goodmanson, *The Future Dying Church*, Center for Church Communication, http://www.goodmanson.com/church/the-future-dying-church (September 15, 2012).

3. Adapted from charts developed by David T. Olson, *The American Church Crisis* (Grand Rapids, MI: Zondervan, 2008), pp. 120 and 176; and by Daniel Sherman, *Pastors Leaving Ministry*, PastorBurnout.com, http://www.pastor-burnout.com/pastors-leaving.html (September 15, 2012).

4. *What Is The Current Divorce Rate In America?* Divorce Statistics, http://www.divorcestatistics.info/what-is-the-current-divorce-rate-in-america.html (September 15, 2012).

5. *Percentage Of Births To Unmarried Women*, Child Trends Data Bank, http://www.childtrendsdatabank.org/pdf/75_PDF.pdf (September 15, 2012).

6. *Child Abuse In America*, Childhelp, Inc., http://www.childhelp.org/pages/statistics.

7. *FBI Releases 2010 Crime Statistics*, The Federal Bureau of Investigation, http://www.fbi.gov/news/pressrel/press-releases/fbi-releases-2010-crime-statistics?utm_campaign=email-Immediate&utm_medium=email&utm_source=fbi-in-the-news&utm_content=32573 (September 15, 2012).

8. Owen Allen, *Spiritual Excellence: An Evaluation of Spiritual Effectiveness in Individuals and Denominations in America* (Ann Arbor, MI: ProQuest, 1991), endnotes for chapter 4, note 5, p. 271. This book is the author's doctoral dissertation for a degree in organizational behavior from the Union Graduate School of Union University, Cincinnati, OH. The dissertation resulted from three years of full-time research between 1988 and 1991 on First Century original Christianity and Fourth Century institutional Christianity. This dissertation is the basis of most of the references, facts, history, and principles in this book.

9. *Spiritual Excellence*, notes for chapter 4, note 6, p. 272.

10. *Spiritual Excellence*, notes for chapter 4, notes 9, 10, 12, 13, p. 272.

11. *Spiritual Excellence*, notes for chapter 4, note 17, p. 272.

12. *Spiritual Excellence*, notes for chapter 4, note 18, p. 272.

13. *Spiritual Excellence*, notes for chapter 4, note 19, p. 272.

14. *Spiritual Excellence*, notes for chapter 4, note 20, p. 272.

15. *Spiritual Excellence*, notes for chapter 4, note 21, p. 272.

16. *Spiritual Excellence*, notes for chapter 4, note 29, p. 273.

17. Owen Allen, *Preactive Leadership* (Denver, CO: Management House Books, 2012) pp. 253-288.

18. *Preactive Leadership*, pp. 440-442.

Chapter 3

1. *"Religion: Weekly Attendance At Religious Services,"* Public Broadcasting System, http://www.pbs.org/fmc/book/pdf/ch6.pdf (October 5, 2012). The 50 percent attendance figure is based on the year 1955 in the graph. The projections for the year 2050 are computed from the chart in David T. Olson, *The American Church Crisis* (Grand Rapids, MI: Zondervan, 2008), p. 180.

2. Examples of the traditional whitewashing of Constantine's life can be seen at: "*Constantine the Great - The Roman Emperor Constantine I*," About. Com, http://ancienthistory.about.com/cs/people/p/constantine.htm (October 5, 2012). Wikiquote, *"Constantine the Great,"* http://en.wikiquote.org/wiki/Constantine_the_Great (October 5, 2012).

3. The account of Constantine's life and career in this book comes from an extensively researched and referenced study approved by a committee of eleven scholars and published in the author's doctoral dissertation, *Spiritual Excellence: An Evaluation Of Spiritual Effectiveness In Individuals and Denominations In America* (Ann Arbor, MI: ProQuest Company, 1991). Among the books used for research on Constantine were such books as: Burckhardt, Jacob. *The Age of Constantine the Great*. New York, NY: Pantheon Books, 1949. Coleman, Christopher Bush. *Constantine the Great and Christianity*. New York, NY: The Columbia University Press, 1914. Baynes, Norman H. *Constantine the Great and the Christian Church*. London, England: The British Academy, Humphrey Milford House, 1932. Alfoldi, Andrew. *The Conversion of Constantine and Pagan Rome*. London, England: Oxford University Press, 1948. Grant, Michael. *Constantine The Great: The Man and His Times*. New York, NY: Barnes & Noble Books, 1993. And Lietzmann, Hans. *From Constantine to Julian: A History of the Early Church, Vol. 111*. New York, NY: Charles Scribner's Sons, 1950.

4. Most history books assert that the "odd sign" that Constantine supposedly saw in his dream at the Milvian Bridge, and that he used as his "Salutary Sign" in battle, was the ancient Christian *Chi-Rho* symbol – formed by the Greek letter

Chi (χ) overlaid by the Greek letter *Rho* (ρ) – and thus Constantine is the person who "invented" the Christian *Chi-Rho* symbol. However, that cannot be true, since the Christian *Chi-Rho* symbol has been found in First and Second Century catacombs under Rome; and because it has also been found in early Greek and Latin manuscripts and on early coins, all of which *predate* Constantine's life. Instead, the Salutary Sign that Constantine used in battle was a unique symbol found nowhere else in history. This author hypothesizes that Constantine saw the Christian *Chi-Rho* symbol etched on the walls of the Emperor Diocletian's dungeons when he was a young man (etched there by Christians being tortured), and that it was a hazy memory of these *Chi-Rho* symbols that Constantine saw in his dream; or that he somehow remembered; and it was this hazy memory of the *Chi-Rho* that led to the creation of Constantine's unique "Salutary Sign" at the Milvian Bridge. Summary: Constantine didn't invent the Christian *Chi-Rho* symbol because it predated him. However, he had a hazy memory of it from his youth, and that led to him to the creation of a similar symbol in his Salutary Sign.

Chapter 4

1. Fabrizio Mancinelli, *Catacombs and Basilicas: The Early Christians in Rome* (Florence, Italy: Scala, Istituto Fotografico Editoriale, 1981), p. 64.

2. Graydon F. Snyder, *Ante Pacem: Archaeological Evidence of Church Life Before Constantine* (Atlanta, GA: Mercer University Press, 1985), p. 166.

3. Leonardo B. Dal Mas, *Rome of the Caesars* (Florence, Italy: Bonechi Edizioni, 1987), p. 8.

4. E. Manzione and L. Pazienti, *Rome and the Vatican* (Rome, Italy: Soc. Editrice Fi. Da. Ro., 1983), p. 12.

5. The Fourth Century Byzantine Greek phrase coined in Constantinople in the Fourth Century from which today's English word "church" evolved is: *kuriakon doma*. It literally means "building of the Lord" or "the Lord's building." Originally, the words *kuriakon doma* had no meaning other than the *physical structure* of a religious building – either Christian or non-Christian. This is confirmed in such references as: William Evans, *Great Doctrines of the Bible* (Chicago, IL: Moody Press, 1974), p. 182. Everett F. Harrison, *Baker's Dictionary of Theology* (Grand Rapids, MI: Baker Book House, 1960), p. 123. J. D. Davis, *Illustrated Davis Dictionary of the Bible* (Nashville, TN: Royal Publishers, Inc., 1973), p. 146. A. R. Fausett, *Fausett's Bible Dictionary* (Grand Rapids, MI: Zondervan Publishing House, 1963), p. 130. Special note: Constantine's Roman basilicas were sometimes called "houses of God" in Latin

(*Domus Dei*) in later years. However, today's English word "church" originated with the Greek word *kuriakon* in Constantinople in the Fourth Century – and after that was improperly used to translate the first English Bibles in England in the Middle Ages.

6. Christopher B. Coleman, *Constantine the Great and Christianity* (New York, NY: The Columbia University Press, 1914), pp. 32-33.

7. *Ante Pacem*, pp. 26-29.

8. The Greek word that today's *Bibles* translate as "cross" is *stauros*. *Stauros* (pronounced "stah-<u>rahss</u>'") is correctly translated into English as an "upright pole," "post," or "stake," especially a large one with a pointed end. Such stakes were driven into the ground to build fences and fortifications. But they were also used as execution tools to impale or crucify victims in various ways (with ropes, nails, upside down, etc.). The crucifixion process is also referred to in the Bible as being "hung on a tree" (the Greek word for "tree" is *xulon*); and actual trees were also used as tools for impalement and crucifixion. Nobody knows factually what kind of crucifixion the Romans used to execute Jesus in Jerusalem in the First Century. Was it a pole? Was it a tree? Was it shaped like an "**X**"? Was it shaped like a "**T**"? The Romans even crucified victims by nailing them or tying them to walls and rooftops. Thus, today's Christian cross (seen on church steeples, jewelry, and in pictures) originated with *Constantine*. Thus, to conform to the tradition started by Constantine, the Greek word *stauros* is always translated into English as "cross" in today's *Bibles*. These meanings of *stauros* and *xulon* are verified in such reference books as: *Ante Pacem*, pp. 26-29; James Strong, *The Exhaustive Concordance of the Bible* (Nashville, TN: Abingdon Press, 1890), pp. 50 and 66; *Baker's Dictionary of Theology*, p. 152; and W. E. Vine, *An Expository Dictionary of New Testament Words: Volume I* (Old Tappan, NJ: Fleming H. Revell Company, 1940), p. 256 and *Volume IV*, p. 153.

9. Ralph Waldo Emerson, the American essayist, lecturer, poet, and philosopher made this statement in his essay, *Self-Reliance*, in 1841. http://www.national-center.org/SelfReliance.html. (07-25-13)

Chapter 5

1. Graydon F. Snyder, *Ante Pacem: Archaeological Evidence of Church Life Before Constantine* (Atlanta, GA: Mercer University Press, 1985). Dr. Snyder (1930-2016), whom the author knew personally, was a gifted scholar of First Century Christian life. Yet he used the word "church" in the title of his books. But there *was* no "church" before Constantine. Constantine himself coined the

word "church" in the Fourth Century, 300 years *after* Christianity was founded. It is therefore *revisionism* for historians to write about "church" life before Constantine. Correctly used (if it is used at all), the English word "church" should only refer to a *building* that is being used for religious purposes, either by Christians or non-Christians.

2. The English prefix "para-" comes from the Greek preposition, *para* (pronounced " puh-<u>rah</u>'"), meaning by the side of, or near, or parallel to. Thus, the para-groups solution means to operate small groups by the side of a traditional parent congregation without either interfering with the operations of the other. This meaning of *para* is verified in: *An Expository Dictionary of New Testament Words: Volume IV*, p. 20.

Chapter 6

1. Owen Allen, *Preactive Leadership* (Denver, CO: Management House Books, 2012) pp. 88-96.

2. Owen Allen, *Spiritual Excellence: An Evaluation of Spiritual Effectiveness in Individuals and Denominations in America* (Ann Arbor, MI: ProQuest, 1991), notes for chapter 3, note 19, p. 268.

3. In the Early Christian letters, "false teachers," "false apostles," and "false prophets" are repeatedly condemned – as they are in chapter 2 of *Second Peter*, verse 1; chapter 11 of *Second Corinthians*, verse 13; and chapter 4 of *First John*, verse 1, in the New Testament portion of the Bible.

4. "People's Troubles are the Same Everywhere." *Greensboro (NC) News & Record* (August 3, 1995).

5. The Greek word for a "natural" person, or an "unspiritual" person, or a "non-Christian" is the *same* word. It's the Greek word *psuchikos* (pronounced "sue-hee-<u>cahss</u>'"), which can be translated as any of those terms – or simply as a person who does *not* have the Holy Spirit within them. The best known use of the word *psuchikos* is by Paul in *First Corinthians,* chapter 2, verse 14. These meanings are verified in such reference books as: W. E. Vine, *An Expository Dictionary of New Testament Words: Volume III* (Old Tappan, NJ: Fleming H. Revell Company, 1940), p. 102; James Strong, *The Exhaustive Concordance of the Bible* (Nashville, TN: Abingdon Press, 1890), p. 79; Alton Bryant, ed. *The New Compact Bible Dictionary* (Grand Rapids, MI: Zondervan Publishing House, 1967), p. 389; Millard J. Erickson, *Concise Dictionary of Christian Theology* (Grand Rapids, MI: Baker Book House, 1986), p. 102; *The Englishman's Greek Concordance of the New Testament* (Grand Rapids, MI:

Zondervan Publishing House, 1970), p. 808; and *The Analytical Greek Lexicon* (Grand Rapids, MI: Zondervan Publishing House, 1973), p. 443.

6. Adapted from *First Corinthians,* chapter 2, verse 14.

7. William Evans, *Great Doctrines of the Bible* (Chicago, IL: Moody Press, 1974). p. 129. Evans states that all of the major religions of the world have a doctrine that states in some form or fashion that humans are a "fallen race," that human nature is primarily "selfish," and that all humans are born to live in "sin."

8. The Greek word for our "flesh" (our selfish human nature) is *sarx. Sarx* (pronounced "sarks") can also be translated into English as carnal, worldly, earthly, sinful, or temporal. Literally, the word "flesh" can refer to our bodily tissue but, figuratively, the Early Christians used it to refer to the egotistical motivations of our selfish human natures. These meanings are verified in such reference books as: *An Expository Dictionary of New Testament Words: Volume II,* pp. 107-108; *The Exhaustive Concordance of the Bible,* p. 64; *The Analytical Greek Lexicon,* pp. 363-364; Everett F. Harrison, *Baker's Dictionary of Theology* (Grand Rapids, MI: Baker Book House, 1960), pp. 222-223; *Concise Dictionary of Christian Theology,* p. 58; A. R. Fausett, *Fausett's Bible Dictionary* (Grand Rapids, MI: Zondervan Publishing House, 1963), p. 233; and *The New Compact Bible Dictionary,* p. 176.

9. Adapted from *Psalms,* Psalm 14, verses 2 and 3.

10. Adapted from *Galatians,* chapter 5, verses 19 through 21.

Chapter 7

1. The Greek word for human "sin" (meaning negative behavior motivated by our selfish human natures) is *hamartia. Hamartia* (pronounced "hah-mar-tea'-ah") can also be translated into English as an offense, a trespass, or a fault against God or other people. These meanings are verified in such reference books as: James Strong, *The Exhaustive Concordance of the Bible* (Nashville, TN: Abingdon Press, 1890), p. 10; and W. E. Vine, *An Expository Dictionary of New Testament Words: Volume IV* (Old Tappan, NJ: Fleming H. Revell Company, 1940), p. 32.

2. The Greek word for the human "mind" is *nous* (pronounced to rhyme with a hangman's "noose'.") It can be translated into English as: our understanding; our ability to make decisions; or our will power. The Early Christians taught that our mind has no morals or ethics of its own. Instead, it produces the behavior of whatever force is motivating it – good or bad. These meanings

are verified in such reference books as: *The Exhaustive Concordance of the Bible*, p. 50; *An Expository Dictionary of New Testament Words: Volume III*, p. 69; *The Analytical Greek Lexicon* (Grand Rapids, MI: Zondervan Publishing House, 1970), p. 280; and Everett F. Harrison, *Baker's Dictionary of Theology* (Grand Rapids, MI: Baker Book House, 1960), p. 355.

3. Adapted from *Matthew*, chapter 9, verse 4. The Greek word for the human heart is *kardia* (pronounced "car-<u>dee</u>'-ah"). But *kardia* is also a popular synonym for the human mind. This is verified in such reference books as: *The Exhaustive Concordance of the Bible*, p. 39; *The Analytical Greek Lexicon*, p. 213; and *An Expository Dictionary of New Testament Words: Volume III*, pp. 206-207.

4. The Greek word for "spirit," referring to the Holy Spirit – or referring to the spirit inside human beings – is *pneuma* (pronounced "<u>new</u>'-muh"). The same word can be used for both, except that when referring to the Holy Spirit is should be capitalized. These meanings are verified in such reference books as: *The Exhaustive Concordance of the Bible*, p. 58; Arndt and Gingrich, *A Greek-English Lexicon of the New Testament and Other Early Christian Literature* (Chicago, IL: The University of Chicago Press, 1957), p. 680; *The Analytical Greek Lexicon*, p. 67; and *An Expository Dictionary of New Testament Words: Volume IV*, p. 62.

5. Adapted from *Luke*, chapter 8, verses 54 and 55.

6. Adapted from *Acts*, chapter 7, verses 59 and 60.

7. The Greek word for the human "soul" (as a synonym for the inner spirit in human beings) is *psuche'* (pronounced "sue-<u>hay</u>'"). This is verified in such reference books as: *The Exhaustive Concordance of the Bible*, p. 79; *A Greek-English Lexicon of the New Testament and Other Early Christian Literature*, p. 680; *The Analytical Greek Lexicon*, pp. 67 and 331; and *An Expository Dictionary of New Testament Words: Volume IV*, p. 54. However, *psuche'* is a confusing Greek word because it can also be translated "life," referring to the overall *life* of a human being in the sense of "He lost his life (*psuche'*)." But the fact that *psuche'* can be a synonym for the human spirit is shown in references such as *Acts*, chapter 2, verse 27; *Second Corinthians*, chapter 12, verse 15; *First Peter*, chapter 1, verse 9; and *Hebrews*, chapter 10, verse 39. For example, the reference in *First Peter* reads "… you are receiving the end result of your faith, the salvation of your souls (*psuche'*)."

8. Adapted from *Luke*, chapter 12, verse 20.

9. Adapted from *Ephesians*, chapter 2, verses 1 through 5. The Greek word for "dead" that Paul is using is *nekros* (pronounced "nay-crahss'"), literally meaning dead, but figuratively meaning "as if dead" or "inactive" or "incapable of Spiritual motivation." This is verified in such reference books as: *The Exhaustive Concordance of the Bible*, p. 49; *An Expository Dictionary of New Testament Words: Volume I*, p. 273; and *A Greek-English Lexicon of the New Testament and Other Early Christian Literature*, p. 536.

Chapter 8

1. Adapted from the episodes where the disciples argued among themselves about who was the "greatest" in *Mark*, chapter 9, verse 34; *Luke*, chapter 9, verse 46; and *Luke* chapter 22, verse 24, in the New Testament portion of the Bible.

2. Adapted from the episode where the disciple Judas betrayed Jesus in *Matthew*, chapter 26, verses 47 through 50.

3. Adapted from the episode where the disciples, Peter, James, and John went to sleep instead of praying with Jesus in *Matthew*, chapter 26, verses 36 through 45.

4. Adapted from the episode where the disciple Peter denied he ever knew Jesus in *Matthew*, chapter 26, verses 69 through 74.

5. Adapted from the episode where the disciples hid behind locked doors for fear of being recognized as disciples of Jesus on the streets, in *John*, chapter 20, verse 19.

6. Adapted from the episode where the disciple, Thomas, demanded proof of Jesus's resurrection, in *John*, chapter 20, verses 24 through 28.

7. The Early Christian letters make it clear that, during the period that the frightened disciples were hiding in a house in Jerusalem, the Holy Spirit had *not* yet come in His fullness to indwell human beings and to give them a new second source of inner motivation. Adapted from *John*, chapter 7, verse 39, where the apostle John explains Jesus's statement in the temple courts by saying, "By this, (Jesus) was referring to the Holy Spirit, whom (the disciples) ... were *later* to receive; (because) up to that time, the Spirit had *not* been given." In chapter 14, verses 16 and 17 of *John*, Jesus says to the disciples, "I will ask the Father, and He will give you ... the Spirit of truth ... for He (now) lives *near* you (but soon He) will be *in* you." In chapter 15, verse 26 of *John*, Jesus says, "When the (Spirit) comes, whom I will send to you from the Father ... He will testify about me." Finally, in chapter 20, verses 21 and 22 of *John*, there is a

dramatic scene in which Jesus illustrates symbolically to the disciples what is about to happen to them. He blows a puff of air on them with His mouth and says, "As the Father has sent me, I (am going to) send you ... (and this is how you will) *receive* the Holy Spirit." Thus, while the Holy Spirit had been in the world since creation, and had been "with" or "near" key people in both the Old and New Testaments, at this point in world history, He was *not* yet available to the disciples as a permanent inner source of Spiritual motivation within them.

8. Adapted from *Acts*, chapter 1, verse 3.

9. Adapted from *First Corinthians*, chapter 15, verses 5 through 8.

10. Adapted from *Acts*, chapter 1, verses 4, 5, and 8.

11. The Greek noun "baptism" (as in the *baptism* in the Holy Spirit) is *baptisma* (pronounced "bop'-teas-mah"). The verb "baptize" (as in to *baptize* in the Holy Spirit) is *baptizo* (pronounced "bop-teed'-zo"). In the First Century culture in which Jesus used the word, to "baptize" something meant to immerse it in another substance (such as dye, oil, water, etc.), and to keep it submerged until it soaked long enough to change its basic nature. For example: *baptizing* vegetables in vinegar until they became pickles; *baptizing* cloth in dye until it changed colors; *baptizing* swords in oil until they were tempered; *baptizing* bread in wine until it was soaked. Also, sunken ships, waterlogged timbers, and drowned people were said to have been *baptized*. Thus, when Jesus told the disciples that they were going to be Spirit-baptized, His words had a specific cultural meaning to them. His words meant that their inner spirits were going to be immersed in the Holy Spirit and soaked in power until they were permanently awakened Spiritually. Special note: Jesus's First Century use of the noun "baptism" to refer to Spirit-baptism should *not* be confused with today's use of the same word in the Christian celebration of *water-baptism*. The two baptisms are completely different things. Water-baptism is a symbolic celebration involving an immersion in water to demonstrate that a person has *been* Spirit-baptized and is a Christian. Water has no Spiritual properties and does not change a person in any way, and failing to make a clear distinction between these two baptisms is a common mistake that Bible translators, preachers, priests, and theologians make – since some Bible verses are talking about one baptism, and some Bible verses are talking about the other one – and translators often do not make clear which is which. These meanings of the Greek word "baptism" are verified in such reference books as: James Strong, *The Exhaustive Concordance of the Bible* (Nashville, TN: Abingdon Press, 1890), p. 18; Arndt, William F. and F. Wilbur Gingrich. *A Greek-English*

Lexicon of the New Testament and Other Early Christian Literature (Chicago, IL: The University of Chicago Press, 1957), p. 131.

12. Adapted from *Joel*, chapter 2, verses 28 and 29.

13. Adapted from *Matthew*, chapter 3, verse 11; and *Luke*, chapter 3, verse 16.

14. Adapted from *Acts*, chapter 1, verses 13 and 14; and chapter 2, verses 1 through 13. The date and time of the Holy Spirit's arrival are verified by Gene Edwards, *The Early Church* (Goleta, CA: Christian Books, 1974), pp. 9-29; Alton Bryant, *The New Compact Bible Dictionary* (Grand Rapids, MI: Zondervan Publishing House, 1967), p. 111; William Evans, *Great Doctrines of the Bible* (Chicago, IL: Moody Press, 1974), p. 181; Henry B. Halley, *Halley's Bible Handbook* (Grand Rapids, MI: Zondervan Publishing House, 1965), p. 561; and Merrill F. Unger, *Unger's Bible Dictionary* (Chicago, IL: Moody Press, 1966), p. 205.

15. Adapted from *Acts*, chapter 2, verses 1 through 3.

16. Adapted from *Acts*, chapter 2, verse 4. The First Century writer of *Acts* opens verse 4 with the Greek word *kai* (pronounced "kye'"), and then uses it a *second* time later in the *same* verse. *Kai* is a complex Greek word that can be translated many ways as: "but," "also," "then," "and then," "and so," "likewise," "indeed," and other such terms, depending on the context of the sentence. These meanings of *kai* are verified by such reference books as: *The Exhaustive Concordance of the Bible,* p. 39; and *A Greek-English Lexicon of the New Testament and Other Early Christian Literature*, pp. 392-394. The trouble with translating *Acts*, chapter 2, verse 4 into English, is that today's denominational translators, who often don't *understand* what's actually happening in the verse, either *omit* the first *kai* at the opening of verse 4, or translate *kai* in *both* places in the verse simply as "and." But such weak translations do not make it clear that *Acts* chapter 2 is describing *three* separate Spiritual experiences: a) The disciples were *baptized* in the Holy Spirit in verse 3. b) in verse 4, they were temporarily *filled* with the Holy Spirit. c) After that, they received a *gift* from the Holy Spirit. So if the Greek word *kai* is included in both of the places in verse 4 where it is in the original Greek – and if it is translated with fuller meanings than simply "and," a stronger translation of verse 4 is: "*Then*, all of them were filled with the Holy Spirit, *and also* began to speak in other languages as the Spirit gave them the words." This kind of translation makes it clear that verse 4 is reporting that *two* additional and separate, Spiritual experiences followed the baptism in the Holy Spirit that the disciples had received just moments before in verse 3.

17. Adapted from *Acts*, chapter 2, verses 5 through 13.

18. Adapted from *Acts*, chapter 2, verses 14 through 36.

19. Adapted from *Acts*, chapter 2, verses 37 through 41.

20. Adapted from *Matthew*, chapter 8, verses 31 through 32; and *James*, chapter 2, verse 19.

21. Adapted from *First Corinthians*, chapter 6, verse 19.

Chapter 9

1. Tim Dowley, ed. *Eerdman's Handbook to the History of Christianity* (Berkhamsted, Herts, England: Lion Publishing Company, 1977), pp. 114, 117.

2. James A. Kleist, ed. *Ancient Christian Writers* (New York, NY: The Paulist Press, 1948), pp. 16-17, 37, 45-46, 50, 59, 65. Kleist is quoting from two ancient Christian training manuals, *The Teaching of the Twelve Apostles* and *The Epistle of Barnabas*.

3. Adapted from *First Corinthians*, chapter 2, verses 1 through 5.

4. Adapted from the opening line of *Didache* (pronounced "di-duh-kay'," or "di-duh-key'") in chapter 1, verse 1; as published in James A. Kleist in *Ancient Christian Writers*, p. 15. The *Didache* is a First Century training manual for infant Christians. Its Christian author is unknown, but some researchers think it was written in the city of Ephesus in Turkey around 90 AD, since it was discovered in Istanbul in 1883. Other researchers think the apostle Paul helped write the manual in Antioch, Turkey around 60 AD. However, all researchers agree that it was written in Turkey in the First Century – and that it is one of the most important Early Christian documents ever found outside of the Bible.

5. The Greek word for "life" (as in The Way of *Life*) is *zoe* (pronounced "zoh-aa'"). Depending on the context of the sentence, *zoe* can mean eternal life in heaven. Or, it can mean Spiritual life on earth; i.e., the inner motivational power of the Holy Spirit that gives Christians the character of the Holy Spirit. These meanings are verified in such reference books as: Everett F. Harrison, ed. *Baker's Dictionary of Theology* (Grand Rapids, MI: Baker Book House, 1960), p. 323; Alton Bryant, ed. *The New Compact Bible Dictionary* (Grand Rapids, MI: Zondervan Publishing House, 1967), p. 324; and W. E. Vine, *An Expository Dictionary of New Testament Words, Volume II* (Old Tappan, NJ: Fleming H. Revell Company, 1940), p. 348. The latter meaning is shown in the Early Christian letters in such places as: *John*, chapter 1, verse 4 and chapter

8, verse 12; *Acts*, chapter 2, verse 28; *Romans*, chapter 8, verses 2, 6, and 10; First John, chapter 3, verses 14 and 15. Likewise, the Greek word for "death" (as in The Way of *Death*) is *thanatos* (pronounced "than-uh-<u>tahss</u>'"). It can mean eternal damnation. Or, it can mean unspiritual life on earth; i.e., the inner motivational power of the selfish human nature that gives Christians the behavior of non-Christians. These meanings are verified in such reference books as: *Baker's Dictionary of Theology*, p. 158; *The New Compact Bible Dictionary*, p. 128; and *An Expository Dictionary of New Testament Words, Volume I*, p. 276. The latter meaning is shown in the Early Christian letters in such places as: *Luke*, chapter 1, verse 79; *John*, chapter 6, verse 16; and *Romans*, chapter 7, verse 5, and chapter 8, verse 6. The difficulty with the two words "life" and "death" in Christian writing is that they can refer to inner motivation in some verses – and they can refer to the eternal destinations of heaven and hell in other verses. This confuses readers. As a result, the terms "light" and "darkness" are more helpful and are used by this author.

6. Adapted from *The Epistle of Barnabas*, chapter 18, verse 1, as published in *Ancient Christian Writers,* p. 61. *Barnabas* is another First Century training manual for infant Christians. Its Christian author is unknown, but researchers think it was written in Egypt around 120 AD because of its content and its style. Thus, while *Barnabas* was written by a different author, in a different country, between 35 and 65 years after the *Didache* – *Barnabas* teaches exactly the same motivational principles as the *Didache*.

7. Millard J. Erickson, *Concise Dictionary of Christian Theology* (Grand Rapids, MI: Baker Book House, 1986), p. 97.

8. Merrill F. Unger, *Unger's Bible Dictionary* (Chicago, IL: Moody Press, 1966), p. 661. The Greek word used in these ancient training manuals is *phos* (pronounced "<u>foce</u>'"), meaning "light." The word "light" is being used here in the motivational sense in which it's used in other First Century letters such as: *Matthew*, chapter 5, verses 14 through 16; *Luke*, chapter 11, verses 35 and 36; *John*, chapter 1, verses 4 and 5, and chapter 3, verse 19, and chapter 8, verse 12, and chapter 12, verse 46; *Acts*, chapter 26, verse 18; *Second Corinthians*, chapter 4, verse 6, and chapter 6, verse 14; *Ephesians*, chapter 5, verses 8 and 9; *First Thessalonians*, chapter 5, verse 5; *First Peter*, chapter 2, verse 9; and *First John*, chapter 1, verse 5, and chapter 2, verses 9 and 10.

9. Adapted from *Galatians*, chapter 5, verses 22 and 23. The Greek word translated here into English as "produce" is *karpos* (pronounced "car-<u>pahss</u>'"). *Karpos* means the "result of" or the "effect of" something, or it means what something "produces." But it can also be literally translated "fruit." In England

in 1611, the translators of the *King James Version* of the Bible translated it as "fruit," and denominational translators have followed that lead ever since. This is where today's popular Christian phrase "the fruit of the Spirit" comes from. However, "fruit" is a weak and confusing translation for Twenty-First Century readers, since it masks the fact that Paul is writing about motivation and behavior. These meanings of *karpos* are verified in: *An Expository Dictionary of New Testament Words, Volume II*, p. 133.

10. The First Century teaching on "Light and Darkness" (representing the two opposing inner motivations in Christians) is taught in at least nine of the New Testament letters, including: *Matthew, Luke, John, Acts, Second Corinthians, Ephesians, First Thessalonians, First Peter,* and *First John*, and it's implied in several others.

11. Adapted from *Galatians*, chapter 5, verses 19 through 21.

12. Adapted from *John*, chapter 7, verses 38 and 39. This teaching by Jesus is a clear prophecy of the Day of Pentecost and of the inner motivational power of Spirit-filling that was to begin for Christians on that dramatic day, the birthday of Christianity. As a side note, there are over a dozen other *Old Testament* verses that Jesus may have been referring to in this temple episode. But most scholars believe He was referring to *Isaiah*, chapter 12, verses 2 and 3.

13. Adapted from *Ephesians*, chapter 5, verse 18.

14. Adapted from *Acts*, chapter 2, verse 4.

15. The apostle Paul used the Greek word for "Spiritual" (*Pneumatikos*, pronounced "new-mah-tea-cahss'") for the first time in history in 49 AD in *Galatians*, chapter 6, verse 1. This was 19 years *after* Christianity was founded on the Day of Pentecost, on May the 30th, in the year 30 AD. The word "Spiritual" was not used by any other Greek, Roman, or Jewish religion before this time; and thus, the word "Spiritual" is uniquely a Christian word. That is important to know, since humans could *not* be Spiritual *before* Christianity was founded. Spirituality was only possible for humans *after* Christianity was founded, and it can still only be experienced by Christians. For that reason, the word "Spiritual" does *not* appear in *Matthew, Mark, Luke,* or *John* because they were written about events that occurred before Pentecost. *Spirituality* is a completely post-Pentecost experience.

16. The Greek word for "Spirit" (referring to the Holy Spirit) is *Pneuma* (pronounced "new'-mah.") The word for "Spiritual" is *Pneumatikos* (pronounced "new-mah-tea-cahss'"), and comes *from* the word *Pneuma*. Thus, Spiritual

behavior *only* comes from the Holy Spirit. Spirituality is an expression of the indwelling power of the Holy Spirit within Christians. Therefore, since the words "Spirit" and "Spiritual" refer to the third Person of God, they should always be *capitalized*. These meanings are verified in such reference books as: *The Exhaustive Concordance of the Bible*, pp. 58-59; *A Greek-English Lexicon of the New Testament and Other Early Christian Literature*, pp. 680-685; *An Expository Dictionary of New Testament Words, Volume IV*, pp. 62-65; and *Baker's Dictionary of Theology*, pp. 493-497.

17. The Greek word for "holy" (as in Holy Spirit) is *hagios* (pronounced "hog'-ee-ahss"). The word means separated from sin, devoted to God, and set apart for His service. More completely, it means human behavior that's ethical, moral, sacred, pure, and worthy of God. It means a withdrawal from worldliness to live a Christ-like life. These meanings are verified in such reference books as: *An Expository Dictionary of New Testament Words, Volume II*, pp. 226-227; *A Greek-English Lexicon of the New Testament and Other Early Christian Literature*, pp. 9-10; and *The New Compact Bible Dictionary*, p. 230.

18. Adapted from *Ephesians*, chapter 4, verses 22 through 24; and *Romans*, chapter 12, verse 2.

Chapter 10

1. Adapted from *Second Chronicles*, chapter 15, verses 1 and 2 in the Old Testament; and from passages such as *Matthew*, chapter 6, verse 33; *Acts*, chapter 17, verse 27; *Hebrews*, chapter 11, verse 6; and *James*, chapter 4, verses 2 and 3, in the New Testament.

2. Adapted from *Matthew*, chapter 5, verse 6.

3. Adapted from *Luke*, chapter 11, verses 9 through 13.

4. Adapted from *Romans*, chapter 7, verses 18 through 20.

5. Adapted from *Romans*, chapter 7, verses 22 and 25.

6. Adapted from *James*, chapter 4, verse 1.

7. Adapted from *First Peter*, chapter 2, verses 11 and 12.

8. In the First Century, Christians had two Greek words for "war" when writing about the inner battle between Light and Darkness within Christians. The first word was the verb *strateuo* (pronounced "strah-too'-oh"), meaning "to go to war" or "to wage a military campaign." The second word was the noun

polemos (pronounced "pah'-luh-mahss"), meaning a "war." These two words indicate the determination with which a Christian's selfish nature fights the indwelling Holy Spirit within him or her. These meanings are verified in such reference books as: James Strong, *The Exhaustive Concordance of the Bible* (Nashville, TN: Abandon Press, 1890), pp. 59 and 67; W. E. Vine, *An Expository Dictionary of New Testament Words: Volume IV* (Old Tappan, NJ: Fleming H. Revell Company, 1940) p. 197; William F. Arndt and F. Wilbur Gingrich, *A Greek-English Lexicon of the New Testament and Other Early Christian Literature* (Chicago, IL: The University of Chicago Press, 1957), p. 778; and Everett Harrison, *Baker's Dictionary of Theology* (Grand Rapids, MI: Baker Book House, 1960), p. 496.

9. Adapted from *Diognetus*, chapter 6, verse 5, in *Ancient Christian Writers* (New York, NY: The Paulist Press, 1948), p. 140.

10. The Greek verb for "filled" (as in Spirit-filled) is the verb *pimplemi* (pronounced "pim'-play-me"). Its tense – the aorist participle – indicates that it's a *temporary* condition, not a *permanent* condition. It means to *temporarily* provide some substance (in this case, the Holy Spirit) to fill a container (in this case, a Christian's mind) for the limited period of time in which the substance is needed. Examples of how the verb was used in the First Century include: filling a sponge with vinegar; filling a boat with fish; filling a wedding reception with guests; filling a ship's sails with wind, and filling a house with noise. The point is, such "fillings" are *temporary*. Sponges dry out; fish are eaten; wedding guests leave; wind dies in a ship's sails, and a house becomes silent again. This means that when a Christian is "filled" with the Spirit, his or her mind is *temporarily* motivated by the Holy Spirit for the limited time period in which His power is *needed* for that specific situation. Then, when His power is no longer needed, it subsides in the Christian's mind until needed again. Thus, Spirit-filling is *cyclical* in a Christian's mind like the ocean's tides. These meaning are verified in such reference books as: *The Exhaustive Concordance of the Bible*, p. 58; *An Expository Dictionary of New Testament Words, Volume II*, p. 97; *A Greek-English Lexicon of the New Testament and Other Early Christian Literature*, p. 676, and Harold E. Monser, ed. *The Logos International Study Bible* (Plainfield, NJ: Logos International, 1972), p. 2445.

11. The Greek word for a "disciple" (as in a Christian disciple) is the noun *mathetes* (pronounced "mah-thay-tace'"). It comes from the Greek verb "to learn" and thus means a learner, student, trainee or, more importantly, a follower of a set of knowledge or a style of behavior. *Mathetes* implies a person who is a dedicated believer in the teachings of a mentor. Thus, Followers of The Way in the First Century were "disciples," since they were students and trainees

learning to live as Spiritually mature Christians. These meanings are verified in such reference books as: *An Expository Dictionary of New Testament Words, Volume I*, p. 316; *The Exhaustive Concordance of the Bible*, p. 45-46; *Baker's Dictionary of Theology*, p. 166-167; Millard J. Erickson, *Concise Dictionary of Christian Theology* (Grand Rapids, MI: Baker Book House, 1986), p. 44; and Alton Bryant, ed. *The New Compact Bible Dictionary* (Grand Rapids, MI: Zondervan Publishing House, 1967), p. 133.

12. Adapted from *Ephesians*, chapter 4, verses 11 through 14.

13. Adapted from *Second Peter*, chapter 1, verses 5 through 8. The Greek word that Peter uses here that is translated as "increasing measure" is the verb *pleonazo* (pronounced "play-ah-<u>nod</u>'-zo"). It means to cause something to grow, or to increase, until it abounds and becomes superabundant. These meanings are verified in such reference books as: *The Exhaustive Concordance of the Bible*, p. 58; and *An Expository Dictionary of New Testament Words: Volume I*, p. 18.

14. Adapted from *First Corinthians*, chapter 1, verse 7; added to chapter 3, verses 1 through 3. These verses show clearly that many of the Christians in the small groups in the city of Corinth, Greece were "infant" Christians – their behavior was fleshy, carnal, and like non-Christian behavior. Yet, they expressed *all* of the Spiritual gifts in their lives. This proves the principle that immature Christians can express gifts and can express them immaturely: in unspiritual, inappropriate, and embarrassing ways.

15. Adapted from *John*, chapter 3, verse 6.

16. Adapted from *First Corinthians*, chapter 3, verse 16; and *Ephesians*, chapter 3, verses 14 and 16.

Chapter 11

1. Adapted from *Matthew*, chapter 21, verses 28 through 31. This riddle was told by Jesus in order to confront the chief priests and elders in the temple – and it illustrates the behavioral principle that what Christians *think, believe, and say* is less important than how they *behave* Spiritually each day by displaying the Holy Spirit's supernatural power in their lifestyle. Many Christians have been taught to approach Christianity "intellectually" emphasizing what they "believe" about various traditional denominational doctrines, rituals, and programs. However, the key to the Christian life is to be *motivated* more and more by the indwelling Holy Spirit – producing more and more Spiritual *behavior*.

Then, given enough time, the Holy Spirit will reveal everything that a Christian needs to know about doctrines, rituals, and programs.

2. In England in 1604, King James the First ordered the committee of 47 priests appointed to translate the new *"King James Version"* ("KJV") of the Bible to make certain that their translation *conformed* fully to the doctrines, policies, rituals, and hierarchy of the Church of England denomination. The king even appointed archbishop Richard Bancroft to serve as "chief overseer" of the project to insure that the priests did as ordered. They did, and this explains why so many verses of the KJV Bible reflect the terms and practices of institutional Christianity rather than the terms and practices of the Early Christians. For example, in the KJV Bible, Christian *small groups* are called "churches," and Christian *elders* are called "pastors," and to *declare* the Christian message is called "preaching," and so forth.

3. Adapted from *Galatians*, chapter 5, verses 22 and 23. The Greek word translated here as "fruit" is *karpos* (pronounced "car-pahss'"), literally meaning the physical fruit harvested from trees, vines, and gardens. However, a stronger translation of *karpos* is: the "produce" of the Spirit; or what the Spirit "produces"; or the "result" of the Holy Spirit's motivation. But the priests in England in 1611 who translated the *King James Version* of the Bible translated the Greek word *karpos* literally as "fruit" – and of today's translations have followed that obsolete translation. This is where today's popular phrase "the fruit of the Spirit" came from. But "the *fruit* of the Spirit" confuses today's readers because it masks the fact that Paul is writing about Christian *behavior*, not the "fruit" of trees, vines, and gardens.

Chapter 12

1. The Greek word for "gift" (when referring to a gift of the *Spirit*) is the noun *charisma* (pronounced "har'-is-mah"). *Charisma* is from a Greek verb meaning to do something in a kind, and forgiving, and gracious way. So *charisma* refers to a miraculous and supernatural free gift from God – one given solely as a gratuity by divine favor; one given by God to a recipient who has done nothing to earn it or to deserve it. Spiritual gifts are different from human talents, skills, and abilities, and are *not* created by the tissues and organs of the human body. Spiritual gifts are expressed by the will of the Holy Spirit through Christians, and by Christians, and for Christians. Non-Christians cannot express them, and they are only rarely used for the benefit of non-Christians. These meanings are verified in such reference books as: James Strong, *The Exhaustive Concordance of the Bible* (Nashville, TN: Abandon Press, 1890), p. 77; and W. E. Vine, *An Expository Dictionary of New Testament Words: Volume II* (Old Tappan, NJ: Fleming H. Revell Company, 1940), p. 147; Everett Harrison,

Baker's Dictionary of Theology (Grand Rapids, MI: Baker Book House, 1960), p. 497; and William F. Arndt and F. Wilbur Gingrich, *A Greek-English Lexicon of the New Testament and Other Early Christian Literature* (Chicago, IL: The University of Chicago Press, 1957), p. 887.

2. Adapted from *First Corinthians*, chapter 7, verse 7, and chapter 12, verse 11.

3. Adapted from *First Timothy*, chapter 4, verse 14; and *Second Timothy*, chapter 1, verse 6.

4. Adapted from *First Peter*, chapter 4, verse 10. Paul presents this principle in slightly different words in *First Corinthians*, chapter 12, verse 7.

5. Adapted from *First Peter*, chapter 2, verse 9.

6. Adapted from *Acts*, chapter 2, verses 5 through 11; and chapter 6, verses 1 through 10.

7. Adapted from *First Corinthians*, chapter 12, verses 12 through 26.

8. Adapted from *First Corinthians*, chapter 12, verse 31. Many Bibles translate this verse from the Greek into English as "the best gifts" or "the greater gifts." But that is misleading because it seems to indicate that a hierarchy of gifts exists, and one does not. The Greek word Paul uses in this verse is the adjective *kreitton* (pronounced "cry'-tone"), meaning "the more useful," or "the more serviceable," or "the more advantageous" gifts. What *kreitton* actually means in this context is to express the gifts that *best satisfy the needs* of the other Christians in a small group in the time and place they are needed. These meanings are verified in such reference books as: *The Exhaustive Concordance of the Bible*, p. 43; *An Expository Dictionary of New Testament Words: Volume II*, p. 122; and *A Greek-English Lexicon of the New Testament and Other Early Christian Literature*, p. 450.

9. Adapted from *First Corinthians*, chapter 1, verse 7; chapter 3, verses 1 through 3; and chapter 5, verses 1 through 11.

10. Adapted from *First Corinthians*, chapter 12, verses 9, 28, and 30. The Greek words for "gifts of healings" are the nouns *charismata iamaton* (pronounced "harr'-is-muh ee'-uh-muh"), both of which are *plural* words. This indicates that there are many kinds of illnesses from many different causes, but that the Holy Spirit can cure them all, if He wills to do so. These meanings are verified in such reference books as: *An Expository Dictionary of New Testament Words: Volume II*, p. 204; and *Baker's Dictionary of Theology*, p. 261.

11. Adapted from *Joel*, chapter 2, verses 28 and 29, in the Old Testament. Joel prophesied about *three* of the Spiritual gifts that would be given to Christians when Christianity was founded on the Day of Pentecost in the First Century. He foretold the coming of the Spiritual gifts of prophecy, dreams, and visions. But in our list in this chapter, we deleted duplications in the gifts, and since we wanted to list the gift of *prophecy* in one of Paul's New Testament references, we only credited Joel with the gifts of Spiritual dreams and Spiritual visions.

12. Adapted from *Romans*, chapter 12, verses 6 through 8; *First Corinthians*, chapter 12, verses 8 through 10 and verse 28; and *First Corinthians*, chapter 14, verses 3 and 27.

13. Adapted from *First Corinthians*, chapter 14, verses 2, 4, 5, 14, and 18.

14. Adapted from *First Corinthians*, chapter 14, verse 4. The Greek word for "edify" that Paul uses in this verse (in saying that the gift of speaking other languages "edifies" Christians) is the verb *oikodomeo* (pronounced "oye-cah-dah-may'-oh"). It comes from a Greek word that means to build a house. So *oikodomeo* literally means to build, repair, restore, and establish things. Figuratively, it means to help a Christian grow in wisdom, grace, virtue, holiness, blessedness. So expressing the gift of speaking other languages helps Christians grow Spiritually. These meanings are verified in such reference books as: *The Exhaustive Concordance of the Bible*, p. 51; *An Expository Dictionary of New Testament Words: Volume III*, p. 18; and *Baker's Dictionary of Theology*, p. 177.

15. Adapted from *First Corinthians*, chapter 14, verses 6 through 9, with 11, 16, 19, and 23.

16. The "Pentecostal movement" was founded by a 27-year old college dropout and itinerate preacher named Charles Fox Parham (1873-1929). In October 1900, Parham rented a large empty house known as "Stone's Folly" in Topeka, Kansas and named it the "Bethel Gospel School." He then recruited 34 local young students, and began teaching them a confused mixture of "end times baptism," "holiness," and "missionary" doctrines that he had learned the previous summer in a Christian commune at Shiloh, Maine. Then, on the night of December 31, 1900, the students held a New Year's Eve prayer service and, at midnight, Parham laid hands on them and prayed for them "to receive the end-times baptism" that he had been teaching about. To their surprise, the students began expressing the Spiritual gift of speaking other languages (none of them knew what it was), and the Pentecostal movement was born. Parham closed the school in the spring (it was only open six months), and in 1901 went back

on the road as an itinerate preacher – only this time he was teaching his "end times baptism" doctrine and telling people about the events at the school. His travels eventually led to the "Azusa Street Revival" in Los Angeles in April, 1906. And by 1914, Pentecostal denominations were springing up across the country. Summary: The Spiritual gifts that Parham's students expressed were valid. One student was interviewed by local language professors and found to be speaking Chinese. The problem was that their understanding of the events was innocently mistaken in several ways. They had been taught that they were having a "second" experience that Christians can only have "after" salvation; and that the "sign" of this experience was the gift of speaking "in tongues." However, none of that conforms to the First Century Christian teaching on the gift of prayer languages presented in this book.

17. The "Charismatic movement" was founded by a 44-year old Episcopal priest named Dennis J. Bennett (1917-1991) in Van Nuys, California on April 3, 1960. On that date, Bennett announced from the pulpit of St. Mark's Episcopal Church that he had "received a personal Pentecost with the gift of speaking other languages," and that other members of the congregation were also having the experience. An uproar began in the congregation pro and con that lasted for three weeks and, to make peace, Bennett resigned his position. Meanwhile, his story made the local newspapers, was picked up by the wire services, ended up in *Time* and *Newsweek* magazines, and the "Charismatic movement" was born. Dennis Bennett and his wife, Rita, traveled, spoke, and wrote books for the rest of Bennett's life. Summary: The Charismatic movement was actually the Pentecostal movement invading the mainline denominations, and was primarily an underground movement. Its big mistake was adopting the fuzzy doctrines of the Pentecostals that expressing Spiritual gifts is a "second" experience that comes "after" salvation, and that the only "sign" of it is the Spiritual gift of speaking other languages.

18. When the gift of speaking other languages made its debut in history on Pentecost morning at the founding of Christianity on May 30th, 30 AD, the words used to describe the event (*Acts*, chapter 2, verse 4) were the three Greek words *laleo heteros glossa* (pronounced "lah-<u>lay</u>'-oh <u>heh</u>'-tuh-rahss <u>glow</u>'-suh"). Translated correctly into today's English, these three words mean: *to speak other languages*. By the supernatural power of the indwelling Holy Spirit, each of the 120 disciples began to speak in a language *other* than any that he or she could normally speak. However, the non-Christian pilgrims in the streets recognized the languages because the languages were the pilgrim's *own* languages from their home countries. Sadly, these three Greek words (*laleo heteros glossa*) were translated in the *King James Version* of the

Bible in 1611 as "to speak with other tongues." Thus, millions of Christians today are suspicious of the gift of "tongues," since this Medieval word makes the gift seem mysterious and strange. The result is that many Christians avoid it and miss the Spiritual strength and faith-building it could give them.

19. Adapted from *First Corinthians*, chapter 14, verse 4.

20. Adapted from *First Corinthians*, chapter 14, verse 23.

21. Adapted from *First Corinthians*, chapter 14, verses 27 and 28.

22. Adapted from *Acts*, chapter 2, verses 8, 12, and 37; and *First Corinthians*, chapter 14, verse 22.

23. Adapted from *First Corinthians*, chapter 14, verse 23.

Chapter 13

1. Adapted from *First Corinthians*, chapter 2, verses 1 through 5.

2. The Greek word for "faith" (as in "Christian faith") is the noun *pistis* (pronounced "pis'-tiss"). It comes from the Greek verb "to be persuaded," and means confidence, conviction, and trust in something – especially in the fact that God, Christ, and the Holy Spirit are real and that our relationship with them is real. These meanings are verified in such reference books as: James Strong, *The Exhaustive Concordance of the Bible* (Nashville, TN: Abandon Press, 1890), p. 58; and W. E. Vine, *An Expository Dictionary of New Testament Words: Volume II* (Old Tappan, NJ: Fleming H. Revell Company, 1940) p. 71.

3. Adapted from *First Peter*, chapter 2, verses 5, 9, and 11.

4. Adapted from *John*, chapter 14, verse 26.

5. Adapted from *Hebrews*, chapter 3, verse 8.

Chapter 14

1. Dozens of references to Early Christian small group gatherings in homes are mentioned, either directly or indirectly, in the New Testament. References are in: *Acts*, chapters 1, 2, 5, 8, 10, 12, 16, 17, 18, 19, 20, 21, and 28; *Romans*, chapter 16; *First Corinthians*, chapters 1, 11, 14, and 16; *Colossians*, chapter 4; *First Timothy*, chapters 3 and 5; *Second Timothy*, chapter 2; *Titus*, chapter 1; *Philemon*, chapter 1; and *Hebrews*, chapter 3. The names of dozens of First Century Christians who participated in these small groups are also mentioned.

Finally, Christians are admonished in *Hebrews*, chapter 10, verse 25, *not* to abandon the habit of gathering in small groups. Special note: This verse in *Hebrews* is frequently misapplied by today's pastors of institutional congregations to pressure their members to continue attending their institutional programs.

2. Adapted from various verses in *Romans*, chapter 16.

3. The Greek word incorrectly translated as "church" in today's English Bibles is the noun *ekklesia* (pronounced "eh-clay-see'-ah"). It comes from two Greek roots that mean "to call a gathering." Thus, *ekklesia* can be translated as: a gathering, assembly, congregation, or body of Christians. But most simply, it can be translated as a *group* of Christians. Specifically, it refers to a small group of Christians gathering for prayer, worship, and fellowship in their homes. These meanings are verified in such reference books as: James Strong, *The Exhaustive Concordance of the Bible* (Nashville, TN: Abandon Press, 1890), p. 26; and W. E. Vine, *An Expository Dictionary of New Testament Words: Volume I* (Old Tappan, NJ: Fleming H. Revell Company, 1940), p. 84; Joseph T. Shipley, *Dictionary of Word Origins* (New York, NY: The Philosophical Library, Inc., 1945), pp. 80-81; Hans Kung, *The Church* (New York, NY: Shed and Ward, 1967), p. 81; William Evans, *Great Doctrines of the Bible* (Chicago, IL: Moody Press, 1974), p. 182; Everett F. Harrison, ed., *Baker's Dictionary of Theology* (Grand Rapids, MI: Baker Book House, 1960), p. 123; Alton Bryant, ed., *The New Compact Bible Dictionary* (Grand Rapids, MI: Zondervan Publishing House, 1967), p. 111; J. D. Davis, *Illustrated Davis Dictionary of the Bible* (Nashville, TN: Royal Publishers, Inc., 1973), p. 146; and A. R. Fausett, *Fausett's Bible Dictionary* (Grand Rapids, MI: Zondervan Publishing House, 1963), p. 130.

4. Adapted from *Romans*, chapter 16, verses 3 and 5.

5. Adapted from *Second Corinthians*, chapter 6, verses 14 through 17.

6. The Greek word for "weak faith" (referring to a Christian who has weak trust in God, or referring to an actual non-Christian) is the adjective *apistos* (pronounced "ah'-peh-stahss"). It comes from Greek roots meaning "without trust," and can be translated as unfaithful, faithless, doubting, unbelieving, finding something too incredible to accept. Or, it can literally be translated as a non-Christian. Thus, the word *apistos* can refer to a non-Christian, or a Christian whose faith is weak. For example, in the "Doubting Thomas" story in *John*, chapter 20, verse 27, Jesus uses this same Greek word (*apistos*) when He says to the apostle Thomas, "Stop *doubting* and believe!" Now, Thomas was

one of the original twelve disciples and he continued as a disciple after Jesus returned to heaven. So Jesus was *not* accusing Thomas of being a non-Christian. Jesus was warning Thomas to *stop* being a Christian "doubter" and having "weak trust" as a Christian. Likewise, in *Second Corinthians*, chapter 6, the apostle Paul isn't only warning Christians against socializing with non-Christians – he's also warning them against excessive socializing with infant Christians because of the negative peer pressure. These meanings are verified in such reference books as: *The Exhaustive Concordance of the Bible*, p. 14; and *An Expository Dictionary of New Testament Words: Volume I,* p. 117; and William F. Arndt and F. Wilbur Gingrich, *A Greek-English Lexicon of the New Testament and Other Early Christian Literature* (Chicago, IL: The University of Chicago Press, 1957), p. 85.

7. *The Human Group* was written by George Casper Homans (1910-1989) of Harvard in 1950, and published by Harcourt, Brace & World, Inc., in New York City. Homans was a sociologist and founded the field of behavioral sociology. To write the book, he studied small group behavior for several years in industrial plants, boy's street gangs, pacific island villages, and the citizens of small towns. His discoveries are still valid today, and the principles that he discovered apply to Christian small groups as well as secular small groups.

8. The Greek word for "house" or "household," in verses such as *Acts*, chapter 16, verse 15, is the noun *oikos* (pronounced "oye'-cahss"). It can be translated as house, household, home, or family, depending on the context of the sentence. Its frequent use in the First Century Christian letters clearly indicates that Early Christian worship and prayer groups were based on small family units meeting in private homes. These meanings are verified in such reference books as: *The Exhaustive Concordance of the Bible*, p. 51; *An Expository Dictionary of New Testament Words: Volume II,* pp. 236-237; and *A Greek-English Lexicon of the New Testament and Other Early Christian Literature*, pp. 562-563.

9. Adapted from *Matthew*, chapter 18, verses 19 and 20. The amazing Spirituality promised in this passage is *not* fully revealed in the words of today's Bibles. In the First Century, doing something "in another person's name" meant to do it with that other person's full power and authority – and the only time Christians have the full power and authority of Jesus is when they're *Spirit-filled*. Thus, when Jesus says Christians must meet in "His name," He's saying they must be *Spirit-filled* when they meet. Further, it's a weak translation of the Greek in verse 20 to have Jesus saying that He'll be "with" Christians when they meet in Spirit-filled small groups. The Greek word in the verse is the adjective *mesos* (pronounced "meh-sahss'"), which is better translated that Jesus will be *in the*

middle of, in the midst of, and among small groups of Spirit-filled Christians. These meanings are verified in such reference books as: *The Exhaustive Concordance of the Bible*, pp. 47 and 52; *An Expository Dictionary of New Testament Words: Volume III*, pp. 65 and 100; and *A Greek-English Lexicon of the New Testament and Other Early Christian Literature*, pp. 508 and 574.

10. Adapted from *Romans*, chapter 8, verse 9; *Philippians*, chapter 1, verse 19; and *First Peter*, chapter 1, verse 11.

11. Adapted from *Colossians*, chapter 1, verse 18; and *Ephesians*, chapter 1, verse 22.

12. The Greek noun *kephale* ("cath-ah-lay'") literally means the physical head of a person or animal. Figuratively, it refers to a person who is the superior, or headmaster, of a group. In this context, it refers to Jesus *guiding* small group worship through the indwelling power of the Holy Spirit in the group's participants. This means the guidance is only performed by the group's permission, since Jesus and the Holy Spirit never override human will power. Then if the group does permit the guidance, it is implemented only with Spiritual behavior (love, joy, peace, patience, etc.) and Spiritual gifts (visions, healings, miracles, revelations, etc.).

13. The Roman emperor Flavius Theodosius Augustus was born in Spain in 347 AD, and died in Rome in 395 AD. He is also known as Theodosius I, or Theodosius the Great, in some history books. He was emperor of Rome from 379 to 395 AD, and was the last emperor to rule over a unified Roman Empire. He passed a law known as the *Lex Fidei* (Latin for the *Law of Faith*, pronounced "lex fee'-day") on February 28, 380 AD in the Fourth Century. This decree outlawed *small groups* in the empire, and thus ended the original Christian small group culture that had been the key to Christianity's success for 350 years. Theodosius completed the dismantling of Spiritual Christianity that Constantine started.

Chapter 15

1. Adapted from a blend of *Ephesians*, chapter 1, verse 23; and *Hebrews*, chapter 10, verse 25. In the *Hebrews* verse, Christians are warned *not* to abandon the habit of gathering together in small groups. This verse is often incorrectly applied by the pastors in today's traditional congregations to mean that members should be loyal to the congregation's formal programs. In the First Century, "pastors" and "congregations" as we know them today did not exist, so the verse is referring to small groups.

2. Adapted from *Ephesians*, chapter 4, verses 29 and 30. The Greek word for "grieve" (as in grieving the Holy Spirit) is the verb *lupeo* (pronounced "loo-pay'-uh"). It comes from a Greek root meaning to annoy, to cause to mourn, or to cause to hold a grudge. Thus, *lupeo* means to do something to someone (in this case, the Holy Spirit) that annoys him or her, that causes a heaviness in him or her, or that causes him or her to hold a grudge. These meanings are verified in such reference books as: James Strong, *The Exhaustive Concordance of the Bible* (Nashville, TN: Abandon Press, 1890), p. 45; and W. E. Vine, *An Expository Dictionary of New Testament Words: Volume II* (Old Tappan, NJ: Fleming H. Revell Company, 1940), p. 178.

3. Adapted from *Isaiah*, chapter 55, verses 8 and 9.

4. Adapted from *Matthew*, chapter 18, verses 19 and 20. In the First Century, to do something "in another person's name" meant to do it with that person's *full power and authority*. However, the only time Christians have the full power and authority of Jesus is when they're *Spirit-filled*. Also, the word "with" in this passage (*mesos*, pronounced "meh-sahss'") is better translated to say that Jesus will be *in the middle of, in the midst of,* or *among,* groups of Spirit-filled Christians. These meanings are verified in such reference books as: *The Exhaustive Concordance of the Bible*, pp. 47 and 52; *An Expository Dictionary of New Testament Words: Volume III,* pp. 65 and 100; and *A Greek-English Lexicon of the New Testament and Other Early Christian Literature*, pp. 508 and 574.

5. Adapted from *Revelation*, chapter 4, verses 10 and 11. The Greek verb "to worship" is the word *proskuneo* (pronounced " prahss-coo-nay'-oh"). It comes from the Greek root for a dog. Thus, it means to kiss the face of God and lie lovingly at His feet like a faithful household pet. Because of this, First Century Christians usually worshiped on their knees and often prone on the ground in a posture of complete submission. We see this in *Matthew*, chapter 28, verse 9; *Mark*, chapter 15, verse 19; *Luke*, chapter 5, verse 8; and *Ephesians*, chapter 3, verse 14. Note that this totally submissive attitude is quite *different* from today's Christian "worship" in which well rehearsed performers on a stage sing and play musical instruments while the audience applauds their skill. These meanings are verified in such reference books as: *The Exhaustive Concordance of the Bible*, p. 61; *An Expository Dictionary of New Testament Words: Volume IV*, p. 235; Everett Harrison, *Baker's Dictionary of Theology* (Grand Rapids, MI: Baker Book House, 1960), p. 560; and William F. Arndt and F. Wilbur Gingrich, *A Greek-English Lexicon of the New Testament and Other Early Christian Literature* (Chicago, IL: The University of Chicago Press, 1957), p. 723.

6. Adapted from *Ephesians*, chapter 1, verse 22; chapter 4, verse 15; chapter 5, verse 23; and *Colossians*, chapter 1, verse 18. Note that in all these references, the improper Constantinian word "church" should be replaced with the proper First Century word *group*. The word "church" did *not* exist in the First Century and was unknown to the Early Christians. Thus, Jesus is the Head of the Body of Christ, and also the Head of any *small group* that meets as a unit of the Body of Christ.

7. Adapted from *John*, chapter 4, verses 23 and 24.

8. The Greek word for "truth" (as in worshiping the Father in truth) is the noun *aletheia* (pronounced "ah-lay'-thay-ah"). It refers to what is factual and real in a situation. More specifically, it refers to a Christian's Spiritual duty in a situation. Thus, worship to the Early Christians meant to submit to what was factual and real in their relationship with God, and to what was their Spiritual duty toward Him. This meant to worship Him directly and personally (without human mediators) through the Spiritual power of Spirit-filling. These meanings are verified in such reference books as: *The Exhaustive Concordance of the Bible*, p. 9; *An Expository Dictionary of New Testament Words: Volume IV*, p. 159; and *A Greek-English Lexicon of the New Testament and Other Early Christian Literature*, p. 35.

9. Adapted from *Second Corinthians*, chapter 3, verse 17.

10. Adapted from a blend of *First Corinthians*, chapter 14, verse 26; *Ephesians*, chapter 5, verse 19, and *Colossians*, chapter 3, verse 16. Note the consistency of these three First Century passages. Christians are meant to be Spirit-filled when they worship; and, as influenced by the Holy Spirit, each Christian is meant to participate individually in the worship experience, serving the other Christians in the small group with gifts of the Spirit as the Spirit guides.

11. Adapted once more from a blend of *First Corinthians*, chapter 14, verse 26; *Ephesians*, chapter 5, verses 19 and 20; and *Colossians*, chapter 3, verses 16 and 17, giving another view of what Spirit-guided, true, and free Christian worship is like.

12. Adapted from *Philippians*, chapter 3, verse 3.

Chapter 16

1. Adapted from *John*, chapter 10, verse 10; and *Matthew*, chapter 13, verse 19.

2. Adapted from *Revelation*, chapter 12, verse 9.

3. Adapted from *John*, chapter 8, verse 44; and *Revelation*, chapter 12, verses 9-10.

4. Adapted from *Second Corinthians*, chapter 4, verse 4. Also see *John*, chapter 12, verse 31, chapter 14, verse 30, and chapter 16, verse 11; and also see *Revelation*, chapter 12, verse 12.

5. Adapted from *James*, chapter 4, verse 7.

6. The source of the "white and black dog" metaphor is unknown. Some researchers have suggested that the source is Cherokee; others have guessed it's Russian; others have claimed it's African. Regardless of the source, people have used the metaphor for years. For example, Sir Winston Churchill, the prime minister of England during the 1940s, is said to have talked about "beating back his black dog" during the stresses of leading England in World War II.

7. Adapted from *Luke*, chapter 11, verses 11-13. Bible researchers say that these verses can be translated two different ways. They can be referring to the basic experience of being indwelled and becoming a Christian; or they can be referring to Christians becoming Spirit-filled.

8. Adapted from *First Corinthians*, chapter 14, verses 2, 4, and 14.

9. Adapted from *Romans*, chapter 8, verse 26; and *First Corinthians*, chapter 14, verses 2, 4, and 14.

10. Scientific studies over the years (some made by non-Christians who didn't know what they were studying and who rejected all involvement by God in their findings) have found that prayer languages really are human languages. A few such studies include: Goodman, Felicitas D. (1972) *Speaking in Tongues: A Cross-Cultural Study in Glossolalia.* Chicago, IL: University of Chicago Press. Samarin, William J. (1972) *Tongues of Men and Angels: The Religious Language of Pentecostalism.* New York, NY: Macmillan. Harris, Ralph W. (1973) *Spoken By the Spirit: Documented Accounts of "Other Tongues" From Arabic to Zulu.* Springfield, MO: Gospel Publishing House.

11. Adapted from *First Corinthians*, chapter 14, verse 5, using the English Standard Version (ESV). Paul's Greek word *glossa* is translated here as "prayer languages."

12. The Christian motto "*Shun Evil*" ("*Avoid Evil*"), appears throughout Early Christian writing. It appears with various wording in *Polycarp* (Philippians, chapter 11, verse 1); *Didache*, chapter 3, verse 1; and *Barnabas*, chapter 4,

verse 1, published in James A. Kleist, *Ancient Christian Writers* (New York, NY: The Paulist Press, 1948), pp. 16, 40, and 81. It is also with various wording in *Romans*, chapter 12, verse 9; *First Thessalonians*, chapter 5, verse 22; *Second Timothy*, chapter 2, verse 16; *First Peter*, chapter 3, verse 11; and *Third John*, verse 11. The Greek word "shun" is the verb *periistami* (pronounced "perry-is'-tuh-me"), meaning to turn one's back on something, to avoid something, or to stay away from something. These meanings are verified in such references as: James Strong, *The Exhaustive Concordance of the Bible* (Nashville, TN: Abandon Press, 1890), p. 57; and W. E. Vine, *An Expository Dictionary of New Testament Words: Volume I* (Old Tappan, NJ: Fleming H. Revell Company, 1940), p. 91.

13. The Greek word for "evil" is the adjective *kakos* (pronounced cah-cahss'"). It refers to any behavior that is morally and ethically wrong, wicked, injurious, destructive, harmful, or bad for Christians or for other people. *Kakos* not only refers to the works of Satan, it also refers to the inner drives of a Christian's own selfish nature. These meanings are verified in such references as: *The Exhaustive Concordance of the Bible*, p. 39; and *An Expository Dictionary of New Testament Words: Volume I*, p. 50.

14. Adapted from *James*, chapter 3, verses 14-18; and chapter 4, verse 1. The apostle James says that envy, selfishness, disorder, fights, quarrels, and all other such "evil" behavior in Christians comes from the "war within" them (their inner battle between Spirit and flesh). James says that this evil behavior doesn't come from heaven. Instead, it is *unspiritual* and comes from Satan.

15. Adapted from *Philippians*, chapter 4, verse 8.

16. The Greek word for a "saint" is the adjective *hagios* (pronounced "hog'-ee-ahss"). It comes from roots that mean to be chaste, modest, sacred, blameless, pure, clean, and without fault. So the word refers to Christian *behavior* – not to what Christians say or believe. The word "saint" was (and is) a generic term for all Followers of The Way. We see that in *Romans*, chapter 1, verse 7; *Second Corinthians*, chapter 1, verse 1; and *Ephesians*, chapter 1, verse 1; and so on. These meanings are verified in such references: *The Exhaustive Concordance of the Bible*, p. 7; and *An Expository Dictionary of New Testament Words: Volume III*, pp. 314-315.

17. Adapted from *Ephesians*, chapter 1, verse 1.

18. Adapted from *John*, chapter 13, verse 35.

19. The Greek word for "love" that Jesus used in *John*, chapter 13, verse 35, is the noun *agape* (pronounced "ah'-guh-pay"). It refers to a powerful supernatural emotion from the Holy Spirit that was unknown to ancient people before Christianity. It is a uniquely Christian emotion that other religions do not experience, and it is the chief characteristic of Christianity as well as the chief characteristic of God. As such, it is the foundation of Christian fellowship, and true fellowship cannot exist without it. The two are expressions of one another. These meanings are verified in such references as: *The Exhaustive Concordance of the Bible*, p. 7; and *An Expository Dictionary of New Testament Words: Volume III*, pp. 20-21.

20. Adapted from *First John*, chapter 1, verse 7.

21. The Greek word for "fellowship" is the noun *koinonia* (pronounced "coin-ah-knee'-ah"). It means to participate in the lives of other Christians in a deep and supernatural way, and to share Spiritual behavior, gifts, and experiences with them. It also means sharing physical time, talent, and treasure with them, and even implies forming partnerships with them in a business sense. So the word *koinonia* is much stronger in the original Greek than it is in today's English. It is used in these senses in *Acts*, chapter 2, verse 42; *Second Corinthians*, chapter 8, verse 4; *Galatians*, chapter 2, verse 9; *Philippians*, chapter 1, verse 5; and *First John*, chapter 1, verses 6-7. These meanings are verified in such reference books as: *The Exhaustive Concordance of the Bible*, p. 42; *An Expository Dictionary of New Testament Words: Volume II*, p. 90; Atone T. Bryant, *The New Compact Bible Dictionary* (Grand Rapids, MI: Zondervan Publishing House, 1967), p. 175; Millard J. Erickson, *Concise Dictionary of Christian Theology* (Grand Rapids, MI: Baker Book House, 1986), p. 56; and William F. Arndt and F. Wilbur Gingrich, *A Greek-English Lexicon of the New Testament and Other Early Christian Literature* (Chicago, IL: The University of Chicago Press, 1957), pp. 439-440.

22. The Greek word for "servants" (apostles, prophets, teachers, etc.) is the noun *diakonos* (pronounced "dee-ah'-cuh-nahss"). It refers to people in service positions: such as personal attendants, table waiters, and others who serve people at the expense of their own time and interests. This is the word that the Early Christians used to refer to the full-time calls to Christian service. The word appears in such verses as *First Corinthians*, chapter 3, verse 5; *Second Corinthians*, chapter 6, verse 4; and *Ephesians*, chapter 6, verse 21. These meanings are verified in such references as: *The Exhaustive Concordance of the Bible*, p. 22; and *An Expository Dictionary of New Testament Words: Volume III*, p. 72.

23. Apostles, elders, evangelists, prophets, and teachers are mentioned in *Ephesians*, chapter 4, verse 11, as well as other verses. Deacons are mentioned in *Philippians*, chapter 1, verse 1, as well as other verses.

24. Adapted from *Romans*, chapter 11, verse 29. This verse says that God's gifts and calls are *irrevocable* and can never be *withdrawn*. That means the six calls to fill-time Christian service, founded by the Holy Spirit in the First Century, still exist today; and that a Christian who has one of these calls on his or her life can never shake it off.

25. Adapted from *Acts*, chapter 13, verses 1-4. "Saul" was the apostle Paul's Jewish name in Hebrew, and "Paul" was his Roman name in Latin. Thus, in Bible episodes involving Jews, he's called "Saul," and in episodes involving Romans and Greeks, he's called "Paul."

26. The Greek prefix *para*- (pronounced "puh-<u>rah</u>'") refers to something that's beside something else, or that's near something else. So a para-group is a group that is beside another group, or near another group, or parallel to another group. These meanings are verified in such references as: *The Exhaustive Concordance of the Bible*, p. 54; and *An Expository Dictionary of New Testament Words: Volume IV*, p. 28.

27. On the Discovery Channel on October 27, 2010, the American-Australian television program, "MythBusters," used magnetoencephalography and functional magnetic resonance imaging to scan the brain of a person doing a mental task, and the equipment showed that up to 35 percent of the person's brain was used during the task. http://www.discovery.com/tv-shows/ myth-busters/ mythbusters-database/ten-percent-brain. (07-14-19)

28. Adapted from *Romans*, chapter 6, verse 4; also implied in *Acts*, chapter 5, verse 20; and in *Second Corinthians*, chapter 3, verse 6; as well as other verses.

29. Adapted from *Jude*, verses 24-25.

Bibliography

Alfoldi, Andrew. *The Conversion of Constantine and Pagan Rome*. London, UK: Oxford University Press, 1948.

Allen, Owen. *Preactive Leadership*. Denver, CO: Management House Books, 2012.

Allen, Owen. *Spiritual Excellence: An Evaluation of Spiritual Effectiveness in Individuals and Denominations in America*. Ann Arbor, MI: ProQuest, 1991.

Arndt, William F. and F. Wilbur Gingrich. *A Greek-English Lexicon of the New Testament and Other Early Christian Literature*. Chicago, IL: The University of Chicago Press, 1957.

Atkerson, Steve, ed. *House Churches: Simple, Strategic, Scriptural*. Atlanta, GA: New Testament Reformation Fellowship, 2008.

Barna, George and William Paul McKay. *Vital Signs: Emerging Social Trends and the Future of American Christianity*. Westchester, IL: Crossway Books, 1984.

Barna, George. *Revolution*. Wheaton, IL: Tyndale House Publishers, 2005.

Banks, Robert. *Paul's Idea of Community: The Early House Churches in Their Historical Setting*. Grand Rapids, MI: William B. Eerdmans Publishing, 1988.

Bass, Diana Butler. *Christianity After Religion: The End of the Church and the Birth of a New Spiritual Awakening*. New York, NY: Harper One, div. HarperCollins, 2012.

Baus, Karl. *History of the Church: Volume I: From the Apostolic Community to Constantine*. New York, NY: A Crossroad Book, The Seabury Press, 1980.]

Baynes, Norman H. *Constantine the Great and the Christian Church*. London, England: The British Academy, Humphrey Milford House, 1932.

Berardio, Angelo Di, ed. *Patrology: Volumes I-IV*. Westminster, MD: Christian Classics, 1988.

Berry, George Ricker. *The Interlinear Literal Translation of The Greek New Testament With the Authorized Version*. Grand Rapids, MI: Zondervan Publishing House, 1974.

Borowski, Oded. *Daily Life in Biblical Times*. Atlanta, GA: Society of Biblical Literature, 2003.

Bryant, T. Alton, ed. *The New Compact Bible Dictionary*. Grand Rapids, MI: Zondervan Publishing House, 1967.

Burckhardt, Jacob. *The Age of Constantine the Great*. New York, NY: Pantheon Books, 1949.

Cairns, Earle E. *Christianity Through the Centuries: A History of the Christian Church*. Grand Rapids, MI: Zondervan Publishing House, 1981.

Colson, Charles W. and Ellen Santilli Vaughn. *The Body: Being Light in Darkness*. Dallas, TX: Word Publishing, 1996.

Carson, D. A. *Becoming Conversant with the Emerging Church: Understanding a Movement and its Implications*. Grand Rapids, MI: Zondervan, 2005.

Cho, Paul Yonggi and Harold Hostetler. *Successful Home Groups*. Plainfield, NJ: Logos International, 1981.

Coleman, Christopher B. *Constantine the Great and Christianity*. New York, NY: The Columbia University Press, 1914.

Comby, Jean. *How To Read Church History: Volume 1*. New York, NY: The Crossroad Publishing Company, 1985.

Dal Mas, Leonardo B. *Rome of the Caesars*. Florence, Italy: Bonechi Edizioni, 1987.

Day, Colin A. *Roget's Thesaurus of the Bible*. New York, NY: Barnes & Noble Books, 1992.

Davaris, Dimitris G. *Patmos: The Sacred Island Where St. John Wrote the Apocalypse*. Athens, Greece: Nikopoulou-Dressos, 1990.

Davis, J. D. *Illustrated Davis Dictionary of the Bible*. Nashville, TN: Royal Publishers, Inc., 1973.

Dickerson, John S. *The Great Evangelical Recession: 6 Factors That Will Crash the American Church ... and How to Prepare*. Grand Rapids, MI: Baker Books, 2013.

Dowley, Tim, ed. *Eerdman's Handbook to the History of Christianity*. Berkhamsted, Herts, England: Lion Publishing Company, 1977.

Duin, Julia. *Quitting Church: Why the Faithful are Fleeing and What to Do About it.* Grand Rapids, MI: Baker Books, 2008.

Earle, Ralph. *Word Meanings in the New Testament: One-Volume Edition.* Grand Rapids, MI: Baker Book House, 1986.

Edersheim, Alfred. *The Life and Times of Jesus The Messiah.* Peabody, MA: Hendrickson Publishers, Inc., 2004.

Edwards, Gene. *The Early Church.* Goleta, CA: Christian Books, 1974.

Ehrman, Bart D. *The New Testament: A Historical Introduction to the Early Christian Writings.* Oxford, England: Oxford University Press, 2004.

Ehrman, Bart D. *The New Testament and Other Early Christian Writings.* Oxford, England: Oxford University Press, 2004.

Ehrman, Bart D. *After the New Testament: A Reader in Early Christianity.* Oxford, England: Oxford University Press, 2004.

Ehrman, Bart D. *Christianity in Late Antiquity: 300 – 450 C.E.* Oxford, England: Oxford University Press, 2004.

Erickson, Millard J. *Concise Dictionary of Christian Theology.* Grand Rapids, MI: Baker Book House, 1986.

Evans, William. *Great Doctrines of the Bible.* Chicago, IL: Moody Press, 1974.

Everyday Living: Bible Life and Times. Fascinating, Everyday Customs and Traditions From the People of the Bible. (*The Everyday Series.*) New York, NY: MJF Books, with Thomas Nelson, 2006.

Fausett, A. R. *Fausett's Bible Dictionary.* Grand Rapids, MI: Zondervan Publishing House, 1963.

Gallup, George, Jr. and D. Michael Lindsay. *Surveying the Religious Landscape: Trends in U.S. Beliefs.* Harrisburg, PA: Morehouse Publishing, 1999.

Gallup, George, Jr. *The Next American Spirituality: Finding God in the Twenty-First Century.* Colorado Springs, CO: Victor, an imprint of Cook Communications Ministries, 2000.

Gibbon, Edward. *The Decline and Fall of the Roman Empire: Volumes 1-6.* Chicago, IL: The Great Books of Encyclopedia Britannica, Inc., published with the University of Chicago, 1952.

Goodman, Felicitas D. *Speaking in Tongues: A Cross-Cultural Study in Glossolalia*. Chicago, IL: University of Chicago Press, 1972.

Gower, Ralph. *Manners and Customs of Bible Times*. Chicago, IL: Moody Press, 1987.

Grant, Michael. *Constantine The Great: The Man and His Times*. New York, NY: Barnes & Noble Books, 1993.

Gustafson, James M. *Treasure in Earthen Vessels: The Church as a Human Community*. New York, NY: Harper & Row, Publishers, 1961.

Hall, Christopher A. *Reading Scripture With the Church Fathers*. Downers Grove, IL: InterVarsity Press, 1998.

Halley, Henry B. *Halley's Bible Handbook*. Grand Rapids, MI: Zondervan Publishing House, 1965.

Harris, Ralph W. *Spoken By the Spirit: Documented Accounts of "Other Tongues" From Arabic to Zulu*. Springfield, MO: Gospel Publishing House, 1973.

Harrison, Everett F., ed. *Baker's Dictionary of Theology*. Grand Rapids, MI: Baker Book House, 1960.

Hill, Julian V., ed. *Common Life in the Early Church*. Harrisburg, PA: Trinity Press International, 1998.

Homans, George C. *The Human Group*. New York, NY: Harcourt, Brace & World, Inc., 1950.

Hostetler, Bob. *Quit Going to Church*. Abilene, TX: Leafwood Publishers, 2012.

Hughes, Robert. *Rome: A Cultural, Visual, and Personal History*. New York, NY: Alfred A. Knopf, 2011.

Huttman, Maude Aline. *The Establishment of Christianity and the Proscription of Paganism*. New York, NY: Columbia University, 1914.

Jacobsen, Wayne. *The Naked Church*. Eugene, OR: Harvest House Publishers, 1987.

Johnston, Jeremiah J. *Unimaginable: What Our World Would Be Like Without Christianity*. Minneapolis, MN: Bethany House, 2017.

Jones, Tony. *The New Christians: Dispatches From the Emergent Frontier*. San Francisco, CA: Jossey-Bass/Wiley, 2008.

Kinnaman, David. *You Lost Me: Why Young Christians Are Leaving Church and Rethinking Faith*. Grand Rapids, MI: Baker Books, 2011.

Kleist, James A., ed. *Ancient Christian Writers*. New York, NY: The Paulist Press, 1948.

Kraut, Robert E. and Paul Resnick. *Building Successful Online Communities: Evidence-Based Social Design*. Cambridge, MA: The MIT Press, 2012.

Kung, Hans. *The Church*. New York, NY: Shed and Ward, 1967.

Leedom, Tim C. and Maria Murdy. *The Book Your Church Doesn't Want You to Read*. New York, NY, Cambridge House Press, 2007.

Lietzmann, Hans. *From Constantine to Julian: A History of the Early Church, Vol. III*. New York, NY: Charles Scribner's Sons, 1950.

Lohfink, Gerhard. *Does God Need the Church?* Collegeville, MI: The Liturgical Press / Michael Glazier Books, 1999.

MacDonald, Gordon. *Who Stole My Church: What to Do When the Church You Love Tries to Enter the 21st Century*. Nashville, TN: Thomas Nelson, 2007.

MacDonald, James. *Vertical Church: What Every Heart Longs For. What Every Church Can Be*. Colorado Springs, CO: David C. Cook, 2012.

Mancinelli, Fabrizio. *Catacombs and Basilicas: The Early Christians in Rome*. Florence, Italy: Scala, Istituto Fotografico Editoriale, 1981.

Manzione, E. and L. Pazienti. *Rome and the Vatican*. Rome, Italy: Soc. Editrice Fi. Da. Ro., 1983.

Marshall, Alfred. *The Interlinear NASB-NIV Parallel New Testament in Greek and English*. Grand Rapids, MI: Zondervan Publishing House, div. HarperCollins, 1993.

Marshall, Catherine. *Something More*. New York, NY: McGraw-Hill Book Company, 1974.

Marty, Martin E. *The New Shape of American Religion*. New York, NY: Harper & Row, 1959.

McVey, Steve. *52 Lies Heard in Church Every Sunday*. Eugene, OR: Harvest Home Publishers, 2011.

Mead, Frank S. *Handbook of Denominations in the United States*. Nashville, TN: Abingdon Press, 1985.

Meinardus, Otto F. A. *St. Paul in Greece*. Athens, Greece: Lycabettus Press, 1973.

Miller, Keith. *The Taste of New Wine*. Waco, TX: Word Books, 1965.

Monser, Harold E., ed. *The Logos International Study Bible*. Plainfield, NJ: Logos International, 1972.

Olson, David T. *The American Church in Crisis*. Grand Rapids, MI: Zondervan, 2008.

Paulk, Earl. *Spiritual Megatrends: Christianity in the 21st Century*. Atlanta, GA: Kingdom Publishers, 1988.

Perschbacher, Wesley J. *The New Analytical Greek Lexicon*. Peabody, MA: Hendrickson Publishers, 1990.

Pollinger, Seth. *The World Jesus Knew: Life, Politics, and Culture in Judea and Around the World*. Worthy Books, Worthy Publishing Group, 2017.

Putnam, Robert D. *Bowling Alone: The Collapse and Revival of American Community*. New York, NY: Simon & Schuster, 2000.

Reno, Russell R. *In the Ruins of the Church: Sustaining Faith in an Age of Diminished Christianity*. Ada, MI: Brazos Press, div Baker Publishing Group, 2002.

Renwick, A. M. *The Story of the Church*. Downers Grove, IL: InterVarsity Press, 1958.

Rutz, James H. *1700 Years is Long Enough: A Guide to Creating an Open Church*. Costa Mesa, CA: Open Church Ministries, 1990.

Rutz, James H. *The Open Church: How to Bring Back the Exciting Life of the First Century Church*. Beaumont, TX: The SeedSowers, 1992.

Samarin, William J. *Tongues of Men and Angels: The Religious Language of Pentecostalism*. New York, NY: Macmillan, 1972.

Schaff, Philip. *History of the Christian Church: Volume I*. Grand Rapids, MI: William B. Eerdman's Publishing Company, 1910.

Scott, Ernest. *The Nature of the Early Church*. New York, NY: Charles Scribner's Sons, 1941.

Sefton, Henry. *A Lion Handbook: The History of Christianity*. Oxford, England: Lion Publishing, 1988.

Shanks, Hershel and Ben Witherington III. *The Brother of Jesus: The Dramatic Story and Meaning of the First Archaeological Link to Jesus and His Family*. New York, NY: Harper Collins Publishers, 2003.

Shipley, Joseph T. *Dictionary of Word Origins*. New York, NY: The Philosophical Library, Inc., 1945.

Shook, Ryan and Josh. *Ditching Secondhand Religion for a Faith of Your Own*. Colorado Springs, CO: Waterbrook Press, 2013.

Simson, Wolfgang. *The House Church Book: Rediscover the Dynamic, Organic, Relational, Viral Community Jesus Started*. Carol Stream, IL: Tyndale House Publishers, 2009.

Snyder, Howard A. *The Problem of Wine Skins: Church Structure in a Technological Age*. Downers Grove, IL: InterVarsity Press, 1975.

Snyder, Graydon F. *Ante Pacem: Archaeological Evidence of Church Life Before Constantine*. Atlanta, GA: Mercer University Press, 1985.

Snyder, Graydon F. *Church Life Before Constantine*. Atlanta, GA: Mercer University Press, 1991.

Snyder, Graydon F. *Inculturation of the Jesus Tradition: The Impact of Jesus on Jewish and Roman Cultures*. Harrisburg, PA: Trinity Press International, 1999.

Spong, John Shelby. *Why Christianity Must Change or Die: A Bishop Speaks to Believers in Exile*. San Francisco, CA: HarperCollins, 1998.

Spong, John Shelby. *A New Christianity for a New World: Why Traditional Faith is Dying and How a New Faith is Being Born*. San Francisco, CA: HarperCollins, 2001.

Strong, James. *The Exhaustive Concordance of the Bible*. Nashville, TN: Abandon Press, 1890.

Sweet, Leonard. *I am a Follower: the Way, the Truth, and the Life of Following Jesus*. Nashville, TN: Thomas Nelson, 2012.

Swindoll, Charles R. *The Church Awakening: An Urgent Call for Renewal*. New York, NY: FaithWords, 2010.

Thayer, Joseph H. *Thayer's Greek-English Lexicon of the New Testament*. Peabody, MA: 2205.

The Amplified Bible. Grand Rapids, MI: Zondervan Bible Publishers, 1965.

The Analytical Greek Lexicon. Grand Rapids, MI: Zondervan Publishing House, 1970.

The Englishman's Greek Concordance of the New Testament. Grand Rapids, MI: Zondervan Publishing House, 1970.

Unger, Merrill F. *Unger's Bible Dictionary*. Chicago, IL: Moody Press, 1966.

Viening, Edward, Ed. *The Zondervan Topical Bible*. Grand Rapids, MI: Zondervan Publishing House, 1969.

Vine, W. E. *An Expository Dictionary of New Testament Words: Volumes I-IV*. Old Tappan, NJ: Fleming H. Revell Company, 1940.

Viola, Frank. *Reimagining Church: Pursuing the Dream of Organic Christianity*. Colorado Spring, CO: David C. Cook, 2008.

Viola, Frank and George Barna. *Pagan Christianity? Exploring the Roots of Our Church Practices*. Wheaton, IL: Tyndale House Publishers, 2008.

Visalli, Gayla, ed. *After Jesus: The Triumph of Christianity*. Pleasantville, NY: The Reader's Digest Association, 1992.

Walker, Williston, Richard A. Norris, David W. Lotz, and Robert T. Handy. *A History of the Christian Church*. New York, NY: Charles Scribner's Sons, 1985.

Walsh, John Evangelist. *The Bones of St. Peter: The First Full Account of the Search for the Apostle's Body*. Garden City, NY: Doubleday & Company, 1982.

Wolfe, Alan. *The Transformation of American Religion: How We Actually Live Our Faith*. New York, NY: Free Press, div. of Simon & Schuster, Inc., 2003.

Zacharias, Ravi. *Has Christianity Failed You?* Grand Rapids, MI: Zondervan, 2010.

Index

Symbols

4,000 Religions on Earth 269
7,000 Languages on Earth 189, 277
51 Percent Rule 147

A

Acceptance of Selfishness 80
Accuser of Christians 266
"Afterglow," After Worship 256
Amplias, Small Group Member 215
Analogy,
 The "Wagon Wheel" 285
Andronicus, Small Group Member 215
Angels 208
Angels in the Coffee Shop 207
Antioch, City in Turkey 7
Apostle Paul's Description of Spirit-Guided Worship 249
Arab Dialects 278
Aramaic, Daily Language of Jews 5
Archaeological Excavations 214
Aristobulus, Small Group Member 215
Athens, City in Greece 147
Attitudinal Mistake in Worship 244

B

Baptisim in the Holy Spirit 99
Barnabas, Early Christian Letter 72
Basic Model of Motivation 88
Basilica Christians 56
Basilica, Latin Word for Courthouse 40
Basilicas, Roman Courthouses 39
Be Habitually Spirit-Filled 151
Behavior of Darkness 118
Behavior of Light 118
Being Born-Again 109
Being Converted 111
Being Redeemed 111
Being Regenerated 111
Being Saved 111
Benefits of Prayer Languages 275
Be Open to New Experiences 144
Best Sequence for Experiences 183
Bethel Gospel School 195
Biggest Mistake in Small Groups 230
Biggest Principle of the Holy Spirit 132
Birthday of Christianity 102
Body of Christ 229, 239
Book, *The Human Group* 221
Buildings, Programs, and Ancestors 55
Bulldozing Christian Buildings 11

C

Calls to Full-Time Servantship 45
Catacombs, Christian Cemetery Tunnels 309

Cause-and-Effect Linkage 168
Cause of World Trouble 77
Challenge to Today's Leaders 292
Changing Christian Ancestors 58
Changing Group Types 225
Charismatic Movement 195
Charles Fox Parham 195
Charles Spurgeon, Evangelist 69
Children Who Wanted a Dog Story 300
Christian Goal 123
Christiani 8
Christianity's Original Symbols 48
Christian Leaders Today 292
Christian Lifestyle Habit #1 269
Christian Lifestyle Habit #2 272
Christian Lifestyle Habit #3 279
Christian Lifestyle Habit #4 282
Christian Lifestyle Today 263
Christian Mind 125
Christian Saints 281
Christians, are a Chosen People 177
Christians, are a Holy Nation 177
Christians, are a Royal Priesthood 177
Christians, are God's Special Possession 177
Christian Statistics 14
Christian Symbols 309
Christus, Latin Name for Christ 35
"Church" Buildings 39
"Churches" That Never Existed 58
"Church", Source of the Word 41
Clement, Early Christian Letter 72
Clerici, Latin Word for Clerks 46

Command to be Filled With the Spirit 269
Confession, The 92
Constantine, Emperor of Rome 26
Constantine, Priest in the Sun God Religion 27
Constantine's Bribes 46
Constantine's Giant Arch 32
Constantine's Giant Statue 32
Constantine's Mysterious Dream 30
Constantine's Odd Symbol 30
Constantine's Salutary Sign 31
Constantine's Wave of new Laws 32
Constantinople, City in Turkey 41
Constantius Chlorus, Father of Constantine 27
Contamination, The 37
Corinth, City in Greece 115
Courthouses, Sun Gods, and Crosses 37
Courthouses, The 37
Crispus, Constantine's Son 50
Crucifixes 48
Current Crisis, The 55

D

Dark Ages of History 51
David, King of Israel 79
Day of Pentecost 121, 124
Deceiver of the World 266
Definition of an Infant Christian 109
Definition of a "Small Group" 221
Definition of a Small Worship Group 239
Definition of Baptism 99

Definition of "Behavior" 114, 271
Definition of "Disciples" 152
Definition of "Fruit" 164
Definition of our Soul 87
Definition of Peer Pressure 218
Definition of Selfish Human Nature 78
Definition of Spiritual 123
Definition of Spirituality 112
Definition of the Word "Fellowship" 287
Definition of the Word Holy 125
Definition of the Word "Para" 293
Definition of the Word "Saint" 281
Definition of the Word Sin 84
Definition of the Word "Worship" 246
Dennis Bennett 195
Desensitized Christians 280
Details of Spiritual Gifts 174
Devil 265
Diagram 1
  Basic Model of Motivation 88
Diagram 2
  The Natural Person 89
Diagram 3
  The Infant Christian 107
Diagram 4
  The Growing Christian 127
Diagram 5
  The Mature Christian 141
Didache, Early Christian Letter 72
Diognetus, Early Christian Letter 72
Discovery of Full-Time Gifts 179
DNA Tests 57

Dramatics of Spirit-Filling 131
"Dream" at Milvian Bridge 29
Dropouts, The 11
Dungeons of Diocletian's Palace 37
Dwight L. Moody, Evangelist 69

E

Early Christian Letters 71
Early Christian Lifestyle xi, xii, xvii, 20, 25, 32, 51, 55, 70, 141, 142, 152, 156, 172, 207, 209, 213, 224, 234, 263
Early Christian Living 292
Early Christian Small Groups 214
Edict of Milan 33
Elizabethan English 165, 195
Ephesus, City in Turkey 91, 117, 121
Every Christian Has All the Part-Time Gifts 176
Every Christian Has One Permanent Gift 174
Evil One 266
Example of Spirit-Guided Worship 250
Excessive Fleshy Emotions 155
Experience of Spirit-Filling 120
Extended Interactions in Small Groups 223

F

Face-to-Face Interaction in Small Groups 222
Fausta, Constantine's Wife 50
Feast of Pentecost 102
Fellowship, Christian 284
Fellowship is Supernatural Unity 287

Festival of Pentecost 100
Festival of Tabernacles 120
Fifth Tip for Spiritual Maturity 149
Fighting Satan 266
Fight the Inner War With Vigor 144
First Bloody Battles 29
First Circle of Motivation 84
First Level of Spirituality 89
First Spiritual Level
  Natural People 67
First Tip for Spiritual Maturity 142
Fish Symbol 2
Five Parts of a Small Group 222
Five Principles of Spiritual Gifts 177
Five Principles of Spirituality 61
Five Small Group Decisions 240
Flavius Valerius Constantinus,
  Constantine's Latin Name 26
Flesh, Mind, and Spirit 83
Followers Lose Their Name 7
Followers of The Way 4, 7, 11, 18, 33, 42, 152
Followers, The 1
Four Habits of Early Christian Living 268
Four Questions Many Christians Ask Themselves 275
Four Spiritual Levels 67
Four Supernatural Experiences 143
Fourth Spiritual Level
  The Mature Christian 137
Fourth Tip for Spiritual Maturity 147
Frequent Interaction in Small Groups 223
Fruit of the Spirit 119, 143, 163, 165

Full-Time Call of Apostles 289
Full-Time Call of Deacons 289
Full-Time Call of Elders 289
Full-Time Call of Evangelists 289
Full-Time Call of Prophets 289
Full-Time Call of Teachers 289
Full-Time Christian Servants 288
Full-Time Servants 288

G

Gaius, Small Group Member 215
Garbage In, Garbage Out 168
George C. Homans 221
Gifts of Healings 174, 184, 273
Glimpses of Heaven 299
god of this World 266
Great Dragon 266
Greatest Gentleman in the Universe 271
Greatest Whitewash 26
Greek Command Tense 121
Greek, Language of Christian Writers 5
Greek Word for Spiritual 124
Greek Word *Pneumatikos* 124
Ground Rule #1
  Define Fuzzy Words 68
Ground Rule #2
  Use Early Christian Definitions 69
Ground Rule #3
  Use Early Christians as a Model 70
Growing Christians 67, 113, 127
Guidance of a Small Group 227
Guidelines for Para-Groups 293

H

Habit of Being Spirit-Filled 269
Habit of Expressing Spiritual Gifts 272
Habit of Prayer Languages 277
Habit of Shunning Evil 279
Habit of Small Group Worship 282
Habits, Styles, and Saints 263
Half-Sisters of Jesus 101
Having Jesus in your Heart 111
Helena, Mother of Constantine 27
Hermas, Early Christian Letter 72
Hierarchy, a Level of Authority 46
Holograms, Hosts, and Outlaws 213
Holy Spirit xvi, 11, 43, 75, 97, 106, 115, 148, 163
Holy Spirit's Lessons 206, 208
Holy Spirit's Locked Closet 245
Hosts in Small Groups 232
How to be Spirit-Filled 270
How to Feed the White Dog 268
How to Know You're Spirit-Filled 271
How to Live Like First Century Christians 268
Human Flesh 78
Human Talents and Skills are not Gifts 179

I

If We Do What They Did 300
Ignatius, Early Christian Letter 72
Imposters Teaching False Theories 73
Improper Use of the Word "Leader" 230
Indwelling by the Holy Spirit 101
Infant Christians 67, 95, 107
Influenced by the Spirit 148
Institutional Christianity 263
Intellectualizing Christianity 164
International Psychoanalytical Congress 73
Istanbul, City in Turkey 41

J

Jacobus Arminius, Reformer 59
Jairus, Synagogue Ruler in Capernaum 87
James, Half-Brother of Jesus 146
James, the Apostle 266
Jan Hus, Reformer 59
Jesus, Christ, Lord, Savior 152, 155, 163, 201, 204, 208, 285
Jesus, Founder of Christianity 7, 26, 33, 42, 58
Jesus Promised to be Present in Small Groups 228
Jesus's Half-Brothers 101
Jesus's Half-Sisters 101
Jesus's Original Disciples Weren't Spiritual 95
Jill, Jim, and Jack Example of Maturity 149
Joel, Hebrew Prophet 100
John Calvin, Reformer 59
John Knox, Reformer 59
John, the Apostle 266
John the Baptizer, Jewish Prophet 100
John Wesley, Evangelist 69
John Wycliffe, Reformer 59
Jonathan Edwards, Evangelist 69

Jordan River, River in Israel 100
Joseph, Half-Brother of Jesus 101
Jude, Half-Brother of Jesus 101
Junias, Small Group Member 215

K

Key to Spirit's Closet 246
Key to Spiritual Growth 221
Kingdom of God 98
Kingdom of Satan 265
King James Version of the Bible 165, 216

L

Laici, Latin Word for Common People 47
Laity, a Word for Common Christians 47
Law of Faith 234
Leadership Decision in Worship 242
Like-Mindedness 227
List of Spiritual Behaviors 167
List of Spiritual Gifts 184, 185
List of the "Fruit of the Spirit" 167
Living Like Early Christians 266
Living Water 121, 141
Lord's Day, Original Name for Sunday 43

M

Marcus Antonius Felix 4
Marcus Maxentius, Constantine's Enemy 30
Martin Luther, Reformer 59
Mary, Mother of Jesus 101, 122

Master Principle 264
Mature Christians 67, 141
Measure Only Average Behavior 149
Milvian Bridge, a Bridge North of Rome 30
Mini-Congregation Mistake 240
Mini-Congregations 231
Miracle of Pentecost 100
Mistakes, Choices, and Puppies 239
Misunderstandings, The 195
Misuse of the Word "Church" 216
Most Serious Troubles 73
Motivational Diagrams 83
Motivational Linkage 168
Motivational System 168
Motivation of Christians 6
Motivator of Darkness 119
Motivator of Light 118
Motivators 168
Motto
  If We Do What They Did 264
Motto for Small Group Worship 245
Motto, "Shun Evil" 279
Museums 214

N

Narcissus, Small Group Member 215
National Polls on Christianity 14
Natural People 3, 11, 67
Negative Peer Pressure 218, 220
Nero, Emperor of Rome 5
New International Version of the Bible 165
New Kind of Humans 3

New Rome, City in Turkey 216
New Spiritual Experiences 144
New Way of Living 300
New York Hotel Room Story 131
Nicodemus, Member Jewish Ruling Council 155
Nicomedia, City in Turkey 28
Nis, City in Serbia 27
Non-Christian Religions 33
Non-Christians 15, 41, 75
Non-Christian Word "Church" 41
Non-Christian Word "Clergy" 44
Non-Christian Words 42
Non-Christian Word "Sunday" 43
Non-Spiritual Motivation 78
Non-Spiritual People 75
No Priorities Among the Gifts 178

O

Old Serpent 266
Oneness in the Spirit 252
Openness to Spiritual Lessons 208
Other Terms for The Way 7
Our Flesh 84
Our Heart 84
Our Mind 84
Our Selfish Nature 84
Our Soul 86
Our Spirit 86
Outlawing of Small Groups 233

P

Papias, Early Christian Letter 72
Para-Groups Solution 293
Participative Organizational Structures 222
Paul's Command to Christians 122
Paul's Law for Spirit-Guided Worship 257
Paul's Three Calls to Full-Time Servantship 290
Paul, the Apostle 145, 156, 165, 175, 185, 202, 215, 219, 255, 266, 269, 276, 279, 281, 289
Pentecostal Movement 195
Personality of the Holy Spirit 168
Peter, the Apostle 146, 152, 175
Phoebe, Small Group Member 215
Pilgrims, in Jerusalem 103
Polycarp, Early Christian Letter 72
Pontifex Maximus, Latin for Greatest Priest 50
Positive or Negative Behavior 168
Positive or Negative Emotions 168
Positive or Negative Habits 168
Positive or Negative Lifestyles 168
Positive Peer Pressure 218, 220
Practical Application 264, 268, 279
Prayer
    Fill Me, Holy Spirit 269
Prayer for Spirit-Filling 129
Prayer Languages 101, 105
Praying in the Spirit 188
Preconceived Notions Mistake 244
Principles of Behavior 114
Priscilla and Aquila, Small Group Members 215
Problem of Unspirituality 19
Process of Spirit-Filling 128

Program Christians 57
Protestant Reformation 59
Province of Galilee 103
Purpose of Prayer Languages 274
Purpose of the Gifts is to Serve Others 175

Q

Quadratus, Elder in City of Athens 147

R

Record of Spirit-Guided Worship 255
Result of Spirit-Guided Worship 257
Rev. John D. Shields, Christian Friend 270
Rivers of Living Water 171, 249, 264
Roger and Millie Story 207
Roman Catholic Denomination 39, 47
Rome, City in Italy 185, 276, 281, 309

S

Saints 281
Satan 265
Satan's Temptations 279
Scientific Studies of Prayer Languages 278
Second Tip for Spiritual Maturity 144
Seek Spiritual Maturity 142
Sequence of Spiritual Events 181
Shunning Evil 279
"Sign" of Spirit-Filling, 153
Sign that a Christian is Spirit-filled 170
Situational Spirit-Filling 148

Six Calls to Full-Time Servantship 288
Six-Part Structure of a Small Group 224, 283
Sixth Part of a Small Group 223
Sixth Tip for Spiritual Maturity 151
Size of Small Groups 222
Small Group Members Are Not "Spectators" 288
Small Group Members are "Participants" 288
Small Groups 143, 177, 179, 191, 213, 216, 239, 293
Small Groups are the Body of Christ 229
Small Group Worship 282
Snapshot at the "Smiths" 251
Social Groups 224
Sol Invictus, the Ever-Victorious Sun 28
Sopater, Constantine's Friend 50
Source of Spiritual Gifts 174
Speaking Other Languages 102, 105
Specifics of Spirit-Guided Worship 248
Spectator-Type Structure 59, 60
Spirit-filled 179, 228, 233, 268, 295
Spirit-Filling 148, 204, 264, 269
Spirit-Guided Worship 243, 254
Spirit-Guided Worship at the "Smiths" 251
Spirit of Christ 228
Spirit of Jesus 228
Spiritual Baptism 122
Spiritual Behavior 7, 11, 101, 163, 164

Spiritual Cycles 149
Spiritual Deadness 91
Spiritual Experiences 201, 204
Spiritual Gifts 173, 185, 272
Spiritual Gifts are to Make us Happy 175
Spiritual Growth 53, 60, 72, 79
Spiritual Interaction in Small Groups 224
Spiritual Maturity 144
Spiritual Motivation 149
Spiritual vs. Fleshy Emotions 169
Spiritual Worship 239
Standard for Christian Spirituality 55
Statue in Rome 31
Steven, Early Christian Deacon 87
St. John Lateran, Basilica in Rome 39
St. Mark's Episcopal Church 195
Story
   Mary's Miracle on the Sun Deck 192
   Non-Christian in Second Century Rome 284
   Prone of the Bedroom Floor 247
   The Car in the Parking Lot 283
   The Children Who Wanted a Dog xi
   The Crucifix 204
   The Fire Pit 170, 271
   The Friday Night Group 105
   The Gas Logs 270
   The Grand Canyon Dream 191
   The Healing in the Hospital Room 173
   The Holiday Inn Breakfast Hug 286
   The Hologram Story 230

The Man Who Wanted a Pastor 242
The Miracle in the Den 191
The Mysterious Phone Call 1
The Pastor's Wife 189
The Pastor Who Didn't Know the Answer xvi
The Puppy in the Sun 257
The Riddle of the Vineyard 163
The Rush Hour Traffic 114
The Shy Young Mother 180
The Stranger at the Luncheon 137
The White Dog 267
The Young Man at Breakfast 201
The Young Woman's Question 258
Trial of the Apostle Paul 4
St. Peter's, Basilica in Rome 39
Straight Jacket of Human Preplanning 245
Structural Mistake in Worship 244
Summary of Chapter 1 8
Summary of Chapter 2 22
Summary of Chapter 3 35
Summary of Chapter 4 51
Summary of Chapter 5 62
Summary of Chapter 6 81
Summary of Chapter 7 93
Summary of Chapter 8 110
Summary of Chapter 9 133
Summary of Chapter 10 157
Summary of Chapter 11 171
Summary of Chapter 12 198
Summary of Chapter 13 210
Summary of Chapter 14 235
Summary of Chapter 15 259

Summary of Chapter 16 295
Sun god Religion 27
SuperChristian, The 15
Supernatural Fellowship 284
Symbol of the Cross 48

T

Table 1
  Spiritual Behavior 167
Table 2
  Spiritual Gifts 185
Teaching Groups 225
Temptations 280
Term "In My Name" 228
Tests for the Spiritual Gifts 179
The Big Key to Spiritual Growth 109
The Fuzzy Word "Christian" 69
The Fuzzy Word "Spiritual" 69
Theodosius, Emperor, Outlawed Small Groups 233
The Reformers 59, 69
The Three Ground Rules 67
The Way of Life and the Way of Death 116
Thin Veneer of Civilization 78, 90
Third Circle of Motivation 86
Third Spiritual Level
  The Growing Christian 113, 127
Third Tip for Spiritual Maturity 144
Three Activities of the Spirit 203
Three Circles, The 83
Three Supernatural Activities 153
Three Types of Small Groups 224
Tiber River, a River in Rome 30

Time Requirement 149
Topeka, Kansas, City in America 195
Troubles are the same Worldwide 74
Tweakers That Failed 59
Two Pillars of Spirit-Guided Worship 250
Two Principles of Spirit-Guided Worship 247
Two Purposes of the 51 Percent Rule 149
Two Tests of Spirituality 125
Two Tests of Spiritual Maturity 149
Two-Way Interaction in Small Groups 222
Two Ways, The 116

U

Units of the Body of Christ 229
Unity, Christian 284
Urbanus, Small Group Member 215
Use of Prayer Languages 188

V

Valerius Diocletian, Emperor of Rome 28, 30
Van Nuys, California, City in America 195

W

"War" Inside all Christians 169
Warlord, The 25
Warm Puppy Story 258
Water-Baptism 113
White Dog, The 267
Why Christians Are Unspiritual 20

William Tyndale, Reformer 59
Word Church 216
Word Clergy 309, 317
World Upside Down 2
Worship Group Like-Mindedness 227
"Worship" is a Fuzzy Word 246
Worship Type Small Groups 239
Wrong "Ancestors" 57

Y

Young Man at Breakfast, The 201

Z

Zulu Dialects 278

Acknowledgments

First of all, I want to acknowledge Patricia K. Hill, a university English instructor who, many years ago, was the first person to ever tell me that I had writing talent. As a young college student, I never had a chance to tell her how much my life changed after she said that. But since that day in her office, I've written millions of words, published hundreds of business reports and manuals, and published ten books. Patricia Hill is in heaven now, and someday I'll be able to thank her there face to face.

I also want to acknowledge the doctoral committee who many years ago gave me the freedom and encouragement to investigate institutional Christianity without restriction or bias. Such freedom was rare in those days. In alphabetical order they were: Rev. Dr. Rudee D. Boan; Dr. Linda B. Brown; Rev. Dr. Robert D. Dale; Rev. Dr. Brian C. Donley; Rev. Gordon E. Miller; Dr. Elizabeth Kamarck Minnich; Rev. Orrin D. Morris; Dr. Halloway C. Sells; Rev. Jack W. Tebbs; Dr. Nellouise D. Watkins; and Dr. Randall P. White.

Next, I want to acknowledge the family members and friends who played key roles in my Spiritual growth over the years. Many of them are also in heaven today. But each knows how God used him or her in my life. They are: My parents, Jesse Owen Allen, Jr., and Hazel Pearson Allen; and my brother, Rev. James Bryan Allen; and Gus Mackris; Rev. Larry Allison; Rev. Wilburn Hendrix; Rev. Larry and Betsy Heath; Dwight Jester; Rev. John and Kay Setzer; Frank Porter; Rev. David Jones; Lynn Powers; Preston Parrish; Rev. Carl Connor; Doug Carty; Bubby and Janet Chamblee; Rex and Elaine Uhl; Rev. Dr. David Burr; Cliff Owen; Jim Clinard; Larry Rayle; Rev. Jack W. Tebbs; Rev. John D. Shields; Rev. Dr. Larry W. Kennedy; Dr. Joshua T. Fischer; Rev. Dr. Marcus B. Putnam; Drs. Rick and Phyllis Webb; and most of all, my beloved wife, Joanna Smith Allen, who never leaves my side, and who never stops loving, forgiving, encouraging, and praying.

I also want to acknowledge my dear brothers and sisters in *The Gathering – A Christian Community*. Their courage and openness in pioneering para-groups changed all of our lives in wonderful and unexpected ways. I pray God's richest blessings on them, each and every one.

Finally, I want to acknowledge Dr. Estrelda Alexander, president of Seymour Press; Vanderlyn Hampton, managing editor; Jan Loy, editor; and Tammy Rose, graphics specialist, for their bold encouragement and aggressive help in publishing this book. As has happened so often in my life, God unexpectedly brought them into my life at the right time and in the right place to perform yet another one of His marvelous miracles.

About the Author

Owen Allen is a former international management consultant and management trainer. He holds a doctorate in organizational behavior with post-doctoral work at Oxford University. He is also a Certified Management Consultant and a Certified Speaking Professional. As the founder and president of Specific Action Corporation, his clients included such blue chip firms as General Electric, General Motors, Hilton Hotels, John Deere, Kraft Foods, and many other major corporations; as well as many local, state, and federal government agencies. His specialty was small group teamwork, and he trained boards of directors and top executive groups in these techniques, as well as groups of middle managers, supervisors, and foremen. His clients bought over 30,000 copies of his management books. His most recent management book was *Preactive Leadership*, which is also used as a university textbook.

After his management training and consulting career, Owen served as the executive vice president, a dean, and a professor, at a Christian university. Today, as the founder and president of The Christian Family Online in America, Inc., a 501(c)(3) public charity, he writes, teaches, speaks, and blogs about the habits of Early Christian small groups, and about how to live in Early Christian type small groups in today's world. Owen has traveled in 65 countries and has researched Early Christian sites, ruins, artifacts, paintings, and symbols in Greece, Israel, Italy, and Turkey. This is his tenth book.

Owen can be reached at: owen@ChristianFamilyOnline.com.

This book is available on the Internet at Amazon Books; B&N Books; Alibris Books; Thrift Books, and other quality book websites. It is also available as an ebook. In addition, it is available in the form of bulk gifts for congregations, Sunday school classes, retreats, small groups, conventions, conferences, and other such uses by tax-deductible donations to The Christian Family Online in American, Inc. To request such bulk gifts, contact:

books@ChristianFamilyOnline.com

Or

Bulk Books Request
Christian Family Online
PO Box 19125
Greensboro, NC 27419-9125
www.ChristianFamilyOnline.com